Someone

Someone

The Pragmatics of Misfit Sexualities, from Colette to Hervé Guibert

MICHAEL LUCEY

The University of Chicago Press
Chicago and London

The University of Chicago Press, Chicago 60637
The University of Chicago Press, Ltd., London
© 2019 by The University of Chicago
Published 2019
Printed in the United States of America

28 27 26 25 24 23 22 21 20 19   1 2 3 4 5

ISBN-13: 978-0-226-60618-7 (cloth)
ISBN-13: 978-0-226-60621-7 (paper)
ISBN-13: 978-0-226-60635-4 (e-book)
DOI: https://doi.org/10.7208/chicago/9780226606354.001.0001

The University of Chicago Press gratefully acknowledges the generous support of the
University of California, Berkeley, toward the publication of this book.

Library of Congress Cataloging-in-Publication Data

Names: Lucey, Michael, 1960–author.
Title: Someone : the pragmatics of misfit sexualities, from Colette to Hervé Guibert /
    Michael Lucey.
Description: Chicago ; London : The University of Chicago Press, 2019. | Includes
    bibliographical references and index.
Identifiers: LCCN 2018028776 | ISBN 9780226606187 (cloth : alk. paper) | ISBN
    9780226606217 (pbk. : alk. paper) | ISBN 9780226606354 (e-book)
Subjects: LCSH: French literature—20th century—History and criticism. |
    Homosexuality in literature. | Sex in literature.
Classification: LCC PQ307.H6 L834 2019 | DDC 840.9/353—dc23
LC record available at https://lccn.loc.gov/2018028776

♾ This paper meets the requirements of ANSI/NISO Z39.48–1992
(Permanence of Paper).

Qu'on me comprenne, qu'on se mette à ma place. Je me demande si quelqu'un voudrait. Quelqu'un.

(Try to understand me, try to put yourself in my place. I wonder if there's someone who would. Someone.)
ROBERT PINGET, *Quelqu'un* (*Someone*)

An essential (constitutive) marker of the utterance is its quality of being directed to someone, its addressivity.
M. M. BAKHTIN, "The Problem of Speech Genres"

Narratives about the most "personal" difficulties, the apparently most strictly subjective tensions and contradictions, frequently articulate the deepest structures of the social world and their contradictions. This is never so obvious as it is for occupants of precarious positions who turn out to be extraordinary "practical analysts": situated at points where social structures "work," and therefore worked over by the contradictions of these structures, these individuals are constrained, in order to live or to survive, to practice a kind of self-analysis, which often gives them access to the objective contradictions which have them in their grasp, and to the objective structures expressed in and by these contradictions.
PIERRE BOURDIEU, "The Contradictions of Inheritance,"
in *The Weight of the World*

I'm always compelled by the places where a project of writing runs into things that I just can't say—whether because there aren't good words for them, or more interestingly because they're structured in some elusive way that just isn't going to stay still to be formulated. That's the unrationalizable place that seems worth being to me, often the only place that seems worth being.
EVE KOSOFSKY SEDGWICK, "This Piercing Bouquet"

That people are different from each other—I still wonder why and how that can remain so difficult to know; how best to marshal theoretical resources for its realization.
EVE KOSOFSKY SEDGWICK, "Affect Theory and Theory of Mind"

Contents

Roadmap to *Someone*

In this book I am working out a methodology that draws on a few different intellectual traditions: Bourdieusian ways of thinking about the functioning of the field of cultural production and about the functioning of works of literature within that field and within a larger social field; sociological and sociolinguistic (or linguistic anthropological) ways of thinking about how utterances operate both sociologically and pragmatically to do more than they say, and how they often do work through features of language that are not semantic in nature (inspiration comes here from people like Bourdieu, Erving Goffman, and Michael Silverstein); and finally a way of describing sexuality as, to use a slightly cumbersome formulation that I'll explain more fully in chapter 6, an effect exerted on certain practices by a shifting structure of relations between a mobile and expansive set of other sociologically pertinent properties. I take sexuality to be both one sociological variable that we use to identify ourselves and others and the effect of a cloud of other variables. (In my explanation of these ideas in chapter 6, I will draw on Bourdieu's way, in *Distinction* and elsewhere, of modeling relations between sets of socially pertinent variables.) This is a way of doing literary, cultural, and social criticism that I have been finding my way to across the past fifteen years or so.[1] I hope this latest effort takes a few steps forward in a number of directions.

As I will explain more fully in chapter 1, my focus here is on what I call misfit sexualities, and the place they hold in a body of texts drawn from the French literary tradition between roughly 1930 and 1990. Misfit sexualities do not exactly correspond to any of the names for sexualities that we most commonly use—lesbian, gay, bisexual, straight, and so on—and sometimes it takes a serious cognitive effort simply to notice that such other sexualities exist. They are often all too easy to miss for a variety of reasons that the following pages will explore. If I say "misfit" instead of "queer," it is for a number of overlapping reasons, pragmatic ones, we could say, having to do with tone and emphasis, and a bit with method. Some versions of the word "queer" as it has evolved in the academy over the past twenty-five years simply do not work for the misfits I am interested in. This, too, I will explain a bit in chapter 6 when I mention what I take to be the differences between my way of thinking about Violette Leduc's experience of sexuality (in relation to other social variables) and earlier accounts of her writing that attempt to assimilate her to an alternate version of a queer project. The version in those earlier accounts is, I think, one variant of what the editors of the 2005 special issue of *Social Text* titled "What's Queer about Queer Studies Now?" called "queer liberalism," and involves considering sexuality in isolation from other social categories, and imagining *queerness* as mainly instantiating a less constrained, more flexible relation to gender and sexual norms.[2]

The usage of "queer" has, of course, always been contentious. In her landmark essay "Critically Queer," first published in 1993, Judith Butler noted that "if the term 'queer' is to be a site of collective contestation, the point of departure for a set of historical reflections and futural imaginings, it will have to remain that which is, in the present, never fully owned, but always and only redeployed, twisted, queered from a prior usage and in the direction of urgent and expanding political purposes."[3] Now it turns out that many of the misfits I look at are, on the one hand, conservative and reactionary, or, on the other, would like nothing more than to be ordinary. Sometimes they are frustrated by the dissonance of their experience, and evince no particular desire to evolve any kind of critical awareness of that experience. They are occasionally almost resentful of the way in which any acuity they have about themselves has been forced upon them by their experience and the social positioning it entails. Sometimes they are more past oriented than future oriented. There are some people we will meet in the pages ahead who might wish to affiliate with queer, others who would not. It is not that I would necessarily have a problem calling someone queer who would not wish to be, but I think there is a quality to the experience I am aiming to investigate that would be missed by doing so.

Further, it doesn't seem to me to be the case that many of the people I have studied for this project are invested in the "futural imaginings" or the "expanding political purposes" Butler mentions, and this has something to do with the quality of their experience of their misfit sexuality. I began working in earnest on the chapters collected here in 2005 and 2006, around the time that the "What's Queer about Queer Studies?" special issue of *Social Text* came out, with its call to "rethink queer critique" (1) and to resituate sexuality itself as one social process that intersects with many others. Much of the work over the intervening years that has heeded that call, particularly queer of color critique, has been helpful to me in trying to think about the French contexts and the French misfits I write about here. José Esteban Muñoz wrote that he hoped his book *Cruising Utopia: The Then and There of Queer Futurity* might be "a resource for the political imagination."[4] Certainly his work, and the work of others that I will mention in the pages ahead, has been that for me. Muñoz comments in his stirring introduction to *Cruising Utopia* that he "think[s] of queerness as a temporal arrangement in which the past is a field of possibility in which subjects can act in the present in the service of a new futurity" (16). Perhaps some of the interactions between misfits that I will be examining could meet that description, although even the utopian longings that provide the energy for many of the most compelling contemporary queer projects sometimes seem to me only weakly present in the figures and texts I write about. Some of them, as I just mentioned, are not lacking in conservative or reactionary impulses. Progressive change, at least as regards sexuality, is not what they hold a brief for. Perhaps alongside or in place of the reactionary impulses of some of these figures is also something different: a simple wish to fit in, a wish that is frustrated by their experience of their sexuality. But in any case, what captures my attention about what they try to describe about sexuality in language, and about language itself, ends up having to do simultaneously with what seems to me to be appropriately characterized as a *misfit* between 1) the physical and social practices that might constitute a sexuality, 2) the language that might be involved in accomplishing those practices or in reflecting on them, and 3) the categories (both practical and theoretical) that structure the social world and provide it with intelligibility. It is the experience of this misfit that provokes the reflections on, or simply the work on, language, sexual practices, and sociality that I have found so remarkable in the authors I study here.

In "Is Kinship Always Already Heterosexual?," Butler, in speaking of "the field of intelligible sexuality," notes that "there are middle regions, hybrid regions of legitimacy and illegitimacy that have no clear names, and where nomination itself falls into a crisis produced by the variable, sometimes violent boundaries of legitimating practices that come into uneasy and sometimes conflictual contact with one another." Butler emphasizes that

> these are not precisely places where one can choose to hang out, subject posi-
> tions one might opt to occupy. These are nonplaces in which one finds oneself

in spite of oneself; indeed, these are nonplaces where recognition, including self-recognition, proves precarious if not elusive, in spite of one's best efforts to be a subject in some recognizable sense. They are not sites of enunciation, but shifts in the topography from which a questionably audible claim emerges: the claim of the not-yet-subject and the nearly recognizable.[5]

Most of the misfits we will encounter in *Someone* do find themselves at some moment or other negotiating their sexualities in something like what Butler here calls nonplaces. The sexualities they negotiate, with varying degrees of success, involve, again in Butler's words, "social practices, specifically sexual practices, that do not appear immediately as coherent in the available lexicon of legitimation."[6] What is interesting is that these sexual misfits are often perfectly recognizable subjects in other ways, and also that they can, under the right circumstances, negotiate a tenuous form of recognition, one usually *not* involving nomination, that allows them to share with another person or a few other people, in a fragile moment of time and an indefinite region of social space, a misfit sexuality. One of my major preoccupations in *Someone* is the pragmatics of such simultaneously awkward and delicate endeavors.

It strikes me that these authors constitute a somewhat odd set of people to group together: Colette, Genet, Leduc, Beauvoir, Duras, Guibert, Pinget. They are, of course, all writers. Bourdieu notes early on in *Distinction* that "the individuals grouped in a class that is constructed in a particular respect (that is, in a particularly determinant respect) always bring with them, in addition to the pertinent properties by which they are classified, secondary properties which are thus smuggled into the explanatory model." He notes as well that for any given class, "a number of official criteria in fact serve as a mask for hidden criteria."[7] Misfits are, we might say, people who discover that they don't belong to the class that they have been taken (by themselves or by others) to belong to, because some criteria that nobody had ever mentioned (or would ever think to mention) has not been satisfied, or because they either lack an essential secondary (or tertiary) property or possess a disqualifying one. It could be that the absence or presence of such a hidden or secondary property or criterion is not even apparent until a certain event or interaction occurs, until a certain context emerges, or until a certain situation arises. In any case, suddenly or not so suddenly, some kind of a call to order transpires, or some kind of expectation emerges, as a result of which they find themselves unfit or misfit, decategorized, but to an uncertain degree, faced with the project of understanding the terms, the profile we might say, of their misfittedness, and faced with seeing if there is anything that can be done about it—which there may or may not be, depending on who they are otherwise and where precisely they find themselves located in social space. The different things people might do in such circumstances constitute the subject of these pages.

There is a logic to the way the chapters of this book are ordered, but it strikes me that they could be read in any order. Chapter 1, "Colette and (Un)intelligibility," on Colette and one of her texts from the 1930s, is an overture introducing all the themes that will be treated in the rest of the book. Chapter 2, "Sexuality and the Literary Field," slightly more sweeping in its historical coverage, lays out the reasons for my interest in Bourdieusian field theory and proposes various adjustments to the way it is often deployed that seem necessary to me in order to arrive at an understanding of texts dealing with misfit sexualities in twentieth-century France. Chapter 3, "Metapragmatics, Sexuality, and the Novel: Reading Jean Genet's *Querelle*," develops my interest in pragmatic and metapragmatic forms of analysis of both utterances and cultural formations (e.g., genres of interaction and sexualities), using Genet's novel *Querelle de Brest* as both its object of analysis and a source of theoretical inspiration. Chapters 4 and 5 are a methodological pair dealing with two different authors (Beauvoir and Duras) in a similar way, taking a set of writings from a certain time period and trying to show how an experience of a misfit sexuality is sometimes registered not within the confines of any given text, but rather in the set of contextual relations that can be drawn between parts of a sociotextual array. Rather than offering a reading of a particular text, these chapters attempt to capture a moment in an ongoing semiotic process, a process in which a given literary text could be said to be caught up. The goal is to see how misfit sexualities might register themselves within that ongoing process more than they do in any given text.

Chapter 6 takes up a different strand in Bourdieu's work—his ways of thinking about people who find themselves precariously positioned within a given social universe, and the kinds of awareness their vulnerabilities may produce regarding the functioning of the social order. It applies this strand of Bourdieu's thought to misfit sexualities as they can be found in the works of both Violette Leduc and Hervé Guibert, doubtless an odd couple, but, I think, an analytically productive pairing. The work of both Leduc and Guibert involves urgent forms of address from sociologically precarious positions, utterances that struggle to become felicitous because they traffic in unintelligibility, because they constitute an expression of a difference that, on the one hand, seems imperceptible and, on the other, asks to be shared. In fact, this entire book is essentially about those predicaments, and about the literary interest a certain set of writers took in them.

(Some people might find the inclusion of Hervé Guibert in a book about misfit sexualities odd since it might at first glance seem uncontroversial to think of him as prototypically gay. Yet even a prototypically gay man [if that's what Guibert was] could find himself caught up in an encounter with someone else [maybe a man, maybe not, maybe gay, maybe not] that pushes him toward an experience of a sexuality that somehow fails to conform to what is intelligible [to him and others] as gay. This is, I take it, part of the experience that Guibert has with Eugène Savitzkaya. Furthermore, one aspect of his experience with HIV and AIDS that Guibert registered carefully was the way it produced unexpected new forms of intimacy with unexpected people that carried with them new potential for misfittedness. These are the two aspects of Guibert's experience and writing that explain his inclusion here.)

Chapter 7 is a coda in a certain way, reviewing most of the themes of the book by means of a reading of three novels by Robert Pinget, an underread but brilliant New Novelist whose technical virtuosity in thinking about misfit sexualities and their way of existing in language has been mostly unnoticed until now.

The problems I address in this volume are not limited to the temporal period I cover here (mainly 1930 to 1990). I addressed a related set of issues in an earlier volume on Balzac and nineteenth-century forms of sexuality, for instance.[8] I have the sense that to carry the analysis further forward in time requires a significant shift both in the conceptual framework being used and in the precise problems under discussion. To deal with literary productions of the post-1990 period (I am almost tempted to say the post-1980 period, or even post-1970 in some ways) in a satisfactory way would involve developing a fuller account of the impact of several phenomena on the myriad sexual cultures that exist in France and on certain acts of literary expression. Those phenomena include, on the one hand, decolonization and the various correlate kinds of immigrations and other population shifts that characterize the 1960s and following decades, and, on the other hand, the AIDS epidemic, understood as both a global and a local phenomenon with a significant impact not only on sexual cultures but also on literary practices dealing with sexuality. I hope to address both of these phenomena in future work.

On a practical note of a different kind: When an English translation of a French text is given, but no reference to a published translation is provided, the translation is mine. When a published translation is cited, I will occasionally have made silent modifications to it in order to highlight a certain pragmatic effect, or to bring out a certain nuance of meaning or a certain tonal feature.

Colette and (Un)intelligibility

Colette's 1932 publication *Ces plaisirs . . .* (These pleasures . . .) has a lot to say about misfits, and it is a misfit text as well. Colette reworked and republished the volume in 1941 as *Le pur et l'impur* (*The Pure and the Impure*), the title by which it is mostly known today. (I will mostly refer to it in this chapter as *Ces plaisirs . . .* because I am interested in its presence in the context of 1930s France.) In this first chapter, I reconstruct some of the contexts in which *Ces plaisirs . . .* was written and some of the forms of address in which it was caught up in order to allow certain implicit meanings to emerge out of the interplay between text, context, and public.

In earlier work, I approached this volume of Colette's in a different way. There I was interested in the example Colette's book offered of a particular rhetorical gesture that I noticed regularly coming up in discussions of same-sex sexualities by French writers throughout the twentieth century, a gesture that consists in referencing and describing some such sexuality (even declaring one's allegiance to it or participation in it) but not offering it as a place from which someone could speak: speaking *about* it, but neither *for* nor fully *as* a participant in it. Indeed, in the case of *Ces plaisirs . . .*, Colette seemed to go so far as to insist that certain of these sexualities (ones between women) were not a place from which anyone *could ever* speak in any authoritative way. As I put it in the epilogue to *Never Say I*, Colette's purpose seemed to be to describe "an identity that functions as a social category, but not one to which a woman can durably belong, not one with any political potentiality, any future."[1] The first person that was invoked and authorized in order to speak of such identities had somehow to delimit with caution the very terms of their existence, and in such a way that inhabitants of those identities could not ever actually be imagined to speak so as to advocate for themselves.

It was at the end of the pages in *Ces plaisirs* . . . that Colette devoted to the Ladies of Llangollen, Eleanor Butler and Sarah Ponsonby, who ran off together in 1778 and lived together in Wales for the next fifty or so years, that she offered a critique of Proust for his way of portraying women interested in other women. The terms of her critique have intrigued and troubled numerous commentators over the years:

> Can we possibly, without apprehension, imagine two Ladies of Llangollen in this year 1930? They would own a democratic car, wear overalls, smoke cigarettes, have short hair, and there would be a liquor bar in their apartment. . . . Eleanor Butler would curse as she jacked up the car, and would have her breasts amputated. . . . And already, twenty years earlier, Marcel Proust had endowed her with shocking desires, customs, and language, thus showing how little he knew her.[2]

Colette here both suggests and also exemplifies the perils of translating certain kinds of identities across time (as well as across geographic and cultural space). Such an act of translation can involve associating an attribute taken as an index of an identity at one moment of time and in one set of cultural circumstances with an attribute taken as an index of another identity at a later time and a different culture, assuming we will concur both in the parallelism of the two identities and the parallelism of the attributes or emblems associated with them. If, for Colette, there was probably little that could be called "democratic" about the lives of Eleanor Butler and Sarah Ponsonby, what is it that makes the cars of couples of automobile-owning women who are Colette's contemporaries worthy of this attribute? Colette also makes an imaginative link between one member of a couple of women from an earlier time and a surgical procedure that we would nowadays associate with trans-people. (The editors of the Pléiade edition of Colette's works suggest that Colette's contemporaries would most likely have understood her to be making a reference here to the athlete Violette Morris, notably successful in soccer, various track and field events, and race-car driving. Morris had an elective mastectomy in 1929, ostensibly to make it easier to fit behind the wheel of the cars she was racing. Breast-reduction surgery was in fact a topic in the air in various Parisian circles in the late 1920s, and I will return below to a discussion of the cultural work Colette is performing by referencing the topic here.)[3] She disputes the terms of a prior literary representation of the category of persons she is imagining here, the representation found in Proust's *In Search of Lost Time*. Proust, she claims, knew what he was doing in representing same-sex sexuality among men, but not among women:

When he assembles a Gomorrah of inscrutable and depraved [vicieuse] young girls, when he denounces an entente, a collectivity, a frenzy of bad angels, we are only diverted, indulgent, and a little bored, having lost the support of the dazzling light of truth that guides us through Sodom. . . . Puberty, boarding school, solitude, prisons, aberrations, snobbishness—they are all seedbeds, but too shallow to engender and sustain a vice that could attract a great number or become an established thing that would gain the indispensable solidarity of its votaries. (139)

It seems Colette sees no durable and identity-based solidarity among the diversity of women who might, at one point or another of their lives, take a sexual and/or affective interest in other women, and faults Proust for suggesting otherwise.

We might nowadays want to resist the tendency seen here in *Ces plaisirs . . .* to conflate what we would now take to be distinct lesbian and transgender identities; we might also want to stand up for Proust's representations of lesbians and note that the passage of time has amply demonstrated the capacity of lesbians to build durable forms of identity and community.[4] Yet, despite our quarrels, we might also want to find a way to hear something else in Colette's utterances here. Perhaps we could learn to be attentive to her attempt to make a place for another sexuality—or other sexualities—that are being only implicitly referenced in the way she puts her text together. This is where the project of *Someone* gets going, in an effort simply to notice other sexualities that it is often all too easy to miss. One of the central hypotheses of the present book is that certain kinds of misfit sexualities sometimes exist in language and culture without ever being *explicitly* talked about or *explicitly* laid claim to, that in some ways talking *about* them is nearly impossible given the way a particular language and culture work, that these sexualities leave other kinds of traces, more pragmatic than semantic ones. We might, for instance, know in some practical kind of way that there are important differences between the sexualities of different individuals without having the words to say what those differences are. We might make distinctions in practical dealings with people around sexuality about which we are inarticulate. In short, we often *know* more about sexuality in practice than we can actually *say*. What would it mean for an author to write about a phenomenon about which she knows more than she can say, to write about aspects of it that she cannot actually articulate? Often, such writing becomes a space that is meant to activate the implicit pragmatic cultural knowledge of a reader through which inarticulate differences are apprehended. (Of course, the success of such a strategy is only possible should the reader in question have the required practical knowledge available for activation.) Such writing will need to develop techniques to focus readerly attention on some of the myriad ways we regularly draw on inarticulate bits of cultural knowledge in order to act in the world, to understand other people, to interact successfully with them.[5]

One way of glossing Colette's claim about the difference between Sodom and Gomorrah that she says Proust has missed would be to say that she is implicitly asserting that women are more likely to be bisexual than men, and that most women who become involved with other women at some point in their lives are bisexual. (As we shall see shortly, to gloss this statement in such a way involves suggesting that an utterance can be simplified or reduced to some kind of propositional content that can subsequently be restated without distortion using other words.) Implicit in what she might be taken to be suggesting would be that being bisexual is, in her view, not a cultural or personal identity around which women might affiliate, but rather something that is simply observable in people's behavior. Obviously, she does not use this kind of terminology. Such ways of speaking wouldn't really even be possible for several more decades. Colette's register and terminology are decidedly unscientific and unsociological. We might even say that they are determinedly old-fashioned for her time. Evidence of her old-fashioned stance might be her use of words like "vice" and "vicieuse" in the passage just cited in order to mean sexually nonnormative, or her fondness in other places for the word "unisexual," whose vogue in the final decades of the nineteenth century and first few decades of the twentieth had clearly passed by the time she was writing. *Ces plaisirs . . .* , she wrote to her friend Hélène Picard in June 1931, as she worked away at the manuscript and debated what its title should be, "stirs up old things having to do with love, and gets itself mixed up in unisexual love stories."[6]

I am here extrapolating from Colette's text in order to imagine something of the cultural universe out of which it seems to be generated; I am working to imagine the array of cultural concepts regarding sexuality Colette is invoking (perhaps highly idiosyncratic ones that few of Colette's contemporaries even shared with her) as she writes. I have also just called attention to the register in which she couches her observation. Use of a particular linguistic register is itself often a way of making an identity claim. Both the conceptual point of view on sexuality that Colette is putting forth and the register she is using to do so (a register that contributes to the self-positioning Colette is doing without being easily translatable into propositional content) are part and parcel of the presentation of sexuality in *Ces plaisirs . . . .* What I mean to pursue throughout *Someone* are those aspects of sexuality that are not denotated or asserted propositionally in language, but that are conveyed through other aspects of language use such as register, tone, and implicit frames of reference.

Registers, Asif Agha notes, "are historical formations caught up in group-relative processes of valorization and countervalorization, exhibiting change in both form and value over time. For instance, when prestige registers used by upper-class/caste speakers are imitated by other groups, the group whose speech is the sought-after variety often innovates in its own speech habits, seeking to renew or transform the emblem of distinction."[7] There are, of course, many features to a register. What I would like to call attention to in connection with *Ces plaisirs* . . . is register understood as, in Michael Silver-stein's words, "context-appropriate alternate ways of 'saying the same thing' such as are seen in so-called 'speech levels.'"[8] At stake in the discourse on sexuality in *Ces plaisirs* . . . is not only the sense of what "context-appropriate" ways of talking about marginal sexualities might be (the range of possible alternatives), but also negotiated agreements as to what constitutes "the same thing" and what doesn't. In speech or writing about sexuality, just as in other forms of speech or writing, registers serve to index different kinds of social distinctions between speakers and to allow for different kinds of social positioning. As Agha puts it, "processes of enregisterment [are] processes whereby distinct forms of speech come to be socially recognized (or enregistered) as indexical of speaker attributes by a population of language users. . . . Encounters with registers are not merely encounters with voices . . . but encounters in which individuals establish forms of alignment . . . with social types of persons, real or imagined, whose voices they take them to be."[9] One assumes (and not always correctly) that one's audience recognizes the import of a selection (not necessarily a conscious one) from a contrasting set of possibilities encompassed in a given set of registers—or one hopes one's audience appreciates the import of an improvisation that adds a new register to a set of otherwise well-known ones.[10] Is or was what Colette was doing with registers in *Ces plaisirs* . . . recognizable as an act of position-taking in relation to the marginal sexualities that are her subject in the book? Of course Colette, through her choice of lexicon, positions herself as old-fashioned, and as resistant to certain newfangled sexual identities she sees around her that she loosely but perhaps revealingly characterizes as "democratic." (Or at least she applies that adjective to the motor vehicle she imagines some inhabitants of those identities to be driving around in.) But we also see a more complex use of register to suggest something about sexuality (about Colette's own sexuality) that it is harder to characterize semantically or taxonomically. My flat-footed gloss of a claim about sexuality Colette may or may not have been making (that women

re likely to be bisexual than men, and that most women who become
ved with other women at some point in their lives are bisexual) is clearly
active of the complexity of what she was communicating about sexuality,
both her own and sexuality in general.

Speech about bisexuality (the word existed in Colette's time although the
range of speakers who knew it and its range of uses were probably not as wide
as is the case today) often highlights the fact that there are forms of cultural
knowledge about sexuality that cannot easily be done justice by taxonomies.[11]
Consider the following observations from the 2011 report by the LGBT Advisory Committee of the San Francisco Human Rights Commission, "Bisexual
Invisibility: Impacts and Recommendations":

> The term *bisexual* is imperfect at best. It implies a duality of genders that many
> people feel erases transgender and gender-variant people. For others, it con-
> notes a requirement of an exact balance between someone's attractions for
> women and men, or attractions only to women and men who identify with
> the genders they were assigned at birth. . . . The good news is that more and
> more people are comfortable navigating the complexities of human sexuality
> and gender as they are actually lived. The bad news is that the English language
> has not yet caught up in expressing that complexity. At this time, there is no
> clear "best practice" for terminology that fully honors gender diversity while
> not reinscribing invisibility for non-monosexuals.
>
> At this moment in the movement for full equality and dignity for people
> of all sexual orientations and gender identities, *bisexual* is the term that is
> most widely understood as describing those whose attractions fall outside an
> either/or paradigm. It is also (along with MSMW and WSMW) the term most
> often used in research.
>
> As people become increasingly fluent in the dynamics of gender and sex-
> uality, the language will evolve as well. For now, and with full awareness of its
> limitations, *bisexual* is the word used in this report.[12]

We might think of this report and of Colette's text as sharing certain generic
features.[13] They intend to communicate official and unofficial forms of knowledge about diverse sexualities, and to provide authoritative language for doing
so.[14] They critique previous invocations of lexical items and previous applica-
tions of categories. They struggle with denotational language and do other
things with language in the meantime. Because language does not work only
denotationally, we might hazard a guess that the hope of the authors of "Bisexual Invisibility" that language will someday "catch up" with the complexity
of "sexuality and gender as they are actually lived" is a bit of a forlorn one. To
imagine a moment when language might have caught up with sexuality seems
for the authors of the report to be to imagine the creation of new terms with

which to denote a wider range of sexualities and genders. But language will never only function through the denotational application of terms, however conceptually nuanced an understanding those terms may be drawn from. It also does not seem self-evident that the social forms of sexuality extant in a given culture would ever hold still long enough for denotational language to catch up to them.

In "'Cultural' Concepts and the Language-Culture Nexus," Michael Silverstein helpfully distinguishes between what he calls "lexically explicit '-onomic' structures," on the one hand, and "cultural concepts beyond lexicalization," on the other, both of which represent different kinds of knowledge. "The way we denote what we consider 'real-world' things by lexical expressions" is one kind of knowledge, classificatory knowledge, and "to investigate a culture's concepts, in this approach, one tries to extract or induce the semantic consistencies in such lexical usage and model them in terms of -onomies. If one can, one tries to give the intensional principles of conceptual classification that lie behind such an -onomy's structure, more or less identifying these principles with the conceptual meanings—senses—of the critical theoretical terms, the lexical labels of the systematizable culture."[15] Part of Colette's remarkable achievement in *Ces plaisirs . . .* (about which more in a few pages) is her ability simultaneously to play with the limitations of her culture's taxonomic resources for sexuality and to communicate other nonsystematizable (or at least not yet systematized) aspects of sexuality with which we are, to greater or lesser degrees, conversant—just not through processes of lexicalization. The kind of knowledge Silverstein designates as represented by "cultural concepts beyond lexicalization" is "indexically invoked in and by the use of certain language forms in context, but the concepts will never be systematizable" through any series of queries about semantic consistency in lexical usage. That is, we regularly do things with language in a way that indicates we possess (practically) certain kinds of conceptual knowledge about various subjects about which we would have difficulty being articulate.[16] One of the major features of talk about sexuality that falls into this domain and that *Ces plaisirs . . .* could be said to highlight would be the ways many of us use language to localize certain sexualities, sexual identities, and sexual practices (including our own) in time and space, whereas these are aspects of sexuality (its timeliness or lack thereof, its locatability) that our most readily available taxonomic systems in general take no account of or even obfuscate.[17]

We not only have ways of delimiting the geographic or temporal boundaries we would assign to this or that aspect of sexuality, we also actively situate ourselves on various timelines we understand to be part of the history of sexuality (ours or others') or on various kinds of internalized maps of sexuality and

sexual cultures. *Ces plaisirs* . . . , for the most part a retrospective account of
Colette's journalistic or ethnographic interest in the diverse sexual cultures of
the belle epoque in France (thus sexual cultures extant several decades prior
to its writing and publication), is deeply invested in these kinds of activities.
The passage about the Ladies of Llangollen is the oddest piece of the puzzle
that the book constitutes, the only piece that extends the temporal and geographic boundaries of the represented world outward and backward beyond
the limits of France and the belle epoque. I will have more to say about the
significance of the inclusion of this "foreign" material in the text toward the
end of this chapter, but for now suffice it to say that it offered Colette, as she
represented herself in the moment of writing, the occasion to triangulate her
current (1930s) point of view on sexuality with Proust's recent representation
of modern lesbian subjects, and with a couple of women living in Wales more
than a century earlier in order simultaneously to refuse, in an old-fashioned
register, Proust's modernity, while still acknowledging that sexual cultures and
identities evolve over time. For instance, when Colette writes, in the course of
the same passage, that "Sapphic libertinage is the only unacceptable one" (le
libertinage saphique est le seul qui soit inacceptable), and that "we can never
sufficiently blame those occasional Sapphists one meets in restaurants, in
dance halls" (il n'y aura jamais assez de blâme sur les saphos de rencontre, celle
du restaurant, du dancing),[18] she could be taken to be pontificating against
forms of lesbian sociability that were coming to a certain prominence in Paris
in the late 1920s and 1930s. The singer Suzy Solidor, for instance, would open
her famous café-cabaret, La Vie Parisienne, in 1933. It advertised itself as being
open in the afternoons as a "tea room for unaccompanied women" and became famous as a cabaret frequented by chic gays and lesbians, as well as other
women interested in women (those Colette refers to as "saphos de rencontre,"
occasional Sapphists). It was a place where Solidor herself could be heard
singing unambiguously erotic songs about women, such as "Obsession" or
"Ouvre."[19] Colette's claim that "we can never bring enough twilight, silence,
and gravity to surround the embrace of two women" (il n'y aura jamais trop de
crépuscule ménagé, de silence et de gravité sur une étreinte de femmes) seems
antithetical to Solidor's imperatives in performing and recording "Ouvre":

> Open your two trembling knees
> Open your thighs
> Open all there is to open
>
> (Ouvre tes deux genoux tremblants
> Ouvre tes cuisses
> Ouvre tout ce qu'on peut ouvrir)

The passage Colette writes on the Ladies of Llangollen seems almost to be written as a reproach to the burgeoning lesbian culture that surrounded her in Paris, a somewhat paradoxical demonstration of how to represent something in twilight rather than in the light of day, how to speak of something in silence rather than in words. Colette might here be offering an excellent example of someone who is "feeling backward," to use the suggestive phrase of Heather Love.[20]

To develop a sense of what we might refer to as Colette's backwardness, let us return for a moment to her way of referencing the topic of breast reduction or breast amputation: "Can we possibly, without apprehension, imagine two Ladies of Llangollen in this year 1930? They would own a democratic car, wear overalls, smoke cigarettes, have short hair, and there would be a liquor bar in their apartment. . . . Eleanor Butler would curse as she jacked up the car, and would have her breasts amputated." We could say that her tone here is odd, hard to get a fix on. To begin to get a fix on it, it helps to know that she is referencing a discourse on breast reduction that was circulating in the world around her. More than providing that bit of context, we need not only to reconstruct the kinds of cultural work being done by the various instances of media representations of breast-reduction surgery Colette was implicitly indexing in her remark; we also need to hypothesize about the nature of the work Colette was attempting to perform through both the tone and the propositional content of her own invocation of the topic.

The art and culture magazine *Fantasio*, to which Colette had occasionally been a contributor, is a prime location for finding discussions of breast-reduction surgery in the years just prior to the publication of *Ces plaisirs . . . .* It publishes articles discussing the topic on March 15, 1927, April 15, 1929, and April 15, 1930. The 1929 article gives us the name of one of the prominent surgeons performing the operation, "Professeur Gosset," and the 1930 article profiles Violette Morris among other examples of people who have undergone the surgery.[21] In 1927, *Fantasio* editorializes about the rise of this new specialty in plastic surgery, and refers to this new category of medical specialist, the "ablateur de sein" (breast amputator), as an expert who has understood something about "today's woman." Toward the end of its comments on this new trend, *Fantasio* opines: "There are nothing but androgynous busts left. Give it a few years and the female breast will be nothing but a memory" (Il n'y a plus que des poitrines androgynes. Encore quelques années, et le sein féminin n'existera plus qu'à l'état de souvenir). This article suggests that the motivations for breast-reduction surgery are mostly cosmetic, "to keep up with fashion" (pour satisfaire à la mode), and implies that women's interest in the androgynous look causes them to forget their maternal duties: "Small children, yearning for their mother's milk, will look in vain for the exact spot, and, upon discovering a scar, will cry out: 'Hey, mom, you've cut yourself!'" (Les petits enfants, avides du lait maternel, chercheront en vain l'emplacement exact, et, découvrant une cicatrice, s'écrieront: "Tiens, maman, tu t'es coupée!")[22]

For some, then, breast reduction was taken to be a way of keeping up with the fashion for a more androgynous feminine silhouette. The example of Violette Morris indicates, of course, that there could be other motivations for the surgery. If Morris was one name regularly associated with this topic, another was Maryse Choisy, the author in these years of a series of investigative exposés—on prostitution (*Un mois chez les filles*, 1928); on the all-male monasteries of Mount Athos (*Un mois chez les hommes*, 1929); on prison sexuality (*L'amour dans les prisons*, 1930)—as well as a fourteen-page illustrated spread on lesbianism for the comic magazine *Le Rire* in May 1932. When writing on all these topics, Choisy regularly falls into a tone of light, even comic, banter. In *Un mois chez les filles* (My month with the working girls), while describing a scene in which she is filling out a questionnaire for a "dating agency," she tells of the woman proprietor reaching over to feel her breasts to check on their firmness, then noting in her register, "Breasts: firm, although a bit large for today's tastes." Choisy then adds a footnote: "I have since had my breasts reduced by the most famous female surgeon in Paris."[23] This may, of course, have been a bit of ironic repartee rather than an actual statement of fact, but Choisy did also mention breast reduction on a number of other occasions, including suggesting that it was part of the disguise that was necessary for her to sneak into an all-male monastery for her next book.[24] Choisy (who would later convert to Catholicism, attempt to remove as many copies of her earlier books as possible from circulation, undergo psychoanalysis, and become an analyst herself) thus suggests that the fashion was running toward smaller breasts ("a bit large for today's tastes") and proffers a professional motivation for her surgery (to be able more easily to pass as a man as part of her undercover investigation of monks).[25]

Violette Morris would also claim that her surgery had professional motivations. In the article "Vous gênent-ils?" (Do they get in your way? or Do they bother you?) penned for *Fantasio* in 1929, Edmond Tourgis mentions that "one of our all-around women athletes had her breasts removed because they got in her way, or so she says. Why would you let such a thing get in your way nowadays, when so many miracles are possible?" (Une sportive intégrale s'est fait trancher les seins parce qu'ils la gênaient . . . dit-elle. A quoi bon se gêner, en une époque si fertile en miracles?)[26] Tourgis spends the rest of his article recounting the replies of various actresses of stage and screen to his query as to whether their breasts were a problem for them, and reports himself reassured to learn that the actresses were uniformly happy with their breasts and saw no need for modification. When *Fantasio* returns to the topic a year later, the writer juxtaposes two female figures. The second is an anonymous singer who claimed that over time her breasts, large even when she was young, had become heavier and ever more annoying. She underwent surgery, she says, to bring them back to reasonable proportions. Her audience, mostly but not entirely female, is fascinated by her story and by her exhibition of the results. Many take down the name of the doctor involved. However, the article begins by remembering an encounter between the author and "Mlle Violette" that took place a few years earlier: "She obviously was or wished to be of a new sex. She wore short trousers and a jacket. She had apparently had her breasts removed. The ablation rid her of an excessively large bust." (Elle était, évidemment, ou voulait être d'un nouveau sexe. Elle portait la culotte courte et le veston. Il paraît qu'elle a supprimé ses seins. L'ablation l'a débarrassée d'une poitrine excessive.)[27] Here, then, is a different understanding of breast-reduction surgery, one related to questions of sex and gender identity.

Throughout all these writings on breast-reduction surgery, regular mention is made of the legend of the Amazons, mythic women warriors who sacrificed their right breast to enhance their prowess with a bow. That legend brings together questions of the body image of women, their sexual independence, same-sex communities and sexualities, relations between the sexes, the distribution of sex roles in any given society, and the social construction of maternity. Much of the discourse in Colette's world around the topic of elective breast-reduction surgery seems to have to do with questions of fluctuating images of the female body and of female fashion. But any of these other questions regarding same-sex sexuality, gender politics, or the social construction of maternity can easily come up. In fact, we could say that the discourse is constantly implicitly posing questions regarding the relation of all of these topics to each other. When Colette wonders if we should be apprehensive in imagining the Ladies of Llangollen transported forward from the late eighteenth to the early twentieth century, the apprehension is related to the vague aversion she seems to feel in imagining their modern avatars with short hair, smoking and drinking, driving and doing their own work on "democratic" cars, and one of them having breast-reduction surgery. It's an amazingly compact evocation she provides of all the ideological components of the ambient discourse that tangled together issues of cosmetic surgery, body image, gender identity, feminist politics and practice, same-sex sexuality, and emergent discourses of transgenderism and transsexuality. What it clearly isn't is progressive. It seems neither particularly feminist nor particularly favorably

inclined to emerging notions of transgender identities. It seems rather to be
mourning something lost, and that loss is figured in the loss of the modern Eleanor's breasts.[28] (I will return to develop this possibility a bit more toward the
end of this chapter.) We might speculate that the apprehension Colette gives
expression to here is one of the signs of a certain misfit she experiences in her
own sexuality, a sexuality that feels less and less at home in the modern world
around her. In *Feeling Backward*, Heather Love notes that in studying people
who feel temporally out of place in their sexuality, it often becomes crucial to
"focus on the negative affects—the need, the aversion, and the longing—that
characterize the relation between past and present."[29] (Perhaps unsurprisingly,
negative affects will frequently appear around the figures of sexual misfits we
will encounter in the chapters to come.) The production of this negative affect
will not always be indexed to a temporal relation. It sometimes seems to be
more a result of the semiotic experience of the misfit of categories. Such an
experience may have a relation to temporality or to geography, but that needn't
always be the case.

If, in the passage on Proust and the Ladies of Llangollen, hers is an old-
fashioned, recalcitrant relation to modernity, in an earlier passage from *Ces
plaisirs . . .* , when Colette represents her younger self in conversation with
"La Chevalière," an aristocratic, masculine woman sexually interested in other
women, a different time frame is laid out for us. ("La Chevalière" is, as a good
portion of Colette's readership would probably have recognized, based on
Mathilde de Morny—called "Missy" by her friends—with whom Colette had
had a relationship lasting several years in the first decade of the century.)[30]

> With such distinguishing marks as pleated shirt front, hard collar, sometimes
> a waistcoat, and always a silk pocket handkerchief, I frequented a social set
> that was dying out, mostly cut off from the rest of society. Although various
> kinds of habits, good and bad, haven't changed in the past twenty-five or thirty
> years, aristocratic class consciousness [l'esprit de caste], in killing itself off,
> gradually undermined the debilitated clique I am referring to, which tried,
> trembling with fear, to live in a different atmosphere from the one in which it
> could breathe, hypocrisy. It claimed the right to "personal freedom," and set
> itself up as the equal of the ever imperturbable and solid world of pederasty. . . .
> Where could I find, nowadays, the likes of those invited to La Chevalière's table,
> emptying her wine cellar and her purse? Baronesses of the Empire, canonesses,
> lady cousins of Czars, illegitimate daughters of grand-dukes, exquisites of the
> Parisian bourgeoisie, and also some aged horsewomen of the Austrian aristoc-
> racy, hand and eye of steel. . . . I witnessed and paid homage to the decline of
> these women. Once their charm had vanished, they struggled to tell its story,

to explain it. They tried to render intelligible for us their success with and their defiant taste for women. The astonishing thing is that they were successful in doing so.[31]

Here are some of the claims Colette appears to be making in this passage, claims to which we may or may not want to give our full assent: Sexual identities and sexual cultures come and go, Colette suggests, and they often, while they exist, have specific class locations. As the class position inhabited by Missy and her friends disappears, so does the social form of their sexuality. There may seem to be a continuity between past sexual cultures and present ones, but in fact there is no guarantee that that sense of continuity is real, just as there is no guarantee of a past culture remaining intelligible to a later one. The claim laid by Missy and her circle to certain kinds of rights and freedoms bears no necessary relation to any claims to rights that may be made by future sexual minorities. The world of a certain kind of male same-sex relations (the world named pederasty here) has a different kind of existence in time than any women's same-sex culture might have.

In *A Coincidence of Desire: Anthropology, Queer Studies, Indonesia*, Tom Boellstorff notes that "subject positions (socially extant categories of selfhood) do not necessarily exist in unbroken timelines." He speaks of the ways new organizations of sexuality emerge by "overlapping rather than displacing earlier cultural logics," and he analyzes a "layering" effect in which both previous and emergent understandings and enactments of sexuality are linked to other changes in the social field.[32] Elizabeth Freeman has wondered about how time "wrinkles and folds" as sexual presents reach out to sexual pasts or as "the materials of a failed and forgotten project of the past find their uses now, in a future unimaginable in their time."[33] Carolyn Dinshaw has similarly referred to a "felt experience of asynchrony."[34] All of these observations and conceptualizations could help us parse how Colette, in the passage just cited, and throughout *Ces plaisirs . . .* , is situating herself and her sexuality in time and in cultural space, help us parse the implicit claims about her own sexuality and the idiosyncratic (somewhat unintelligible, we might even say) point of view on sexuality that she proffers by means of her book. She associated with this older group of women, wearing signs they would recognize, and was sexually involved with one of them, but without sharing their sexuality. She couldn't share their sexuality because she came from a different time and class. Yet her sexuality overlaps with theirs. When she folds the Ladies of Llangollen into her book, she makes use of them to combat a vision of the sexual present that she finds asserted by Proust's representation of lesbians in his novel. One has the odd sense of Colette as feeling temporally and culturally proximate to the Ladies, temporally and culturally distant from Missy and her set (who interest her ethnographically and personally to the extent that she becomes a participant observer in their lives), yet also temporally and culturally distant from a present moment that she insists cannot include the kinds of girls Proust represents even though it would seem to include modern day Sarah Ponsonbys and Eleanor Butlers with their democratic cars, short hair, dungarees, propensities to work on their automobiles and to seek out the kinds of medical interventions that now belong to what is called sex-reassignment surgery. (Not incidentally, it was apparently Una Troubridge, Radclyffe Hall's companion, who put Colette on to the Ladies of Llangollen.)[35]

Colette writes as if both her own sexuality and her own framework for understanding sexuality—the cultural concepts she implicitly invokes by the way she presents the sexuality of others—should be easily intelligible to her reader. She is an ethnographer/journalist with an interest "in certain privileged creatures and their steadiness in what seems like an impossible balancing pose, and especially in the diversity and steadfastness of that part of their sensuality that was for them a point of honor. Not just a point of honor, but a kind of poetry."[36] The poetry she sees, and helps interpret for us, could perhaps be understood as what Bourdieu calls the "labour of representation" that is required to assert social identities whose intelligibility has no institutional guarantee.[37] People inhabiting these identities would be occupants of the "precarious positions" Bourdieu writes about in *The Weight of the World*: "occupants of precarious positions . . . turn out to be extraordinary 'practical analysts': situated at points where social structures 'work,' and therefore worked over by the contradictions of these structures, these individuals are constrained, in order to live or to survive, to practice a kind of self-analysis, which often gives them access to the objective contradictions which have them in their grasp, and to the objective structures expressed in and by these contradictions."[38] Colette writes as if it were the subjects of her inquiry—those acrobats of the sensual world, miraculously balanced at a point in time or in cultural space, the difficult poetry of whose balancing act she interprets for us in the face of its disappearance—whom we would be hard-pressed to comprehend.

And yet there is also something acrobatic about the position she constructs for herself in this text; her own intelligibility, the frameworks and concepts she invokes in presenting minority sexual cultures and sexual subjects and the self-figuration she creates through these invocations seem anything but self-evident. They require of us a labor of reconstruction and an effort of conceptualization and contextualization. It is as if *Ces plaisirs . . .* is an attempt to put certain frameworks of understanding into circulation, but an effort that has been somewhat stymied. Its frameworks are not to be found close to hand. Her chosen register, we could say, is in some way too idiosyncratic, too unofficial.[39]

In *Never Say I*, I investigated the uneven establishment of what have become the dominant social forms for modern lesbian and gay identities in France, and the construction of certain genres and rituals, of certain literary and social practices, that enabled those identities to be taken up and elaborated in the first person (both in public life and in literary texts)—the first person being itself understood as a social form or artifact that is collectively produced, sustained, and ratified. In *Someone*, my goal is to think about misfit relationships to gay and lesbian identities once they are established. That is to say, I am particularly interested in the conceptualization (or the *difficulty in conceptualizing*) and the representation (or the kinds of writerly work done in the attempt to represent something that resists representation, or something that representation itself resists) of same-sex sexualities that do not manage to correspond to mainstream gay and lesbian identities, once the social form of those identities has been rendered legible and has been somewhat widely disseminated both socially and in literature. The noncorrespondence between these misfit sexualities and lesbian and gay ones may have to do with an odd temporal relation to those identities, the feeling of being somehow before or after them, or with questions of geographical location (the perpetuation of older sexual forms in nonmetropolitan areas, for instance, forms whose durability is precisely linked to their location in regions where time, so to speak, moves more slowly). It may have to do with a discordance between the way gender identity and sexual identity are articulated in particular cases as opposed to in the general image of lesbian and gay identities. It may have to do with the nonpermanence or nonexclusivity of same-sex practices within a given person's sexual history, to the way those practices are distributed between public and private areas (or conscious and unconscious areas) of that person's being. It may have to do with how someone experiences a body in relation to what we might refer to as "sexual intercourse so-called,"[40] how the body is mapped and experienced erotically, and so on. It may have to do with an instance in which two people of "opposite" sexes, but one or both of whom sustain an involvement in "same-sex" identities, find themselves living out their sexuality together, and so on.

A number of the literary texts from the French tradition that I will be examining in this volume are interested not so much in the project of gaining or of furthering social recognition for a particular set of same-sex sexual identities (or simply of being able to write about them). Rather, they seem to want to call a strange sort of attention to sexualities that escape dominant or even emergent categories of apprehension; they develop very particular resources for calling a glancing form of attention to those sexualities that paradoxically resist representation by the way they fail to conform to the categories that normally enable the apprehension of sexuality. The authors and texts that I will be dealing with in the chapters that follow are for the most part ones interested in same-sex sexuality mostly when it falls outside the contours that have come to be instituted for recognized groups. In these cases, it is often difficult to *refer* to or to *denote* the sexualities in question, because they don't exactly have a name, or because naming them with an extant name would betray something about them. If they can't exactly be referred to, if they don't have a strong *semantic* existence, they can nonetheless be gestured at; they can exist pragmatically. That is, if they exist at all (which they do), and if they can be perpetuated (which they can), it is usually in practical (as opposed to theoretical or representational) ways that escape both easy representation and easy conceptualization.

What does it mean to say that nonmainstream, unofficial, misfit sexual forms and cultures almost necessarily have a heavily pragmatic or indexical (a diminished semantic) existence? Their transmission, perpetuation, and survival depend on the transmission and circulation of, on the one hand, the frames of reference that grant them whatever modest intelligibility they have and, on the other, the implicit metapragmatic functions (codes or rules of use that govern, structure, and render recognizable certain social situations) that provide the possibility of a shared framework for particular kinds of practical social and sexual interactions.[41] Without practical knowledge of these metapragmatic functions (which themselves exist and evolve as social forms) people would be unable to participate meaningfully in certain kinds of social and sexual activities. We might wonder in this regard how Mathilde de Morny and her friends successfully render intelligible to Colette the particular nature of their interest in women. (The "astonishing thing," we remember Colette emphasizing, "is that they were successful in doing so.") Here is part of the scene where the ethnographer/journalist Colette interviews her native informant on this question:

> For more than forty years, this woman with the bearing of a handsome young man endured the pride and punishment of never being able to establish a forthright, viable friendship with any woman. It was not for lack of trying, because she asked nothing better or worse. But the salacious expectations of women shocked her very natural platonic tendencies, which resembled more a restrained quivering, or the diffuse emotion of an adolescent, than the precise demands a woman might make. Twenty years ago she tried, with bitterness, to explain herself to me. "I do not know anything about completion in love,"

she said, "except for the *idea* of it that I have. But they, the women, have never allowed me to stop at that point . . ."

"Not a single one of them?"

"Not one."

"Why?"

"I'm sure I don't know." . . .

"But what is it that they hope for, in going further? Are they so invested in sensual pleasure itself, in the idea of sensual pleasure?"

"No doubt," she said, uncertainly.

"They must at least have an opinion about that special pleasure. Do they fling themselves upon it as upon a panacea, do they see it as a kind of consecration? Do they demand it, or accept it, more simply, as a proof of mutual trust?"

La Chevalière averted her eyes, flicked off the long ash on her cigar, waved her hand as a discreet man might do.

"That's beyond me. It's really not any of my business."

"And yet . . ."[42]

Now if this reconstructed conversation or something like it actually did take place twenty years earlier, it was probably taking place while Colette and Missy were in a relationship together. The subject of the conversation, as Colette reconstructs it, has to do with frustrations that occur in Missy's relations with women. It would seem that the frustrations arise from the fact that when Missy is with a woman, two different sexual identities, two different sexual practices, collide with less than satisfactory results. Colette, in the version of herself presented retrospectively here, tries to imagine why all these women demanded of Missy a relationship to sexual pleasure for which she had no inclination. She offers Missy a list of choices as to why the women with whom Missy was involved were so insistent on the experience of orgasm. Missy resists this line of questioning. (One might at this point ask why Colette is posing these questions to Missy rather than to herself, given that she is a member of the group of women with whom Missy has been sexually involved.) Again, we see here how Colette's sexuality, as well as her attitudes toward the sexual order around her, are implicated in the text. Among other functions, perhaps this passage works to distinguish Colette's sexuality not only from Missy's, but equally from that of Missy's other lovers. But in what, precisely, would either of these distinctions consist? What are the distinctive differences between Colette's sexuality and other sexualities in the sexual order as she presents it to us? Perhaps the answers change over time.

Does Colette manage to render her project in *Ces plaisirs* . . . and the social position from which she writes it intelligible to us? Did she render it intelligible to those of her contemporaries who read *Ces plaisirs* . . . when it was first published in 1932? There are interesting conceptual conundrums behind these questions (mainly regarding assumptions we implicitly or explicitly make regarding the kinds of concepts that are immanent in any given cultural universe—including our own—and the extent to which those concepts are shared, the extent to which they circulate). These conundrums will be at the heart of my analyses throughout *Someone*, analyses that necessarily occur at a number of different levels. The first, with which we have already been dealing to a certain degree, regards the question of how literary works end up existing within, and interacting with, a variety of contexts from the moment of initial publication onward throughout their careers, and how they take their meanings from our ability to call those contexts into being as we take that work up at whatever moment we encounter it.[43] Many kinds of meaning depend on the particular construction of a text's dynamic relation to the contexts in which it participates, contexts that we produce in our reading. (I will focus a bit more on the initial contexts of *Ces plaisirs . . .* in the following section.) The problem of recovering evanescent contexts that impact what a given text means in relation to sexuality will be central to the chapters on Simone de Beauvoir and Marguerite Duras that follow. Occasionally works will *explicitly* thematize and reflect upon what is mainly implicit in *Ces plaisirs . . .* : the various problems associated with the pragmatics of a misfit sexuality's cultural and linguistic existence. This will be the case, in particular, of the works by Jean Genet and Robert Pinget that I will be discussing.

I will also be taking up the question of how literary works, as they circulate through time and space, sometimes become the vehicle for the transmission not only of various kinds of practical knowledge about sexuality, but of frameworks through which to organize our perception of sexuality both conceptually and categorically. In 1999, introducing a special issue of *GLQ: A Journal of Lesbian and Gay Studies* titled "Thinking Sexuality Transnationally," Elizabeth Povinelli and George Chauncey pointed to a tension that emerges when thinking about the study of the history of sexuality in transnational terms, "the tension between increasingly powerful global discourses and institutions of homosexuality and heterosexuality and between local sexual ideologies and subjectivities organized in different, often resistant terms."[44] Colette's writing about sexuality in *Ces plaisirs . . .* can already be taken as an illustration and occasionally even an analysis of this tension, as a closer look at her somewhat paradoxical incorporation of the material regarding the Ladies of Llangollen—material drawn from a different time and a different place than the material related to the French belle epoque—will perhaps reveal. (A number of the works I will look at toward the end of *Someone*—see chapter 6 on Violette Leduc and Hervé Guibert—are also built around this tension.) What kind of implicit claims about the circulation of the social forms of sexuality across time and space might Colette be making by writing—in a book ostensibly about the different kinds of nonmainstream sexual subjects and cultures that could be found in belle epoque France—about two women who lived together in Wales at the end of the eighteenth century? Remember the list Colette provides when objecting to Proust's portrayal of "Gomorrah": "Puberty, boarding school, solitude, prisons, aberrations, snobbishness," all of the items listed are, as Colette has it, "seedbeds, but too shallow to engender and sustain a vice that could attract a great number or become an established thing that would gain the indispensable solidarity of its votaries."[45] Colette's claim here seems to be that what happens in certain phases of life or in certain institutional settings should not be abstracted from these limited locations and expanded discursively into some kind of identitarian structure. *Ces plaisirs . . .* thus makes an implicitly contrarian claim faced with a proliferation of other texts in her cultural surroundings (Proust of course, but many other as well)[46] that taken all together could easily count as evidence of what Chauncey and Povinelli call "increasingly powerful global discourses and institutions of homosexuality."

The circulation of information about the Ladies of Llangollen can be understood in similar fashion. For many people, the recovery, recounting, and re-recounting of this information would be part of a project of establishing a secure discursive home for lesbian identities. Colette seems to claim that her representation of material relating to Butler and Ponsonby is for a nearly opposite reason, to check the proliferation of materials being used to build up that discursive home, or to try to design a different home. The resistant stance of Colette's *Ces plaisirs . . .* is paradoxical. At the heart of the paradox is that Colette puts into circulation, or helps remain in circulation, textual material that encourages us to see both the discursive proliferation and the transnational circulation of a variety of social forms of sexuality that are increasingly taken to belong to "global discourses and institutions of homosexuality." So the very act of composing the text of *Ces plaisirs . . .* seems in some ways inherently to undermine whatever resistant stance she is implicitly sketching out. As Benjamin Lee and Edward LiPuma have noted, "circulation is a cultural process with its own forms of abstraction, evaluation, and constraint, which are created by the interactions between specific types of circulating forms and the interpretive communities built around them."[47] I will consider in a later part of this chapter more information about how the circulation of textual material related to the Ladies of Llangollen has precisely to do with the building up of certain kinds of interpretative communities and how the appropriate uptake of this material will be a source of constant dispute. (Understanding conflicting and overlapping patterns of circulation and conflicting and overlapping

interpretive communities will be a key element to reading not only Colette's
Ces plaisirs . . . , but texts by Genet and many others.)

Consider, as a further example of the ways circulation (both of textual
artifacts and of persons) and interpretative communities go together in *Ces
plaisirs* . . . , another list it offers us, this one of the kinds of people found at
Missy's table: "Baronesses of the Empire, canonesses, lady cousins of Czars,
illegitimate daughters of grand-dukes, exquisites of the Parisian bourgeoisie,
and also some aged horsewomen of the Austrian aristocracy, hand and eye
of steel." Whatever characterization of Missy's sexuality one might choose to
give, a very clear claim is being made here that it had a transnational basis,
but a disappearing rather than an emergent one. Colette claims that this is a
sexuality that has lost its social ground, ceased to circulate, and yet here she
is, nudging it back into circulation, retransmitting it, keeping alive its claim
to intelligibility: "they struggled to tell its story, to explain it. They tried to
render intelligible for us their success with and their defiant taste for women.
The astonishing thing is that they were successful in doing so." Of the many
things *Ces plaisirs* . . . turns out to be about, then, one of them is the role
of *interdiscursivity* (the activity of keeping bits of culture in motion by perpetuating them, reciting them, in discourse) in perpetuating or renovating
sexual identities.[48] As Michael Silverstein has recently put it, "We know that
'circulation' of cultural knowledge and values is accomplished by interdiscursivity of communicative events—events of communication linked to and
in various ways incorporating other events of communication linked to and
incorporating other events of communication dot dot dot."[49] Silverstein's "dot
dot dot" suggests a way of understanding the three dots of Colette's title, *Ces
plaisirs* . . . . We can take them to be the mark of the work of indexicality and
interdiscursivity, the sign that Colette's text is continually pointing to bits of
knowledge out there in the cultural universe and to forms of sensual and sexual experience that we are presumed to share, and not only to bits of knowledge and experience, but also to ways of understanding and organizing them.
Silverstein continues: "processes of interdiscursivity move . . . cultural values
through the social space-time of our experience in sometimes characteristic,
sometimes innovative ways. These paths of interdiscursivity become in effect
trajectories of propulsion of cultural knowledge and value, even when they
seem most innocently to be mere reports of happenings or doings of certain
sorts involving people positioned in certain ways to one another."[50] One of
the purposes of *Ces plaisirs* . . . is to propel not only certain bits of knowledge,
but also certain evaluative schemas and stances, forward through time and
outward through space. I'd like now to begin to grapple with the complex

trajectories of knowledge and value that are revealed not only within the textual matter of *Ces plaisirs* . . . but also in the traces we can discover of its early steps out into the world, in the information we have regarding the obstacles to circulation that it encountered in its earliest versions. All of this contextual information can help us in our effort to grasp the peculiarities of Colette's enunciatory position in this complicated text.

Ces plaisirs . . . in Its Context of Origin

There is a story that has been circulating for some time now in the secondary literature about *Ces plaisirs* . . . and its later version, *The Pure and the Impure*. The story circulates widely, and many of us have probably helped propagate it in conversation, in the classroom, or in writing.[51] A concise version of it is offered, for instance, in Elisabeth Ladenson's important 1996 article "Colette for Export Only." Ladenson writes: "Colette's first attempt to publish the text in serial form in the journal *Gringoire* in 1931 came to a bad end, with the fourth installment literally cut off in the middle of a sentence because of the scandalous nature of its contents. When the publisher Ferenczi brought it out in book form the following year, the volume was greeted with cautious incomprehension" (27).

Like many good stories, this turns out to be too good to be true. There is a bit of truth mixed in with much inexactitude that has accumulated over the years. As it happens, the fourth installment was not cut off in the middle of a sentence. Neither the contents of the final sentence nor the contents of the work as a whole can really be considered scandalous either for its time or for the journal in question. The claim that *Ces plaisirs* . . . met with some kind of general incomprehension upon publication needs at least a bit of qualification. Why has this story been so popular, and how did it come to be told in this way?

Maurice Goudeket, Colette's husband, is surely partly responsible. In his 1956 volume *Près de Colette*, he wrote of *Ces plaisirs* . . . :

> While it had begun to appear in the weekly called *Gringoire*, the editor stopped its publication after the second installment, informing Colette in a letter that went something like this: "My dear friend, I'm afraid this time it's gone too far. I'm hearing objections from all sides. I am thus obliged . . ."[52]

In 1973, Elaine Harris, in her book *L'approfondissement de la sensualité dans l'oeuvre romanesque de Colette*, would feel confident asserting that "in 1931 the serial publication of *Ces plaisirs* . . . in the weekly *Gringoire* was cut short. *Le Blé en Herbe* had suffered the same fate in 1923. This kind of prudery [pudibonderie] is less common today, when questions of sexuality have earned the right to be discussed openly." As we shall see shortly, this notion of the prudery that reigned in 1931–32 is highly exaggerated.[53]

Colette herself also bears some responsibility for this myth. Her correspondence from late December 1931 and January 1932 includes a number of exaggerations regarding the termination of the initial publication of Ces plaisirs . . . in Gringoire. She penned several different letters complaining of her treatment at Gringoire, giving slightly different accounts of what happened in each of them. To her friend Hélène Picard, she wrote:

> And now the editor of Gringoire tells me that because the text of mine they are publishing in installments (my next book) isn't meeting with the approval of his "general public" [ne plaisant pas à son "grand public"], he is simply going to cut it short. As proof of which, at the end of the fourth installment, he writes THE END in the middle of a sentence. There was still enough material left for five more installments, more than half. I must say I'm stunned. This has never happened to me before.[54]

To André Dunoyer de Segonzac she writes: "P.S. The editor of Gringoire has informed me that the text of mine they are publishing in installments does not meet with the approval of his 'general public' [ne plaît pas à son "grand public"] and as proof, he simply cuts it without (as yet) any discussion, printing THE END in the middle of a sentence. I confess that this has never happened to me before!" And to her friend and fellow contributor to Gringoire Francis Carco, she writes: "Using the pretext that he has received a few complaints from his 'general public' [qu'il a eu de son "grand public" quelques réclamations], Carbuccia cuts 'Ces plaisirs' off in the middle of a sentence, without (as yet) any discussion. How am I to understand such treatment? He has written me a letter I find unacceptable."[55]

What does it mean, precisely, to say that Colette's text did not appeal to the "grand public" that read Gringoire? Colette, we might note, says nothing about that public being scandalized. And the recipients of her letters would have found it easy to verify in their own copy of Gringoire for December 25, 1931, that Colette was exaggerating for effect in what she wrote to them. The final sentence in the segment of Ces plaisirs . . . published in that issue was perfectly complete. Here it is, along with a few preceding sentences:

> Penetration, the voluptuous gift of wounding! It is, with penetration, just as it is with anything that we consider a kind of paroxysm, or as leading to it. A paroxysm is a measured affair, a recompense accorded to rhythm, to a studied use of oscillation, to "give" and to "take."

A waning force does not wane without appropriating to itself neighboring, consenting forces.

COLETTE   THE END

(Pénétration, don voluptueux de blesser! Il en est de la pénétration comme de tout ce que nous tenons pour paroxysme ou qui nous y mène. Le paroxysme est affaire de mesure, récompense accordée au rythme, à une science des oscillations, du "pris" et du "rendu."

Une force qui décroit ne décroit pas sans s'approprier des forces voisines, consentantes.

COLETTE   FIN)⁵⁶

True, in the book length version of the text that would appear a few weeks later, in February 1932, this concluding sentence occurs in the middle of a paragraph, at least a dozen pages before the end of the book. It is also true that the installment published on December 25, 1931, omitted a number of important passages that would appear in the book. Colette would also revise this passage a bit, so that, in the book version it reads as follows:

Penetration, the voluptuous gift of wounding! A recompense accorded to measured action, to studied progressions and oscillations, to "give" and to "take"! A waning force does not dissipate without in passing appropriating to itself neighboring, consenting forces.

(Pénétration, don voluptueux de blesser! Récompense accordée à la mesure, à la science des progressions et des oscillations, du "pris" et du "rendu"! Une force qui décroît ne s'en va pas sans s'approprier au passage des forces voisines, consentantes.)⁵⁷

It is a passage that caused Colette a good deal of trouble and underwent a considerable amount of rewriting. One can deduce from the rewriting she did that this passage had for her a relation to the complicated closing paragraph of the book, which she also wrote and rewrote numerous times before arriving at a final version.⁵⁸ (I will come back to the final sentences of the book a bit later on.) It is striking to note that Colette herself removes the word "paroxysm" from the passage sometime between its publication in *Gringoire* and its publication in the book. In the version published in *Gringoire*, the penetration being referred to seems in the first place to be related to the probing of the minds of the people Colette is questioning. (For the most part, *Ces plaisirs...* is presented as a sort of ethnographic inquiry in which Colette interviews various informants about the diverse sexual cultures of belle epoque Paris.) Here are the sentences that immediately precede those already cited:

Moreover, I also retain an ease in piercing through, in outwitting, the admirable artifices of children and adolescents. Thanks to this, I am able to savor better than many adults the forbidden pleasure of penetrating that which is young. Ready with their newly invented lies, their artifice both rough and wily, still they do not resent my efforts. To the contrary. My powerful child adversary of many faces enjoys the game, surrenders upon being caught, and displays, blushing with pleasure, the very point that I have struck.

(De plus, il m'en reste une facilité à percer, à déjouer le bel artifice que mettent en oeuvre l'enfance et l'adolescence. Par là je goûte, mieux que beaucoup d'adultes, le plaisir défendu de pénétrer ce qui est jeune. Le frais mensonge, l'art barbare et fin ne m'en font pas grief, au contraire. Mon puissant et puéril adversaire aux multiples visages aime le jeu, se livre quand il est découvert, montre en rougissant de joie le point précis où je l'atteins.)[59]

Yet the use of the word "paroxysm" in the version published in *Gringoire* ("Il en est de la pénétration comme de tout ce que nous tenons pour paroxysme ou qui nous y mène") suggests a double meaning whereby the probing for ethnographic detail seems to acquire a sexual connotation, indeed whereby the ethnographic encounter seems to be quite forthrightly sexualized. It is, of course, true that the version of *Ces plaisirs . . .* published in *Gringoire* stops well before the end of the text Colette had written. Yet it's also the case that it ends at a point that draws our attention to a central feature of Colette's project in her book: to suggest that the process of obtaining information about sexual diversity in the cultural universe in question is itself a kind of sexual activity.[60] Indeed, the acquisition, circulation, and maintenance of information, beliefs, and attitudes about the sexuality of others is surely a part of most any kind of sexuality. There is thus perhaps nothing particularly surprising about the claim that the composition, the publication, and the circulation of *Ces plaisirs . . .* should count as part of Colette's own sexual practices. But finding the appropriate literary form in which to accomplish this sexual act and, at the same time, to make just clear enough to her readers what she was doing, was obviously difficult for Colette. To have chosen to remove the word "paroxysm" from this passage before the book version was published is perhaps a sign of the delicate process of refinement that was part of her ongoing compositional activity.

The half-sexual, half-ethnographic "paroxysm" with which the version of the text appearing in *Gringoire* ends brings us back once again to the question of why Carbuccia, the editor of *Gringoire*, chose to cut off the publication of Colette's text, and why he cut it off at the point in question. *Gringoire* came into existence in 1928, and set itself up in competition with the other major literary weekly of the time, *Candide*. The Gallimard publishing house would launch another literary weekly, *Marianne*, in 1932, in an attempt to compete with both *Gringoire* and *Candide* and to do so from a leftist political position that contrasted with the right-wing positioning of the other two weeklies. At the beginning of the 1930s, many authors and contributors to these journals moved back and forth between all three of them with little concern for the political affiliation of the journal in question. Benjamin Crémieux wrote for both the *Nouvelle Revue Française* and for *Candide*, as did Albert Thibaudet. Works by Colette would appear in *Gringoire*, *Candide*, and *Marianne*. (In fact, later in the 1930s, *Gringoire* would publish her rather brilliant set of short stories, *Bella-Vista*, which could be thought of in some ways as a continuation of the project of *Ces plaisirs . . .* in a different mode.) There were, nonetheless, important differences between the publications, as evinced by their circulation figures. A print run for *Gringoire* could go as high as 640,000 copies; for *Candide* as high as or slightly higher than 300,000; *Marianne*'s circulation figures never rose above 120,000.[61] In an interview from the 1970s, Emmanuel Berl, the editor of *Marianne*, would explain the differences between *Marianne* and *Gringoire* in the following manner:

> On the positive side for us was that our journal was affiliated with the N.R.F. [the *Nouvelle Revue Française*]. That was a guarantee of the quality of our publication. The N.R.F published Claudel, Proust, Valéry. *Gringoire* had no people of that level of quality associated with it. You found a certain vulgarity in the pages of *Gringoire*, a way of offering enticements to its readership [une manière d'aguicher le public].[62]

What were the kinds of enticements offered by *Gringoire* to which Berl refers?

One of the most prominent contributors to *Gringoire* (its literary editor at the time) was the novelist Joseph Kessel. His *Belle de jour* was the first novel to be serialized by *Gringoire* when it began publishing in 1928, and his adventure novel *Fortune carrée* (*Crossroads*) preceded *Ces plaisirs . . .* in its pages in 1931. From July 31 to November 27 of that year, *Gringoire*'s readers were thus following the adventures of Kessel's heroes across mysterious African landscapes, as they fought man and beast and struggled with nature. The book seems still to be popular today. "It is pure adrenaline," writes one reviewer on amazon.fr. Another notes its "short sentences with quick links between the ideas." The contrast with Colette's sinuous, baroque prose and her mastery of indirection as she slowly lays out her thoughts about the diverse sexual cultures of the belle epoque is striking.

Among other items published in *Gringoire* in 1929, 1930 and 1931, one finds a series of articles beginning in July 1930 by Louis-Charles Royer called "Love in Germany," where, of course, all love is deviant. Royer visits gay bars, gay cruising grounds, Magnus Hirschfeld's institute, a lesbian community, and so on. He even offers his readers a summary of Freud's *Three Essays on the Theory of Sexuality*. A year earlier he had written another series of articles for *Gringoire* about his visits to nudist colonies in Germany and elsewhere. This series overlapped with a further one, called "Drug Addicts," by his colleague Marise Querlin,[63] who provided a somewhat scabrous set of investigations of contemporary drug cultures in Paris. The issue published on April 5, 1929, includes Querlin's account of her visit to an opium den:

> That full night that I spent in an opium den rests in my memory as a night both macabre and bleak: a foreshadowing of the grave. Is it really necessary, if you have a death-wish, to kill yourself so slowly, and in a way so dangerous for others? For those who are there watching might be led to believe that this kind of death is full of sensual pleasure. But no. Rather what you have is a disintegration of one's intelligence, one's soul, and then one's body. That's what you get with opium and its 10% of morphine.
>
> These bodies had huddled together as if against the cold. Hands wandered here and there in the open folds of their dressing gowns . . . Here and there a moan would escape. Then everyone would collapse, their heads heavy, filled with monsters or with dreams.[64]

It's hard not to think of the opening scene of *Ces plaisirs . . .* in which Colette recounts her own trip as a journalist to observe the goings-on in an opium den of the belle epoque.

Querlin was also the author of a book published in the spring of 1931 by Éditions de France, the publishing house affiliated with *Gringoire*. The title of the book was *Women without Men*. A brief puff piece for the book appeared in *Gringoire* on March 13, 1931:

> Just like the novel, the investigative report is a literary genre that has become capacious enough to contain many different varieties. So it is that Mlle. Marise Querlin, whose "Cursed Wombs" and "Drug Addicts" have given many readers the chance to appreciate her particular and lucid point of view on certain of humanity's vices, has just published a true study of social mores, one with a suggestive title: "Women without Men." It is our belief that this book will appeal to that large public [immense public] that appreciates all that is extravagant and audacious.[65]

Ces plaisirs . . . was dropped by *Gringoire* because it failed to appeal to its "grand public," and Querlin's *Femmes sans hommes* (which was often found in advertisements in *Gringoire* in spring 1931 alongside Francis Carco's *Prisons de femmes*) is promoted to those in the "immense public" making up its readership who appreciate audacity. As it turns out, interested readers would also have to appreciate huge numbers of misprints and misspellings, a clumsy, lurid style, and a reactionary and fairly repugnant ideology that reveals itself in portraits of drug-addicted and anorexic lesbian sexual predators. In short, it was a book rich in "enticements." (It would be reprinted in the 1950s and in the 1960s, and even translated into English and published in a pulp paperback edition in 1965.)

A reader who did make it all the way to the end of Querlin's volume would discover that *Femmes sans hommes* ends with an incongruously admiring portrait of Renée Vivien: "I am not trying to lay any traps for the reader. Yet it seems to me impossible not to recall, as part of this portrait of these sexual mores, a woman who was one of the greatest poets—and also one of the least recognized—of the early years of this century. It would be an insult to the memory of Renée Vivien to confuse her with others for whom Sapphism was nothing more than a kind of perversion."[66] I mention the pages on Vivien in Querlin's book because Colette's *Ces plaisirs . . .* also contains a portrait of her. The passage on Vivien is one Colette had published privately in 1928 before rewriting it for inclusion in her book in 1932.[67] The subjects Colette took up in *Ces plaisirs . . .* were thus obviously subjects other authors were also writing about quite regularly, employing various manners to do so. There was nothing about the *topic* of Colette's book that would have shocked the readers of *Gringoire*. It seems rather more likely that it was Colette's manner of treating her topic that they would have found too demanding, tiresome, and perhaps insufficient in the titillation they might have been expecting it to provide.

If the serial publication of *Ces plaisirs . . .* in *Gringoire* was not cut off in the middle of a sentence, if there was nothing in Colette's text that would have seemed terribly shocking to the readers of *Gringoire*, might it still not be the case that her difficult prose caused her book to be met with relative incomprehension? Well, yes and no. Even *Gringoire* was able to give an accurate description of the book's project when it mentioned it in its "A l'Étalage" column on April 8, 1932:

> *Gringoire* just recently published extended excerpts from this new book in which the illustrious author of *Chéri* evokes with poetic precision a certain number of figures from the early decades of this century, ones whose portraits called out to be painted; these portraits provide Mme Colette with a pretext for penetrating analyses of love and for descriptive passages that surely should be counted among her most successful pages.[68]

Ces plaisirs . . . was fairly easily recognizable according to the generic possibilities prevailing at the moment of its publication. Historical reportage about the mores of the belle epoque was, it turns out, very much in fashion thanks to a book published a year earlier that had received a lot of attention: Paul Morand's *1900*.[69] When Morand's book was reviewed by Benjamin Crémieux in the *Nouvelle Revue Française* in July 1931, Crémieux made a point of insisting on the importance of the genre of reportage in the literary world of the time, offering as key examples not only *1900* but also Gide's *Voyage au Congo* from 1927. He nonetheless criticized Morand for being overly selective in what he chose to portray about the belle epoque: "Paul Morand ridiculed the fashions of 1900, the books, the fads, its idols. . . . Yet there is another 1900 that needs to be brought forward, one of lasting value, one which deserves a place in history."[70] The same reproach serves as a point of departure for one of the most interesting documents belonging to the initial reception of *Ces plaisirs* . . . , a column written by Fernand Vandérem for *Candide* on February 11, 1932, in which he opposes Colette's book to Morand's. I cite at some length:

> In *1900*, the book that caused such a stir when it was published, one of the most surprising lacuna, the one that we would have expected to stir up the most complaint, was that in which the accursed women [*femmes damnées*, the title of a Baudelaire poem about a pair of women lovers] and their emulators of the opposite sex were left to suffer.
>
> Yet, due either to their pride or to their indifference to publicity, the interested parties did not deign to protest. The upshot was that the omission of these persons, by being allowed to stand, merely helped to accentuate even further the backwards and overly domesticated character that this author wished to lend to the unhappy year in question.
>
> Still, with the passage of time, there is no iniquity which cannot be corrected, as Mme Colette has shown us once again in her new volume, *Ces plaisirs*, where all the depraved and delinquent parties of 1900 at last are given their rightful place in history.
>
> It is not for me to say here with what grace, what humor, and what moving sentiments our great word-charmer carries out this delicate task. Rather, what I wish to emphasize is the immense documentary importance of these delectable pages.
>
> Among the elements described by Colette, all of them dating from the end of the last century or else the beginning of ours, consider, for example, the tragic silhouette of Renée Vivien, the troop of admirers that de Max dragged around with him, the swarm of international pretty young men presided over by Willy's ghostwriter-secretary, or even the moving confession whispered in the weighty silence of an opium den. Then compare these impassioned perversities with the callous flirtations in boarding schools, the schoolboy sadisms

being offered up to us by certain contemporary works like *Pains of Youth*, among many others. You will have to admit that as regards relations of this kind, "1900" easily holds its own not only against 1930, but against any of the most corrupt epochs of the past or the future.

Still, if we are now fully convinced of all of the inversions that existed thirty years ago, things remain a bit obscure when it comes to the domestic mores of this distant epoch. Were the mothers and sons, the fathers and daughters of those years, still wallowing in respectful submission to ancient prejudices and outdated moral attitudes? Or rather could one already find the precursors of the characters in *A Taciturn Man*, at home with the practice of incest, playfully mixing it with homosexuality and tribadism?

If such cases were to be found back then, it would be handy to see them recounted in a novel or a play, such as the one recently offered up by the head of the family group from Cuverville. For that would really be, for once and for all, the complete rehabilitation of "1900"; it could never again be accused of harboring the narrow bourgeois attitudes with which some have claimed it was afflicted.[71]

Among the remarkable features of this article is the careful effort it makes to associate *Ces plaisirs . . .* with a set of other contemporary works, not just Morand's *1900*, but also a play by Ferdinand Bruckner, *Pains of Youth* (*Krankheit der jugend*), which had been produced in Brussels in 1931 as *Le mal de la jeunesse*; a play by Roger Martin du Gard, *A Taciturn Man*, produced in Paris in 1931, in which the protagonist commits suicide after becoming conscious of his own homosexual desires; and perhaps also one of Martin du Gard's stories, *African Secret* (1931), about an incestuous relationship between brother and sister. The article also refers to André Gide's play *Oedipus* (Gide being the "head of the family group from Cuverville"). Like Martin du Gard's *African Secret*, *Oedipus* had been published by the *Nouvelle Revue Française* in the spring of 1931. The play would be produced in Paris in 1932.

Two other features of Vandérem's article merit mention. There is first his way of characterizing Colette as "our great word-charmer" (notre grande charmeuse de mots), and then there is his rather playful manner of juxtaposing Colette's literary project with those of two members of the *NRF* literary group, Gide and Martin du Gard. The basis for the juxtaposition is their shared interest in the topic of nonnormative sexualities. Yet the literary field of the time was marked by a resilient opposition between people like Colette, on the one hand, and people like Gide and Martin du Gard, on the other. Here is what Emmanuel Berl had to say about the members of the *NRF* group:

Often they were led by their "Left Bank" puritanism to commit certain kinds of injustice. Proust may have lived on the Right Bank and associated with the

Countess Greffulhe; that didn't mean he couldn't have a certain kind of genius. Just because Colette lived at the Claridge Hotel and had been in the theater and lived a kind of wild life before the war didn't mean she absolutely lacked talent. . . . There was always a kind of prejudice at the *NRF*, that if you didn't live on the Left Bank, near the Rue Vaneau, which is to say in a somewhat austere and straitlaced neighborhood, then you were some kind of shady character . . . and not a real writer . . . You must be spending all your nights at Maxim's or at the Chabanais.[72]

It is easy to imagine how annoying it must have been for someone as sensitive and priggish as Martin du Gard to see himself mentioned alongside Morand and Colette because of the literary interest he took in sexual questions, easy to imagine the pleasure Vandérem was taking in trying to provoke precisely such annoyance.[73]

As for Vandérem's distinction between Colette the "word-charmer" and Colette the writer of impressive documentary significance, it is worth noting that much of the debate in these years regarding Colette's literary value was organized around this very distinction.[74] If, by marking a separation between stylistic questions and documentary ones, Vandérem runs the risk of missing the heart of Colette's project (since part of her purpose in *Ces plaisirs . . .* is obviously to insist on the impossibility of separating these two aspects of the writing she does), nonetheless he calls our attention to the terms in which people argued over the seriousness of Colette's literary achievements.

We can get a sense of the criteria that were in play in many discussions of Colette's literary status, in decisions as to whether or not to assign this or that kind of value to her achievements, by juxtaposing two judgments of her work, published ten years apart. The first was penned by Jean de Pierrefeu for the *Journal des débats* in 1920, in an article discussing Colette's novel *Chéri*.

Books such as this one, in order to be read, require neither culture nor mental refinement; there is no collaboration between author and reader. Trapped in the magic of these sentences, the reader will either enjoy himself or suffer, but without any of the higher faculties of his intelligence becoming involved.

We thus see the extreme consequences of this art of the senses of which Colette is the most skilled representative. I believe I have established that it leads to the loss of cerebral function, the end of all culture, the definitive impoverishment of the human person, which is reduced to the animal level.[75]

It is a relatively short distance from Pierrefeu's "the magic of these sentences" and "the definitive impoverishment of the human person" to Vandérem's image of a "word-charmer" who carries out the "delicate task" of writing about "depraved and delinquent" human subjects, even if Vandérem seems to be praising Colette, whereas Pierrefeu means to excoriate her. Small wonder that Vandérem would consider himself on more solid ground in dealing with her "documentary" side.

In August 1930, Auguste Bailly would write a review of Colette's *Sido* in *Candide*. Perhaps because this book deals with the figure of Colette's mother and not with the "depravity" of the belle epoque, Bailly is quite forthcoming with his praise of Colette's manner of writing:

> Each word is necessary; each one of them is rich in meaning, imagery, and powers of evocation; each one represents the specific sonority of a given soul, shaken—according to its own modes of sensitivity—by different aspects of or pulls from the external world. . . . Few writers working today can offer us the joy of encountering a way of expressing oneself that never puts a foot wrong, where the most consummate virtuosity never falls into complacency, but always works to further some thought or impression. This is what we encounter from one end to the other of *Sido*.[76]

It turns out that nearly every man who, between 1920 and 1930, undertakes to speak favorably of Colette's writing feels obliged to insist upon the way her writing has evolved, an evolution in which her verbal skills, once devoted solely to the expression of an unregulated sensuality, are now put to service in a more respectable project, "to further some thought," as Bailly has it, or to further some "documentary" project according to Vandérem. As Benjamin Crémieux put it in his article on *Chéri* in the December 1920 issue of the *NRF*, "Colette has taken the measure of her spontaneous art, and now controls her gifts instead of just giving way to them."[77] It's probably not possible to determine the exact extent to which Colette's literary evolution was in fact in some ways a response to the critiques of her work by the likes of Pierrefeu or Crémieux, but her case is one that makes it easy to see the pertinence of a set of questions that Pierre Bourdieu set out in his article "Intellectual Field and Creative Project":

> Even the author most indifferent to the lure of success and the least disposed to make concessions to the demands of the public is surely obliged to take account of the social truth of his work as it is reported back to him by the public, the critics or analysts, and to redefine his creative project in relation to this truth. When he is faced with this objective definition, is he not encouraged to rethink his intentions and make them explicit, and are they not therefore in danger of being altered? More generally, does not the creative project inevitably define itself in relation to the projects of other creators?[78]

At the moment when the serial publication of *Ces plaisirs . . .* in *Gringoire* is interrupted, Colette finds herself confronted by the social truth of her latest text: it deals with sexuality, yet it is not enticing enough to appeal to the large readership of this publication. The "sensuality" of Colette's style had always been a problem for literary folks like Crémieux (and doubtless Gide and his whole circle as well), who had other criteria for taking something seriously as literature. Yet with the passing years, her writing had evolved, with the result that more and more people (including Gide) would concede to her a certain kind of seriousness. This growing recognition is linked to her way of capturing sensual experience in her style as well as to her ways of reflecting upon the social, personal, and interpersonal import of the experience of the sensory world, especially when, as in the case of *Ces plaisirs* . . . , that experience is tied up in a given, nonnormative form of sexuality. All of these different aspects of Colette's situation are palpable in the remarkable passage that brings the 1932 version of *Ces plaisirs* . . . to a close. In reading this passage we might imagine that in it Colette is working to establish a relation to her own past, to her literary style, to the question of sexuality (of her sexuality over time), just as she is working to demonstrate and affirm the difference between her writing and that of a number of her contemporaries.

The ending of *Ces plaisirs* . . . is a reflection on the kind of understanding that might be possible between two women who are fighting over the same man. In the case Colette presents to us, the stronger of the two women (Colette herself), not wishing to cause the weaker woman to suffer, breaks off with the man in question. This provides the occasion for her rival to open her heart to the woman who has chosen to leave the field:

> It is not so easy to ward off sentimental danger, to ward off the now unconfined creature who demands, in the name of her total confidence, tender invasion, and who believes herself pure because some space has been cleared out: "Surround me, besiege me, you are more to me than myself . . . Since you know all there is of me, I am pure . . ."
>
> I heard, I still hear, in that word "pure" that rose up from nothingness, a brief trembling, the plaintive "u," the icy limpidness of the "r." The half-open lips from which it emerged prolonged its unique resonance. In me it awoke nothing so much as the need to hear yet again the word "pure" and to savor that imaginary delight to which we give the name of purity. Yet now that I find myself in that phase of life in which the increasing calmness of certain appetites smiles to see a lessening of certain of the mind's scruples, in which the love of speaking truthfully, of writing truthfully has become an esteemed yet not so burning pursuit, I find that the thirst for purity is a rather ordinary thirst, just as was the thirst that came before it and that told me it was a thirst for impurity. Both of them gather tightly around the word as it wells up, trickles out in an uneven rhythm, moistening them just a bit . . . The word "pure" has

yet to reveal to me its intelligible meaning ... I've only gotten as far as to find a temporary refuge for myself in the transparencies that evoke it, in bubbles, masses of water, prisms, and those isolated, out of reach places at the heart of a crystal.[79]

(Il est moins facile de conjurer le danger sentimental, la créature déclose qui exige un tendre envahissement, au nom de sa confiance totale, et qui se croit pure à force d'être désaffectée: "Investis-moi, je t'aime mieux en moi que moi-même ... Puisque tu sais tout de moi, je suis pure ..."

De ce mot "pur" qui montait du vide, j'écoutais, j'écoute encore le trem-blement bref, l'u plaintif, l'r de glace limpide. Les lèvres qu'il entr'ouvrait prolongeaient sa résonance unique. Il n'éveillait rien en moi, sinon le besoin d'entendre encore le mot "pur" et de savourer le délice imaginaire que nous nommons pureté. Mais, entrée à présent dans cette phase de la vie où la paix croissante des moeurs sourit de voir diminuer les scrupules de l'esprit, où l'amour de dire vrai, d'écrire vrai n'est plus qu'une nonchalance honorable, je tiens que la soif de la pureté est une soif ordinaire comme celle qui la précéda et qui me disait être la soif de l'impureté. Toutes deux se serrent autour du mot qui sourd, dégoutte à temps inégaux et les mouille avarement ... Le mot "pur" ne m'a pas encore découvert son sens intelligible ... Je n'en suis qu'à m'assurer un refuge provisoire dans les transparences qui l'évoquent, dans les bulles, l'eau massive, les prismes, et les sites isolés, hors d'atteinte, au sein du cristal.)

It's a difficult passage, nearly impenetrable, we might be tempted to say.[80] It points in many different directions. It suggests that the relationship between two women that Colette is describing is a fleeting form of sexuality, one that Colette simultaneously resists and accedes to. (The parallels between this pas-sage and the one that we looked at earlier that related penetration and parox-ysm to each other are fairly clear.) One woman watches another pronounce a particular word, and she is transfixed by the sounds out of which the word is made rather than by whatever meaning it may or may not have. This exchange between the two women prompts a reflection, a look back, at the project of the book it brings to a close, a book that was a kind of investigative reporting, full of interviews and various kinds of documentation regarding an earlier period of time. With the passage of time, Colette has arrived at a moment "in which the increasing calmness of certain appetites smiles to see a lessening of certain of the mind's scruples, in which the love of speaking truthfully, of writing truthfully has become an esteemed yet not so burning pursuit." This seems to imply that the quest to render intelligible various sexualities of the belle epoque, the quest that seemed to be at the heart of the book's project, has, by the end of the writing, lost some of its urgency. The documentary aspect of the book recedes and a different dimension comes to the fore, the dimension having precisely to do with the sensual exchange of sounds and of words, with Colette's ambiguous stance toward that sensual element that she shows to be a part of each of the exchanges she records between herself and her informants. The investigative reporting Colette imagined herself doing must, at some point or other, have had something to do with a distinction she wished to draw between the pure and the impure, just as it had to do with a desire to document the facts about the types of relations that could exist between two women, or two men, or a man and a woman, or a man and a series of women, or a man and two women, in certain times and places. Yet it is as if, having come to the end of her project, Colette becomes more interested in accounting not for the meaning of words like pure or impure, but for their sonic and sensual potentials. Perhaps she is finally more interested in accounting for the ways in which her book itself, and her actions in writing it, participate in the circulation of certain kinds of sensual relations to the world, to both men and women, and to words. It seems that certain kinds of probing that are part of various verbal exchanges have something to do with the production of a peculiar form of evanescent sexuality. Yet this unspecified, nebulous sexuality that is linked to the tactile and auditory experience of words (and of the lips, mouths, throats, and breath that produce them) seems more practical and experiential, seems unaligned with more familiar kinds of identities whose rules, regularities, and contours might be something one could establish through the kinds of investigative fieldwork we found Colette enacting elsewhere in the volume. The very experience of producing the book (and perhaps of reading it) overwhelms the character of the investigation it had set out to perform.

The possibility of practicing (in writing and in life) an unspecified sexuality such as this seems a bit different from imagining that you *have* this or that kind of nameable sexuality. It is probably not a possibility that just anyone is able to take up. That is, not everyone could live their sexual life in this manner. Many people encounter circumstances that require them to lay firm claim to a recognizable form of sexuality; indeed, many people seek out situations that enable them to lay claim to a particular sexuality, and would find it frustrating not to be able to do so. The practice of sexuality that we see Colette performing in her book is not simple; it would need time and a certain kind of effort to be acquired, assumed, cultivated, encouraged. (It takes practice.) Perhaps what Colette shows us through the experience of *Ces plaisirs . . .* is the effort of writing and rewriting that goes into keeping such a possibility open across the ongoing span of a life.

On Not Exactly Laying Claim to a Sexuality

Throughout *Ces plaisirs* . . . , then, Colette is signaling various things about her own sexual history, her own practice and experience of sexuality, her own understanding of how categories work to help render certain kinds of sexuality intelligible even as they leave other sexualities (hers?) in some ways unspecifiable. I would like to return, in conclusion, to a fuller discussion of her incorporation of material related to the Ladies of Llangollen into *Ces plaisirs* . . . , to consider what this particular textual moment conveys (and how it does so) regarding Colette's sense of how her own sexuality exists in culture and in time, as well as in relation to other sexualities past and present. To begin with, let us note the ways in which Colette's use of this material reveals that part of the practice of her sexuality is a practice of interdiscursivity.

Consider a letter Colette wrote to Una Troubridge and Radclyffe Hall on March 17, 1932, shortly after the publication of *Ces plaisirs* . . . .[81] The letter is helpful, first of all, in providing yet another set of literary texts to place alongside *Ces plaisirs* . . . . Colette begins by telling Troubridge and Hall that she is trying her hand at a commercial enterprise, the manufacture and sale of a line of beauty products. She goes on to mention that she has just finished reading Hall's *The Well of Loneliness* (a French translation of which was first published by Gallimard in March 1932), and that she was filled with admiration, especially for the scenes of childhood; she continues by mentioning that she has also been reading *Lady What's-her-name's Lover* (a translation of Lawrence's novel had appeared in January 1932), and finds it, in general, adolescent, unsubtle, and boring.[82] Then she turns to the Ladies of Llangollen. She and Troubridge and/or Hall have clearly discussed this couple before.[83] Eleanor Butler and Sarah Ponsonby had returned to the public eye in 1930 thanks to the publication in London of *The Hamwood Papers of the Ladies of Llangollen and Caroline Hamilton*, edited by Mrs. G. H. Bell. Those papers include Eleanor Butler's diaries, which Colette cites in *Ces plaisirs* . . . . It would seem that someone has made Colette a gift of Bell's volume, which she read in English, and also of a reproduction of a portrait of the two ladies. "I have only one picture of them," she writes in *Ces plaisirs* . . . , "a reproduction of a mediocre portrait painted toward the end of their lives."[84] In her letter to Troubridge and Hall, she wishes she could get ahold of a different portrait of the two Ladies that she seems to know is in circulation. She asks her correspondents if it exists as a postcard or in photographic reproduction. Exhibiting the impulse to collect ephemera that marks an avid fan, she wonders if it would be possible somehow to obtain a copy of an issue of *The Strand* magazine from thirty years earlier that apparently referred to the Ladies; finally, she insists to Troubridge and Hall that she adores these two women, notes that as far as she is concerned, it matters not at all whether or not the two Ladies practiced abstinence or had sexual relations, and calls Troubridge a casuist, apparently because of the way Troubridge had insisted during an earlier exchange that the two Ladies must have had sexual relations. She invites Troubridge and Hall to visit soon so that they can discuss the matter further.

Of course, people had been curious about the nature of the relation between the Ladies of Llangollen during their lifetimes and have been ever since. Discussions of them often seem to have gotten stuck on the question of whether or not their relationship was a sexual one (which, of course, requires a prior discussion of what, exactly, we require in order for a relationship to be considered sexual). In her presentation of the Ladies in her book *Intimate Friends*, Martha Vicinus recalls the visit Anne Lister paid to the elderly Sarah Ponsonby toward the end of Ponsonby's life, with part of the goal of Lister's visit being to discuss sexuality. Vicinus writes: "Lister was always on the look-out for signs of lesbian affection and aristocratic manners. She found both in the elderly Ponsonby. . . . Ponsonby and Lister exchanged opinions on books they had read or hoped to read. The intrepid Lister wanted more; she asked, 'if they were classical.' The older woman proudly told her she had never learned Latin or Greek. Probably Ponsonby never knew the Latin and Greek passages on lesbian sex that so fascinated the younger woman."[85] Lister and Ponsonby are in some ways like Troubridge, Hall, and Colette, using discussions of literature to do personal identity work and to attempt to negotiate some common conceptual ground on which to build shared understandings of sexualities.[86] This is interdiscursivity in action, the mobilizing of older texts to current ends, citing or recirculating those earlier texts in order to make knowledge claims and value claims, in order to produce a space of intelligibility for one's own speech and action.

And yet it does not seem that what Colette was attempting by the ways she recontextualized and recirculated information about the Ladies has been all that intelligible. Her use of the material, for instance, has been criticized by Elizabeth Mavor and Terry Castle for what seem like exactly opposite reasons. Mavor's 1973 volume *The Ladies of Llangollen* takes Ponsonby and Butler to be an exemplary instance of romantic friendship:

> The Ladies were celebrated . . . as perfect friends. . . . The two women's relation-
> ship was what we in modern terms would consider a marriage. It was to give
> rise to their own unique and much envied way of life, for did it not combine
> rural innocence and simplicity without lack of comfort and culture; freedom
> from unbridled passion with no loss of pleasure, a balanced reconciliation

between the tiresome polarities of existence? . . . They were aristocratic, they were idealistic, blissfully free, allowing for a dimension of sympathy between women that would not now be possible outside an avowedly lesbian connection. Indeed, much that we would now associate solely with a sexual attachment was contained in romantic friendship: tenderness, loyalty, sensibility, shared beds, shared tastes, coquetry, even passion.[87]

Mavor doesn't here state explicitly that there was no sexual component to romantic friendship; yet when she critiques Colette's way of writing, that implication seems clearer. "Colette . . . incorporated into *Ces plaisirs* only those extracts from *The Hamwood Papers* which suited her theme," Mavor writes. "Her interpretation of the two women, though sympathetic, was very much in terms of her own times as her conclusions show." To make her point, Mavor cites the paragraph in which Colette imagines "two Ladies of Llangollen in this year 1930," with their short hair, car, overalls, rough language, and body manipulation practices. For Mavor, this very gesture of Colette's, imagining what a pair of women like Ponsonby and Butler would be like in 1930, implies that Ponsonby and Butler were themselves lesbian (which means for her, it would seem, sexual). In Mavor's eyes, Colette prepares the way for Simone de Beauvoir, who mentions Ponsonby and Butler in the chapter on "The Lesbian" in *The Second Sex* (for which both *Ces plaisirs . . .* and *The Well of Loneliness* serve as source texts). As Mavor puts it:

By the time Simone de Beauvoir had published *The Second Sex* in 1949 it was taken for granted that Eleanor Butler and Sarah Ponsonby had been lesbians, although, oddly enough, Eleanor was no longer seen as having been the dominant partner. "The union of Sarah Ponsonby with her woman companion lasted for almost fifty years without a cloud," writes Mlle de Beauvoir of them, "apparently they were able to create a peaceful Eden apart from the ordinary world."

Yet there was something incongruous in a vague phrase like "life without a cloud" escaping into a treatise that pretended to be so scientifically specific. We know quite well, and Mlle de Beauvoir could have guessed, that for Eleanor Butler and Sarah Ponsonby, as for anyone else, life was not without a cloud. Could it be that for all her typing and categorizing Mlle de Beauvoir recognized that in both her own and in the popular consciousness the Ladies represented something more than just a lesbian couple?[88]

Something more, or something less? Mavor's own meaning is a bit hard to reconstruct. For them to be more than just a lesbian couple, do we have to subtract whatever we imagine sexuality to be from our understanding of them? Or could there be some sexuality between them, but alongside some other

expansive quality or qualities that causes them to escape the typing and categorizing apparently implied by calling them lesbians?

The reproaches leveled at Colette by Terry Castle, are rather different.
Castle is impatient with anyone willing to portray Ponsonby and Butler as
"the official 'mascots' of the no-sex-before-1900 school." On Castle's reading, "Colette not only reiterated the traditional view of the Ladies as 'two
faithful spinsters,' untouched by any form of 'Sapphic libertinage,' but offered
their story as a paradigm of that 'unresolved and undemanding sensuality'
characteristic (she hoped to convince her readers) of love between women."[89]
For Mavor, Colette inappropriately pushes the Ladies into the future, whereas
for Castle, she quarantines them in an imaginary asexual past. I'm not sure
that either Mavor or Castle has managed to construe the full complexity of
Colette's position. (And I have probably done some injustice to both of their
positions as well, for I have not really dealt with the ways that they, too, are
implicitly taking positions on sexuality and its history via register and other
nonpropositional linguistic channels, just as Colette is.) If neither Mavor nor
Castle seems able fully to give an account of Colette's position, it is doubtless
because that position is and was somehow an unfamiliar one, as well as because Colette often positions herself and her sexuality via implication rather
than by means of explicit statement.

It may well have been the case that in Colette's exchanges with Troubridge
and Hall on the topic of Ponsonby and Butler she had a similar experience of
a dialogue happening at cross-purposes. Why else would she affectionately
call Troubridge a casuist for insisting that it matters that the Ladies had a
sexual relationship? In conversations such as these, Colette evidently has a
position she is trying to stake out, but it seems not to be one that her interlocutors can accept or perhaps even fully understand (to the extent that Colette
understands and can clearly articulate it herself). Colette's fascination with
the Ladies of Llangollen in fact seems to arise from her sense that through
an imaginative relation to them she can experience and express something of
what she experiences in relation to her own misfit sexuality, something that
it is hard for her to articulate and for others around her to grasp. It has to do
with how she experiences sexuality in relation to different time spans (various
moments in the span of her own life, the span of the past few centuries, and the
immediate future), in relation to different groups with differing investments in
same-sex sexualities (an older social formation of cosmopolitan aristocratic
women; not-necessarily-aristocratic cosmopolitan types who passed through
or settled in Paris, such as Hall and Troubridge or Natalie Barney; the modern
lesbians of 1920s and 1930s Paris; etc.), in relation to the "democratic" political

air of the time, and also in relation to bodies—breasts in particular, it would seem.

As for historical time, Colette makes a concerted effort to show the Ladies as somehow having escaped it. They fled to Wales together in 1778. Colette notes that in 1828 one of their visitors referred positively to the "ancien régime" air they had retained about them. She disassociates them and their relationship from all the changes going on in the world around them during the years they spent together:

> In the distance would rumble and then die down the storm of riots in London. The United States would proclaim its independence; a queen and king of France would perish at the guillotine. Ireland would revolt, the British fleet would mutiny; slavery would be abolished ... The universal excitement, the rousing of Europe did not cross the Pengwern Hills that shut in Llangollen, or disturb the waters of the little river Dee.[90]

When Colette considers putting the Ladies back into time, when she re-imagines them in her own time, it is for her, as we have seen, not a happy image that emerges; in the passage where she does that reimagining, the word "democratic" does a lot of work ("they would own a democratic car") to imply something about her own misfit sexuality, a sexuality that seems somehow attached to a nondemocratic ethos in a world where such a way of being was becoming ever less tenable. The Ladies themselves are "beyond time, beyond reach" (128), which apparently means in a permanent ancien régime, a condition to which Colette seems to wish it were still possible to aspire.

If the yoking together of "democratic" and "car" suggests something of the negative affect (or even a vaguely phobic impulse) that arises when Colette thinks about the forms of same-sex sexuality emergent in the culture around her, it would perhaps be horses that represent a bygone era in which she imagines herself as more at home. I suggest this in part because when, in her letter to Troubridge and Hall, Colette praises *The Well of Loneliness*, she praises in particular the childhood scenes involving the protagonist's attachment to her horse, a hunting scene in particular. She finds the scenes involving the horse exalting. And yet any reader could hardly help but notice that cars, too, are everywhere in *The Well of Loneliness*, perhaps not utterly democratic ones (indeed they are mostly signs of wealth), but surely indexes of the same transformations in the social forms of sexuality that Colette was pointing to. Indeed, it is hard not to think of Troubridge and Hall upon reading the passage regarding Ponsonby's and Butler's imaginary descendants.

There are a number of passages in *Ces plaisirs . . .* regarding the Ladies of Llangollen that seem, in fact, like they might be explicitly addressed to the casuistical Una, Lady Troubridge, demonstrating Colette's mastery of the implicit as she tries to express something of her own misfit sexuality that escapes direct statement, and also demonstrating how even published texts can include moments of private address, moments of what Henry Abelove has suggested we might recognize as a kind of "deep gossip," that "is an indispensable resource for those who are in any sense or measure disempowered, as those who experience funny emotions may be," and that is "deep whenever it circulates in subterranean ways and touches on matters hard to grasp and of crucial concern."[91] Here is a brilliantly complex passage filled with indirection in which Colette is speaking of her reading of Eleanor Butler's diary:

> The words "the bedroom" and "our bed" occur but once, if I am not mistaken. English readers, more avid and perverted than I, are free to see in this proof— but of what? Envious of a devotion as imperturbable as this one, some would have it that these two faithful spinsters fell short of purity—but what do they mean by purity? I pick a quarrel with those who consider that patting a young cheek, fresh and warm and velvety as a peach, does not violate the proprieties but that caressing and lightly weighing with the cupped hand a rosy breast shaped like a peach is a cause for blushes, alarmed cries, slurs cast upon the character of the assailant . . . How hard it is for respectable people to believe in innocence! Oh, I know, I know quite well that the cheek remains cool, while the breast becomes excited. Well, so much the worse for the breast! O indiscreet little breast, can you not allow us to hover over you, selfishly meditating and calling up visions of pulpy fruit, rosy dawns, mountains? Can you not allow us to wander among the planets or simply think of nothing? Why are you not like warm marble, impersonal, respectful of the purposeless hand that caresses you? We do not ask your opinion, but there you are, all of a sudden devoid of mystery, imploring, and virile to a degree that is shameful.[92]

Colette reminds us that there are many uses to which the textual material about the Ladies of Llangollen can be put. Bits of that text can be mobilized in all kinds of arguments about the details of their relationship. Yet, Colette says, first we will have to agree what we are arguing over ("proof—but of what?"), and it has to be said that her language seems intended precisely to obfuscate the question. How, precisely, would she know of the role breasts may or may not have played in the intimate relations of Butler and Ponsonby? What part of her own sexual imaginary is she transposing onto them? Is she suggesting that there are kinds of intimate caresses that, because nongenital, are in some way nonsexual—at least for the person doing the caressing, if not for the person being caressed, who may be obliged to have a physical response willy-nilly? Is she suggesting that it is possible to caress someone's breast without meaning for the act to be sexual? Is she preparing us for her mention of breast amputation a few pages later, allowing the way the two passages resonate together to suggest that she finds in certain contemporary relations to the female body a betrayal of what are for her some of its most important erotic features and sexual capacities?

There are perhaps other propositional statements one could offer to gloss the contents of this passage. Yet however interesting those statements would be, they would, as we know, fail to capture all that the passage is trying to accomplish. This is because much of its work seems to be being done through implication, by indexing nonpropositional knowledge about sexuality, about how sexuality might work, about how it might or might not coalesce into sexual identities, about what those identities might involve and imply. There is a hope in the passage that its reader will prove able to activate a frame of reference that will permit some of its implications to unfold, a hope that the reader will prove able to imagine successfully and then appropriately respond to the sexuality of the person making this utterance. Whether or not anyone is capable of doing so is probably never fully answerable. Some of the evidence we have looked at suggests that the misfit sexuality Colette is offering us here is one difficult for most of us to recognize.

In his book *Foundlings: Lesbian and Gay Historical Emotion before Stonewall*, Christopher Nealon identifies a category of texts—he calls them foundling texts—from the early to mid-twentieth century in which writers refuse an affiliation either with a same-sex sexuality that is based on a model of gender inversion or with a model that views same-sex identities as similar to an ethnic identity. Foundling texts nonetheless, for Nealon, demonstrate "an overwhelming desire to feel historical" and reveal "a movement between solitary exile and collective experience."[93] Nealon works mainly on North American materials, but it's clear that the various models of same-sex sexuality he considers—as well as the affective disaffiliation from them that is the key feature of the texts of most interest to him—circulate transnationally. (Indeed, the transnational circulation of various texts and persons is one of the key elements in the history of these identity forms.) It strikes me that Colette's *Ces plaisirs . . .* might be an interesting French example of a foundling text. The inversion model haunts its pages in, for instance, the material related to Missy and her circle, or perhaps by way of the tutelary presences of Una Troubridge and Radclyffe Hall in the passages devoted to the Ladies of Llangollen. Colette's odd deployment of the material related to Ponsonby and Butler in a book ostensibly meant to reflect on the sexual culture of the belle epoque—a deployment that perhaps best serves to indicate the book's compelling interest in thinking about the existence of (Colette's) sexuality over multiple time frames—makes clear her contrarian attitude toward what Nealon calls "the triumphant, progressive narrative of achieving ethnic coherence" (23). To have included the Ponsonby and Butler material in a narrative structured in that "triumphant" way would have involved reading the way certain "English" readers, "more avid and perverted than I," do, taking Ponsonby and Butler as pioneers in the creation of the ethnic landscape of modern lesbian identities. For Nealon, foundling texts "suggest another time, a time of expectation, in which their key stylistic gestures, choices of genre, and ideological frames all point to an inaccessible future, in which the inarticulate desires that mobilize them will find some 'hermeneutic friend' beyond the historical horizon of their unintelligibility to themselves" (23). It is in some ways an apt description of the problems of intelligibility Colette has had in relation to her sexuality in *Ces plaisirs . . .* and perhaps throughout her life—offering rich, detailed sensual and sexual evocations that suggest a speaking position and a sexual subjectivity whose contours we can't quite grasp, resembling but never coinciding with the set of things we have available to us easily to say about sexuality.[94] Nealon casts the problem in terms of a historical horizon, and this seems appropriate, especially given the complex and intense cross-temporal identification Colette develops with Butler and Ponsonby. But it is also a semiotic problem, related to the way sexuality exists in language, related to the fact that we use language in nonpropositional ways, and that much of sexuality's existence in language happens in those nonpropositional linguistic features. I'm not sure if all of the texts I will deal with in the rest of the chapters making up *Someone* could be called foundling texts, but they will all share the semiotic predicament we have found exemplified in *Ces plaisirs . . . .* They will instantiate this predicament, of course, in intense and subtle ways. Most remarkably, they will sometimes, in instantiating it, take this very predicament as an object of study. Indeed, one of the most intriguing aspects of working on this material for me has been to learn to watch authors from various parts of the French literary field collectively develop techniques to deal with the problem of how language can invoke practical but nonreferential understandings of misfit sexualities. We will find versions of Colette's mastery of the art of implication in the writings of all the other authors studied in the pages that follow. ("It is because we are implicated in the world that there is implicit content in what we think and say about it," writes Pierre Bourdieu at the beginning of *Pascalian Meditations.*[95]) Occasionally we will find authors who match her subtlety in insisting that, when it comes to expressing both the existence and the misfit of our sexualities with and within the world around us, implication is not only sometimes our only resource, it is also one of the richest we have.

Sexuality and the Literary Field

Literary works are implicated in the specific cultural field in which they are produced as well as in various other areas of the social world to which author and text belong. It is, in some ways, the intersection or the overlap between the literary field and some of those other areas that interests me throughout this book. When Bourdieu writes, at the outset of *Pascalian Meditations*, that "it is because we are implicated in the world that there is implicit content in what we think and say about it" (9), we can take his observation in several ways. As we have seen, there are pages in Colette's *Ces plaisirs . . .* that seem almost to be addressed to Radclyffe Hall and Una Troubridge. And we have seen that it is possible to reconstruct a whole web of implications in which Colette, Hall, Troubridge, and various written texts they were invested in are caught up. Some of those implications have a literary component, but not exclusively so. On the other hand, Colette and her writing are also caught up in, implicated in, the French literary field that includes journals such as *Gringoire* and the *Nouvelle Revue Française*, critics like Crémieux or Bailly or Vandérem, other writers such as Gide and Proust, or Apollinaire, or Morand, or Kessel. Like Colette, many of the authors I wish to consider throughout these chapters sit uneasily within the structures of the literary field, and I would like to suggest that for most of them, the uneasiness with which they inhabit the structures of the literary field has to do with the fact that as they write they also draw on the resources of various misfit sexual cultures of which they have a practical knowledge in order to achieve their literary aims.

Bourdieu notes that "if the implications of inclusion in a field are destined to remain implicit, this is precisely because there is nothing of the conscious, deliberate commitment, or the voluntary contract, about it" (11). Fields have a "specific logic," and people acting within the field align themselves with

that logic as best they can. Occasionally something happens—*Gringoire* stops
publishing a text you have toiled over—that indicates to you that there is
maintenance work to be done on your relationship with the field in which
you participate. That is, the "specific logic" of the field corresponds (well or
ill) to the "specific habitus, or, more precisely, a sense of the game" (11), that is
incorporated into an individual agent, and any agent, to play well, must always
be recalibrating her or his strategies. Bourdieu elaborates:

> The implicit in this case is what is implied in the fact of being caught up in the
> game, in the *illusio* understood as a fundamental belief in the interest of the
> game and the value of the stakes which is inherent in that membership. . . .
> Each field is characterized by the pursuit of a specific goal. . . . Taking part in
> the *illusio* . . . means taking seriously . . . stakes which, arising from the logic
> of the game itself, establish its "seriousness." (11)

Now what will be interesting about many of the players of the literary game to
be encountered here (not just Colette, but Genet, Leduc, Duras, Guibert . . .)
is that there will often be moments in which something goes awry in their
values and their strategies, something becomes incongruous about their sense
of the "serious." Sometimes, as they play the game, it will seem as if they mis-
understand the rules, or play badly in spite of the knowledge of the rules; or it
may seem that they are simply playing a different game while occupying the
same playing field as everyone else. It is this phenomenon—the ways in which
something about a misfit sexuality can exercise an interference effect within
the literary field—that I wish to explore in the present chapter.[1]

The Literary Field, Autonomy, and Heteronomy

Bourdieu developed the concept of the literary field in order to provide a rigorous way of thinking about a literary work's attachment to the social world
of its production and about the ways it can be understood as participating in
struggles over value and meaning that are specific to that world of literary producers. The literary field, part of the cultural field, is situated within a larger
social world and contains its own local struggles over "symbolic power . . . the
power over a particular use of a particular category of signs, and through that,
on the vision and the meaning of the natural and social world."[2] (Think here
of all the male critics writing about the magic or the charm or the economy
or the excess of Colette's sensual prose.)

The concept of the literary field, as Bourdieu elaborates it, allows for an
effort of what we might call contextualization, but one that does not necessarily involve simply placing a text in relation to other *texts*. It involves, for

instance, reconstructing for a cultural artifact its indexical relations to the social world(s) in which it came to be. To the extent that various signs within the artifact had, have, could have had, could come to have, could be made to have again an indexical function, that function can only be activated by showing where those signs point. (Think of the way Colette's passing reference to breast amputation points to a discussion going on in the culture around her, a discussion implicated in that culture's evolving gender politics.) It is a matter of constructing or reconstructing structures of relevance to which a given artifact was attached so that traces of that attachment can once again exercise a signifying function. (How does writing such as Colette's position itself in relation to writing by someone like Proust, or like Morand, or like Kessel, or like Gide? What are the signs of that effort at positioning?) Such structures of relevance might be, but need not be, textual. Studying an artifact's indexical relations to its contexts of use is not necessarily a study of intertextuality. Textual artifacts make reference to and attempt to manipulate social and discursive structures (including generic conventions) as well as other texts.

Literary fields contain certain structures or patterns or positions or practices that are readily recognizable, and that produce an easy form of comprehensibility for certain kinds of actions or productions within the field, while simultaneously making certain other kinds of action or production less comprehensible—although with the passage of time comprehensibility may accrue to them. (Colette's career, and her constant experimentation with different kinds of topics is interesting to think about in these terms: the success of works such as *La maison de Claudine* [*My Mother's House*] and *Sido*, compared to the difficult reception of *The Pure and the Impure*—despite Colette's deep attachment to this later work—indicates something about the role the structure of a field has—its built-in expectations, its way of positioning authors, its way of shaping publics—in determining the success or failure of this or that work, of this or that author.) The meanings and values that accrue to cultural objects such as works of literature do so thanks to a certain kind of collective labor involving producers, consumers, and various mediating agents, such as publishers, critics, and academics, all of whom collectively sustain the meaning-producing medium—the field—in which cultural works exist. The process is highly interactive, and the meaning is public. As Bourdieu noted in his 1968 essay "Intellectual Field and Creative Project":

> It is in and through the whole system of social relations which the creator maintains with the entire complex of agents who compose the intellectual field at any given moment of time—other artists, critics, intermediaries between the artist and the public such as publishers, art dealers or journalists whose

function is to make an immediate appreciation of works of art and to make
them known to the public (not to make a scientific analysis of them as does
the critic in the proper sense), etc.—that the progressive objectivization of the
creative intention is achieved, and the *public meaning* of the work and of the
author is established by which the author is defined and in relation to which
he must define himself.[3]

A number of structural dynamics within various fields of cultural production that Bourdieu and others who work with his framework consistently
bring out are worthy of mention here, as they will be important to (and sometimes contested by) the analyses I am undertaking in this volume. The first
is the opposition between "heteronomous" and "autonomous" cultural producers. In a field of cultural production that has developed a certain amount
of autonomy within the larger social universe that contains it (meaning, for
instance, that it has dedicated journals, critics, prizes, professional organizations, a wide range of publishers with different profiles, that it is free of censorship, etc.),[4] an autonomous producer is one who seeks (and perhaps achieves)
recognition from others *in the field* for work that resonates in some way with
the specific, expert, aesthetic preoccupations current within the field itself,
and often at the expense of wider forms of recognition and profit. A heteronomous producer would be one who achieves or seeks to achieve recognition
(fame and fortune) not (or not only) from those within the field, but from a
wider public, often by not respecting different forms of rigor that characterize
the work of autonomous producers. It is not necessarily the case that all autonomous producers will be recognized by the *same* peers and experts within
the field. Anna Boschetti provides, for instance, an interesting analysis of the
divergence between Apollinaire and his group (avant-garde poetry) and Gide
and his group (a group of what we might call neoclassical modernists) in the
second decade of the twentieth century:

> Apollinaire's world and Gide's world are opposed on every level, in a way that
> seems almost systematic: by social characteristics, by the dispositions and pre-
> occupations of the writers, by their practices, by the forms of distribution and
> of consecration that they make use of, by the reception they encounter. "Pure"
> literature is at this point split into a space with two different poles.[5]

Indeed, one could easily imagine that the autonomous space of a literary field
could harbor more than two poles. But one might also imagine that too tight
of a focus on this opposition between autonomous and heteronomous producers blinds one to certain other dynamics in the field, or of the field in
relation to the social world in which it is embedded. I will return to this possibility in a moment.

First, let us consider a second opposition key to the analysis of fields of cultural production, an opposition that Bourdieu developed out of his reading of Max Weber's sociology of religion. This is the opposition between heretical and orthodox forms of action and production within a given field. In the case of a religious field, the distinction allows one to contrast kinds of action and discourses characteristic of *prophets* and those characteristic of *priests*, between those who try to produce something outside the mainstream and those who reproduce the mainstream, between those whose actions produce a sense of discontinuity within the culture and those who produce an effect of continuity: "The prophet stands opposed to the priestly body as the *discontinuous* to the *continuous*, the extraordinary to the ordinary, the non-routine to the routine and the banal, in particular where the manner of performing his religious action is concerned."[6] Now obviously a heretical or prophetic form of action or of cultural production stands a chance of success only if it finds a receptive public whose interest in something new counterbalances the opposition it would provoke from more institutionalized and conventional sources of opinion and interest. It finds such a public only if that public was, in some way, already there, waiting to be mobilized:

> The prophet's power rests upon the force of the group he can mobilize. This depends on his ability to give symbolic expression—in an exemplary form of conduct and/or in a (quasi-) systematic discourse—to the specifically religious interests of lay people occupying a determinate position in the social structure. . . . The word and person of the prophet symbolize collective representation that, by virtue of the creative nature of symbolization, they contribute to constituting. The prophet embodies in exemplary conduct, or gives discursive expression to, representations, feelings and aspirations that existed before his arrival—albeit in an implicit, semi-conscious, or unconscious state. In this sense, he brings about, in both his discourse and his person, the meeting of a signifier and a pre-existing signified. . . . Thus the prophet—that isolated individual, a man without a past, lacking any authority other than himself . . .— may act as an organizing, mobilizing force. (129–30)

Heretical producers can thus, if successful, alter the system of relevancies, or part of such a system, that dominates the assignment of value within a given field of production. They do so by mobilizing aspirations and interests that exist in a certain way *elsewhere* than within the field of production in question, and by finding a form in which those aspirations and interests can be introduced into the field of cultural production.

Now, the relation between heretical producers and the autonomous/heteronomous polarity is an interesting one (as, indeed, is the relation between orthodox producers and the same polarity). Bourdieu notes that success for a heretical producer is, of course, to establish a new orthodoxy: "It is necessary for prophecy to die as prophecy, i.e. as a message breaking with routine and contesting the accepted order, for it to survive in the priesthood's doctrinal corpus, where it becomes the daily small-change of the original rich fund of charisma" (127). (Gide's group at the *Nouvelle Revue Française* moves over time from the margins to the center, from being challengers of older orthodoxies to being exemplary of orthodoxy itself.) In the most dramatic cases, a heretical figure or movement can provoke a shift in the systems of relevance and value that prevail throughout a given field. Such success, a kind of "symbolic revolution," amounts to a successful defiance of "the mental structures, the categories of perception and of appreciation," that any cultural practitioner would necessarily have absorbed, have learned to believe in (to a greater or lesser degree) just by virtue of being involved in the cultural field.[7] The most prominent examples Bourdieu gives in *The Rules of Art* (besides Flaubert) of heretical producers who set off successful symbolic revolutions of this kind are Baudelaire and Manet.[8] In both cases, the heretical producer proceeds by way of an allegiance to the autonomous pole of production: "Baudelaire effects for the first time the break between commercial and avant-garde publishing" (67). They force a reevaluation of what it means to be dedicated to and on the cutting edge of painting or poetry or writing or dance or music; they create a model of the kind of painting or poetry or writing or dance that can be experienced as the result of disinterested dedication.

Yet what if the polarity is reversed, what if the challenge to established categories of perception and appreciation comes from a "heretical" producer, perhaps an unwitting one, with affiliations to certain kinds of *heteronomy*— either to a heteronomous space within the field of cultural production or to some kind of social contention that is not yet topicalized within the field of cultural production? Such a heretical producer, witting or unwitting, would almost necessarily address a different public, call a different audience into the field of cultural production. If a heretical producer gains traction by appealing to an unusual or unexpected public, the result can still be a change across time in the balance of interests, and therefore of the values, that organize the field. Clearly the division between avant-garde and traditional artistic or intellectual practice is not the only relevant division around which a heretical/orthodox opposition can be established within a cultural field. Just as, or even more, interesting is the case when a "heretical" writer will mobilize "heteronomous" elements—will gain a public from outside the credentialed literary field, and somehow over time force a shift in the institutionalized system of values of that field. Regionalist writers, writers with an appeal to a certain generation or age group, writers specializing in devalorized genres, ethnic writers, women writers, and writers who deal with marginal sexualities have the potential, regardless of any identifiably avant-garde practices in which they may engage, to produce an effect of this kind—in the process requiring the support of a nonestablished public, a nonmainstream system of distribution and critical reception, as they impose themselves upon more orthodox sensibilities or encourage shifts in critical values. The absence of any mention of Colette in Boschetti's book on Apollinaire and the literary field of his time is intriguing to think about in this regard. It suggests something about the way Colette's (marginal) status is perceived (or the way Colette is simply unnoticeable) from a certain (orthodox) critical point of view. It reproduces the long-standing critical habit of not including Colette in accounts of "serious" literature from the first half of the twentieth century.

Perhaps it could be argued that there is no reason Colette should be mentioned in *La poésie partout*, given that Boschetti is focusing to a large extent on the place of avant-garde poetry within the French literary field between 1898 and 1918. Yet Boschetti also describes Apollinaire's experiments in prose in terms that sometimes seem remarkably relevant to Colette's prose experimentation in those same years. In an observation that might just as well have been made of Colette, Boschetti notes that "Apollinaire often draws on his newspaper columns for his stories without making many changes, and sometimes he makes use of his tales in putting together his columns."[9] The long description she gives of the title story in Apollinaire's prose collection *Le poète assassiné* (*The Poet Assassinated*) could be applied almost word for word to a number of Colette's publications from these same years, such as *Les vrilles de la vigne* (*The Tendrils of the Vine*) (1908), *L'envers du music-hall* (*Music-Hall Sidelights*) (1913), *Les heures longues* (1917), or *Dans la foule* (1918).[10]

> Many of the chapters [in *Le poète assassiné*], conceived and presented as monologues or as scenes, resemble a project for a play. The diverse nature of the different texts is emphasized by abrupt ruptures on every level: of tone, of style, of genre, of setting, of spatial and temporal coordinates. Chapters are short and have their own titles, like poems in a collection. Sentences and paragraphs are often separated from each other, as in poems, by a blank line or by asterisks. Apollinaire mixes in to his stories lines of poetry, poems, bits of songs, a short fable. In short, this kaleidoscopic text introduces into prose narrative the same properties—a crossing of forms, acceleration, a variety of methods, a use of sharp contrasts—that characterize his poetic research in 1914, when "Le poète assassiné" is completed. (263)

Apollinaire had been experimenting with short prose forms even earlier, in *L'enchanteur pourrissant* from 1909 or *L'hérésiarque et Cie* from 1910, around the time of Colette's *Les vrilles de la vigne*, of which, it turns out, he wrote a short review, published in March 1909. There is thus evidence that Apollinaire and Colette were aware of each other's work, and the evidence suggests that Apollinaire understood, and had some ambivalence about, the relevance of Colette's literary practices to his own. Consider the circumstances under which he published his review: under the pen name of Louise Lalanne and as part of a series of texts he wrote devoted to contemporary women's writing. Eugène Montfort, editor of the review *Les Marges* that published Apollinaire's pseudonymous series of columns, explains that he had been looking for someone (preferably a woman) to write such a series of articles. Not finding a woman willing to undertake this assignment, he asks Apollinaire to do it, and together they invent the pen name Louise Lalanne.[11] The second of Louise Lalanne's articles in *Les Marges* opens with two pages devoted to Colette's *Les vrilles de la vigne*. At the end of the third article, Lalanne adds a note indicating that "Colette Willy has written to tell me she finds me horrid" (Colette Willy m'a écrit pour me dire qu'elle me trouvait rosse).[12]

Colette wrote her reply not to Lalanne, but to Apollinaire, it turns out. While scholars have often referred to Apollinaire's article as a positive review, one critic has recently noted its malicious side, and the guarded and ironic quality of the letter in which Colette responds to Apollinaire.[13] Positive or negative, kind or malicious, or some mix of these qualities, what is important here is Apollinaire's way of writing under a woman's name while mentioning, in discussing Colette, both her stage career and her scandalous private life— being married to a man while involved with a woman. Colette's way of leading a very public private life, using that life in her writing, exploiting newspaper coverage of it, having a stage career, and becoming a journalist while also producing literary writing constituted an interesting challenge to standard sets of practices through which one staked a claim for the seriousness of one's literary credentials. Consider, in this light, a single moment from Apollinaire/Lalanne's 1909 column:

> How respectful she is of grammar! Colette Willy's first love was in the masculine because of the singular number this gender demands. But after that one nothing in this world could make her wish to place her loves other than in the feminine.[14]

> (Comme elle respecte la grammaire! Le premier amour de Colette Willy était au masculin à cause du nombre singulier que demande ce genre. Après celui-là pour rien au monde elle ne voudrait mettre ses amours autrement qu'au féminin.)

Apollinaire is referring jokingly to the fact that in literary French, the singular noun *amour* is of the masculine gender, but in the plural, *amours*, it can take the feminine form. Colette began with a husband, but then moved on to women, Apollinaire is implying. In Apollinaire's complex figuration here, grammar—and especially the ability to maneuver carefully in more recondite grammatical regions, is an emblem of belonging to the autonomous regions of literary production. Whereas bringing certain nonmainstream forms of love, or, more specifically, displaying one's own nonnormative sexuality in one's literary production, suggests a belonging to a different (less autonomous) region of the field. By linking her personal life to a fine point of grammar, he clearly means to suggest (without explicitly saying so) that the way her writing makes use of her personal life leaves her seriousness as a writer open to question. Apollinaire's figure is, of course, richly ambiguous. To say of a writer that her grammar is good is obviously to damn with faint praise. Colette is apparently being accused of being heteronomous, but in all the *wrong* ways. That is, Apollinaire, even in the very act of writing as Louise Lalanne, shows *himself* to be perfectly capable of dabbling in heteronomous pursuits—as he will do in various techniques of prose and poetic composition he will develop, and when he pens pornographic novels, for instance. The rivalrous and not entirely convincing claim Apollinaire is making awkwardly in writing (as Louise Lalanne) about Colette would thus seem to be that there are right (his) and wrong (hers) ways of incorporating heteronomous topics and practices into a literary career and a literary work.

However useful the heteronomous/autonomous polarity is for understanding the functioning of fields, then, it needs also to be understood as an ideological weapon that is wielded within the field in skirmishes over symbolic capital. Apollinaire's article, in its ambiguous and ironical way, is an excellent example of this. For all its ambiguity and irony, it is directed against women writers, performers, and people of nonnormative sexualities who are held to be inherently heteronomous in an irrecuperable way.

If Colette doesn't come up in Boschetti's account of Apollinaire's situation within the French literary field, it is surely not because of a lack of proximity within the field they both inhabited (where, in fact, there weren't that many degrees of separation between them). It is more a consequence of the way certain aspects of the structure of that literary field (the tendency of different parties to assign women or people with nonnormative sexualities to the heteronomous regions of the field) have been perpetuated and reproduced by works of literary history and critical analysis, and even by the ongoing evolution of the literary field itself. The juxtaposition of the figures of Colette and Apollinaire, and a consideration of the vexed nature of the consecration Colette has been accorded (particularly in academic circles), might thus lead us to wonder about how certain uses of the opposition between autonomous and heteronomous cultural productions and producers might unwittingly serve to carry forward the orthodox structures of relevance of the literary field under analysis. We might then label as heretically heteronomous producers those who, like Colette, draw on sociocultural contexts and on social contentions (such as those relating to misfit sexualities) from outside the literary field in a way that challenges, sooner or later, the boundaries and internal structures of the field itself. Such literary work may or may not conform to patterns of "sophistication" or "innovation" that are valued at any given moment inside or outside the literary field. Several of the authors to be considered in these pages (Colette, certainly, and also Genet, Leduc, Duras, and Guibert) illustrate this intriguing relation to heteronomy at key points in their careers.[15]

Genet's Heteronomous Publics

To develop a bit further this notion of the heretically heteronomous producer, let us consider the history of Jean Genet's arrival on the French literary scene, and the question of whether or not he belonged to some kind of avant-garde. In Paris in the early 1940s, Genet was helping a young left-wing student friend, Jean Decarnin, run a book stall on the banks of the Seine. While working at the stall, Genet met two young right-wing literary types, Jean Turlais and Roland Laudenbach, with whom he struck up a friendship. Thanks to them, a manuscript he had written, which would become the novel *Notre-Dame-des-Fleurs* (*Our Lady of the Flowers*), found its way into the hands of Jean Cocteau. The story of the circulation of the manuscript of *Notre-Dame-des-Fleurs* is well known. Cocteau discussed the manuscript with or showed it to a series of established writers, apparently including Eluard, Colette, Desnos, Paulhan, Jouhandeau, and Valéry. He then helped make the arrangements for the book to be published privately. Genet's prose style in the novel was, for Cocteau, astonishing and compelling, but sufficiently iconoclastic that Cocteau arranged for one of his acolytes, François Sentein, to read through and repunctuate the manuscript.[16]

All of Genet's early books, perhaps in large measure because of their homoerotic content, were first published privately as collectors' items. *Notre-Dame-des-Fleurs* was originally published in late 1943 in an edition of 350 individually numbered volumes. "Each copy of the original French edition of *Our Lady of the Flowers* cost 5,000 francs, about the equivalent of 1,000 new francs or 150 dollars. . . . Morihien [the publisher] had two friends from the Racing Club de France, his water-polo team, who delivered *Our Lady of the Flowers* and other books to the door of the purchaser the same day they were ordered."[17] *Miracle of the Rose* would first appear in a private edition of 475 copies reserved for subscribers. *The Thief's Journal* as well would first be published privately in a signed edition destined for subscribers. *Querelle* would initially appear in 1947 in a limited noncommercial collector's edition with illustrations by Cocteau. The particular set of private collectors interested in Genet's writing of course included wealthy men drawn to male same-sex eroticism. But from the outset, Genet's writing appealed to literary sophisticates as well. Or perhaps we could say, it appealed to some sophisticates and not to others. It struck some of them as an example of astonishing skill in managing French prose. It struck others as badly written.

Was Genet an enduring artist, or was he a passing pornographic fad? The first page of a first book of an unlikely author with literary pretensions—the first sentence, even—might be taken as a calling card, a totem. Sentein, one of those who chose to see the syntax of the young Genet as a sign of his literary genius, clearly fetishized the opening lines of *Notre-Dame-des-Fleurs*:

> Did he already have a doctrine of his own? I could see it being formulated and taking shape each day. Just like any literature in its infancy, he first wrote in verse. The brief happiness of that innocent moment seemed already behind him. I prefer to his latest poems—which he reads, I have to say, quite badly! accenting them like someone in grade school—I prefer his prose, fresh and novel, with his own syntax once he gets out from under that of Jouhandeau. I earned the right—so to speak—to know this. It was last March when I was obliged to go through *Notre-Dame des Fleurs* from the first line to the last, balancing on the edge of his pen, testing with the winged heel of my own pen if what I was dealing with was a youthful blunder or else already one of those "exploitable errors" of the poetry he was currently producing. Already in the first sentence that was the case. Everyone told me—except Cocteau that is— that the "by not creaking" that didn't come until the end of the sentence, like one of Thucydides' verbs, just wasn't acceptable. But I found that creak admirable, especially after all the effort that had gone into stepping lightly . . . on the part of the thief walking over the tops of the nails.[18]

For Sentein, Genet is someone in the process of elaborating a literary doctrine, someone capable of learning from the prosody of a sophisticated older writer such as Marcel Jouhandeau, and then of taking what he has learned and transforming it, thereby producing an original prosody and syntax, one that, in its nonconformity, shocks certain sensibilities while delighting others. (Sentein's claim for Genet's original syntax is not unlike Apollinaire's "praise" of Colette's grammatical elegance. A particular feature of linguistic competence—or incompetence—is isolated as an emblem of sophistication—or its lack—and autonomy—or its lack.) Here are the first few sentences of *Notre-Dame-des-Fleurs*:

> Weidmann appeared before you in a five o'clock edition, his head swathed in white bands, a nun and yet a wounded pilot fallen into the rye one September day like the day when the world came to know the name of Our Lady of the Flowers. His handsome face, multiplied by the presses, swept down upon Paris and all of France, to the depths of the most out-of-the-way villages, in castles and cabins, revealing to the mirthless bourgeois that their daily lives are grazed by enchanting murderers, cunningly elevated to their sleep, which they will cross by some back stairway that has abetted them by not creaking.[19]

> (Weidmann vous apparut dans une édition de cinq heures, la tête emmaillotée de bandelettes blanches, religieuse et encore aviateur blessé, tombé dans les seigles, un jour de septembre pareil à celui où fut connu le nom de Notre-Dame-des-Fleurs. Son beau visage multiplié par les linotypes s'abattit sur Paris et sur la France, au plus profond des villages perdus, dans les châteaux et les chaumières, révélant aux bourgeois attristés que leur vie quotidienne est frôlée d'assassins enchanteurs, élevés sournoisement jusqu'à leur sommeil qu'ils vont traverser, par quelque escalier d'office qui, complice pour eux, n'a pas grincé.)

The novel begins with a reflection upon the way images circulate in France in the 1930s and 1940s, in this case the image of Eugen Weidmann, the murderer of six people in the second half of 1937, and the last criminal to be guillotined in public in France in June 1939. Weidmann's arrest in December 1937 made him front page news for several weeks. The photograph Genet mentions, in which Weidmann's head was bandaged from wounds sustained during his arrest, was published in *Paris-Soir* on December (not September) 10 of that year.[20] Both French literati and the French general public were fascinated by Weidmann. (Colette would cover Weidmann's trial in 1939 for *Paris-Soir*, for instance.) Genet self-consciously references both this fascination for criminals and a certain kind of circulatory pattern within print culture that allows the fascination to flourish, before moving on to consider, in a tightly crafted image of his own, how this fascination moves from the printed page into the cultural imaginary, into the collective unconscious of bourgeois France, into their very dreams via a metaphoric back staircase up which the criminal quietly sneaks. The opening of Genet's novel thus references the medium within French culture, the genre, we might say, through which he, too, will accede to a public— prurient fascination with criminals, their subcultures, and the crimes they commit. Yet the circulation of his text (personally delivered by friends of the publisher to its exclusive purchasers) is, especially initially, much more limited than that of *Paris-Soir*. Sentein's interest in the syntax of what he calls (either by faulty memory, or because Genet's own original punctuation was different from that Sentein ended up providing) Genet's *first* sentence, dwells particularly on the final words, *n'a pas grincé*. The charming murderer makes his way into bourgeois dreams by means of a servants' staircase that cooperates by not squeaking as the murderer ascends. Apparently, there were those among the first readers of Genet's manuscript, people circulating through Cocteau's apartment where Sentein corrected the manuscript, who found that something about that sentence *did* squeak, that it called out for rewriting. Sentein tells us he chose, partly on Cocteau's authority, *not* to rewrite it—not to reorder the sentence's elements or to reword it—because he heard there, in what other ears perceived as awkwardness, a literary quality, an avant-garde edge, an appropriate stylistic resistance to the norm, that defined Genet for him, that even moved Genet beyond the refined stylistic games of someone like Marcel Jouhandeau.[21]

That squeak in his prose that Sentein and Cocteau chose to value could be said to be the sign that Genet's work belonged to (or addressed) a *literary* public that would differ from the small set of collectors who were initially able to purchase the novel. (Certainly some, or even all, of the collectors might also belong to that literary public, but it would be like a single person belonging to two different clubs.) The novel, in Sentein and Cocteau's understanding, addressed a public of trained literary readers who would value and argue over signs of what they might take to be individual aesthetic genius, readers who value experiments in fine prose. The validity of Genet's claim to such a position as a masterful writer could not be tested in private editions. His texts would need to circulate within the literary field more generally. But what is perhaps most interesting in Genet's case is not so much this initial dichotomy of possible publics for Genet's writing (private collectors of high-end gay pornography, on the one hand, and credentialed readers of cutting-edge literature, on the other), as it is the confusion of possible publics for Genet's writing that would quickly emerge, and the way the coming into being of those publics would not respect what we might take to be the traditional boundaries of the literary field per se.

This confusion of publics is clearly marked in the address of the novel as well. The particular use of *vous* in the opening sentence of *Notre-Dame-des-Fleurs* is often, and it seems to me rightly, taken as a sign that Genet addresses one of the possible publics for the novel in a hostile way. Or, we might say, that *vous* is a sign that he understands it to be possible for the novel to address different publics at different moments, or to address different publics in different ways at the same moment.[22] Didier Eribon makes a distinction among the publics for Genet's novel between "those to whom he addresses himself"

and "those for whom he writes," a critical gesture that recalls a point Michael
Warner makes in *Publics and Counterpublics*, to the effect that "it is . . . possible
to distinguish between an implied addressee of rhetoric and a targeted public of
circulation. That these are not identical is what allows people to shape a public
by addressing it in a certain way. It also allows people to fail if a rhetorical addressee is not picked up as the reflection of a public."[23] In Genet's case, the targeted public of circulation will change with each different form of publication
of the novel; the implied addressee of the first sentence might be taken to be the
rich collectors of the first edition, or a wider literate bourgeois public; whereas
other people implicitly addressed by the novel might be assumed to belong to
a different kind of public altogether, one that the book would, in a certain way,
have to bring into being. Eribon makes a strong case for the idea that "those for
whom he writes" are "a small number of imaginary and ideal readers, 'young
people' and 'inverts,' the true addressees of his books" (41). He recalls here a
passage from Genet's *Thief's Journal*: "I am assembling these notes for a few
young men. I should like them to consider these remarks as the recording of a
highly delicate ascesis."[24] He also recalls that the narrator of *Querelle* says early
on, that that book "addresses itself to inverts."[25] This ideal set of readers—linked
to particular social characteristics that might allow the different experiences
chronicled in his book to resonate with them—has a destabilizing relation to
other possible publics: rich people who buy private editions, literarily sophisticated readers who appreciate an author's ability to manipulate French prose
(and also the novel form) in a skilled way that reveals a knowledge of other
great writers, a more general public that finds some kind of pleasure in "scandalous" writing. These ideal readers might, for instance, relate to the book in a
way that is not considered aesthetically suitable in any orthodox sense by the
standards of more credentialed publics. Consider another observation from
The Thief's Journal to which Eribon calls our attention: "My talent will be the
love I feel for that which constitutes the world of prisons and penal colonies."[26]
The sentence captures a nice contradiction in the address of Genet's novels: his
talent (his *literary* talent? his talent as a prose artist?) may be the love he bears
for those whose experience he chronicles, yet that talent produces the sentences
whose syntax and rhythm fascinate people like Sentein and Cocteau. Moreover,
it would probably also assure a certain kind of illegibility for many of those to
whom his "love" itself is directed. In any case, Genet's work, by way of its formal
characteristics and its subjects, addresses multiple publics: it obviously does
address itself to the literary field, but it clearly imagines sneaking in readers
who currently have no legitimate place within that field.

Genet's prose would first reach the literary field directly when, in the spring
of 1944, an excerpt from *Notre-Dame-des-Fleurs* appeared in the literary jour-

nal *L'Arbalète*, alongside writings by Sartre, Claudel, and Leiris. The publisher of that journal, Marc Barbezat, would soon thereafter put out the first public edition of *Notre-Dame-des-Fleurs*, allowing Genet officially to become a "man of letters," and perhaps to find the public he needed if he wanted to be taken seriously in the literary world.[27] When Genet's collected works were published by Gallimard a few years later, it seems that Genet himself helped cut out certain "offensive" passages, "apparently demonstrating," as Mathieu Lindon puts it, "two different sentiments that run contrary to those usually assigned to him: a sense of social responsibility and an indifference to the literary."[28] Most discussions of the variations between different versions of the text of *Notre-Dame-des-Fleurs* turn around questions of literary autonomy and integrity (in short, about Genet's claim to be a literary artist), and around questions of the way a work addresses its (multiple) public(s). For instance, Bernard Frechtman, who translated *Notre-Dame-des-Fleurs* into English, was obliged to defend his choice of the version of the text he translated, and also to defend Genet's artistic integrity, in the *New Statesman* in 1964: "When Gallimard decided to issue the complete edition of his works, which had been published earlier in limited editions available only to subscribers, Genet revised his four novels. The cuts and other changes which he made were dictated solely by artistic considerations and not by prudence. A comparison of the texts of the Gallimard edition and those of the earlier editions would show that the passages which were dropped do not exceed in violence and frankness others which were retained. This holds for *Our Lady of the Flowers* as well as for the other works. Genet revised but did not censor his books."[29] Close scrutiny of the various versions of the text does not exactly bear out Frechtman's claim.[30] Edmund White, in his biography of Genet, shows much less concern for Genet's artistic integrity (indeed he directly impugns it!) when he suggests that what was at stake was an attempt to redefine the public for the novels, to readdress them: "Obviously the direction of many revisions was away from the crudely pornographic, in keeping with Genet's imagined reader, a middle-class heterosexual man" (207). White's comment oversimplifies the situation, of course, and would seem totally to misidentify "Genet's imagined reader," but it, like Frechtman's, helps us to see how one's sense of Genet's public (and of how his aesthetic practices reveal which public he was addressing) are part of what is at stake in establishing or characterizing or defending his position in the literary field.

Bourdieu writes in "Intellectual Field and Creative Project" of "the continual challenge offered by the mere existence of new creators (or by deliberate provocation on their part) who can arouse in the public (and particularly in the intellectual classes) new demands and rebellious doubts" (109–10). Genet's writing has this capability—Sartre's advocacy of it and the concomitant resistance to it by other writers such as Bataille, Blanchot, and Duras (writers who had a stake in both claiming avant-garde status and in being seen as arbiters of the rights of others to that status) reveal this clearly.[31] Yet to focus only on "the intellectual classes" would be to risk missing other social contexts that are invoked by Genet's writing and by the circulation of his works, the other publics that are addressed by them—or, on the other hand, we might say that it risks missing the way someone from the intellectual class might be addressed in a way that is not "suitable" according to the prevailing rules of public intellectual discourse.

When Bourdieu speaks, in his essay on Weber's sociology of religion, of what makes for a successful prophet, he suggests the following:

> Let us then dispose once and for all of the notion of charisma as a property attaching to the nature of a single individual, and examine instead, in each particular case, sociologically pertinent characteristics of an individual biography. The aim in this context is to explain why a particular individual finds himself socially predisposed to live out and express with particular cogency and coherence, ethical or political dispositions that are already present in a latent state amongst all the members of the class or group of his addressees.[32]

Now clearly some of those in the literary field who found themselves drawn to Genet and his work (and perhaps also some of Genet's readers who had only a marginal relation to the literary field) were so drawn because of the relation they felt between their sexuality and his. They would be faced with a problem regarding what terms to use in order to generate discourse around Genet's work, in what way sexuality could figure in that discourse (if it could), in what way *their* sexuality would be implicated in the act of generating discourse around Genet's writing. Alfred Schütz, in speaking of the phenomenology of social relations, notes that

> in the individual's definition of his private situation the various social roles originating in his multiple membership in numerous groups are experienced as a set of self-typifications which in turn are arranged in a particular private order of domains of relevances that is, of course, continuously in flux. It is possible that exactly those features of the individual's personality which are to him of the highest order of relevance are irrelevant from the point of view of any system of relevances taken for granted by the group of which he is a member. This may lead to conflicts within the personality, mainly originating in the endeavor to live up to the various and frequently inconsistent role expectations inhering in the individual's membership in various social groups.[33]

Schütz could be taken to be speaking of the place of sexuality, and of speech or writing about sexuality, in many public cultural and social arenas. Modern literature turns out to be a place where the personality conflicts of which Schütz speaks, and which might better be thought of as the experience on an individual level of contentions that structure a wider social field, can force their way to public attention. There are heretical writers and works that over time succeed in altering the structure of the literary field by the way they introduce new, previously heterogeneous elements into that field, by introducing new elements, new topics, into current discourse in that field. They succeed by changing the rules for speech and for written discourse; they change structures of relevance; they rearrange which aspects of an individual's life are relevant to the cultural field and to discourse within it. They gradually change the distribution of relevant features and schemas of value within the literary and intellectual fields. They make new kinds of public meaning available. By changing the context, they change what works can mean, what characteristics of those works are perceptible and available to discourse; they change how works are valued and understood.

The long-term success of heretical cultural producers thus may arise not only from their reception within the cultural field, but also from the way they manage, be it initially, or at some specific moment later in their career, or else over time, to address a (heteronomous) public that extends beyond that field, or that extends or redefines the boundaries of that field and, also over time, perhaps produces a change in its structures of value and relevance. Michael Warner's development of a contrast between publics and counterpublics can help clarify what is at stake here. "When people address publics," he notes, "they engage in struggles—at varying levels of salience to consciousness, from calculated tactic to mute cognitive noise—over the conditions that bring them together as a public. The making of publics is the metapragmatic work newly taken up by every text in every reading. What kind of public is this? How is it being addressed?"[34] Works such as Genet's provoke the questions: Who are Genet's readers? What does it mean to be one of Genet's readers? While reading the work, people feel impelled to ask, am I one of Genet's readers? And often, they feel moved to declare that they are not.[35] Or if they are, they feel the need to place certain conditions upon their readership. An example of this would be the odd exchange reported to have taken place between Genet and Sartre. Genet asks: "Since you aren't a homosexual, how is it that you can like my books?" Sartre replies: "It's because I am not homosexual that I like them."[36] These are examples of statements that pursue the metapragmatic work of which Warner speaks, making claims regarding the kind of public that reads or should read Genet, the manner in which he should be read, and the conditions that define the public that reads him.[37]

Warner goes on to note that certain publics, in particular those that form around issues related to sexuality and gender, might better be called *counterpublics*. The forms of address that produce counterpublics are not the same as those that produce publics, says Warner, and the kinds of things that can come to be said in counterpublic discourse, its structures of relevance, differ from those of public discourse:

> Discussion within such a public is understood to contravene the rules obtaining in the world at large, being structured by alternative dispositions or protocols, making different assumptions about what can be said or what goes without saying. This kind of public is, in effect, a counterpublic: it maintains at some level, conscious or not, an awareness of its subordinate status. (56)

When a counterpublic comes to exist around a text, it produces discourse according to the codes in place in that particular counterpublic. Such discourse is never fully contained within the subculture in question (members of counterpublics are members of other publics as well), and it threatens, when it circulates beyond its immediate context of origin, to introduce discontinuities into acceptable public styles of discourse as well. Admitting that one is a reader of Genet and discussing his work produces discourse about aspects of sexuality, for instance, in public spaces where it might not have occurred previously. Warner further notes:

> Like all publics, a counterpublic comes into being through an address to indefinite strangers. (This is one significant difference between a counterpublic and a community or group.) But counterpublic discourse also addresses those strangers as being not just anybody. They are socially marked by their participation in this kind of discourse; ordinary people are presumed not to want to be mistaken for the kind of person who would participate in this kind of talk or be present in this kind of scene. (120)

If the movement of the text, or of versions of the text, or of excerpts of the text of Genet's *Notre-Dame-des-Fleurs* from a private edition, to the literary journal *L'Arbalète*, to a public edition by the small publishing house also called L'Arbalète, to an edition published by Gallimard, is a pattern of circulation that allows Genet to find a literary public, it is also the condition thanks to which his text has the occasion to produce other counterpublics whose impact on public discourse will only be felt gradually, even over generations. But when Sartre says of Genet's books, "It's because I am not homosexual that I like them," that comment indexes a tension between publics and counterpublics; it places Sartre in a certain kind of public, not a sexual counterpublic, for Genet's texts, and asserts the rights of that public to adjudicate the meaning of those texts. It is part of a larger statement by Sartre regarding the appropriate uses (and therefore the public meaning) of Genet's text. The counterpublic uses and meanings of those same texts necessarily take longer to reveal themselves.[38] Bourdieu, in a conversation with Robert Darnton, talked of "an absolutely fundamental problem, which is that of the articulation, within a differentiated society, of a cultural code that is at least vaguely held in common . . . with specific codes associated with sub-universes."[39] This is the problem of the articulation between a counterpublic and an orthodox public culture, brought to a head when a cultural producer such as Genet achieves a certain kind of unstable consecration within the orthodox literary field while simultaneously enabling by way of his writing the production of a counterpublic that both overlaps with and is external to the field of orthodox cultural production. Prevailing schemes of relevance are laid open to change. Genet's writing, his person, and his speech in public and in private all become cultural references productive of further discourse.

The process is not necessarily a quick one. It can be ongoing for decades. Consider the circumstances of an interview with Sartre in 1980, and the responses Sartre gives regarding Genet. The interview was published in *Gai pied*, a monthly gay cultural magazine that had begun to appear roughly a year earlier. This is thus thirty-five or so years after Sartre had asserted of Genet's books that "it's because I am not homosexual that I like them." In that time, social movements around same-sex sexual identities have developed, and journals such as *Gai pied* or *Masques*, which constitute more public organs of expression for these counterpublics, offer them a chance to assert their own structures of relevance in relation to previous discourse and in relation to previous cultural productions:

> —*In your novels, certain characters treat sodomy as if it were an act of domination par excellence, by which one man subjugates another. In "The Condemned of Altona," Frantz declares: "Of two leaders together, either they have to kill each other or one has to become the woman of the other." Why do you see the passive role in sodomy as a kind of capital punishment?*
>
> —That was more or less the impression that I had and that I developed after some discussions with Genet. When I was writing my book on him, I had the chance to speak to him, and I would come up with my hypotheses and run them by him. . . .
>
> —*The passive homosexual makes an offer and a gift of himself. For you, he loses all his dignity; he becomes, in words you wrote "an imaginary woman who takes pleasure in the absence of pleasure." Why should such a lack of consideration*

fall upon and take in not only passive homosexuals but any woman having het-
erosexual relations?

    —Read Genet: he is the one who gives this impression. He is the one who
says there is no pleasure involved, that he looks for it but can't find it.... In
these matters I relied on Genet, because he was the one I was talking to.

    —*Do you really think that there is an absence of pleasure in every act of
passive sodomy?*

    —No, there's no reason that should be the case. But it's certain that Genet
didn't find much pleasure in it.[40]

For Sartre, very clearly, literature has been a space for thinking about sexuality in sociological, political, philosophical, and psychological terms. Indeed,
Sartrean discourse around literary texts such as Genet's rarely touches upon
what might be considered traditional literary or aesthetic concerns. For Sartre,
Genet is an authority on a particular sexual subculture. The two people interviewing Sartre for *Gai pied*, Jean Le Bitoux and Gilles Barbedette, are also
clearly primarily concerned with ideologies of representation rather than with
literary or aesthetic concerns. Questions regarding Genet's syntax, the archi-
tecture of his novels, the techniques of narration he employs—and the way he
might use aesthetic elements such as those to map diverse kinds of relations
with previous authors such as Gide or Proust or Cocteau or Jouhandeau—are
really not on the table.[41] And yet these kinds of discussions are about the *use*
of literature, about ways of using literature, about the functioning of literary
signs. They are about Genet's literary production and its effects, they make
claims regarding the meaning of his works; they draw upon prior discursive
and cultural formations in order to move public discussions of cultural artifacts in new directions. They take Genet's text, or Sartre's text, and reentextu-
alize it—insert it into a new context in which its meaning evolves.

    Moreover, such discussions could also be said to be about point of view
and address, even if the participants in them don't always fully realize that this
is the case. That is to say, it doesn't take much thought to realize that Genet
must have had a particular way of addressing Sartre. Sartre must have had a
particular point of view on Genet. We can assume that Genet crafted what he
said to Sartre in the light of his sense of whom he was addressing. He didn't
just spout "the truth" about "sodomy." (Also, you don't even have to pay particularly close attention to a novel like *Querelle* to notice that there are characters in Genet who enjoy passive anal intercourse, and who don't consider
participating in it to be an act of submission or of feminization.) Genet was
hyperattentive to forms of address and their function, as we have already seen.
He understood that forms of address shape whatever "information" it is that is
being exchanged. He made this attention to address into an aesthetic concern.

As we shall see, this attention to the pragmatics and metapragmatics of speech about sexuality becomes an ongoing subject, a topic of research, we might say, for other authors interested in sexuality. Among the authors I will be treating in this volume, Leduc and Pinget are prime examples of people who share Genet's simultaneously social and aesthetic concern with the pragmatics and metapragmatics of address in speech about sexuality.

The exchange between Le Bitoux, Barbedette, and Sartre in 1980 might remind us of the kinds of conversation Colette must have been having with Hall and Troubridge—negotiations regarding how sexuality is organized in life and in language, what its history has been, and how meanings related to sexual practices shift over time. In the case of Colette, Hall, and Troubridge, their private conversations had an impact on the writing of *Ces plaisirs* . . . , whereas here, the conversation with Sartre seems to be part of an attempt to contest the kinds of meanings ascribed to certain sexual acts, meanings that Le Bitoux and Barbedette seem to believe Sartre and Genet helped circulate. What I am tracing is the way the topic of same-sex sexuality impacted the structures and contours of the French literary field; the ways in which literary texts occasionally served as vehicles for the transmission both of various kinds of practical knowledge about sexuality, and of frameworks through which to organize our perception of sexuality both conceptually and categorically; and the ways in which certain literary works would themselves learn to reflect upon how sexuality exists in language, in both propositional and nonpropositional ways. All of these processes are interrelated, involving struggles over status both as readers and as producers in the literary field, involving the prevalence and prestige of different kinds of uses of literary works among various publics and counterpublics, and involving the development of various aesthetic techniques and currents of critical reflection within the literary works themselves.

Let's develop for a few more pages our sense of the manners in which certain literary works might have been read, used, understood by counterpublics (say, how Violette Leduc, Jean Sentein, and Jean Cocteau could all read Beauvoir's *L'invitée* [*She Came to Stay*] in 1943 and 1944 and understand it to be a text about female same-sex sexuality, even if such sexuality is never represented in the novel)—in ways that would perhaps be seen as illegitimate or immature or inappropriate by defenders of various kinds of literary or critical orthodoxies. These very counterpublic uses and understandings of specific literary works can themselves be read as contestations of the values and codes that help determine what counts as an appropriate usage of a literary text, that help determine what texts are, in fact, literary, or, indeed, attempt to contest the limits of the literary field itself. Take as exemplary here the trajectory between two moments in writings by Violette Leduc, the first from *La Bâtarde*, the second from *La folie en tête* (*Mad in Pursuit*). In *La Bâtarde*, Leduc describes her relation at about age sixteen to a provincial bookstore:

> I also walked in the Place d'Armes on Saturday nights. The lighted storefronts crackled before my eyes. I was attracted, intrigued, spellbound by the yellow covers of the books published by the Mercure de France, by the white covers of the Gallimard books. I selected a title, but I didn't really believe I was intelligent enough to go into the largest bookstore in town. I had some pocket money with me (money that my mother slipped me without my stepfather's knowing), I went in. There were teachers, priests, and older students glancing through the uncut volumes. I had so often watched the old lady who served in the shop as she packed up pious objects, as she reached into the window for the things that people pointed out to her. . . . She took out Jules Romains' *Mort de quelqu'un* and looked at me askance. I was too young to be reading modern literature. I read *Mort de quelqu'un* and smoked a cigarette as I did so in order to savor my complicity with a modern author all the more. . . . The Saturday after that I stole a book which I didn't read; but I paid cash down for André Gide's *Les Nourritures terrestres* and a sculpture of a dead bird. Later, under my bedclothes, when I went back to boarding school, I returned to the barns, to the fruits of André Gide by the glow of a flashlight. As I held my shoe in the shoe shop and spread polish on it, I muttered: "Shoe, I will teach you to feel fervor." There was no other confidant worthy of my long book-filled nights, my literary ecstasies.[42]

Leduc paints here a number of the ways in which she experiences her relation to books, bookstores, and literature as illegitimate, a number of ways in which, we might say, she feels excluded from the literary field (for which the lighted interior of the bookstore is here a synecdoche), and even when she enters the literary field (goes into the store), she feels that she does so in a way that fails to respect its most common understandings of itself (she will read neither as teacher, priest, or student). We could say that she experiences herself more as a member of a counterpublic than as a member of a public. She is too poor, too uncultivated, too young, too enthusiastic a reader to approach literature appropriately. Her reading is tied to other sensual experiences (cigarettes and the smell of shoe polish) in a way that enhances her sense of its illicitness.[43] It's not clear that there is much rhyme or reason to her choice of authors, other than that they have their books in the front window and exude an aura of modernity. And yet it turns out that she, like many other alienated young people, often people exploring nonnormative sexual experiences, develops an affiliation with Gide's *The Fruits of the Earth*, a countercultural classic of the early to mid-twentieth century, with its call to a certain kind of sexual dissidence, to an experience of fervent sensuality.[44]

Later in *La Bâtarde*, Leduc will recount her first evening walk in Paris: "Psychology books, philosophy books, science books, astronomy books . . . The desire to lift that bookstore bodily off the ground and carry it off on my back, to feel the green embrocation of the covers on my shoulders. That was my first pious halt before the bookstore of the Presses Universitaires. Another day I stood and drank in the titles of the Garnier classics draught upon draught" (114–15). Her relation to literature is one of perhaps excessively sensualized, self-torturing worship. She understands Parisian bookstores, unlike the one in her small town, as somehow holding not only a wider variety of books, but something more essentially literary. She imaginatively undertakes some kind of herculean task as part of her quest to be anointed with that essence. Her ambitions at this point in time do not seem to include writing. Perhaps emphasizing how unlikely it seems to her that someone of her low social standing, someone with her lack of application as a student, could ever occupy a legitimate position as a producer in the literary field, she tells her mother, "I will become a bookseller; I will get a job in a bookstore" (124), to which end she enrolls in courses at the Maison du livre. Those courses seem to tip the balance in her favor when she is interviewed for a menial position in the advertising department at the Plon publishing house a bit later on.

La Bâtarde tells multiple intertwined stories: of the development of a powerful investment in literature and the literary world, but of the enduring sense that the form of her relationship to literature and the literary world, her abject (and abjectly sensual) relation to the authors and the writing she admires, are irrevocably illegitimate, unorthodox, inappropriately sensual, insufficiently intellectual, linked to all kinds of dissident sexual attachments and failures of sophistication. Leduc conveys a clear sense that the literary world is a place in which knowledge of dissident sexualities can circulate, that that is, indeed, one of the functions of works of literature, but not one of its public functions. It is an aspect of modern literature that somehow cannot be spoken of directly. Institutionalized manners of dealing with literature often find ways of simply not noticing this aspect of literary texts, or the role sexuality plays in a variety of literary relations. That Leduc should ever come to imagine herself a writer is perhaps itself remarkable, given the degree to which she understood her relations to the literary world and to literary objects as inappropriate ones. *La Bâtarde* and its sequel *Mad in Pursuit* offer a compelling case study of how a member of a literary counterpublic manages to make a career for herself as a writer, marginal in all sorts of ways, one whose success will also perhaps never be a public one, but always a counterpublic one, whose recognition will always also be a kind of misrecognition, precisely because her investment in literature differs in such profound ways from standard kinds of investments:

her relation to such forms of value (as they were usually conceived in the literary field around her) as sophistication or innovation or social engagement
are not normative; she doesn't easily fit any notion of avant-garde writing, and
so on.[45]

Thanks to the encouragement and intervention of a number of figures
(including most notably Maurice Sachs and Simone de Beauvoir), Leduc does
become a published author, but success of various kinds eludes her. Here is a
scene that captures some of the particularities of Leduc's situation. Described
in *Mad in Pursuit*, it takes place shortly after the publication of her first book,
L'asphyxie (1946), which received only meager and unkind critical notices despite an excerpt having been published in Sartre's *Les Temps Modernes*, and
despite the book having appeared in a collection edited by Albert Camus:

> One afternoon I was preparing an assortment of vegetables to make my soup,
> a wild hope seized me, the knife fell onto my one sad leek. I threw on my
> clothes. The journey to the Bac station was interminable. I arrived in front
> of the Gallimard bookstore on the Boulevard Raspail, in front of its eclectic
> windows, completely out of breath. But it must be in them. It wasn't. The large-
> format books, the rare editions of Valéry, of Gide, of Apollinaire, disdainful
> and withdrawn, rejected me utterly. The bastions of modern literature cannot
> be overthrown just to make way for your little pile of turds. Oh God, how I
> begged outside those windows . . . If I had only been sure of what I was writing,
> I should have been saved . . . Baudelaire and Rimbaud, were they sure of them-
> selves? But I wasn't Baudelaire, I wasn't Rimbaud. Ten new books published
> every day. How can you expect them to display such a flood? An hour, even if it
> were just for an hour, each of us in turn . . . Where has it gone since I dedicated
> all those copies? Where has it gone to earth? Have the bookstores received
> it? I should die of shame if I had to ask them. Writing must be a sin, or why
> should I prefer to conceal it? My guilt was coming back. Window displays and
> bookstores whispered to me in the night: "You'll never amount to anything,
> you'll never amount to anything at all," just as my mother had once dinned
> those words into me in the past. I shall hand in my cards. Hand in your cards
> to whom? To the bookstores, to their windows, to the publisher.[46]

Perhaps foolishly, Leduc grants the window of the bookstore run by the publishing house Gallimard on the boulevard Raspail a particular kind of sa-
credness. True, *L'asphyxie* was published by Gallimard, so why shouldn't they
put it in their window? For Leduc, to be on display in its window alongside
other Gallimard authors such as Valéry and Gide would seem to be consecration itself. Yet how could someone who was obliged to express her excessive
youthful enthusiasm for Gide's *Les nourritures terrestres* to her poor shoes as
she shined them, someone who only moments ago was chopping up leeks

for soup (and how differently Leduc turns this into a gendered performance than Colette would have . . .), expect to find her book on the other side of the glass in the bookstore window, especially when the book itself seems even to her somehow so inappropriate. She seems aware that "true" artists would not feel the abject and self-defeating need for the kind of recognition she seeks: Baudelaire and Rimbaud would simply have known they deserved a spot in the window display even if they would also have known they were unlikely to get one. They wouldn't have been such pathetic victims of their longing for the spot in the window. As Anna Boschetti puts it, in a way that sounds almost as if it could be understood as a reproach directed at Leduc: "In fields such as the artistic or the literary, the fundamental form of interest for anyone aspiring to true greatness consists in the search for perfection, which often carries with it the implication of absolutely complete disinterestedness as regards material or social advantages."[47] (Does "anyone"—*ceux* in the original French—here have a gender?) Yet perhaps what Leduc is seeking without knowing it, or what she is learning to seek in this awkward, uncomfortable moment when she is feeling hungry in all sorts of ways, and also especially downtrodden by the reviews of *L'asphyxie* published by Roger Kemp in *Nouvelles littéraires* or André Rousseaux in *Figaro littéraire*, when she knows she doesn't have enough standing among the huge number of authors Gallimard publishes to merit a place in their window (yet), perhaps what she "wants" is not "true great-ness," is not perfection, is not disinterestedness. Perhaps what she is looking for, mostly without knowing it, is a counterpublic, rather than a public. And perhaps the "innovation" of her work could only be perceived critically if the notion of innovation itself were to evolve to include the ability of her work to address that previously unassembled group of people who would become the counterpublic of her readers.[48]

Within counterpublics, books of the kind that are not often found on dis-play in bookstore windows (idiosyncratic books by idiosyncratic authors for idiosyncratic readers) often circulate by word of mouth (and perhaps this was even more true in the middle of the last century than it is today):

> My cheeks still wet with tears, I ran into the antique dealer Hagnauer, who was only too delighted to give me the news that Cocteau had read my book and was telling everyone else to read it. Encouraged, I walked round for hours and hours. I had developed a method: that of the bird's nester. I slowed down when I was twenty yards away from the bookstore, then I stole up on it very gently so as to surprise my book in the window and receive a shock from it. But all the nests were empty. Except once. Where? The dispiriting window of the Polish bookstore on the Boulevard Saint-Germain. How old and worn it looked in the very back row! If I buy it from them, then they'll take it out of

the window; if I buy it from them, it will become a dusty rectangle after I leave. I looked at it for a long time.[49]

Cocteau helps her book find readers in informal ways; its formal place in bookstores remains highly tenuous. Leduc is learning, we might say, that she is a stranger within the literary field, much in the way Alfred Schütz talked about a stranger as "a border case outside the territory covered by the scheme of orientation current within the group. He is, therefore, no longer permitted to consider himself as the center of his social environment, and this fact causes again a dislocation of his contour lines of relevance."[50] As time goes by, and she makes the acquaintance of Genet and becomes aware of his writing and his own relation to the literary field, it only confirms her in the kind of "stranger" attitude she has always experienced toward that same field. Genet's *Miracle de la rose* is recommended to her by Simone de Beauvoir, but it is not a text that is easily available. It only exists in a hand-printed 475-copy edition published by Arbalète, Marc Barbezat's small publishing house. Beauvoir promises Leduc she will leave her copy of the novel for Leduc with the cashier at the café Les Deux Magots.

> The lady at the desk of the Deux-Magots handed me the copy of *Miracle de la Rose* Simone de Beauvoir had left there for me. It's heavy, I commented. Yes, it's heavy, the lady at the desk replied. . . . That evening *Miracle de la Rose* weighs down my bed. The book is inside a chest, between two covers that fit together. I have brought a deluxe edition home with me: it's a first. . . . The size and weight are almost those of a Bible at the foot of a pulpit. They require a lectern, special arrangements. I lean my elbow on the pillow, we tilt, the book and I together, towards the wall, and we begin to give ourselves to one another. I am falling into my reading of *Miracle de la Rose* as one falls in love.[51]

Genet's book comes to Leduc through unofficial channels, we might say, and her reading of it resembles her reading of Gide's *The Fruits of the Earth*, involving a combination of secrecy, sensuality, and sacrality. There is a lesson to be learned about the combination of these two phenomena, unofficial circulation and a certain kind of fervent reading: they link both Genet and Leduc to a kind of heretical "stranger" heteronomy, a sexual counterpublic "within" the literary field. We could also say that Leduc's aspiration for recognition within the literary field has been shaped in a particular way by the impact the circulation of social forms of sexuality through literature has had on her: she has been addressed by literature in a counterpublic kind of way, and seeks to rebroadcast that address. The kind of recognition that happens within such a counterpublic can never find an easy equivalent within the display window of a bookstore, which gives a certain poignancy to Leduc's futile and despairing fantasy of finding a way to offer everyone an equal share of recognition: "Ten new books published every day. How can you expect them to display such a flood? An hour, even if it were just for an hour, each of us in turn." An hour in the Librairie Gallimard's window would bring her nothing, unless the right reader accidentally walked by and had already been primed to notice her. Leduc is thus learning something about being a new author, and something about the consequences of addressing a counterpublic in a public forum. Not only "a new author," of course, but also a woman. Her imaginary literary pantheon may include Gide and Genet alongside Simone de Beauvoir, her literary supporters may include Sartre, Camus, and Cocteau, still (more on this topic in chapter 6) the literary field is obviously structured to the disadvantage of women, and women and men will not be able to find and address counterpublics in parallel fashion.[52]

As Bourdieu puts it, "to inquire into the origins of this public meaning is to ask oneself who judges and who consecrates, and how the selection process operates so that out of the undifferentiated and undefined mass of works which are produced and even published, there emerge works which are worthy of being loved, admired, preserved and consecrated."[53] Leduc's early work does come to be admired by much the same set of people who admired Genet's early work. Some of these people are on their way to being well-established agents in the literary field who do what they can to provide for her recognition there (Sartre, Beauvoir, Camus); some of these people are already well-established agents in the literary field, but contribute more to a kind of unofficial circulation of her work (Cocteau); and some, such as the book-collecting industrialist Jacques Guérin, who helped arrange for a private, luxury collectors' edition (143 copies) of her second book, *L'affamée*, clearly helped the book circulate *outside* the literary field per se. It was, in fact, in the form of this private edition that Leduc's book would find itself where she had always dreamed it would be. As her biographer, Carlo Jansiti, notes, the private edition "comes off the presses in September 1948. Paul Morihien, rue de Beaujolais, dedicates a window to it."[54] Morihien was, of course, also the publisher of the private edition of Genet's *Our Lady of the Flowers*. But this is a bookstore even more difficult for ordinary people to enter than those we have already seen Leduc standing outside of. The exclusive material form of the book, whatever sensual atmosphere it may provide should you be lucky enough to get into bed with it, is a sign of the limited nature of the public that can receive its address. The more affordable, regular Gallimard edition published a few months later was more accessible—and sold poorly.[55] Leduc was slow to find her (counter)public.

In the case of both Leduc and Genet, then, we could speak of the parallel histories of the counterpublic and the public meanings of their works, and we could notice how certain key figures participate in both these histories, perhaps engaging different sides of themselves as they do so. (Cocteau would seem to be exemplary of this.) We should also note how the different meanings these works can hold for different publics reveal more than divisions within the social field. They may also reveal different ideologies regarding the uses of literature that struggle for dominance within the literary field per se. (The discussion of various kinds of nonnormative or misfit sexual practices and cultures, the circulation of information about those practices and cultures, may not strike some people as literary.) The circulation of certain literary works "outside" the literary field (as well as within it) implies the accumulation by those works of meanings that arise from contexts that are not simply literary, and that are as likely to be situated outside, or astride the boundaries of, what many are likely to construe or construct as part of the literary field. In the cases of Leduc and Genet, as well as a number of other authors to be considered in these pages, the circulation of literary works turns out to have a relation to the circulation of various social forms through which misfit sexualities are experienced, enacted, and (sometimes) recognized. Leduc's and Genet's works show both a practical and a theoretical understanding of this phenomenon of social semiotics. Additionally, they do "aesthetic" work on this phenomenon, or they use it as part of an aesthetic endeavor. Thus Genet's *Querelle* (along with other of his novels) can be seen to analyze the way individuals circulate through sexual forms (with or without being aware of it) as they move through different social universes; on another level, the novel participates in the redistribution of knowledge regarding certain forms of sexuality within a culture—and thereby, as it circulates, accumulates value, meaning, as more and more reentextualizations accrue to it, it contributes to changes in the functioning of the cultural field itself. On yet another level, it has a linguistic and aesthetic interest in how language functions in order to do all these things. In *Querelle*, as we shall see in the next chapter, Genet seems particularly interested in studying both the highly structured, predictable set of sexual forms through which people usually move in their daily round, so to speak, and also the situations that arise when some kind of foreign social agent appears and then moves through those forms unpredictably, speaking and acting in untoward ways, throwing standard schemes of perception and relevance, along with standard uses of language, out of kilter. *Querelle*, along with Genet's other books, functions in a similar way within the literary field.

As people negotiate their way through the social world, their success depends on their mastery of recognizable and socially acceptable patterns, forms, or genres for all kinds of interaction, including sexual interaction—patterns, forms, or genres with which they improvise as best they can to achieve their goals. The complexity of the semiotic negotiations involved in sexual interactions outside the norm gradually becomes a topic, an area of investigation we could even say, in literary writing about sexuality in twentieth-century France. Consider, as one small instance of this, the following passage from *La Bâtarde*, in which the young Violette, still newly arrived in Paris, furthers her acquaintance with Gabriel, a fellow she met in the cinema one day, and who has started coming to meet her every day when she gets out of school:

> He was a buyer for a firm in Clermont and his job was to buy in Paris all the things the women didn't have down there: dressmaking articles, porcelain, hardware. Our freedom at four in the afternoon went to my head. He tried to make me smoke in the street and his daring stunned me.
>
> "Last week you went to the Galeries with your mother and your brother. You got on an 'S.'"
>
> "What? How do you know?"
>
> "I followed the bus in a taxi."
>
> His eyes added: "Don't make a fuss. That's how it is."
>
> "Your mother ordered a lemon juice. You had an ice. Your mother was in a bad temper."
>
> "You were there!"
>
> I said: I have a girl friend.
>
> "We'll go to Montparnasse!"
>
> I said: before her I had Isabelle.
>
> "We'll go to the Dôme!"
>
> I said: I have a girl friend. I write her every day.
>
> "We'll go to the Select."
>
> I said: She writes me every day.
>
> "We'll go to the Jockey, my little one, we'll go to the Jockey together."
>
> "I've got a girl friend!"
>
> Gabriel understood; his sacrifices increased. (119–20)

This passage is, in part, about the circulation of sexual knowledge, about the negotiation of misfit sexual relations, about how someone finds out what understandings an interlocutor has of various forms of sexuality and in the process refines their own understanding of available cultural concepts for apprehending sexuality, about how two people might establish some kind of common understanding under which a relationship could continue. Both Gabriel and Violette are revealing things to each other about their sexuality—that he is some kind of a voyeur interested in girls just finishing high school, that she has "une amie" and a sexual history with women. Both of them are insistent on revealing something about which neither of them can be said to be clear or explicit. They are negotiating a shared sexuality without it or its component parts being named, perhaps because the terms established for that sexuality are such that it will not conform to any name that might be available. Gabriel, by referencing a series of places in Montparnasse in which various kinds of sexual misfits might congregate, offers an arena in which they might pursue their relation, even if the spots he mentions seem, in some ways, beyond their means, and even if the two interlocutors might not yet share any understanding of what those place names connote. Nonetheless, naming places in the way he does serves to let her know that there may be, in fact, places for people like them—even if "people like them" has no clear referent.

One sees in a passage such as this how the act of representing a negotiation related to marginal sexualities can raise all sorts of linguistic anthropological questions. We could say that our practical or pragmatic success in the social world depends on our evolving attempts to master a constantly evolving set of metapragmatic forms, novel interaction genres, and imaginary geographies that offer a structure for pragmatic action that might have, or might acquire, some wider kind of social legibility. In literary texts about misfit sexualities we regularly see scenes representing this practical training in the use of the fleeting interaction genres for the construction or maintenance (or dissolution) of these sexualities. On occasion, as, perhaps, in the scene we have just been looking at, the representation of these scenes becomes more than just an act of representation. It becomes an instance of a specifically literary concern with implicitness, with pragmatics and metapragmatics. As I observed in the previous chapter, nonmainstream, unofficial, transitory, misfit sexual forms and cultures almost necessarily have a heavily pragmatic existence. They exist in language implicitly. The participants in these activities are involved in them in ways of which they may be mostly unconscious or to which they may have great difficulty giving explicit verbal expression (which need not be exactly the same thing). People such as Genet, Leduc, and also, as we are about to see, Robert Pinget, produce a variety of innovative literary practices that manage to demonstrate how certain kinds of sexuality sometimes inhere within language, yet not within the sphere of its referential functioning. Rather they are to be found in the indexical or pragmatic functioning of language, and thus would ordinarily tend to evaporate with the moment of enunciation. Yet occasionally there are literary texts that seem to have become so interested in this representational conundrum that they find a way around it. In *Querelle*, for instance, Genet studies (among other things) a disruption in the easy flow between the pragmatic and metapragmatic levels on which sexual encounters occur. Novels such as *Querelle* turn out not simply to be spaces of representation, spaces in which various referential aspects of culture, in particular, of sexual culture, can be recorded. They are certainly that, and in being that, they contribute to the circulation of knowledge regarding certain social forms of sexuality. They enact that circulation, and, to some degree, effect a redistribution of knowledge every time they are, so to speak, reused. But they are also instruments that call to our attention the myriad ways we implicitly invoke culture to act in the world, thereby occasionally provoking in some of us a sense of our participation in the nonreferential, nondenotational aspects of our use of language and of cultural forms.

Authors such as Genet or Leduc or Pinget develop literary techniques, modes of writing, to deal with the problem of how language, in the context of its use, invokes cultural forms in which practical but nonreferential knowledge about sexuality exists. They become interested in studying what Michael Silverstein has called metapragmatic functions. Remember the observation by Silverstein already cited in the previous chapter: "Metapragmatic function serves to regiment indexicals into interpretable events of such-and-such type that the use of language in interaction constitutes (consists of). Understanding discursive interaction as events of such-and-such type is precisely having a model of interactional text."[56] What Leduc shows her younger self negotiating with Gabriel is a coherent bit of interactional text that would encompass a shared understanding of, a cultural form for, a sexuality they both want to share, but whose form cannot simply be stated. People like Leduc, or Genet, or Pinget, thus use literary means to arrive at an understanding of the relationship between culture and language use quite similar to the one laid out by someone like Silverstein, in which certain kinds of "cultural concepts" are "revealed in cultural practices—among them the always indexical social action of using language." This kind of "presumptively shared knowledge" has a practical existence that is "access[ed]" and "renew[ed]" on each occasion in which a shared cultural form for the sexuality becomes the basis for a new interaction. Such shared cultural forms "are empirically investigable once we abandon the idea that they are analogues . . . to lexically coded concepts."[57]

One consequence of the predominantly practical existence of these non-lexically coded cultural forms in which misfit sexualities often transpire is that meanings are hard to hold on to. This is the case, of course, for the coherence of an ongoing set of interactions forming the history of a shared sexual experience, but it is also the case for efforts to study this aspect of language use in relation to meaning. It requires a particular context, as well as a particular way of attending to context, to bring out this aspect of the work of people like Colette, or Genet, or Beauvoir, or Duras, or Leduc, or Pinget. I am arguing that some of these authors (Pinget most particularly, but also Colette in her own way, as we have seen, and Genet, as we shall see shortly) worked directly on this sociolinguistic topic in its relation to sexuality. But the same difficulties with regard to the transitory nature of contextually fleeting meanings can be noted about counterpublic uses of literary texts such as Beauvoir's *L'invitée* (*She Came to Stay*) that were in and of themselves not explicitly studying this aspect of language; rather they were simply caught up in it—serving for certain readers to invoke relationships between women such as the ones Beauvoir herself was involved in at the time she wrote the novel without ever representing them. The invocation of these relationships in *L'invitée* was possible because of the way the text existed within certain strikingly impermanent contexts that can only be reconstructed with some effort. As Silverstein notes, cultural knowledge of this kind "*lives and dies in textual occasions.* We create it on occasions of use of particular words and expressions in particular cotextual arrays one with respect to another, as much as, on subsequent occasions of use of them, we try to presume upon the knowledge previously experienced and, perhaps finding our presumption being questioned, have to create it again or modify it for some new interlocutor."[58]

The introduction of the topic of nonmainstream and misfit sexualities into the literary field allows for repeated representations of occasions of language use that depend on the presumed practical knowledge of misfit sexual forms or that work to recreate or modify such knowledge, and also allows, in the case of certain authors, for a kind of technical reflection on the semiotic characteristics upon which such exchanges rely. This technical reflection can itself sometimes be difficult to perceive, not only because the features of language use being reflected upon are so hard to maintain an awareness of, but also because the study of this kind of language use is happening in relation to sexuality—which various features of the literary field might otherwise create a propensity to ignore, or to avoid contributing to discourse about. Yet through such reflection and its concomitant technical experimentation, we can see writing on the semiotics of misfit sexualities finding its way into some of the most technically sophisticated (autonomous and experimental) regions of the literary field—finding its way, we might say, to another kind of inaccessibility, since understanding the work of rigorously experimental texts such as some of Robert Pinget's novels will in itself require a good deal of technical and conceptual preparation on the part of the reader. Pinget is, to my eye, in some ways the most technically sophisticated of the authors I will treat in this volume, and also, for the reasons I have just mentioned, probably the least well known, the least read, and the least well understood. His 1965 novel *Someone* (*Quelqu'un*) is, of course, referred to in my title, but my analysis will also focus on his 1962 *The Inquisitory* (*L'inquisitoire*) and his 1968 *The Libera Me Domine* (*Le Libera*). All three could be thought of on one level as representations of aspects of the sexual culture of French village life (with the prominent inclusion of same-sex sexualities) in the post–World War II decades. Yet they are in fact representations of how that culture exists *in speech*. This is what allows them also to be theoretical or technical investigations of what Pinget referred to as "tone": those aspects of language that carry meaning without performing a referential function, that allow something to be accomplished by a voice in an interaction without certain kinds of explicit mention coming into play. That is, superficially, his novels continue to advance the traditional realist project of an evolving referential relation to the world, while, on another level, the novels take as their object of investigation those nonreferential aspects of language that are an important component of the medium through which various social realities, including misfit sexualities, perpetuate themselves. Indeed, reading Pinget allows us to appreciate how the nonreferential aspects of language constitute a lion's share of the medium in which the social forms of misfit sexualities exist.

"Tout ce qu'on peut dire ou *signifier* ne m'intéresse pas, mais la *façon de dire*," Pinget would write in the text that became the "Author's Note" at the end of *The Libera Me Domine*: "It is not what can be said or *meant* that interests me, but *the way in which it is said*."[59] He would also use the word "tone" to describe "manner," all those features of language that didn't have to do with the "matter" at hand. It would be a tone of voice, a manner of speaking that he needed to discover, to hear in his ears, in order to begin writing: "And once I have chosen this *way*—which is a major and painful part of the work, and which must therefore come first—it imposes both composition and subject-matter on me. And once again, I am indifferent to this subject matter." Two different aspects of Pinget's project are worth insisting on. One is the way he posits what he is attempting to do as an interesting aesthetic challenge: "Personally, what I am attempting to do is to translate into writing the tone of language. It is tone that gives language its quality." (Ce que personnellement je cherche, c'est de traduire dans l'écriture le ton de la langue. C'est le ton qui fait la qualité d'un langage.)[60] Pinget couches his endeavor in the language of an autonomous work of art. If he insists that the matter of what is being said is indifferent to him, it is because what is aesthetically essential is found in other linguistic features. A book of conversations with Madeleine Renouard that he published in 1993 begins with a section comprising an alphabetical list of terms for which he provides short definitions. Here is one:

Sex
Cannot work as the subject of a great work. Sometimes in literature if the occasion presents itself, the subject can be touched upon quickly, in a flash. Nothing more than that.[61]

(Sexe
Ne peut être le sujet essentiel d'une grande oeuvre. En littérature si l'occasion se présente on peut l'aborder rapidement, une flambée. Pas au-delà.)

Spoken, we might say, like someone laying a claim to be understood as an autonomous literary producer, not someone it would make any sense to accuse (remember Apollinaire writing about Colette) of having heteronomous (unaesthetic) kinds of interests in broadcasting things about sexuality (one's own or others). And yet the very fact that Pinget would make such a (seemingly indefensible) claim is simply evidence that he was caught up in the same field dynamics as all the other writers we've been considering. The reviewers for the *Figaro littéraire* who penned early reviews of *The Inquisitory* and of *The Libera Me Domine*, for instance, would both make a point of comparing Pinget to Jouhandeau, not for stylistic reasons, but for reasons of subject matter: sexuality and small-town life. Both reviewers refer to Jouhandeau's cycle of texts about the small town Chaminadour and the various kinds of sexual misfits and other odd people whose stories Jouhandeau tells.[62] Part of what they seem to want to imply is that you wouldn't write about this kind of subject matter if you weren't somehow personally implicated in it. (Remember the question Genet supposedly asked Sartre: "Since you aren't a homosexual, how is it that you can like my books?" It's not a question one could ever imagine Pinget wanting to ask.) Pinget would never, as far as I know, explicitly address the relationship between tone and sexuality that we will see him working out in his novels—perhaps partly because of the image he wanted to project as an autonomous literary producer. He would also (again perhaps partly because of wanting to project that image) in general be charmingly coy about his own sexuality. Being coy, we could say, is a matter of tone. It is a way of walking the edge between the explicit and the implicit. Consider two other entries from his 1993 dictionary:

Urinals
Those were the good old days. They've all been removed from the streets of Paris so no one knows where to go to piss anymore. (189)

Wee-wee
Little boys at the very least are bound to know what this is. (205)

(Urinoirs
C'était le bon temps. Ils sont tous supprimés dans les rues de Paris et on ne
sait plus où pisser.

Zizi
Tous les petits garçons en tout cas savent ce que c'est.)

Surely these entries are exercises that study the relationship between tone and
sexuality. Perhaps the entry on public urinals is also the sign (the index) of
an affiliation not only with a sexual culture but also with a literary tradition
(including Proust and Genet, for instance) in which what goes on between
men in public urinals finds representation. What goes on in a train station
men's room will come up in *The Libera Me Domine*, we might recall. And we
will see in the chapter on Pinget how the account of what goes on there is
tied into the novel's experimental study of how sexual knowledge circulates
through implication. So then, perhaps Pinget's project is about sexuality (in
language), even if he would never say so *explicitly*. A literary critic who was
one of Pinget's big advocates, Madeleine Chapsal, wrote the following in an
early review of *The Libera Me Domine*:

> It's voice for voice's sake, writing for writing's sake. It takes hold of the reader,
> who becomes its witness, and is carried away, intoxicated by speech. There may
> well be something that is being kept hidden from the reader, for this voice too
> often takes on an accusatory tone for it not to be dissimulating some kind of
> culpability, some kind of alarm.[63]

Chapsal's prose captures nicely the ambiguity of Pinget's project. Is it a voice
portrayed for its own sake at the heart of the project, or writing for its own
sake, or the aesthetic daring of trying to capture "tone" in writing? Or is it what
is "behind" the voice, perhaps not so much something secret as something
that is being spoken without being said? We could say that Pinget's writing
"about" sexuality and the things he said "about" his books that are "about"
sexuality as it exists in speech, enact the predicaments of a misfit sexuality's
pragmatic existence in language. Pinget gives perhaps no finer example of this
predicament than the remarks with which he closes the "Author's Note" to *The
Libera Me Domine*:

> It remains to be seen who speaks in the tone of *The Libera Me Domine*. This
> time I don't know. Contradictory remarks are reported by someone . . . who
> hasn't revealed his identity to me. (238)

"Someone" (the word) stands throughout the present book as a token not only
of the misfit whose utterances struggle to enact something in language for

which there are no readily available words, but also of the hope for an inter-locutor who would prove capable of understanding an evanescent message about the experience of sexuality that cannot exactly be stated in so many words, but that is nonetheless being put forth in language in the hopes of founding a community of shared understanding, however small, however awkward, however fleeting.

Metapragmatics, Sexuality, and the Novel: Reading Jean Genet's *Querelle*

Metapragmatics

The term "metapragmatics" has come up briefly in each of the preceding chapters in relation, on the one hand, to the codes or rules of use, or presuppositions that need to be negotiated or transmitted in order that misfit sexualities can continue to be enacted, however tenuously, and, on the other hand, in relation to the making of publics and counterpublics for works of literature that deal with sexuality, misfit or otherwise. It is time to develop a fuller understanding of the term. In order to do so, I begin this chapter by juxtaposing a couple passages from Charles Sanders Peirce's 1907 essay "Pragmatism" with a couple passages from Jean Genet's novel *Querelle de Brest*, first published in December 1947. Peirce's ideas about semiosis are one of the key origin points for thinkers who work on, to quote Michael Silverstein, "language-in-use . . . as the cultural medium par excellence."[1] Focusing on language-in-use might be taken to be a nonhermeneutical interpretive move, one that furthers an interest in *public* meaning rather than in some kind of meaning that could be imagined to reside "within" an aesthetic artifact. Pragmatics is about use and contexts of use of language, and metapragmatics is about pragmatics.

Metapragmatic statements are a subspecies of metalinguistic statements, famously characterized by Roman Jakobson as one of the six functions of language, the one we invoke "whenever the addresser or the addressee needs to check up whether they use the same code."[2] As Jakobson notes, "Any process of language learning, in particular child acquisition of the mother tongue, makes wide use of . . . metalingual operations" (76). It's possible to make a distinction, among the different kinds of metalinguistic queries, between metasemantic ones and metapragmatic ones. Inquiring about the meaning of a word, or about a particular speaker's meaning, is usually initially metasemantic, although this quickly gets complicated. Consider, in this regard the two queries, "what does homosexual mean?" and "what do you mean by homosexual?" The latter query has already taken on more of a metapragmatic cast. Moving further into the metapragmatic realm might be a query such as "what's the difference between homosexual and faggot?" although again it's complicated. A reader of Genet's *Our Lady of the Flowers* (*Notre-Dame-des-Fleurs*) might want to ask a question that is both metapragmatic and metasemantic about a sentence like this one: "And all of them, the girl-queens and boy-queens, the aunties, fags, and nellies of whom I am speaking, are assembled at the foot of the stairway" (Toutes, les tantes-filles et tantes-gars, tapettes, pédales, tantou-zes, dont je vous parle, sont réunies au bas de l'escalier).[3] Are there semantic or pragmatic differences, someone might want to ask (and what kind of metalinguistic question would that be?) between all those designations? And what are the rules of use in play that cause them to take the feminine gender (toutes . . . réunies) in French? In general, citing Silverstein again, we could characterize pragmatics as "including the notion of how systematic variations in 'saying the same thing' in discourse constitute *social identity markers* of participants in the communicative act."[4] And we could think about metapragmatics as having to do with large cultural functions, genres, perhaps, that we invoke in order to carry out our pragmatic endeavors.

Now, naming people is a pragmatic endeavor, and the passage from Peirce that I want to look at first has to do with proper names. Proper names, Jakobson, reminded us in his essay "Shifters and Verbal Categories," "take a particular place in our linguistic code: the general meaning of a proper name cannot be defined without a reference to the code."[5] That is to say, if we take the statement "Jean Genet wrote a novel called *Querelle de Brest*," it's not exactly sensible to pose the metasemantic question, "What's a Jean Genet?" As Jakobson has it, "the name means anyone to whom this name is assigned" (387). Or as Silverstein puts it: "such lexical items as so-called kinship terms or personal names in any society can hardly be characterized by a 'semantic' analysis. It is the pragmatic component that makes them lexical items to begin with."[6] The passage from Peirce that I want to consider first has precisely to do with the pragmatic component of proper names:

> Suppose I chance to overhear one man at a club say to another "Ralph Pepperill has bought that mare Pee Dee Kew." Never having heard before either of Ralph Pepperill or of Pee Dee Kew, it means to me only that some man has bought some famous trotter; and since I knew already that some men do make such purchases, it does not interest me. But the next day I hear somebody inquire where he can find a copy of Steven's edition of Plato; to which reply is made that Ralph Pepperill says he has a copy. Now although I never was knowingly acquainted with any purchaser of crack trottinghorses, yet I should not have

supposed that such a person would be aware of possessing an old edition of Plato whose chief value is due to the circumstance that modern citations from the Dialogues usually refer to it. After this, I begin to pay attention to what I hear of Ralph Pepperill; until, at length, that which the name means to me probably represents pretty fairly what it would mean to an acquaintance of the man. This imparts, not merely an interest, but also a *meaning* to every little scrap of new information about him;—scraps that would have conveyed no information whatsoever, had they first introduced his name to my ears. Yet the name itself will remain a designation devoid of essential signification, and so much of the accidental kind as it may at any time have acquired will not have been derived, in however slight measure, from the utterer of any sentence which it may furnish with informatory interest;—at least, not from him in his capacity as utterer of that sentence.[7]

Peirce offers this example as part of an effort to understand how a verbal sign (either a message or part of a message, an utterance or a component of an utterance) exists between the utterer and the person who hears it. For Peirce, Ralph Pepperill is a sign with an object—"that by which the sign is essentially determined in its significant characters in the mind of the utterer" (409). The person who hears the utterance has to construct some version of the object in order to make sense of the utterance, but as Peirce notes, to do so requires knowledge that "must come from some previous or collateral source" (404). To construct the object of the sign is to cause to be produced what Peirce famously calls an "interpretant." It's a notoriously difficult notion. Here's how William Hanks describes it:

> An interpretant might be a simple sign, or it might be an entire elaborate discourse. That is, it might be greater than a single sign ... an interpretant may be derived from the original sign plus other knowledge or experience that the addressee has at her disposal. . . . More than a mere sign, the interpretant is like an ideological horizon, a background of evaluative "glosses" that actors in a social group apply to any sign.[8]

Consider any of the "getting to know you" exercises that form a part of certain cultural repertoires. They mostly consist in helping create associations between proper names and cultural schemas, so that we know something about the kind of person to whom a name is attached. Associations call upon previous experience within a culture. Peirce notes in a related vein that "in all cases [the interpretant] includes feelings; for there must, at least, be a sense of comprehending the meaning of the sign" (409). In the case of our budding acquaintance with Ralph Pepperill, that "feeling" goes by the name of interest. At first there is none. We aren't interested in playboys who buy racehorses, but then when we discover that a racehorse-buying playboy also collects scholarly editions of Plato, our curiosity is piqued. Somehow now we have something to make sense of, a social identity to register and contemplate. Still the "meaning" will not be *in* the name, it will be in the indexical relationships between that name and any number of bits of cultural information that we collect. The ability to form interpretants adequate to a given interaction is a form of cultural literacy, we might say; the patterns of interest we reveal in forming interpretants (disdaining an interest in Pee Dee Kew, but perking up one's ears upon hearing of someone who knows the value of Steven's edition of Plato) also reveal the way in which we form and communicate our own cultural identities often quite implicitly via the indexical or pragmatic aspects of communication. Not being interested in someone or something is productive of identity.

What we have in this example from Peirce is one instance of how, citing Silverstein again, "discursive interaction brings sociocultural concepts into here-and-now contexts of use—that is . . . interaction indexically 'invokes' sociocultural conceptualizations."[9] Further, it invokes "the *nonuniformity* of knowledge within a community."[10] I am not part of the group of people up-to-date on thoroughbreds in the vicinity, nor do I care to be, but as for editions of Plato . . . I am intrigued by the existence of someone both interested in racehorses and old editions of Plato, even if that might suggest Pepperill's interest in editions of Plato is the economic or bibliophilic interest of a collector rather than that of an intellectual. I want to know more; I am curious about the way different cultural streams might intersect in a given person, curious about how a new manifestation of some feature of the social order through which I move might be about to become apprehensible in a way that reveals something unexpected about that very order.

Part of the reason for the juxtaposition of Genet and Peirce that is about to take place is that I wish to call attention to a certain amount of theoretical work going on not just in *Querelle*, but in all of Genet's novels, on the topic of indexicality (the way both individual statements within interactions and the interactions themselves point to, invoke, valorize, challenge, or rework specific cultural frameworks of intelligibility). The interest in indexicality found in a novel like *Querelle* bears specifically on its relation to the production of oneself as a social subject (for I take it that that's also what the Peirce passage was about) and, more specifically in the case of Genet's novel, as a sexual subject.

The passage from *Querelle* that I want to consider occurs on board the ship *le Vengeur*, docked in Brest, a port in Brittany, and involves the Lieutenant Seblon and his orderly, Querelle. Seblon, identified by the novel as a pederast, finds Querelle a source of endless erotic fascination. Querelle, who flirts with Seblon in his own ambiguous way, will be having sex with a number of other men in the novel, without any precise label being fixed upon him. The novel repeatedly puts on display a category of men who have come in the past thirty years or so to be called MSMs, "men who have sex with men"—a category developed in HIV prevention work in order to identify those men who have sex with other men without inhabiting any identity category that might be associated with those acts. At one point, in discussing the policeman named Mario (one of the men Querelle has sex with), the novel notes: "Indeed, nei-ther Mario, nor any of the other heroes of this book (with the exception of the lieutenant Seblon, but Seblon is not *in* the book) is a pederast; and for Mario those people were of two kinds—those who want to get fucked and pay for it and are called fairies, and the others" (En effet, Mario, ni aucun des héros de ce livre [sauf le lieutenant Seblon, mais Seblon n'est pas *dans* le livre] n'est pédéraste, et, pour lui, il y a: ceux qui se font mettre et qui payent et sont des tantes, et les autres).[11] There's plenty that could be said about that particular sentence, but for now it will serve merely to point up the novel's interest in the invocation of identity categories, and the conditions of their applicability, in the idea that there might be competing and incompatible sets of identity categories extant in a single society. These kinds of interest, central to the novel as a whole, are also at the heart of the passage I'm moving toward here.

Querelle is, among other things, a drug smuggler who has only the pre-vious evening snuck some opium past customs with the help of another sailor whom he then casually murdered. Immediately following the murder, he vis-ited one of Brest's brothels, "La Feria," at which he engaged in homosex with Nono, the fellow who runs the place. The French language has a particular slang term for certain men who have sex with men for which there is no easy equivalent in English, *enculé*. I've altered the published translation here slightly, inserting in the place of *enculé* a neologism that captures a bit of its semantic content, if not its pragmatic force: buttfuckee. The other crucial word in this passage, *pédé*, a shortened form of *pédéraste*, is translated with reasonable accuracy, at least in North America, as "faggot."

> The Lieutenant, standing in front of Querelle, whom he desired but did not dare approach, made an almost imperceptible gesture, nervous, quickly with-drawn. Querelle noted all the waves of uneasiness passing across the eyes firmly fixed on his without letting one of them escape him—and (as if such a weight had, by squashing Querelle, caused his smile to broaden more and more) he kept on smiling under the gaze and the physical mass of the Lieu-tenant, both bearing down on him so heavily that he had to tense his muscles against them. He understood nonetheless the gravity of that stare, which at that moment expressed total human despair. But at the same time, in his mind, he was shrugging his shoulders and thinking:

"Faggot!"

He despised the officer. He kept on smiling, allowing himself to be lulled by the monstrous and ill-defined notion of "faggot" sweeping back and forth inside his head.

"Faggot, what's a faggot? Is it a buttfuckee?" he wondered. And gradually, his lips narrowing slightly, the corners of his mouth prepared to form themselves into a disdainful smirk. But then the thought of this sentence dissolved the smirk into a vague feeling of torpor: "I'm a buttfuckee, too." He couldn't quite grasp this thought clearly, though he did not find it repulsive, but he experienced the sadness it carried when he realized he was pulling his buttocks in so tight (or so it seemed to him) that they no longer touched the seat of his trousers. And this fleeting, yet quite depressing thought generated, up his spine, an immediate and rapid series of vibrations which quickly spread out over the entire surface of his black shoulders and covered them with a shawl woven out of shivers. (87–88)

(Le lieutenant, debout en face de Querelle qu'il désirait et n'osait approcher, avec la main fit un geste presque imperceptible, nerveux, vite rentré. Querelle enregistrait, sans en laisser échapper une, toutes les ondes d'inquiétude des yeux fixés sur les siens, et, comme si un tel poids eût, en écrasant Querelle, de plus en plus élargi son sourire, il souriait sous le regard et la masse du lieutenant appesanti sur lui au point qu'il se raidissait pour les supporter. Il comprenait, cependant, la gravité de ce regard et que tout le désespoir d'un homme, en cet instant, s'y trouvait exprimé. Mais en même temps qu'il faisait dans le vide un large mouvement d'épaules, il pensa:

"Pédé!"

Il méprisa l'officier. Il souriait encore et se laissait bercer par le mouvement dans sa tête de l'idée énorme et mal équilibrée de "pédé."

"Pédé, qu'est-ce que c'est? Pédé? C'est un enculé?" pensait-il. Et doucement, pendant que sa bouche se refermait un peu, la commissure des lèvres s'organisait pour un pli méprisant. Cette phrase pensée le diluait en une vague torpeur: "Moi aussi, j'suis un enculé." Pensée qu'il distinguait très mal, qui ne le révoltait pas, mais dont il éprouva la tristesse quand il s'aperçut qu'il serrait les fesses au point—lui paraît-il—qu'elles ne touchaient plus la toile du pantalon. Cette très légère, mais très désolante pensée déclencha dans son échine une immédiate et rapide succession d'ondes qui s'étalèrent sur toute la surface de ses épaules noires et les couvrirent d'un fichu tissé de frissons. [319])

This is a literary text doing theoretical work in its own way, and a certain amount of commentary is required to make its theoretical focus more apparent. The passage describes an interaction in which both men understand that more is going on than can be said. The lieutenant's rapidly controlled gesture and intent gaze are the signs of his obsession with Querelle. Querelle's smile and his entire bodily stance indicate the seductive performance in which he constantly engages when in Seblon's presence. Their interaction is structured by the identities they perform: an adoring, somewhat closeted older man and a sensual, handsome, and putatively straight rough youth. "Pédé" is precisely what someone like Querelle is supposed to call someone like Seblon. But suddenly the invocation of that word produces an effect—mental and corporeal—different than the one in the script Querelle had thought he was enacting. The passage insists, as do a number of passages in the novel, on Querelle's verbal inarticulateness. It is not that Querelle isn't linguistically talented, or that he's not very bright. The problem here is that what is at stake is happening on a linguistic and cultural level that it is particularly difficult to be aware of. Querelle poses to himself a series of metalinguistic questions, which we could interpret as follows: Are the words *pédé* and *enculé* equivalent? Can you be one but not the other? Can the work they do to assign someone to a position of social vulnerability be separated from the work they do in describing something a person is or does? If Querelle is a semantic *enculé*, how does that affect his relation to Seblon's pragmatic condition as a *pédé*? Do they both now share something, and is that sharing somehow enacted by the shivers that Querelle's body imposes upon him? And what would happen if Seblon "knew" that Querelle was an *enculé*? That is maybe a badly posed question, for it is not entirely clear if, in fact, he could pragmatically ever be that for Seblon.

In short, what may have seemed initially like a question of semantics ("Pédé, qu'est-ce que c'est?") turns out to be something else. This is not a scene of what a linguistic anthropologist might refer to as "the pragmatic constitution of social categories through speech,"[12] although that's what it might have been had Querelle been able to successfully call Seblon a *pédé*—even if only to himself. It's a failed pragmatic event, in a certain way, the failure being caused by the agency of the sentence, "Moi aussi, j'suis un enculé," which stops a scornful smile in its tracks, and turns the scene into a strange metapragmatic event, where Querelle, instead of successfully constituting a social position for himself in relation to Seblon, has to reflect upon the use of pragmatic aspects of speech in the constitution of social positions.[13] It's also an interesting moment in which Querelle admits to himself that he doesn't exactly know how sexuality works, either personally or culturally.[14] Suddenly he has a sense of lacking the authority to successfully deploy a set of socially legible sexual categories that would include his own biography.[15]

Sexuality

When it comes to sexuality (and it is obviously not the only social arena that is like this), people often carry themselves through tricky encounters with reasonable amounts of practical intelligence, but without being able to talk in any coherent way about what they do. Such certainly seems to be the case with the sailors who come to Brest and to the brothel that is at the heart of *Querelle*.

> For the ships' crews, Brest will be the city of La Féria. Far from France, sailors never talk about this brothel without cracking a joke or laughing a bit too hard . . . and they evoke the proprietor and the proprietress with the help of expressions like these:
> —Let's roll the dice for it. Like at Nono's!
> —That guy, for a piece of ass he'd even go so far as to play with Nono!
> —That one over there, he'd go to La Féria to lose.
> While the Madam's name is never mentioned, the names of "La Féria" and "Nono" must have traveled all around the world, murmured by the lips of sailors or tossed out in a mocking retort. On board there never is anybody who actually knows what La Féria is, nor does anyone know precisely what the rules of the game are for which it has such a reputation. But no one, not even the greenest recruit, dare ask for an explanation; every sailor would have it be known that he knows what's up. Thus the establishment in Brest appears ever in a fabulous light, and the sailors, as they approach that port, secretly dream of that house of ill repute of which they'll only speak in a joking way. Georges Querelle, the hero of this book, speaks of it less than anyone. He knows that his own brother is the Madam's lover. (English, 5–6; French, 239–40)

What does it mean to think of sexuality as a game everyone plays but with rules no one knows? Let's limit ourselves for the moment to the verbal aspects of sexuality, to sexuality considered as an exchange of utterances, verbal signs.

Michel Foucault suggested in *The Archaeology of Knowledge* that sexuality could be thought of as a set of possible things that could be said about a set of objects that was itself constructed by the utterances that would reference them:

> Instead of studying the sexual behavior of men at a given period . . . instead of describing what men thought of sexuality . . . one would ask oneself whether, in this behaviour, as in these representations, a whole discursive practice is not at work; whether sexuality . . . is not a group of objects that can be talked about . . . a field of possible enunciations . . . a group of concepts . . . a set of choices.[16]

In *The Archaeology of Knowledge*, Foucault maps out an archival practice and a practice of reading in which individual texts are studied as part and parcel of larger discursive masses; the boundaries of individual works, in this kind of study, can be seen as somewhat arbitrary delimitations within a larger discursive field. The intent of the study is to investigate the establishment of discursive regularities, or of slow shifts within the overarching regularities of a given discursive formation. Matters related to the internal workings of a particular text are likely to be somewhat left in the background in this kind of work. For Foucault, an archaeology of sexuality of this sort "would reveal, not of course as the ultimate truth of sexuality, but as one of the dimensions in accordance with which one can describe it, a certain 'way of speaking'" (193). This practice—assembling a mass of data (a huge set of utterances) and then analyzing it to establish certain regularities that transcend any particular utterance—is modeled to a certain extent on a Saussure-inspired linguistics, which involves a particular way of distinguishing between what Saussure famously called *langue* and *parole*. Let's recall a few aspects of this distinction. (I've been developing the case for an understanding of a kind of practical knowledge that people use to enact their sexualities, but cannot always house in language, so obviously Foucault's focus in *Archaeology* on utterances and "ways of speaking" will need to be developed and qualified to take account of that practical understanding. The links between Genet and Foucault and Saussure, *langue* and *parole* that I wish to draw out will, I hope, become clear quite shortly.)

Saussure wrote of a particular faculty characteristic of human beings, the faculty for articulated speech. It is given, he said, "first by our organs and then by the play that we can obtain from them." He notes, however, that "it is only a faculty, and it would be materially impossible to exercise it without another thing which is given to the individual from outside, *la langue*." "*La langue*," Saussure says, "is the social product whose *existence* allows the individual to exercise the faculty of language."[17] From time to time, Saussure would make an interesting and problematic comparison of *la langue* to a musical work. "A musical work," he wrote on one occasion, "exists only by means of the sum total of performances that are made of it. Yet any performance is indifferent to the work. A symphony is a reality that exists even without being executed. Just so can the execution by means of *parole* of that which is given in the *langue* be taken to be inessential." At another point, he says, "the individual performance is what resides in the individual faculty, that is what is allotted to the individual. But this is comparable to the performance of a musical masterwork by an instrument; there are many who can execute it but the piece itself is perfectly independent of these diverse executions."[18]

Pierre Bourdieu offered a well-known critique of Foucault's way of thinking about the relationship between an utterance and the discourse to which it belongs, observing that Foucault's fidelity "to the Saussurean tradition" meant that "he refuses to look outside 'the field of discourse' for the explanatory principle of each of the discourses in the field." For Bourdieu, "it is not possible to treat cultural order . . . as an autonomous and transcendent system."[19] That is, for Bourdieu, the "individual performance" references more than just the *langue* as it produces meaning. It also references different structures of the social order, or different contentions within the social order, different features of the sociohistorical situation in which it takes place. This tension between, on the one hand, the structure of *langue* or discourse and, on the other, the articulation of the discursive realm with the realms of practices and of social and political relations, a tension Bourdieu and Foucault both spent a great deal of time thinking about, is also part of what is at stake in Genet's writing about sexuality.

Sociological and discursive accounts of sexuality, loosely speaking, those that locate the structure of sexual experience outside of the individual and in both the sociocultural realm and the realm of discourse often seem highly counterintuitive in everyday contexts. The scene we have just looked at in *Querelle* reveals someone suddenly caught short by the fact that he has received an inkling that his sense of himself exists in relation to cultural patterns of regularity and that relation urgently requires some recalibration. Otherwise his speech risks becoming nonsense and his actions risk unintelligibility.

In his 2004 article "'Cultural' Concepts and the Language-Culture Nexus," Silverstein asks a resonant set of questions that situates itself slightly differently in relation to the *langue/parole* distinction and that perhaps can thereby advance our understanding of the kind of analysis of sexuality that seems to interest Genet. Silverstein asks:

> Is there . . . a sociocultural unconscious in the mind—wherever that is located in respect of the biological organism—that is both immanent in and emergent from our use of language? Can we ever profoundly study the social significance of language without understanding this sociocultural unconscious that it seems to reveal? And if it is correct that language is the principal exemplar, medium, and site of the cultural, then can we ever understand the cultural without understanding this particular conceptual dimension of language?[20]

At a certain point in the article from which this citation is drawn, Silverstein is particularly interested in a conceptual dimension of language that is, as he puts it, beyond lexicalization. This would be a conceptual dimension that structures individual perceptions and actions, but that an individual could not articulate, could not refer to. It exists in language only pragmatically, and resists (it is a semiotic resistance, not a psychoanalytic one) being brought into the referential realm. (I have already used this notion of concepts that are beyond lexicalization in the first chapter to think about the ways in which Colette situates different social forms of sexuality in relation to historical time.)

> The way we denote what we consider "real-world" things by lexical expressions reveals at least one kind of knowledge, for example, that certain plants and animals are members of a category and that members of that category have certain properties. . . . To investigate a culture's concepts, in this approach, one tries to extract or induce the semantic consistencies in such lexical usage. . . . If one can, one tries to give the intensional principles of conceptual classification that lie behind such [a] structure. . . . the lexical labels of the systematizable culture. Unfortunately, cultural concepts of the kind we are focusing on here just do not work in this fashion; they are indexically invoked in and by the use of certain language forms in context, but the concepts will never be systematizable. (634)[21]

We have already seen some reference to this kind of non-lexically-systematizable way of understanding certain aspects of the social world in the description of the way Mario (even as he himself engages in homosex) has practical ways of dividing people into categories that are partly sexual, partly economic: "Indeed, neither Mario, nor any of the other heroes of this book (with the exception of the lieutenant Seblon, but Seblon is not *in* the book) is a pederast; and for Mario those people were of two kinds—those who want to get fucked and pay for it and are called fairies, and the others" (79). Not just Mario, but the narrator (or the novel) also in this same passage engages in practical acts of categorization that it cannot explain systematically.[22]

These nonlexical concepts, the kind that enable the gestures of categorization in which sexuality seems closely wound up, Silverstein tells us, "turn out to be . . . revealed in cultural practices. . . . They are empirically investigable once we abandon the idea that they are analogues . . . to lexically coded concepts." They constitute a kind of "presumptively shared knowledge," and people "indexically access it and experientially renew it each time words and expressions are used in the emerging 'poetic' structure of denotational and interactional textuality."[23] Think of what we mean when we sometimes ask the question, "You know what I mean?" We are often checking in about a level of meaning that is not being spoken, checking in to make sure that shared presuppositions are in fact shared. But the kind of presupposition in question here is perhaps presupposed in such a deep way that we couldn't even articulate it as a presupposition.[24]

Sometimes we act or interact knowingly, according, perhaps, to what Erving Goffman called interaction entities, but that knowledge is purely practical, and wouldn't necessarily involve being able to be articulate about what we are doing, or imagining that our actions relate to something that might be called an identity. In his classic essay "Where the Action Is," Goffman takes an interest in forms of doing (like the sex Querelle engages in) that are sharply distinctive. As he puts it, "By the term *action* I mean activities that are consequential, problematic, and undertaken for what is felt to be their own sake."[25] Ordinarily, Goffman points out, our interactions avoid sharply distinctive actions; that is to say, we are more commonly disposed toward interactions that are well carried out and are *not* fateful or consequential (Goffman's terms) or distinctive in the sense of producing some kind of social friction.

> The ceremonial order sustained by persons when in one another's presence does more than assure that each participant gives and gets his due. Through the exercise of proper demeanor, the individual gives credit and substance to interaction entities themselves, such as conversations, gatherings, and social occasions, and renders himself accessible and usable for communication. Certain kinds of misconduct, such as loss of self-control, gravely disrupt the actor's usability in face to face interaction and can disrupt the interaction itself. The concern the other participants have for the social occasion, and the ends they anticipate will be served through it, together ensure that some weight will be given to the propriety of the actor's behavior.[26]

Our interactions are not only forms of exchange; they also serve to reference and confirm "interaction entities" (genres for interaction, we might say, forms that exist socially and exert a structuring influence on interaction). In practice, we negotiate, confirm, reject, or innovate with respect to these entities in every interaction we undertake. Querelle's way of conducting himself in sexual interactions seems, whether intentionally or not, to involve him in fateful and consequential interactions in which, in theory, his "usability" for future interactions should be severely compromised.

Laud Humphreys made interesting use of Goffman's thinking about where the action is (and *what* action is: "action is to be found wherever the individual knowingly takes consequential chances perceived as avoidable"[27]) in writing his book *Tearoom Trade: Impersonal Sex in Public Places*. At a certain point in his research, he informs us, he chose to abandon trying to analyze the psychological motivations of the participants in the interactions he was observing, and instead decided to work to understand how the participants gave themselves over to interactions that were somehow prestructured forms of consequential action. Tearooms revealed for Humphreys "ritual means of achieving collective action," and revealed a set of roles specific to the ritualized behavior in question. "A role unfolds," Humphreys noted, "becoming evident only as the action approaches showdown . . . Even the actor may not know his role until the action is finished." He concludes:

> If we may view role performance as shaped by the end of the action and identifiable only in terms of the payoff, it may help us to understand the difficulties sex researchers have with applying traditional, psychologically oriented analyses of gender identity to actual patterns of homosexual performance.[28]

Humphreys's use of Goffman's framework is a helpful challenge to the prevailing tendency in much critical discourse to locate sexuality too exclusively in the psychological realm, to think of it in terms of identities and taxonomies, and to neglect the extent to which it is lived and experienced as a set of evolving cultural forms into which, within which, and through which agents move. Through the figure of Querelle, Genet seems to be offering a similar understanding of the experience of sexuality.

Interaction entities are indexed, we could say, evoked, by gesture and by language-in-use. We call upon them, but usually don't think about naming them. Perhaps they don't leave much of an explicit trace within the written record, except to the extent that we can attempt to reconstruct the way some exchange of language, some moment of language-in-use, some act of *parole* implicitly points to their existence. Silverstein insists that this is why it is *parole*, and not *langue*, that counts if you want to see culture in action: "it is language-in-use—a socioculturally inflected *parole*—that makes of language a substantive part and parcel of culture, as well as a more fruitful exemplar of the cultural and a guide into it."[29] Perhaps, though, when it comes to dealing with literary artifacts, it might be prudent not to jettison the concept and the implications of *langue* quite so quickly. *Langue* and *parole* might both be relevant foci for different moments within a single analytic enterprise.

For instance, it does not seem to me correct, in the final analysis, to associate the Foucauldian archaeology of discourse exclusively with *langue*. For Silverstein, "cultural knowledge *lives and dies in textual occasions*. We create it on occasions of use of particular words and expressions in particular cotextual arrays one with respect to another, as much as, on subsequent occasions of use of them, we try to presume upon the knowledge previously experienced and, perhaps finding our presumption being questioned, have to create it again or modify it for some new interlocutor."[30] How long is a "textual occasion," and where does cultural knowledge go outside of those occasions? Advocates of *parole* could be said to have a preference for seeing cultural knowledge as revealed only in short-term interactive textual occasions. Foucault, the archaeologist of textual artifacts, could perhaps be said to be interested in a materialized form of such knowledge (mostly printed text on paper). Silverstein is, as he says, mainly interested in "here-and-now contexts of use," in the indexical invocation of sociocultural conceptualizations in specific, punctual discursive interactions.[31] When it comes to textual artifacts, what draws Silverstein's interest is "not the denotational text directly or simply, but rather indications of more originary interactional text(s) of inscription. We seek the residue of past social interaction carried along with the sign vehicle encoding the semantic, or denotational, meaning in denotational text."[32]

Foucault was not interested in the "denotational text directly or simply," either, as it turns out. I think that what Foucault imagined himself doing was, in fact, creating an image of past arrays of cultural knowledge that enabled— that formed the background for—given acts of meaning production. One might even choose to say that *The Archaeology of Knowledge* is, at least in part, a book about discovering the indexical relations that tie together different cultural or discursive formations over a longer span of time:

> We must grasp the utterance in the exact specificity of its occurrence; determine its conditions of existence, fix at least its limits, establish its correlations with other statements that may be connected with it, and show what other forms of statement it excludes. . . . An utterance is always an event that neither the language (*langue*) nor the meaning can quite exhaust. . . . Like every event, it is unique, yet subject to repetition, transformation, and reactivation . . . it is linked not only to the situations that provoke it, and to the consequences that it gives rise to, but at the same time, and in accordance with a quite different modality, to the statements that precede and follow it.[33]

Genet's *Querelle* is interesting to me as a textual artifact partly because I think it's a good example (along with Genet's other novels) of how long it can take for a textual artifact like this one to be understood in relation to all the cultural variables and schemas it invokes. It has to accumulate an interpretative tradition. Its public meaning is still evolving, we could say, still revealing itself. I am, of course, also interested in *Querelle* because it seems to be a theoretical inquiry into the way certain specific utterances about sexuality take on meaning within a given situation. And then, of course, it is itself a masterfully crafted utterance of this kind—one to which we (you and I) are still in some way responding.

Consider the scene of the throw of the dice toward the beginning of the novel. The rule of the house, confusing to so many sailors, is not that hard to reconstruct. It is as follows: should you want to have sex with Madame Lysiane, you have to have sex with Nono first, but whether Nono fucks you or you fuck Nono is determined by a game of dice. (The novel doesn't seem to consider the possibility of a woman coming to the brothel looking to have sex with Madame Lysiane.) Sometimes guys, as one might expect, say they want to have sex with Madame Lysiane in order to be able to have sex with Nono. Genet lays out for us a structured system of sexual interactions, in which a kind of accident determines the roles into which you will fall regardless of how you imagine yourself motivated by "your" desire. The novel presents a clear sense that there is a mimetic imbrication between individual actions, and even individual motivations, and the structured system. Bourdieu's description of this kind of imbrication is a classic one:

> All the schemes of perception and appreciation in which a group deposits its fundamental structures, and the schemes of expression through which it provides them with the beginnings of objectification and therefore of reinforcement, intervene between the individual and his/her body. Application of the fundamental schemes to one's own body, and more especially to those parts of the body that are most pertinent in terms of these schemes, is doubtless one of the privileged occasions for the incorporation of the schemes, because of the heavy investments placed in the body.[34]

For Bourdieu, these schemes of perception, which are part of what produce regularity and intelligibility within a culture, are, of course, not acquired consciously. "The process of acquisition . . . [which] has nothing in common with an *imitation* that would presuppose a conscious effort to reproduce a gesture, an utterance or an object explicitly constituted as a model—and the process of reproduction . . . tend to take place below the level of consciousness, expression and the reflexive distance which these presuppose."[35]

Querelle could be taken to be a theorization by Genet of the process of acquiring those structures that ground sexual interaction and sexual expression; it could be taken to be an ethnography of the interaction entities that occasionally make coherent sexual interaction possible in a multicultural environment (and, of course, occasionally fail to do so as well). The novel also studies individual attempts to be expressive within those entities, as well as the accidents attendant on witting or unwitting improvisation within a ritually defined interaction entity. In the process, it almost necessarily depicts the various forms of semiotic friction that given acts of expression or improvisation can produce within the system. Does Querelle (or anyone else in the novel) know when he breaks the rules, improvises in unexpected ways, fails to conform to standard patterns? Querelle, as macho looking a fellow as one could like, asks to sleep with Madame Lysiane and then cheats at the game of dice in order to make sure that he will be the one getting fucked by Nono. The cultural expectation is understood to be that someone like Querelle should cheat toward a different end.

This wasn't the first time a well-built lad had asked for the Madam in order to sleep with the brothelkeeper. One thing intrigued him: which one would get to bugger the other. . . . He pulled out a die from his waistcoat pocket. . . . Norbert bent down and threw the die on the floor. He rolled a five. Querelle took the die. He felt certain of his skill. Nono's well-trained eye noticed that Querelle was going to cheat, but before he could intervene the number "two" was sung out by the sailor, almost triumphantly. For a moment Norbert remained un-decided. Was he dealing with some kind of joker [blagueur]? At first he had thought that Querelle wanted to get it on with his own brother's mistress. This fraudulent trick had proved that was not so. Nor did the guy look like a fag [pédé]. Perturbed all the same by the care this prey took in assuring its own perdition, he shrugged lightly as he rose to his feet and snickered. Querelle, too, stood up. . . . Into what would he be transformed? A buttfuckee [enculé]. The thought terrified him. What makes up a buttfuckee? From what stuff is it put together? From what angle do you have to look at one to know what it is? (English, 69–70; French, 301)

From what we understand to be the rules of the game (but where does that easy understanding come from if the rules are never explicitly given?), Querelle would seem to be headed for his downfall, his social destruction, loss of honor, loss of prestige, and so on. This would seem to follow from the way he has taken part in the game as it is set before us. Yet, even as he gives way to the rules of the game, somehow Querelle seems also to change the game itself. He challenges the forms of legibility it provides. The novel will end (at least in the most complete French version; the English translation, having been made from a less complete edition, ends somewhat differently) with a postcoital Querelle kissing Madame Lysiane on either cheek as he leaves her bedroom to head back to sea. The game of dice has thus played itself out to an expected end. And yet Querelle's pathway through the social forms of sexuality that surround him is not exactly an expected one: he cheats to make sure he gets fucked by Nono, and assumes the consequences of that action over the long term (consequences having to do with character, honor, masculinity—a few of the currencies of sexual exchange, as well as consequences for his imagi-nation of his own body), while still finding his way to Madame Lysiane's bed. The novel uses Querelle to confront the regularized patterns of distinction that form a normative scheme of sexual perception with a series of unpredict-able actions. Querelle's actions instantiate semiotic unpredictability. "He had appeared among them with the suddenness and elegance of the joker in the pack. He scrambled the patterns, yet gave them meaning" (269), comments the narrator toward the end of the novel. (Il était apparu au milieu d'eux avec la soudaine promptitude et l'élégance du joker. Il brouillait les figures mais leur donnait un sens [515].)[36] His unexpected moves produce new meanings out of the arrangement of the same traditional game pieces. Genet's interest in *Querelle* seems to be both in the highly structured, predictable set of sexual forms through which people usually move and in the phenomenon of an agent (a joker, a special case of a misfit) who moves through those forms in unpredictable ways, throwing standard schemes of perception out of kilter. Consider, in that light, this remarkable conversation between Querelle and Nono well into the novel, evidence of a lasting sexual relationship between the two of them:

Once they'd buttoned up their trousers, they looked at each other, smiling.
—Wow, what a bunch of dicks we are, aren't we?
—What do you mean, dicks? We aren't hurting anyone.
—But do you like it, giving it to me in the ass?
—Me, sure, why not? It's not bad. I can't say as I've got a crush on you; that'd be a lie. A crush on a guy, never understood that. It happens, of course. I've seen it. But it's not going to happen for me.
—Same here. I get buggered because I don't give a damn, it's fun, but don't ask me to fall for a guy.
—But have you ever tried fucking a young guy?
—Never, no interest.
—A cute little fellow with smooth skin, you wouldn't go for it?
Querelle, lifting his head which had been tipped forward to tighten his belt buckle, shook it left and right, and made a face.
—So what you are into is just taking it up the butt.
—Whatever. Who gives a fuck? I tell you, it's just about having a good time. [My translation; this passage is not included in the published English translation.]

(Quand ils s'étaient boutonnés, ils se regardaient en souriant.
—Tu parles! On est bien des cons, tu crois pas?
—Pourquoi, des cons? On fait de mal à personne.
—Mais ça te plaît, à toi, de me le mettre au cul?
—Moi, ben alors, pourquoi pas? C'est pas mauvais. Je peux pas dire que j'ai le béguin pour toi, ça je mentirais. Le béguin pour un homme, j'ai jamais compris. Ça existe, remarque. J'ai vu des cas. Seulement moi je pourrais pas.
—C'est comme moi. Je me laisse endaufer pasque je m'en fous, moi je trouve ça marrant, mais faudrait pas me demander d'avoir le béguin pour un type.
—Et baiser un jeune, t'as jamais essayé?
—Jamais. Ça m'intéresse pas.
—Un petit mignon, avec la peau douce; ça te dirait rien?
Querelle, la tête baissée pour serrer la boucle de la ceinture, la relevait en la secouant de droite à gauche et en faisant la moue.

—En somme ce qui te plaît, c'est de te faire encaldosser?

—Ben après. Tu parles ce que j'en ai à foutre. Je te dis c'est plutôt histoire de se marrer. [449–50])

We see here a certain particular speech genre being invoked, a genre that might be labeled the "post-coïtal moment of intimacy."[37] Both Nono and Querelle seem well versed in the genre. It is a part of their linguistic habitus, we could say. In this genre, nosy questions about sexual proclivities are allowed, and answers to them are provided. Nono and Querelle collaborate well on a standard performance of the genre. They both make an effort to construct what Silverstein would call "conversationally usable biographies" using "emblems of identity" sufficiently widespread in a culture that their interlocutor will accept them.[38] Querelle will seem to include and exclude certain specific sexual acts from his repertory, seem to exclude sentiment from his sexual exchanges (at least here), and yet insist that his sexual choices are not indexed to his desire ("ce qui te plaît," as Nono says), but to something more ambiguous ("histoire de se marrer," a question of having a good time—but in what way?). We see in general in *Querelle* a theoretical interest in the efforts of any number of individuals not simply to assimilate the system for successfully invoking an identity, but to improvise with the elements system and produce a possible identity construct that is, to some degree, potentially unintelligible because of its improvisatory character, perhaps an emergent social form, perhaps not. And perhaps Genet's use of the genre of the novel needs to be understood as a parallel kind of improvisation on another level, working to produce effects whose legibility is similarly difficult to establish.[39]

The Novel

Genet was mostly living in Paris during the early 1940s, the years of the German Occupation. He supported himself in part by helping out a friend, Jean Decarnin, who sold books from one of the stalls along the Seine. He occasionally stole books to stock the stall. He gradually became friends with a circle of young literary types, a number of them members of various right-wing groups such as the Action Française before the war and supporters of the Vichy regime during the war. By way of various of these friends, Genet was introduced to Jean Cocteau, who was impressed enough by Genet's poetry and prose to help arrange for the clandestine publication of what would be Genet's first novel, *Notre-Dame-des-Fleurs*. It would appear in 1944.

On May 29, 1943, Genet was arrested for stealing a deluxe edition of Paul Verlaine's *Fêtes Galantes* from the Librarie de la Chausée d'Antin. In a letter from prison (where he is awaiting trial, writing poetry, and working on the manuscript of his second novel, *Miracle de la rose*) dated June 16, 1943, to François Sentein, Genet writes: "What's the title of the work on language by Saussure? I need it. Thanks."[40] This was a period in which Sentein was doing everything he could to avoid being sent to Germany as part of an STO group (Service de travail obligatoire, a work detail). Such service was for many a death sentence. Sentein had reenrolled as a university student as part of his plan to avoid being sent to Germany, and was attending lectures on linguistics. His journal records a number of reflections on Saussure, suggesting that Genet would have gained his acquaintance with the Swiss linguist in conversations with Sentein. We have learned to think of Saussure as primarily the linguist of *langue*, the fixed set of differential relations that enable meaning in language. But Saussure's course was also about language change. (The preeminence of his discussion of *langue* might be to some extent produced by the choices of Saussure's editors.) Indeed, it was Saussure's comments on change that caught Sentein's attention. In particular, Sentein cites in his journal entry for December 12, 1942, this passage from the opening pages of the third part of Saussure's *Course in General Linguistics*, where Saussure speaks briefly about literary language:

> The river that is language flows without interruption. Whether it flows calmly or rapidly is a secondary consideration.
>
> It is true that this uninterrupted evolution is sometimes hidden from view by the attention we pay to literary language; for literary language is superimposed on natural language, and its existence is subject to other constraints. Once it has been formed, it usually remains fairly stable; it tends to remain identical with itself. Its dependence on writing gives it special guarantees of preservation. So it is not literary language that will allow us to see the degree to which natural languages are variable when freed from all literary regulation.[41]

Sentein was himself apparently not a fan of language change. Here are some of the reflections that round out his journal entry on the subject once he has copied out that passage from Saussure and another passage on the same topic from Saussure's disciple and editor, Charles Bally:

> I'll say again that a communicative system is all the more "alive"—a stupid enough word to use for a thing, in any case—the more it facilitates communication; that a code communicates all the better the more stable and widespread it is; that the most "living" language is therefore the one that evolves the least across time and varies the least across space; that the masters of a language who help it remain alive are those who prevent as much as possible its evolution and its variation; but that they then make a serious error when they oppose with

their whims and wishes an evolution that has really taken place; and that, as
for linguists, their job should be to describe this process, not to push it along,
and certainly not to sing its virtues.[42]

Such a rigid, authoritarian attitude might seem like a strange one for someone
who is, at the same time as he is penning these thoughts on Saussure and Bally,
acting as one of Genet's literary supporters. Genet's literary language, as we
have seen, was far from standard or stable. And, as we saw in the last chapter,
more than just a supporter of Genet, Sentein was instrumental in the production of Genet's first novel, Cocteau having apparently assigned him the task
of "correcting" the punctuation of the manuscript of Notre-Dame-des-Fleurs.
It was in July of 1943, while the court proceedings regarding Genet's theft of
Verlaine are taking place, that Sentein read a newspaper account of the proceedings in which a few of Genet's verses were reprinted. It was reading those
verses that provoked Sentein to offer the reflections we looked at already in
the previous chapter:

> Did he already have a doctrine of his own [when he wrote those verses]? I could
> see it being formulated and taking shape each day. Just like any literature in its
> infancy, he first wrote in verse. The brief happiness of that innocent moment
> seemed already behind him. I prefer to his latest poems—which he reads,
> I have to say, quite badly! accenting them like someone in grade school—I pre-
> fer his prose, fresh and novel, with his own syntax once he gets out from under
> that of Jouhandeau. I earned the right—so to speak—to know this. It was last
> March when I was obliged to go through Notre-Dame des Fleurs from the first
> line to the last, balancing on the edge of his pen, testing with the winged heel of
> my own pen if what I was dealing with was a youthful blunder or else already
> one of those "exploitable errors" of the poetry he was currently producing.[43]

It is intriguing, the way Genet's literary language impressed some literary
people and made others uncomfortable—perhaps especially those whose
ideology of language was harshly conservative. (Sentein is an interestingly
confused case here.) Surely understanding Genet's writing requires a different
understanding of the functions of literary language than the one offered by
Saussure in the passage that Sentein copied out. Both Genet's language and
his thinking about language might even be taken to offer a kind of challenge
to Saussurean linguistics precisely because of his interest in pragmatic and
metapragmatic aspects of language use, in what language can be used to do,
and in what it means to notice what language is doing (besides just "meaning"
things).[44]

Consider the following passage from Querelle:

Already, at the age of fifteen, Querelle had smiled the smile that was to be peculiarly his for the rest of his life. He had chosen a life among thieves and spoke their argot. We'll try to bear this in mind in order to understand Querelle whose mental representative faculty and whose very feelings depend upon, and assume the form of, a certain syntax, a particular orthography. In his speech we find expressions like "sitting on our thumbs," "my dogs are barkin'," "light a fire under it!," "don't let the door hit you," "he's gone all red," "what a sucker!," "hey babe, feel how happy I am to see you," "go easy cowboy . . ." and so on, expressions that are never pronounced clearly, but muttered in a muffled sort of voice, and as if from within, without really seeing them. They are not projected, which means Querelle's language didn't really shed any light on him, or maybe we could say it didn't really draw an image of him. These expressions seemed, on the contrary, to enter through his mouth, to pile up inside him, to settle and form a thick mud deposit, out of which, at times, a transparent bubble would rise up, exploding delicately on his lips. A slang word had risen. (11)

(A quinze ans Querelle souriait déjà de ce sourire qui le signalera toute sa vie. Il a choisi de vivre avec les voleurs dont il parle l'argot. Nous essaierons de tenir compte de ce détail pour bien comprendre Querelle dont la représentation mentale, et les sentiments eux-mêmes, dépendent et prennent la forme d'une certaine syntaxe, d'une orthographe particulière. Dans son langage nous trouverons ces expressions: "laisse flotter les rubans . . . ," "J'suis sur les boulets . . ." "magne-toi le mou . . ." "faut pas qui ramène sa crêpe . . ." ". . . il a piqué un soleil" ". . . comment qui grimpe à l'échelle le gars . . ." ". . . dis donc, poupée, je marque midi . . ." "laisse couler . . ." etc . . . expressions qui n'étaient jamais prononcées d'une façon claire, mais plutôt murmurées d'une voix un peu sourde, et comme en dedans, sans les voir. Ces expressions n'étant pas projetées, son langage n'éclairait pas Querelle, si nous l'osons dire, ne le dessinait pas. Elles semblaient au contraire entrer par sa bouche, s'amasser en lui, s'y déposer, et former une boue épaisse d'où parfois remontait une bulle transparente explosant délicatement à ses lèvres. C'était un mot d'argot qui remontait. [245])

There may be an interesting kind of challenge to typical ways of thinking about language here. Remember that Saussure characterized *langue* as "comparable to a musical work" and noted that "a musical work exists only by means of the sum total of the executions of it. Yet any execution is indifferent to the work. A symphony is a reality that exists even without being executed. Just so can the execution by means of *parole* of what is given in the *langue* be taken to be inessential."[45] What Genet seems to offer in Querelle is a person in whose use of language something other than this hypothesized relation between *langue* and *parole* occurs—a relation in which the *parole* reveals other aspects of itself and its relation to culture than those traditionally associated with a Saussurian paradigm. To carry on Saussure's metaphor, we could perhaps say that when Querelle speaks, what catches the ear is a way in which his speech is out of tune—and then as a result, the very identity of the tune is put into question, shifts. In the experience of Querelle's language, something is communicated, but it is not communication. Something is indicated about the way language functions, something is called to attention about the way language is foreign to its speakers, implanted in them, passing through them. And yet that passage occasionally produces something unpredictable, something that seems almost not quite to be language, but that by not quite being language, forces us to notice something about the functions of language that usually escapes our awareness.

Genet's Querelle, as we have seen, exhibits a certain kind of pragmatic finesse as regards sexual interactions that leave those around him inarticulate. Indeed, Querelle is inarticulate himself about the way he moves within the sexual cultures that surround him. Genet thematizes inarticulateness at various points in the novel, including in the following difficult sentence toward the beginning of the novel. The published translation gets the sentence wrong—not hard to do, given how hard it is to understand, how compressed is its meaning. I provide the French first:

> Nous aimerions que ces réflexions, ces observations que ne peuvent accomplir ni formuler les personnages du livre, permissent de vous poser non en observateurs mais en créatures ces personnages qui, peu à peu, se dégageront de vos propres mouvements. (255)

It means something like this:

> I would like these reflections, these observations that the characters of this book can neither complete nor even formulate, to permit me to present you these characters not simply as observers but as creatures, who, bit by bit, will emerge from—or will liberate themselves from—your own movements. (20)[46]

The reflections referred to in this passage have to do with the relations that might exist between the proximity of two men, the experience of sexual arousal, the attempt to account for that arousal in one's own imagination, and the speech and other sounds (including a *râle assourdi*, a "muffled groan") that result from that arousal. The inarticulateness of the characters about their own relation to sexuality allows the novelist room to reflect upon it. Their inarticulateness is not a failing, so much as an opportunity to recognize that we know more about sexuality, or we live and act out more of sexuality, than we can say. Genet's goal vis-à-vis his characters and his reflections is therefore complex. The characters are not meant to be simply representational; they are not to be assigned the role of mapping out some territory for us. What cannot be articulated by the characters about sexuality in their world might only be "understood" by the reader should the novel somehow activate the pragmatic cultural knowledge (the invisible presuppositions) of that reader (and should the reader have the practical knowledge in question available for activation). Genet understands his novel not simply as a space of representation in which various referential aspects of culture can be recorded. He works to make it an instrument that calls to our attention the myriad ways we invoke culture to act in the world. It is as if the book wants to make us feel as acutely as possible our participation in the nonreferential aspects of sexual culture (which is not necessarily where *identities* happen, even as sex may be taking place), to feel culture happen as we read, in particular that part of a culture that cannot be found in the denotational value of the words on the page. This brings us to our final framing of the novel in relation to metapragmatics, a framing that a citation from Michael Warner's essay "Publics and Counterpublics" can help provide. Warner writes:

> There is no speech or performance addressed to a public that does not try to specify in advance, in countless highly condensed ways, the lifeworld of its circulation. This is accomplished not only through discursive claims, of the kind that can be said to be oriented to understanding, but also at the level of pragmatics, through the effects of speech genres, idioms, stylistic markers, address, temporality, mise-en-scène, citational field, interlocutory protocols, lexicon, and so on. Its circulatory fate is the realization of that world. Public discourse says not only: "Let a public exist," but: "Let it have this character, speak this way, see the world in this way." It then goes out in search of confirmation that such a public exists, with greater or lesser success—success being further attempts to cite, circulate, and realize the world-understanding it articulates. Run it up the flagpole, and see who salutes. Put on a show, and see who shows up.[47]

Here is Genet's shorthand version of Warner's observation, from only the second page of his novel, where he stops to criticize a sentence he wrote on the novel's first page, but then notes that its failings were in fact due to its desire to address and have an effect on a certain public:

> In that very long sentence beginning "it envelops him in clouds . . . ," we did indulge in facile poeticisms, each of the propositions being merely an argument in favor of the author's weaknesses. It is admittedly under the sign of a very singular inner feeling that we would set down the ensuing drama. We would also like to say that it is addressed to inverts. (4)

> (Dans la très longue phrase débutant par: "il enveloppe de nuées . . ." nous nous sommes abandonnés à une facile poésie verbale, chacune des propositions

n'étant qu'un argument en faveur des complaisances de l'auteur. C'est donc sous le signe d'un mouvement intérieur très singulier que nous voulons présenter le drame qui se déroulera ici. Nous voulons encore dire qu'il s'adresse aux invertis. [238])

The novel understands and presents itself as a move in the same game that Querelle and Nono play; it both is and imagines itself as an utterance standing between the utterer and the reader the way the words *pédé* and *enculé* stand between Seblon and Querelle, or the way the proper name Ralph Pepperill existed for Peirce. It is not what the words denote (or even connote); it is how they act upon our interests, how we take them up. *Querelle de Brest* was first published in a very limited private edition studded with erotic drawings by Cocteau. When the novel tells us it is addressed to inverts, it might have meant, it might have ended up meaning, those inverts with money who collect limited private editions of somewhat pornographic literature illustrated with pornographic drawings by Jean Cocteau. It is not only the case that not everyone would have been interested such a book. Not many could have afforded it. Gallimard would publish it later in a more affordable form, and also in an altered text (a number of the passages I have addressed in these pages were cut, for instance—only to be reinstated in a different edition several decades later). Without these later publications, rendered possible in part by Sartre's interest in Genet, as well as the interest of people like Cocteau and Sentein, and then by the evolution of Genet's reputation, the book might have remained as interesting to us as the Ralph Pepperill who bought Pee Dee Kew was to Peirce. Genet, I think, knew as much, and knew that if he wanted to be read differently, it was not the book per se that would have to change, but the forms of interest it could attract and the ways in which it could circulate. Genet would, so to speak, have to make sure that Pepperill not only collected racehorses and owned a rare edition of Plato, but that he did some reading and thinking. Genet understood that it wasn't enough to have written a novel like *Querelle*. He also had to become the author some people might choose to read in the way I've been reading him.[48] That is not *in* the text. Or perhaps I should say it is not enough that it merely be in the text. It also has to be part of the text's uptake. We have to know how to look to find this particular theoretical Genet (Genet, a semiotic joker in his own right) in his text, and we have to want to. If we do so, it is thanks in part to ongoing literary, cultural, and political history, to the evolution over time of the public for certain kinds of literature; it is the history of the novel (the history of *this* novel), and the history of sexuality in action together.

4

Simone de Beauvoir and Sexuality in the Third Person

In this chapter I want to develop a bit further the hypothesis that certain kinds of misfit sexualities can exist in language and culture without ever being explicitly talked about, that in some ways talking *about* them is nearly impossible given the way a particular language and culture work, that these sexualities leave other kinds of traces, more pragmatic than semantic ones. An understanding of such pragmatic misfit identities, I want to show, is helpful to a certain way of reading a novel like Simone de Beauvoir's *L'invitée* (1943, translated as *She Came to Stay*), which registers relationships between women such as the ones Beauvoir herself was involved in at the time she wrote the novel without ever representing them. It registers them in relation to contexts whose very availability is characterized by a variety of kinds of impermanence, and thereby calls our attention to those forms of meaning that reside in the always shifting relations between texts and contexts. In both this chapter and the next one, on misfit sexualities in Duras, what I want to demonstrate about the existence of misfit sexualities cannot be done through what we usually think of as a reading "of" a text—a novel, a letter, a journal, and so on. The traces of the misfit sexualities I will be looking for here and in the following chapter often exist in the spaces between texts. That is, I am interested in how certain literary works that do not necessarily represent a given misfit sexuality can nonetheless, when viewed as part of a certain sociotextual array, be seen as involved in registering the existence of misfit sexualities. Constructing such arrays is perhaps not exactly an act of textual interpretation, not an act of what we often refer to as reading, so much as it is an effort to capture a moment in an ongoing semiotic process, and to see how that process might count in the history of what a text is and what it becomes, the history of what it could be said to mean or to have meant.

Dos Passos Style

Both Beauvoir and Sartre were deeply struck by the technical achievements of John Dos Passos in his USA trilogy when they encountered it in the 1930s. They attested to their admiration in a number of ways and in a number of places. They would take up and rework various aspects of Dos Passos's narrative practice in the novels they were working on in the late 1930s: Beauvoir's *L'invitée* and Sartre's *L'âge de raison* (*The Age of Reason*). But more than that, they would take up this narrative practice as a tool for apprehending their own daily life. As Beauvoir puts it in the second volume of her memoirs, *The Prime of Life*, Dos Passos had "invented a distance with regard to his main characters, which meant that they could be, at one and the same time, drawn as detailed individuals and as purely social phenomena."[1] This dichotomy between an understanding of an individual as possessing internal origins for various aspects of its being and becoming, and an understanding of an individual as an instance of social inscription, with external origins for its being and becoming, is one central to Beauvoir's thought and writing in these years. The distance Beauvoir refers to in Dos Passos's handling of his characters is created for her by the particular version of free indirect discourse (or represented speech and thought) he practiced, even if she doesn't avail herself of either of those terms.[2] "Sartre and I frequently attempted to take up this double point of view on others or especially on ourselves," Beauvoir notes, declaring that Dos Passos furnished them with a new "critical tool" with which to shed light on their lives:

> For instance, we sketched out our conversation in the Café Victor as Dos Passos might have handled it: "The manager smiled in a satisfied way, and they both felt furious. Sartre drew at his pipe, and said that perhaps it was not enough merely to sympathize with the revolution. The Beaver [Beauvoir's nickname] pointed out that he had his own work to do. They ordered two large beers, and said how hard it was to sort out what you owed other people from what you owed yourself. Finally they declared that if they had been dock workers they would undoubtedly have joined the Communist Party, but in their present position all they could be expected to do was always side with the proletariat." Two *petit bourgeois* invoking their unwritten work as an excuse for avoiding political commitment: that was the truth, and indeed we had no intention of forgetting it. (113–14)[3]

For Beauvoir, this shift from speaking about oneself in the first person, to a particular manner of speaking of oneself in the third is "cruel" (113) and yet clarifying. The cruelty has to do with the affective experience produced by the uptake of the relation between the two instances yoked together within what she refers to as this "doubled" point of view.[4] In the essay Sartre published on Dos Passos's novel *1919* in 1938, he observed, in similar fashion, that performing this doubling is a sure way to make you hate yourself:

> Yesterday you saw your best friend and expressed to him your passionate hatred of war. Now try to relate this conversation to yourself in the style of Dos Passos. "And they ordered two beers and said that war was hateful. Paul declared he would rather do anything than fight and John said he agreed with him and both got excited and said they were glad they agreed. On his way home, Paul decided to see John more often." You will start hating yourself immediately. It will not take you long, however, to decide that you *cannot* use this tone in talking about yourself.[5]

Sartre's choice to refer to this narrative device as a "tone" is intriguing; he thereby underlines the extent to which he and Beauvoir were striving for ways of conveying particular affects by way of certain narrative techniques.[6] Why would Sartre characterize this tone as unbearable? After all, even if he says you can't use it in talking about yourself, in fact he did just that, as did Beauvoir. In his *War Diaries*, the journal he kept during the so-called phony war in the fall of 1939 and the spring of 1940, he recounts a tense conversation he had with a pair of his fellow soldiers, regarding their reasonably privileged positions within the French military apparatus. (Sartre was mobilized in Alsace as a meteorologist attached to an artillery unit.) About this conversation from mid-November 1939, Sartre writes:

> But all the same, as I return with Paul to the room we share I feel ridiculous, and just like one of Dos Passos's characters (Richard). So I recite the story to myself in Dos Passos style: "And Sartre lost his temper and said they ought to be living in privation because it was wartime. And he condemned Pieter, because Pieter had got people to pull strings for him. And he declared that they were all bastards, himself included, and that they ought to sleep on straw or in mud like the soldiers at the front. It struck nine and everyone went home. Sartre greeted his landlady, then retired to a comfortable bed with an eiderdown over his feet." It would be a bit thick, even as something out of Dos Passos.[7]

Both Sartre and Beauvoir have philosophical points to make about the implications of this kind of narration, but they are also intrigued by the affectivity (cruelty, self-critique, self-hatred) they see being put into play. Both the affectivity and the philosophical points are related to and produced by, among other things, the distribution of pronouns that occurs in their texts when they decide to switch into Dos Passos mode.

Of course there's no guarantee that the affective effect of a given way of mobilizing pronouns will be perceived identically by different speakers and readers. (Indeed, as Brian McHale notes, "There is of course no question of FID [free indirect discourse] functioning in a given context . . . unless it can be recognized by the reader and interpreted appropriately." He adds, "It is obvious that no one kind of index is uniquely constitutive of FID in all cases."[8]) As Niko Besnier observes in a review article on the scholarly and critical literature related to language and affect, language often carries affect in those of its channels that are most indexical. "Most linguistic affect," Besnier notes, "is itself a metamessage."[9] This means affect is often communicated ambiguously or inventively, that people innovate in their use of various indexicals in their effort to convey affect, that techniques for the display of affect are not fixed in time or across cultures. Besnier again: "For language users, the multifunctionality of affective devices is often a communicative resource, rather than a problem. Because they may signal more than one referent, and often more than just affect, affect-laden structures are particularly useful when ambiguity is a useful or necessary communicative strategy; indeterminacy itself becomes a communicative resource" (429). When Sartre and Beauvoir narrate to themselves bits of their lives in the third person of a certain kind of free indirect discourse that they associate with Dos Passos, there is no guarantee that their experience of the affect involved will coincide with anyone else's. Readers of the novels by Sartre, Beauvoir, and Dos Passos, for instance, might not experience the same "feel" that the authors imagine themselves conveying through their use of these narrative practices. Sartre's and Beauvoir's statements about how they experience and intend certain ways of distributing pronouns count as metapragmatic statements that are meant to explain the pragmatics of what may be their very particular idiolect. And for our purposes, it may be the case that what Beauvoir achieves pragmatically by way of this narrative technique is something different from what she tells us she was trying to achieve.

Another way of putting this would be to point out the extent to which the appropriate or successful apprehension by a reader of the purport of a given narrative technique is made possible by that reader's access to a collective social understanding of the rules of use of that technique. When someone tries to establish new rules of use, only time will tell if those rules will be widely adopted. Vološinov, in *Marxism and the Philosophy of Language*, speaks of the "steadfast social tendencies in an active reception of other speakers' speech, tendencies that have crystallized into language forms." He notes that "the mechanism of this process is located, not in the individual soul, but in society."[10] A bit further along, he comments that "indirect discourse 'hears' a message differently; it actively receives and brings to bear in transmission different factors, different aspects of the message than do . . . other patterns" (129). Beauvoir and Sartre are offering us lessons in how to hear the discourse they represent, how to distinguish between the different elements of what Vološinov calls "the verbal envelope of an utterance and its referential meaning" (132), or how to perceive the different "intonations" (138) that can inhabit the same utterance in which speech or thought is represented. (One of the more common understandings of free indirect discourse is that it involves hearing two conflicting voices in the confines of a single utterance, where the narrator can be understood as the owner of the utterance, and yet "what is involved, in general, is a mode of expression perceived as incompatible with the narrator's voice."[11] Or, we could say, even if the narrator leaves no trace of their own point of view, or their own intonation in the utterance, their presence somehow remains, creating some kind of a distance, often an ironic distance, between narrator and character.) Those "intonations" of a written text are only perceptible if the reader is capable of grasping not only the purport of various syntactic features of the text but also various ways in which the text is caught up in and draws meaning from (indexes) the larger textual, discursive, and social universe in which it exists, including sometimes ephemeral register effects of language, durable or fleeting distinctions tied to this or that aspect of an aesthetic practice, social positionings of authors, and so on. (As McHale writes: "The reader, far from having *a priori* mastery of the voices in a text, must be gradually 'schooled' by the novel itself to organize its semantic continuum into the appropriate voices, whether these are fictional speakers or nonpersonified 'interpretative positions' or 'linguistic ideologies.'"[12]) My argument is that there are things to be heard in Beauvoir's technique about which it would be unreasonable to expect her to be fully articulate on the metapragmatic level.[13]

Beauvoir says that the cruelty of this Dos-Passos-esque way of using pronouns in narrative resides in the way it allows us to "perceiv[e] men simultaneously through the spectacle of freedom they would play out inside themselves and as fixed reflections of their own situation."[14] Sartre puts it slightly differently:

> Even if you've let yourself become stuck within collective representations, you had first to experience them as an abdication of your individuality. We are neither mechanical objects nor possessed souls, but something worse; we are free. We exist either entirely *within* or entirely *without*. Dos Passos's man is a hybrid creature, an interior-exterior being. Here we are with him, within him, experiencing his vacillating individual consciousness, when suddenly it gives way, loses strength, and becomes lost in the collective consciousness. We follow along and suddenly we are outside without even noticing it.[15]

For both Sartre and Beauvoir, the affective experience of Dos Passos's mobilization of pronouns produces a philosophical reflection on the first person's relation to the experience of subjecthood. Sartre implies that the first person is the necessary locus of the experience of freedom, and yet the integrity of this experience is always on the point of collapse as that first person is revealed to be awash in various exterior, collective currents that make personhood itself a tenuous experience. Sartre's claim that you cannot talk about yourself in the mixed way he finds in Dos Passos without hating yourself is an interesting one. It is hard to decide if he means that such a hatred would be the result of coming to *misperceive* ourselves as the kind of hybrid creatures he found in Dos Passos, or if it would be the result of our then having to perceive something accurate about our relation to collective experience that we are in general more comfortable not knowing: if the freedom he mentions—freedom here being more or less dependent on a certain deployment of the first person, and a certain reception of that deployment—is a kind of delusion produced by a regime of pronoun usage, a delusion that another pronoun usage regime could disrupt, or if the narrative and pronominal technique of Dos Passos runs the danger of producing a debilitating but nonauthoritative frame for experiencing the world and conceiving human action within it.

Sexuality and "Interior Life"

The project of representing a certain kind of struggle for freedom in their novels was for Sartre and Beauvoir complicated by an aesthetic agenda they also took up regarding the novelistic representation of "interior life." "Interior life" was most tellingly represented for Sartre and Beauvoir by the novelistic practice of Marcel Proust, and that practice was one they mostly sought to eschew in their own novels. Thanks to a rigorous application of phenomenology, Sartre wrote in another essay from 1939, "nous voilà délivré de Proust"— finally we are done with Proust. And if we are finally free from Proust, it is coincident with our freedom from interior life itself: "finally, everything is outside, everything, even ourselves: outside, in the world, among all the others."[16] In some of the examples we have seen so far, Sartre and Beauvoir have been turning themselves inside out by means of a turn to the third person: a way of exposing a certain kind of class positioning they can't seem to experience fully in themselves in the first-person mode. That is to say, from inside the first person, Sartre and Beauvoir seem to think it will be a problem to represent certain aspects of one's own subject formation. Subject formation is not a first-person kind of experience, not part of the narration of interior life. Would this mean that Sartre and Beauvoir would also think about sexuality as belonging to the outside and subject to these same vagaries of experience, to think of it as something that cannot be fully experienced in the first person (but perhaps also not fully in the third)? For if Proust is a novelist of interior life, he is also, for Sartre and Beauvoir, a novelist of sexuality, of same-sex sexuality in particular, and it turns out to be part of their novelistic agendas to continue working with the representations of same-sex sexuality central to their immediate precursors (say André Gide and Proust), as well as to closer contemporaries such as Julien Green or Marcel Jouhandeau or, a few years later, Jean Genet and Violette Leduc. That is, an interest in same-sex sexualities flourished in French literature at this time for personal, political, and ideological reasons—but also for technical ones. It poses questions about the relationship between techniques of representation and the object of representation, questions writers deal with on both technical and philosophical levels.

Proust's error as a novelist, Sartre wrote rather bluntly in 1945, was to imagine that he could use his own homosexual experience as a basis for presenting the heterosexual love of Swann for Odette. Proust "believes in the existence of universal passions whose mechanism does not vary substantially when there is a change in the sexual characteristics, social condition, nation, or era of the individuals experiencing them. Having thus 'isolated' those immutable emotions, he can attempt to reduce them, in turn, to elementary particles. Faithful to the postulates of the analytic cast of mind, he does not even imagine that there might be a dialectic of feelings—he imagines only a mechanics."[17] Sartre's quarrel with Proust on this question has to do with a contrast he wants to draw between an analytics of "universal passions" and a synthetic approach to an individual in her or his specific situation. For Sartre, sexuality is part of the way individuals manifest their situation. The act of manifesting something, as Sartre and Beauvoir conceptualize it, will exceed the capacities of any first person—however unpleasant and cruel any such person might find it to be to face up to this fact. A given manifestation of sexuality is particular to an individual, it is a folding in of an outside that is subsequently re-revealed in ways specific to a given person in a given time and place. "We are of the opinion," Sartre writes, "that a feeling always expresses a specific way of life and a specific conception of the world that are shared by an entire class or an entire era, and that its evolution is not the effect of some unspecified internal mechanism but of those historical and social factors" (259). A given sexuality will thus define a class of people at a given moment, even if each person, as a specific unity, will manifest that sexuality differently: "We maintain that the various sentiments of an individual are not juxtaposed, but that there is a synthetic unity of one's affectivity and that every individual moves within an affective world specifically his own. . . . Every affect—like, for that matter, every other form of psychical life—*manifests* his social situation" (260). Maurice Merleau-Ponty says something similar in *Phenomenology of Perception* (hardly surprising given the tightness of the intellectual exchanges between him, Sartre, and Beauvoir in these years): "Sexuality," writes Merleau-Ponty, "is neither transcended in human life nor figured in its center by unconscious representations. It is at all times present there like an atmosphere."[18] That is to say, the reflexive human consciousness cannot ever simply master the sexuality of the embodied person to which it is attached, it cannot grasp it in a bounded act of intellectual apprehension; nor can sexuality be theoretically envisioned as having its origin in some nonreflexive and interior instance of representative action such as a psychoanalytic unconscious. It is for Merleau-Ponty, as for Sartre, and as for Beauvoir, an outside folded in. "Sexuality," he continues, "without being the object of any deliberate act of consciousness, can motivate central forms of my experience" (169). It is, in short, and using the word in its phenomenological sense, an *intentionality* that brings together, among other things, a physical and social world, a perceiving and responsive body, and a reflexive consciousness that is never fully adequate at grasping the forms of intentional action performed by the perceiving and responsive body in question. Sartre and Beauvoir's interest in pronouns, both for the writing of novels and for the apprehension of their own lives, is consonant with this understanding of sexuality, one that lies, for instance, at the heart of Beauvoir's project for her first novel, *L'invitée*. In this novel, it turns out that the relation between the first and the third persons can indicate something about one of the sexualities "in" the novel, even if neither Beauvoir nor the novel have the resources to be articulate about the phenomenon in question.

Sexual Experience and the Distribution of Pronouns

In late 1939 and early 1940, the period of the *drôle de guerre* during which Sartre is mobilized in Alsace, Beauvoir is working assiduously on the manuscript for *L'invitée*. Her letters to Sartre in these months, along with a journal she had begun keeping, recount certain details of her sexual relationships with three of her former high school students: Olga Kosakievicz, Bianca Bienenfeld (who is referred to in the correspondence as Louise Védrine), and Nathalie Sorokine. (Beauvoir taught in high schools in Rouen and then Paris until 1943, at which point, in the midst of the Occupation, she would be relieved of her teaching duties following the investigation of a complaint lodged with the authorities by Sorokine's mother regarding inappropriate relations with her daughter.)[19] The sexual relationships with Bienenfeld and with Sorokine overlapped in late 1939. Beauvoir was constantly comparing the three young women to each other and dissecting the differences in her responses to each of them. Here is an excerpt from a letter to Sartre dated December 21, 1939, which begins with a reference to Beauvoir tutoring Sorokine in French philosophy:

> I had had to use a lot of energy to explain Descartes to Sorokine; I was all wound up, but in a happy way, because I had given a good lesson: all told, it amounted to a nervous overflowing of vitality, mixed with a compulsory amiableness, and also a certain awkwardness on my part [j'étais en état de tension, et de tension heureuse vu que j'avais donné une excellente leçon: ça faisait un débordement nerveux de vitalité, avec consigne d'amabilité, et un certain manque d'adaptation]—I think it is for similar reasons that these days Kos. is *funnier* than usual in my eyes, because of her friends it would seem. There is a way of keeping an eye on one's relaxed appearance, of abandoning control in a controlled way, of losing touch with reality while remaining conscious of it that energizes people in relation to themselves, transposed to a social level—it's a kind of art of the same kind of bad faith as in Faulkner or Dos Passos and which produces ambiguous objects. [Il y a une façon de surveiller son laisser-aller, de s'abandonner avec contrôle, d'être désadaptée sans perte de conscience qui monte les gens dans leurs rapports avec eux-mêmes, transposés en social—une espèce d'art d'assez mauvais foi que celui de Faulkner ou Dos Passos et qui crée des objets ambigus.] That's how I experienced my behavior towards Védrine; I don't know if you can see what I mean because I'm never like that with you.[20]

The lesson on Descartes with one appealing young woman had gone well, but left Beauvoir a bit agitated; her agitation is tinted with an amiableness she feels obliged to enact and with a sense of being a bit off kilter. The feeling she has about her own psychological state reminds her of her recent impressions of Olga Kosakievicz (still a close friend and neighbor). Olga is now moving with a circle of friends who have induced in her a newly elevated level of what we might call hypomania, a condition that Beauvoir finds familiar. This personality change apparently strikes Beauvoir as producing a sense of artificiality. The sentence that begins "there is a way of keeping an eye on one's relaxed appearance" is, in French, particularly interesting because of the way the possessive pronoun *son* of "Il y a une façon de surveiller son laisser-aller" hesitates slightly in its reference. When one first encounters it, it seems like it might be referring back to Olga ("She has a way of keeping an eye on her relaxed appearance"), whereas its reference ends up being impersonal—an impersonal third person anchored in the word "people" (*les gens*). In this case "people" would include both Beauvoir and Kosakievicz, each of whom seems caught up in a slightly dissociative and hypomanic state, a state of self-doubling, in which you feel nearly out of control, but in a controlled kind of way, with the result that the gap between your out-of-control behavior and the internal sense of control produces a dual, ambiguous state that registers for her as artful or in bad faith. And yet this bad faith seems not so much an ethically dubious position as a state that is organically and socially produced.

We might posit at this point that "bad faith," that famous category of analysis for Beauvoir and Sartre, is a term that attempts to capture the relation between a certain experience and the registering of that experience within a discourse structured by a particular affectively colored pronoun system: a surge of nervous energy produces behavior that is somehow socially irregular, and somehow a person simultaneously enacts that out-of-control behavior, observes it, and recounts the enactment to herself—thereby seemingly existing simultaneously in the first- and third-person modes, existing simultaneously personally and socially, simultaneously as narrator (first person) and as character (third person).[21] The experience of this state reminds Beauvoir of effects in the representation of character produced by the narrative techniques of Dos Passos and Faulkner. She seems in her letters and her journal to apply the bad faith she speaks of to herself as the chronicler (both for herself and for Sartre) of her own relationships with these three women, in particular with Védrine, where the manifestation of her own sexuality is apparently sometimes painful to her and inassimilable in its totality to her first person, and where she thus exposes her own sexuality as a social object most expressible in third-person discourse—but perhaps not fully expressible even there. Her experience of this sexuality is divisive, compartmentalizing, highly anxiogenic. She writes to Sartre on November 12, "Yesterday we talked from 7 to 10 in my room, then went to the 'Sélect' to eat and then went off to bed: an intense, passionate night, I was nauseated by passion, it's like foie gras, but bad foie gras on top of it all—and I wasn't looking forward to the day today—but surprisingly, she was pleasant."[22] A few days earlier she had written, "we spent a passionate night together; the strength of her passion is crazy; sensually speaking, I was more caught up in it than usual, with, it seems, a vague and loutish idea that I should draw as much 'profit' as possible from her body—there was a touch of perversity there, of which I cannot approve, and which seems basically to have been an absence of tenderness, or so I think: it was the awareness of experiencing sensual charms without tenderness, something that in short had never happened to me before" (247–48).

There is clearly a problem with Beauvoir's first person in relation to the women she has sex and sleeps with, a problem whose investigation involves her way of distributing the first and third persons in and around these relationships. "I am never like that with you," she tells Sartre, as if in context with him, she can arrive at a first person that is trustworthy, in which there can be a kind of coincidence between consciousness and experience.[23] In these months she is working on her novel (following a rigorous practice of the blending of first and third persons as learned from Dos Passos: "In each successive chapter I identified myself with one of my characters, and excluded any knowledge or notion beyond what he or she would have had"[24]). One of the unspoken subjects of the novel might well be said to be an investigation of the third-person component of the sexuality of women who have sex with women.[25]

(Let me open a long parenthesis here to add that I hold no allegiance myself to any kind of analytic project that would invoke too seriously the concept of "bad faith," even though I am obviously interested in the role the concept plays in Beauvoir's and Sartre's writing. To imagine one can invoke the concept rigorously is usually to imagine that one can grasp a coherent, durable referent for the first-person pronoun, and that is not a claim I am making here. Consider statements such as this one, from Richard Moran's *Authority and Estrangement: An Essay on Self-Knowledge*: "The special features of first-person awareness cannot be understood by thinking of it purely in terms of epistemic access . . . to a special realm to which only one person has entry. Rather we must think of it in terms of the special responsibilities the person has in virtue of the mental life in question being *his own*. In much the same way that his actions cannot be for him just part of the passing show, so his beliefs and other attitudes must be seen by him as expressive of his various evolving relations to his environment, and not as a mere succession of representations (to which, for some reason, he is the only witness)."[26] Even the most appealing analyses—such as this one—of the authority and responsibility that may or should adhere to the first person can usually, with a slight shift of perspective, be seen instead as rules of use for the first-person pronoun, as guidelines for the use of specific genres of speech or thought, guidelines that wish to act as anchors for, or limits to, the potential referentiality of the first person. The analysis of "bad faith," self-deception, or related concepts could then be seen as requiring a particular set of prior beliefs about the referential range and the referential stability of the first-person pronoun—a range and stability that are in fact produced by the limited set of generic performances to which the analysis refers. Such stability is probably only possible as long as certain normative rules of use within certain specified genres can be successfully enforced, as long as certain genres of speech and patterns of thought can be widely inculcated and successfully and regularly reinvoked.[27])

At the same time that she is working on her novel, Beauvoir begins keeping a journal alongside her extensive letters to Sartre. In order to think about her practice of the first person in the writing of this journal, she conscientiously undertakes to read and reflect upon recently published literary journals by figures such as André Gide and Julien Green. Of Green's *Journal* she writes to Sartre in October 1939,

> I read Green's *Journal*; in the end it becomes amusing the degree to which this guy is nothing but a facade [apparence]; that doesn't make sincerity impossible, but there's a sincerity in the realm of appearances themselves . . . and for the rest of it he is so industrious that it recalls Ginette Lumière—when he speaks of paintings or a landscape or recounts small anecdotes, one feels inclined to say to him, "my dear sir, you certainly are working rather hard at this."[28]

Arguably, what she experiences as Green's artificiality is an affective reaction to the use of a particular linguistic or literary register. And in point of fact, the sensation of bad faith produced in her by her reading of Green's *Journal* may not be all that different from her experience of herself in her encounters with Védrine, or in the accounts of them she writes for Sartre.

The idea of being nothing but an appearance is one that is for Sartre and Beauvoir related to a particular practice of the first person that they observed in the world around them, and it is a subject the two of them seem to have talked about frequently in the 1930s. In her memoirs, Beauvoir tells us that it was in relation to one of her colleagues in the high school in Rouen where she taught in the early 1930s that discussions of this topic reached a turning point:

> One of my younger colleagues was a mine of dogmatic opinions and violent moods in the teachers' lounge; but when I tried to talk to her privately, I found myself plunging into mental quicksands. This contrast disconcerted me, till one day light dawned: "I've got it," I told Sartre. "Ginette Lumière is unreal, a sort of *mirage* [apparence]." Thenceforth we applied this term to anyone who feigned convictions or feelings for which they held no surety: we had discovered, under another name, the idea of *roles*.[29]

The first person is, then, as much the pronoun of bad faith as the pronoun of authenticity. The third person, used in the "Dos Passos mode" to speak of yourself, corrects the excesses of the first person, chastens it, breaks the role, requires that one have the strength of one's pronoun's convictions, but perhaps also reveals things the first person, even in its most honest manipulations, could not encompass.

For Beauvoir (and Sartre) there is an area of experience, of "vitality," out of which sometimes arise behaviors that are assimilable only with difficulty to the "authentic" first person that we seem to have some cultural obligation to assume. These experiences can sometimes be painfully assimilated in the chastening narrative style of Dos Passos, which produces "ambiguous" figures whose condition is divided between first- and third-person perspectives. Those unwilling, incapable, or simply uninterested in chastening themselves in this way can be seen as merely a collection of roles wittingly or unwittingly enacted in particular contexts.

If sexuality is so central to the thinking of Beauvoir and Sartre about these pronominal problems, it is because sexual behavior is linked for them both to certain notions of spontaneity and privacy, to a kind of experience that might seem least given to inauthenticity, and to the performance of socially constrained roles. There will be, in their writing, an intriguing contrast between the space of a bed in a hotel room or a bedroom, for instance, the space where sexual acts often occur, and the arena constituted by a café table, where sexuality can be thought about in public, or where public interactions with sexual partners will occur. The café is the ideal stage for bad faith. We might, putting a Goffmanian spin on things, say that for Sartre and Beauvoir, the bed is a place where a sexual self presents itself to you, and the café table is the place where you present (in person) and represent (in writing) yourself (your sexual and your social selves) to yourself and to others. Except that this is not a fully Goffmanian spin on things, because for Goffman, more explicitly than for Beauvoir and Sartre, there is no region in which the self is not already caught up in representation through the invocation of some kind of social form for interaction. As he puts it at the end of *The Presentation of Self in Everyday Life*, "a correctly staged and performed scene leads the audience to impute a self to a performed character, but this imputation—this self—is a *product* of a scene that comes off, and is not a *cause* of it. The self, then, as a performed character, is not an organic thing that has a specific location, whose fundamental fate is to be born, to mature, and to die; it is a dramatic effect arising diffusely from a scene that is presented, and the characteristic issue, the crucial concern, is whether it will be credited or discredited."[30]

During his analysis of the presentation of self, Goffman elaborates two notions, back region and front region, which are useful for understanding the structural relations between café table and bedroom, between journal and novel, between first persons (of which there may be several for any given person) and third persons, that are key to the reading I wish to offer of Beauvoir's novel. He writes:

> A back region or backstage may be defined as a place, relative to a given performance, where the impression fostered by the performance is knowingly contradicted as a matter of course. There are, of course, many characteristic functions of such places. It is here that the capacity of a performance to express something beyond itself may be painstakingly fabricated; it is here that illusions and impressions are openly constructed. (112)

For Ginette Lumière, the teacher's lounge is a front region, a place of active, intentional performance. Julien Green's (expurgated) journal is also a front region, one where Beauvoir feels the signs of the fabrication of the performance remain too legible. Beauvoir wishes to find the authentic person, even if it means going backstage to do so, and is frustrated when the trip backstage does not, in and of itself, produce a successful performance of authenticity: "when I tried to talk to her privately, I found myself plunging into mental quicksands." Her *manque d'adaptation* after an intense session of tutoring with Sorokine or her difficulty in claiming all the aspects of the experience of her sexual encounters with these women disconcert her because, in fact, she cannot tell in these circumstances where her behavior is manufactured, cannot tell if she herself is front stage or back. (This is perhaps characteristic of her experience of what I am calling a misfit sexuality.) But in fact as Goffman and our own experience both testify, a region can switch from back to front and back again with less than a moment's notice:

> And, of course, a region that is thoroughly established as a front region for the regular performance of a particular routine often functions as a back region before and after each performance, for at these times the permanent fixtures may undergo repair, restoration, and rearrangement, or the performers may hold dress rehearsals. To see this we need only glance into a restaurant, or store, or home, a few minutes before these establishments are opened to us for the day. In general, then, it must be kept in mind that in speaking of front and back regions we speak from the reference point of a particular performance, and we speak of the function that the place happens to serve at that time for the given performance. (127–28)

This mobile distinction between back and front regions (or, we might add, the possibility that a given place is simultaneously back region and front region for two overlapping performances) interests me for a number of reasons: it helps us to understand how Sartre and Beauvoir use the distinction between the café and seemingly private places such as a hotel room to structure and to apprehend their lives (the café being the place where, allowing yourself to be seen writing in public, you present your own back region to the public, and where, through your writing itself—often about the bedroom—you strive, in a different manner and for a different public, for a similar end); it helps us to understand what interested them about the narrative technique they thought they learned from Dos Passos (that it pulls down the curtain protecting a backstage area, ruining a performance of self); and it helps to understand the particular relationship between a journal and a novel that was gaining increasing visibility in the 1930s—when Gide began his project of publishing regular sections of his own journal, as if voluntarily offering insight into the back region preparations both for a public presentation of self and for a public presentation of finished literary works. The distinction also returns us to the question of affect. For if Sartre says you will hate yourself if you resort to the Dos Passos mode for too long, if Beauvoir feels nauseous after a sex act that solicits her participation and enjoyment without soliciting her allegiance, if the amiability toward Sorokine invoked in her by her tutoring session seems alien to her, this is because it is generally (but not universally) experienced as unpleasant to come up against the presentational limits of oneself, to become a spectator to one's own performance.

Both Gide and Green were, in their journals, faced with problems similar to Beauvoir's at this time: what are the means for representing same-sex sexuality in fiction, and also in journals? As one constructs a journal as a genre that provides access to a backstage region in which fictions are constructed, how will the personal motivations for the fictional representation of same-sex sexuality be dealt with? What does one risk exposing about oneself? In his journal, Julien Green writes about discussing this problem with Gide: "I was telling him that I had carelessly left my journal open on my worktable and that the servants had surely taken a look at it, and he replied that as far as he was concerned the curiosity of servants seemed flattering, and that he intentionally left insignificant kinds of papers out on his desk to satisfy their desire to know."[31] But to know what? Or how much? It is no surprise that Beauvoir, whose journal was quite explicit about her sexual relations, panics one day when she discovers she has left it behind in a café. This was in early January 1940, on the day she was taking Sorokine back to her hotel room to have sex with her for the first time. She writes to Sartre:

> We went up to my room, where I was horrified to discover I had left my black notebook behind at la "Coupole"; I was frightened out of my wits that it might get picked up by just anyone, and I rushed back there; happily, I found it. We came back and sat down side-by-side and after 10 minutes of chatting we had gotten as far as kissing; after 15 minutes of kisses we were in bed, having modestly turned out the lights . . . Certainly it's not the same as it was with Kos. but I really do like her body and find these moments extremely pleasant, especially the faces she makes, which are quite moving. . . . She also asked me if we were criminals and if we'd be put in prison if we were discovered like this. I said no, which made her sad; she had found the idea charming.[32]

Maybe a sexuality such as Beauvoir's leaves its record not in any particular representation, but in the pattern of the scattering of its traces across different platforms with different generic requirements, through different voices resulting from the different expectations of the various genres—a scattering caused by extant notions of private and public, by the particular representational games of a given literary moment, by the interlocking social and personal experiences of the person whose sexuality is in question, by that sexuality's relation to the linguistic environment (including the pronouns) in which it occurs, as well as by various cultural and political forces existing in its own particular historical moment.

How private is the piece of foolscap on which someone writes a letter while seated at a café table, or a black notebook in which someone keeps a journal, and thanks to what sets of circumstances are we able to read the words inscribed on that paper and in that notebook today? Beauvoir could sit at a café table with one of her girlfriends and write a letter to Sartre about having sex with her. The first person of the letter and the first person at the table cannot be the same, and that very division is part of the experience and the manifestation of her sexuality, which presents itself differently in different places (say cafés and hotel rooms) as well as in different genres (journals, letters, novels)— genres whose relationships to publicity and privacy are different—different in the moment of enactment or inscription, of course, and also variable over time, at least for those that continue to exist on some kind of material support.[33] Beauvoir's letters to Sartre and her journal were not published until 1990, four years after her death. The versions of Gide's and Green's journals that Beauvoir was reading in 1939 and 1940 were expurgated ones. Fuller versions of these journals would also be published only much later, in Gide's case after his death. Nevertheless, there are a certain number of passages in the version of Green's *Journal* that she was reading that must have resonated in some way with Beauvoir as she read them. The following, for example, dated March 29, 1930, is one she could nearly have written herself, substituting "heroine" for "hero" and "girl" for "boy":

> Thought, this morning of the story I'm writing at the moment. I have my back up against the wall. If I hesitate about speaking of the hero's love for a boy, I distort the truth, and, in order to seem to conform to acceptable moral standards, I commit a prudent act that will make me lose all esteem for myself. That's how one ends up becoming a man of letters.[34]

One becomes a man of letters through an act of self-dissociation, but then one recovers one's self-esteem by attempting to sew back together various parts of oneself by publishing parts of a journal revealing the back region supporting the novel's performance.

Beauvoir's relations during these years with her girlfriends and with her one boyfriend other than Sartre were discussed in detail in her journal and her letters to Sartre. *L'invitée* tells the story of a couple, Françoise and Pierre, who decide to invite a young woman, Xavière, to join them, transforming their intimate couple into an intimate trio. The novel is able to represent Françoise (the character who most resembles Beauvoir) sharing with Pierre (the character who most resembles Sartre) her sexual involvement with another male character, Gerbert, yet the novel will not represent any sexual behavior between Françoise and Xavière, although it can hint at it—for instance, by having other characters wonder about the possibility. Elisabeth, Pierre's sister, has invited the threesome over for dinner, and upon seeing them, thinks to herself "Pierre was certainly sleeping with Xavière, she was sure of that. And the two women? It was quite possible—they made such a perfectly symmetrical triangle."[35] And yet they weren't sleeping together. Here we see how Beauvoir's deployment of free indirect discourse, where "any knowledge or notion beyond" the ken of the character through whom the narration is focalized is "excluded," becomes a kind of symbol of, or objective correlative for, her own complicatedly disassociative sexuality.[36] The traces of female same-sex sexuality left in the novel, the very difficulty of its inscription there, have in fact something to tell us about any number of things: the kinds of significance that can accrue to certain literary techniques such as free indirect discourse; the possibilities for certain kinds of speech about certain manifestations of same-sex sexuality in Paris in the early 1940s (during the Occupation); the particular experience of sexual identity that was Beauvoir's; and, of course, the way people use pronouns in relation to "their" sexuality.

Without expanding the way we consider pronouns to include studying their distribution within a practice of the self and of sexuality, it is difficult to comprehend the extent to which specific understandings of sexuality might depend on a particular practice of pronoun distribution, and the ways in which an ability to apprehend certain kinds of sexuality (such as Beauvoir's) might be hindered precisely by available ways of mobilizing pronouns.[37] It may be that the sexuality Beauvoir practices, records in her journal, but cannot quite record in her novel, is a sexuality that does not coincide with the normative pronoun distributions for sexual expression within her specific cultural circumstances, that if it finds its expression not in any one textual location but through the contradictory traces it leaves across multiple textual locations, this is because there is no more direct means to expression available for this sexuality, or even that, in a certain way, this is not a sexuality that seeks direct expression (or both at the same time).

L'invitée

Part of my goal in the first part of this chapter has been to arrive at a point where I could weave together a few moments from Beauvoir's *L'invitée*, and through this entextualization both do a little bit of something we might call the history of sexuality and reflect on that doing. By entextualization, I mean the bringing to bear of a particular context on the novel in a way that allows certain meanings that might not otherwise be palpable to make a serious claim on our attention, and I mean for it to be noticeable that particular contexts (and therefore particular meanings) become available to certain people at certain times, and that these contexts have different kinds of lifespans.[38] The meanings I wish to point to exist on the level of narrative technique, on the level of what the novel represents (or cannot represent—although it can leave traces of this nonrepresentation in the novel itself and also in its paratexts), on the level of its philosophical ambitions, and also in the way in which it could be thought of as participating (implicitly and explicitly, intentionally and unintentionally) in some of the sexual cultures of its time and place. All of the material I've presented so far should help us to grasp a number of its achievements in its investigation of certain forms of sexuality, an investigation intricately involved with its deployment of pronouns, since, obviously, part of the history of sexuality—especially of its misfit rather than its mainstream forms—is the history of the difficulty of establishing enunciatory positions from which to speak of, about, or from those social forms. The less closely tied the sexual practices involved are to any practice or formation of a sexual identity, the more difficult it is to establish any such enunciatory position and the more tenuous that position will be.

L'invitée was Beauvoir's first novel. It was published in 1943, but Beauvoir had begun work on it in the late 1930s, and was working steadily on the manuscript in late 1939 and early 1940, when Sartre was mobilized in Alsace. The plot of the novel is set in motion by a fascination that grows between Françoise and the younger Xavière. The trio they form with Pierre sometimes seems to sustain itself on the energies produced by the characters *not* acting on any of the new sexual possibilities their three-way intimacy would seem to suggest. Certainly it seems as if Beauvoir, her girlfriends, Sartre, and their immediate circle would have been incapable of reading the novel as *not* being to some extent about women who have sex with women, even if that legibility was limited to a small group of privileged readers at the time and takes some effort to reconstruct today.[39]

Chapter 2 of the first part of the novel reaches its most racy moment in the following passage, in which, seated together in a café in the early morning hours, Françoise is doing her best to convince Xavière to leave her family in Rouen and move to Paris to try to make her life there, a move that will involve, at least at the outset, depending on Françoise for support:

> [Françoise] caressed the warm hand that lay trustingly in hers. "You'll see, you'll have a beautiful, rich, little life."
>
> "Oh, I do want to come," said Xavière. She let herself go, relaxing all her weight against Françoise's shoulder; for some time they remained motionless, leaning against one another. Xavière's hair brushed against Françoise's cheek, and their fingers remained intertwined.
>
> "It makes me sad to leave you," Françoise said.
>
> "Me too," Xavière rejoined softly.
>
> "My dear little Xavière," murmured Françoise. Xavière looked at her, her eyes shining, her lips parted; soft and yielding, she had given herself over to Françoise completely. Henceforth it would be Françoise who would lead her through life.[40]

Beauvoir would write in her memoirs that Xavière was based to some extent on Olga Kosakievicz, with whom she and Sartre had been involved in Rouen before 1935 and then later in Paris.[41] She would suggest to her biographer Deirdre Bair that some of the less pleasant aspects of Xavière's character were drawn from the personality of Olga's sister, Wanda.[42] It would seem, in fact, that Beauvoir drew inspiration for her portrayal of the relationship between Françoise and Xavière from her experiences with all three of her girlfriends of these years. Yet when, later in life, she would talk about the genesis of the novel with people like Bair, she would not mention Bienenfeld or Sorokine in this regard. In general, when she would talk about her relationships with Olga Kosakievicz, Nathalie Sorokine, or Bianca Bienenfeld (Védrine), she would not speak of the sexual aspects of these overlapping relationships, as if the extant cultural forms for sexuality to which she could have referred were disabling rather than enabling, leaving her no way to construct what we have already seen Michael Silverstein call in the previous chapter a "conversationally useable biography."[43] Unsurprisingly, then, there was no way she could speak or write of their cumulative importance to the development of the novel itself.[44]

Yet if Beauvoir, in the course of the remainder of her life—and probably for different reasons at different moments in her life—could not speak (at least to most people) in the first person about her sexual experiences with women during the late 1930s and early 1940s, this does not mean L'invitée could not itself in some way be *about* these experiences. It is surely important in this regard, given that her (and Sartre's) investigation of the uses and possible meanings of free indirect discourse had to do precisely with what people were able to conceive about themselves, that the character of Françoise becomes a locus for the display of a certain articulate inarticulateness about sexuality. (Somehow her inarticulateness seems not to give her the same semiotic power it gave to Querelle, the joker in his pack, as we have already seen.) As she and Xavière are dancing together in a nightclub in the second half of the novel, we read, "Dancing made her head spin a little. She felt Xavière's beautiful warm breasts against her, she inhaled her sweet breath. Was this desire? But what did she desire? Her lips against hers? This body unresisting in her arms? She could think of nothing. [Elle ne pouvait rien imaginer.] It was only a confused need to keep this amorous face forever turned toward hers, and to be able to say with passion, 'She is mine'" (247). *Elle ne pouvait rien imaginer.* She could come up with no relevant images, we might say. Françoise is here being required to exemplify a way of thinking about the relation of an "image" to a sexuality that Beauvoir shared with Sartre, where an image functions as a kind of form (as much a social form as an individual one) that allows a sexuality to coalesce into existence out of the raw materials of sense impressions and reactions to them. Sartre, in *The Imaginary* (published in 1940), wrote that sexual desire, or hunger, or disgust, all undergo "a significant modification while passing through the imaging state":

> They were concentrated, made more precise, and their intensity increased. . . . Desire and disgust exist at first in a diffuse state, without precise intentionality. In being organized with a piece of knowledge into an imaging form [avec un savoir dans une forme imageante], the desire is made precise and is concentrated. Enlightened by the knowledge, it projects its object outside itself.[45]

What Françoise lacks is the know-how (perhaps something like "cognitive capacity" would be a better translation for *savoir* in this passage from Sartre than "a piece of knowledge") to synthesize her confused sensations by means of an imaginary form. And yet it is not that she and Xavière don't know lesbians exist. Xavière has recounted to her earlier in the novel an evening out with Pierre during which the two of them found themselves in a queer bar in Montmartre. There they met, among others, "two women at the bar, completely drunk":

> She added confidentially, "Pederasts."
> "You mean lesbians?" Françoise asked.
> "Isn't it the same thing?" asked Xavière, her eyebrows rising.
> "You only say 'pederast' for men," Françoise replied.
> "Anyway, they live together [c'était un ménage]," Xavière said with a shade of impatience. (184)

The problem is that the category of lesbian does not work as an image to bring coherence to her experience with Xavière. The simple phrase "Elle ne pouvait rien imaginer" (which in this context we might translate as "Her imagination failed her," or, more verbosely, "Her imagination did not have the resources to make her experience articulate") indicates that *L'invitée* belongs to a whole set of texts in which Beauvoir and Sartre are developing a phenomenological and also a sociological account of same-sex sexualities. (The set includes *L'invitée*, *The Second Sex*, *Nausea*, *Being and Nothingness*, *Saint Genet*, *The Age of Reason*.) *L'invitée* stands as one of the most interesting of these texts for a couple of reasons. First, because it is the one in which a same-sex sexuality fails to encounter a recognizable social form, and, corollarily, it is the one where the project to investigate this problem cannot even be fully avowed—doubtless partly because of the choice of the particular version of free indirect discourse employed, partly because of the constraints of the historical moment of the Occupation, and partly because of various forms of ambivalence particular to Beauvoir herself. (Even so, we can notice a similarity between this scene in which Françoise feels her head spin and wonders if she is having an experience of desire and wonders further what that possible desire would require of her, and the scene we noticed in the previous chapter where Querelle grips his buttocks and feels a shiver run up and down his spine as his body experiences, and his mind tries to apprehend, what it means to be an *enculé* without being a *pédé*.)

The chapter in which Françoise and Xavière dance together, like the second chapter of the novel, which concludes with them seated in a café with fingers entwined, is focalized through Françoise. (Indeed, the novel rigorously refuses ever to focalize anything through Xavière, so we never see a representation of their relation from Xavière's point of view.) And because we know to read the novel as if it were being written by Dos Passos, we know that Françoise's point of view is somehow being ironized—or perhaps it would be better to say that Sartre and Beauvoir were, in their novelistic experimentation of these years, interested precisely in exploring how this literary technique could be used to portray the limits of what a consciousness was able to conceive and articulate about itself.[46] Think of *L'invitée*, then, as being, at least for certain people, a novel about women who might have sex with women—yet are understood by those concerned not to be identical with lesbians—and about the difficulty of such people finding an enunciatory position from which to speak about their sexuality. More generally, *L'invitée* might be taken as a novel about that part of sexuality that cannot be lived in the first person, and part of which might (or might not) be captured by a swerve into third-person contemplation—a technique allowing us to view people as somehow awash in sexuality—and manifesting their own as a kind of eddy within larger tides and currents. Finally, *L'invitée* might be taken as a novel about the way nameable and unnameable forms of sexuality wash through all of us, and provide only some with a context in which to manifest our sexuality as a text that others can read; whereas others manifest in fragmentary ways pieces of a variety of sexual forms that may or may not suffice, but that don't amount to anything easily cognizable, recognizable, or entextualizable for most people around us.

Consider, in support of this line of thought, a few more details regarding the context of the writing of *L'invitée* and its first reading by those in Beauvoir's immediate circle. In February 1940, Beauvoir is eagerly awaiting Sartre's return to Paris from Alsace for a two-week leave. They plan to read and discuss the manuscript of each other's novels. On February 1, 1940, Beauvoir notes in her journal: "I meet up with Védrine at the bar of the 'Sorbonne' and work sitting next to her. I ponder chapter 10, and come up with a lot of wonderful ideas and an outline for an entire new beginning, which is the part that needed the most work."[47] Sartre arrives in Paris on February 4, and from February 4 to 14 they spend a few hours most days sitting in cafés reading and discussing each other's manuscripts. Sartre returns to duty on February 15. On March 9, Beauvoir reports to Sartre on a night in which she goes out with Olga to a famous Parisian nightspot, the Martinican bar in the fifteenth arrondissement known as the Bal Nègre.[48] Certain details in the description in her letter to Sartre make it seem likely that this trip was the source for some of the material we find in the scene in *L'invitée* where Françoise and Xavière visit the same club and dance together. On March 12, Beauvoir tells Sartre of having a long conversation with Nathalie Sorokine about her novel while seated together in the Luxembourg Gardens. By late April she has a manuscript of about four hundred pages that she is getting ready to show to Brice Parrain, an editor at Gallimard. In early May, while they are awaiting Parrain's reaction, Beauvoir apparently recounts (in a letter that has been lost) another night out on the town, this time in the company of Nathalie Sorokine, whose affectionate public conduct toward Beauvoir left her feeling rather uncomfortable. Sartre replies to her on May 4:

> As for Sorokine, like you, I find that her instability is annoying, but you should take into account that there are many tender gestures that even a well-mannered man can permit himself in a dance-club with a woman, and which a woman with another woman must not allow herself. That must be a little annoying for her. In any case, she loves you in a rough-and-ready kind of way, and your story makes me laugh, my dear.[49]

Arguably, then, the scene in *L'invitée* that takes place in the Bal Nègre (from which we have looked at one passage already) is a kind of palimpsest for the production of which Beauvoir drew on her experience of Parisian nightlife in the company of a couple of her girlfriends on a couple of occasions.

Of writing about Paris dance halls like the Bal Nègre, where Caribbean dances such as the beguine were introduced to a French public, Brent Edwards observes that it often includes "claims of authenticity, testimonies to rapid cultural transformation dramatized among the diversity of dancers and parasitic onlookers in a single dance hall, all in addition to the familiar straining to describe this 'dance of love' while invoking all the old deep-set desires, all the familiar 'exotic accessories,' all the echoes of the literary *doudou* suddenly staged among a modern and cosmopolitan crowd."[50] A version of the figure of the *doudou*, the "smiling, sexually available black or colored woman (usually the latter) [of the French West Indies] who gives herself heart, mind, and body to a visiting Frenchman (usually a soldier or colonial official) and is left desolate when her lover abandons her to return to France,"[51] is clearly present in Beauvoir's writing about the Bal Nègre. The figure, in Beauvoir's iterations, could certainly be used as further evidence for Daphne Brooks's concise claim that "systematically overdetermined and mythically configured, the iconography of the black female body remains the central urtext of alienation in transatlantic culture."[52] Here is a passage from Beauvoir's letter to Sartre about the trip to the Bal Nègre with Olga Kosakievicz: "I thought it would be kind of fun to go there . . . a whole lot of the St Germain crowd was there, taking up one whole side of the room and part of the gallery; they were agreeable to look at, as well, especially the women, some of whom were quite pretty. There were plenty of negroes and some admirable negresses, and they danced a crazed quadrille—I'd never seen one quite so obscene, the women with their skirts hiked up and their legs apart, wiggling their bottoms."[53] If ever there was a moment where we could wish a switch from first to third person in the Dos Passos mode *might* make you hate yourself at least a little bit, this could be it. But that isn't really what happens in the comparable scene in the novel. As Xavière and Françoise sit in the Bal Nègre and watch the dancing, Xavière becomes fascinated and envious of the dancing of one woman in particular:

> "Ah!" she said, "I'd give one year of my life to be that Negress for just one hour."
>
> "She's beautiful," Françoise agreed. "Her features are not those of a Negress. Don't you think she must have Indian blood?"
>
> "I don't know," Xavière said, looking miserable. Admiration had brought a gleam of hatred to her eyes.
>
> "Or else, I'd have to be rich enough to buy her and keep her locked up. Baudelaire did that, didn't he? Imagine coming home and, instead of a dog or a cat, finding this magnificent creature purring in front of the fireplace!"

> A naked, black body stretched out in front of a log fire. . . . Was that what
> Xavière was dreaming of? How far did her dreams go? (248)[54]

The racialized structure of spectatorship and the racist fantasy of exploitation
do not seem exactly ironized by the narrative, or even a primary focus of
attention. The novel doesn't appear to be thinking very hard about the links
it is putting on display between a racialized spectacle, indeed the memory of
slavery, and a misfit form of sexuality. What we have here would seem to be a
moment in the history of what Sharon Patricia Holland calls in the memorable
title of her 2012 book *The Erotic Life of Racism*. One of the points of Holland's
book is to "suggest that we can't have our erotic life—a desiring life—without
involving ourselves in the messy terrain of racist practice." She discusses Beauvoir's presentation of the importance of erotic experience in *The Second Sex*,
noting that Beauvoir localizes in erotic experience "the revolutionary potential
for a certain autonomy. . . . For Beauvoir, the erotic is a good thing because
it quite simply allows women in particular to possess their own sexuality."
Holland then queries: "But what if our erotic selves have been compelled . . .
by such terms as 'community,' 'home,' and 'race'?"[55] The scene we are looking
at in *L'invitée* seems almost ready to pose part of this question, but then draws
back from doing so.

There is rather a different purpose that this scene seems to serve within a
larger narrative structure, one that has to do with noticing that certain performances of sexuality can probably only be successful in certain kinds of spaces
at certain times. As it pursues that insight, it doesn't take much account of the
specificities of class, race, and ethnicity that may be involved in structuring
the different spaces that it represents in some detail.

Consider the moment, a few pages earlier, when Françoise and Xavière
arrive together at the Bal Nègre.

> "Look, there's Dominique's whole crowd," Xavière said as they walked into the
> dance hall.
>
> There was the Chanaud girl, Lise Malan, Dourdin, Chaillet. . . . Françoise
> nodded to them and smiled, while Xavière cast a veiled glance in their direc-
> tion; she had not let go of Françoise's arm, for she did not dislike having people
> take them for Lesbians when they entered a public place; it was the kind of
> shocking behavior that amused her. . . . Françoise experienced real pleasure at
> feeling herself included in the stupid spite of this bunch of gossips; she felt as if
> she and Xavière were being cut away from the rest of the world and imprisoned
> in an impassioned intimacy. (246)

> (—Tiens, voilà la clique de Dominique, dit Xavière en entrant dans la grande
> salle.

Il y avait la petite Chanaud, Lise Malan, Dourdin, Chaillet . . . Françoise leur adressa un signe de tête souriant tandis que Xavière coulait vers eux un regard endormi; elle n'avait pas lâché le bras de Françoise, elle ne détestait pas quand elles entraient dans un endroit, qu'on les prît pour un couple: c'était un genre de provocation qui l'amusait. . . . Françoise éprouva un vrai plaisir à se sentir enveloppée avec elle par la niaise malveillance de toute cette bande comméreuse, il lui semblait qu'on les isolait ensemble du reste du monde et qu'on les enfermait dans un tête-à-tête passionné. [309])

I have provided both the English translation and the French original, because of the notable discrepancy between them. What kind of a problem in up-take is foregrounded for us when we see that a translator has read "elle ne détestait pas quand elles entraient dans un endroit, qu'on les prît pour un couple" (which might be more literally translated as "it wasn't disagreeable to her when, walking into some joint, they were taken to be a couple") and has chosen to render it "she did not dislike having people take them for Lesbians when they entered a public place"? It is a category problem, that has to do with the difficult legibility of those misfit sexual identities that do not fall within the most widely broadcast parameters. But now suppose that Françoise and Xavière had performed that entrance not at the Bal Nègre, but in Montmartre in the bar in which Xavière and Pierre had met the lesbian couple, a bar about which Xavière had commented, "Perhaps if you went there every evening, they'd finally agree to adopt you" (Peut-être en retournant là-bas tous les soirs, on finirait par se faire adopter) (184). Or perhaps not. The trip to a queer bar in Montmartre and the trip to the Bal Nègre are both examples of kinds of sexual tourism available within a large city such as Paris in the middle of the twentieth century, but with a difference. Two women entering arm in arm in one context would clearly not signify the same way in the other. Perhaps you could not easily have made so successful an appearance as a nonlesbian same-sex couple in a queer bar in Montmartre as you could have at the Bal Nègre. At the Bal Nègre, for instance, Xavière and Françoise are both acutely aware of the presence of other members of their bohemian set from the Saint-Germain neighborhood, the spectators for their site-specific performance of couple-hood. The particular audience could be said to a certain extent to determine not only the success of the performance, but its very possibility. This kind of social know-how (a practical sense of the way that cultural concepts and forms for interaction are unequally distributed across social spaces) regarding when and where to take up a certain role is something the novel displays without articulating; it is a know-how one could probably possess without being able to express.[56]

The Bal Nègre had opened in 1924 as a dance hall for mostly working-class

Martinicans. Two artists, Joan Miro and André Masson, lived on the same street, and in 1926 Robert Desnos moved into their old space. He apparently started bringing his artist and writer friends to visit the club, and soon it was being written up in the press, slowly becoming an attraction not only for Parisians, but for tourists from the United States and elsewhere as well.[57] Many people who write about it describe it as a space of permissiveness, of category blurring, of an openness to not quite specified sexual possibilities, a kind of openness that was perhaps especially important to its white patrons.[58] And certainly this seems to be how it functions in *L'invitée*, not so much as a bar for the West Indian community in Paris as a space to which a certain bohemian crowd will go to spectate, a crowd that exhibits a certain familiarity with, that might even be one of the specific cultural homes for, certain concepts and practices of same-sex sexuality that, even if they can be recognized, are barely named, and perhaps have only the most fleeting relation to identities that could be readily named.[59]

Consider one final instance of Françoise's inarticulateness about her sexuality. It is, we can now see, an index of many things—varieties of censorship in force at the historical moment of the novel's composition, for instance, but also a form of sexuality that resists being named because of certain features of the naming system for sexual forms extant in the culture in which it occurs. Here is the description of the end of the evening the two women spend together at the Bal Nègre, once they are back at the doorway to Xavière's hotel room:

> Silence descended heavily, it wasn't words that would be able to do something about it; Françoise couldn't find a gesture, paralyzed as she was by the intimidating grace of this beautiful body she didn't even know how to desire. . . . She was standing near the door; on a sudden impulse, she took Xavière in her arms. "Goodnight, my dear Xavière," she said, brushing her cheeks with her lips.
>
> Xavière gave way, and for a moment she rested against her shoulder, stationary and supple; what was she waiting for? For Françoise to release her or to hold her tighter still? She lightly disengaged herself. "Good night," she said in a perfectly natural voice. (251–52)

Imagine Beauvoir giving this passage to Kosakiewicz to read, or Védrine, or Sorokine, or Sartre, or anyone else in their circle. They will necessarily see through the camouflage to what remains unrepresented.[60] Yet out of the camouflage Beauvoir has produced something else. Partly we see the representation of the difficulty of producing an enunciatory position from which a woman who has sex with women without being a lesbian can speak. Partly we see a representation of that part of sexuality that cannot be assumed in the first person. These two parts probably go together, for the further one's sexual practices are from being caught up in the form of a sexual identity, the less access they are likely to have, at least in our culture, to first-person expression.[61]

I suggested earlier that Sartre and Beauvoir, in repeatedly explaining Dos Passos to themselves and to us, were trying to establish a certain metapragmatic function, productive of a certain experience of reading, a function and an experience that others might not share and might contest. I have been doing something similar here, in providing a context for reading Beauvoir's letters and her first novel. Sexual forms, and especially nonmainstream, unofficial, misfit ones, have, as I have noted already several times, a heavily pragmatic or indexical (a diminished semantic) existence. Their transmission, perpetuation, and survival depend on the transmission of the metapragmatic functions that enable people to participate in them meaningfully—in practical ways of which they may be mostly unaware or to which they may have great difficulty giving semantic form—and in ways that often do not exist much in the first-person mode. Beauvoir's *L'invitée*, contextualized in this way (and without this context it is perhaps difficult to see in this way), becomes an interesting case of a novel serving instrumentally both as a record and a relay of those pragmatic and metapragmatic functions as they might have been enacted in one very particular sexual culture. The third person of free indirect discourse in *L'invitée* thus recalls of course the difficulty of Beauvoir's own enunciatory position regarding her sexuality, but also that part of a misfit sexuality whose existence is hard to note in any other mode.

Coda: "The Lesbian"

Six years after the publication of *L'invitée* (1943), Beauvoir would publish *The Second Sex*. It appeared in two volumes, one in June and one in November of 1949. Several chapters of the second of the two volumes would appear in the journal *Les Temps Modernes* shortly before the first volume itself was published: "Sexual Initiation" appeared there in May 1949, and "The Lesbian" and part of "The Mother" in June. Much scandal and outrage ensued.[62] It can be difficult for readers today to conceive of the outrage the volumes, and especially the chapters that were published early in *Les Temps Modernes*, provoked in a certain sector of the French reading public, just as it can be difficult to appreciate how important the volume was for many readers eager for public discussion of the topics it broached. It is held by many these days that the volume, and perhaps particularly the chapter on "The Lesbian," hasn't aged well. In an article on that chapter published in 2004, Hazel Barnes is quite blunt: "This is not the best of Beauvoir's chapters. The supporting research is thin. The presentation is not well organized. In certain key passages her writing does not show its habitual clarity, a failing that certain readers have interpreted as a reflection of the author's own uncertainty or ambivalence."[63] Barnes notes in particular that it is difficult to understand why Beauvoir could not have made better use of her own experience here, or the experience of others in her circle. (Beauvoir apparently claimed not to have consulted any of her lesbian acquaintances while writing the chapter.) Some later readers have even gone so far, Barnes notes, as to accuse Beauvoir of writing about lesbianism from a heterosexually biased perspective. For Barnes, on the other hand, it seems clear that Beauvoir is writing about lesbians from the perspective of a bisexual woman, assuming that her discussion of lesbians applies only to women whose sexuality *exclusively* involves other women. We might then say that the chapter offers another example of the problem of register and enregisterment that I discussed in relation to Colette in my first chapter. Different people hear different registers when they read Beauvoir's "The Lesbian." Based on their different pragmatic senses of the available registers for speaking about same-sex sexualities, they construct hypotheses regarding the social position of the speaker in question (Beauvoir). Registers shift over time, as do the social positions they index. Knowledge about them is also (as we saw in Genet's *Querelle*) inconsistently distributed across a social field at any given time, which means people are always guessing, and sometimes metapragmatically inquiring about, the register assumptions and practices of their interlocutors. Is Beauvoir backward-looking like Colette, whom she cites on a number of occasions?[64] Is she sexually modern for her moment? As time has passed, has she been left behind?[65] What is her own involvement in the sexuality she is discussing? What is the genre of the chapter "The Lesbian"?[66] As usual, we position ourselves by taking a position.

Let me here, to round off this chapter, cite just one passage from "The Lesbian." Barnes tells us (330) that it is the passage most frequently cited by those critics of Beauvoir who reproach her for being insufficiently supportive of lesbians. I cite it because of its relevance to *L'invitée* and because it allows us to notice once again the importance of register. The passage comes just before the end of the chapter, when Beauvoir is speaking of the hostility certain "virile homosexual women" feel toward men. Here it is, in English and in French:

> This complex hostility is one of the reasons that leads many homosexual women to flaunt their sexuality; they only socialize among themselves; they form their own kind of clubs to show they have no more need of men socially than sexually. First lesbians play at being men; then being a lesbian itself becomes an act; male dress, at first only a costume, becomes a livery; and the woman who claims to want to escape from male oppression ends up the slave of the very character she has created; she had wanted not to be shut up in a

woman's situation, yet she imprisons herself in that of the lesbian. Nothing gives a worse impression of narrow-mindedness and of mutilation than these cliques of emancipated women.[67]

(Cette hostilité complexe est une des raisons qui conduit certaines homosex-uelles à s'afficher; elles ne se fréquentent qu'entre elles; elles forment des sortes de clubs pour manifester qu'elles n'ont pas plus besoin des hommes socialement que sexuellement. De là, on glisse facilement à d'inutiles fanfaronnades et à toutes les comédies de l'inauthenticité. La lesbienne joue d'abord à être un homme; ensuite être lesbienne même devient un jeu; le travesti, de déguise-ment se change en une livrée; et la femme sous prétexte de se soustraire à l'oppression du mâle se fait l'esclave de son personnage; elle n'a pas voulu s'en-fermer dans la situation de femme, elle s'emprisonne dans celle de lesbienne. Rien ne donne une pire impression d'étroitesse d'esprit et de mutilation que ces clans de femmes affranchies.)

Cited here at the end of this chapter, the passage clearly resonates with the implicit distinction that is drawn in *L'invitée* between the bar in Montmartre frequented by lesbians and the Bal Nègre where Françoise and Xavière are able to dance together and be seen as a couple without being "imprisoned" in an identity. It resonates as well, looking backward in time just a little bit, to the position we saw Colette taking in *Ces plaisirs . . .* , deprecating the female masculinity she associated with certain contemporary forms of lesbianism (arguably in part because it represented for her a way of flaunting one's sex-uality), while honoring a more femino-centric eroticism with a more hazy relation to sexuality, such as that she found in the example of the Ladies of Llangollen. Looking forward in time, it resonates with an ideological position we will encounter in more detail in the next chapter, one hostile to the crea-tion of communities around sexual identities, hostile to identity politics itself. As Scott Gunther notes in *The Elastic Closet*, "In recent decades, the French rhetoric of universalism has stymied French homosexuals from mobilizing politically around sexual identities and has encouraged various manifestations of social respectability along with a surprisingly strong reverence for hetero-normative values."[68] The clash between a universalist ideology and identity politics seems nascent already in this passage from *The Second Sex*.

But if we make the mental effort to hold this passage in the context I have been working to elaborate throughout this chapter, one in which Beauvoir's misfit sexuality registers itself without ever finding a secure platform on which to represent itself explicitly, then what we might hear here, if we tune our ears to a particular register, is a misfit sexuality speaking, pointing to some kind of categorically in-between space in which it exists as best it can. In *The*

Female Complaint, Lauren Berlant calls femininity itself a genre, and clarifies that a genre is "an aesthetic structure of affective expectation, an institution or formation that absorbs all kinds of small variations or modifications." It is a helpful way of looking at things. Berlant continues: "To call an identity like a sexual identity a genre is to think about it as something repeated, detailed, and stretched while retaining its intelligibility, its capacity to remain readable or audible across the field of all its variations."[69] It is not to disagree with Berlant's wonderful description to note that it seems in the case of misfit sexualities, which are also caught up in and lived through genres, or sometimes stuck in the spaces between genres (borrowing from them to patch new ones together, or trying to find fixes to keep old ones viable), that the intelligibility (to the extent that it is even clearly being sought after) is never confirmed, is always in doubt, and that the readability or the audibility of the genre(s) invoked are always being interfered with by various kinds of semiotic noise.[70] This helps us to appreciate how misfit sexualities endure in situations of ongoing denotational incapacity, situations of semiotic frustration that often tax the expressive resources—along with the patience and equanimity—of the people involved.

The Contexts of Marguerite Duras's Homophobia

Similar to my interests in the previous chapter, part of my interest in this chapter on Duras is in a way of thinking about texts in relation to context—in particular the text of Duras's book *The Malady of Death* (along with some of her other writings published around the same time, the late 1970s and early to mid-1980s), which I would like to reinstall, so to speak, in a particular set of contexts, and then to think about how the dynamic relation between text and context itself, rather than the text or the contexts on their own, reveals something about the social pragmatics of misfit sexualities and about the uses of literary texts in the history of these sexualities. Or, put another way, my goal, in examining a particular episode in France in the 1970s and 1980s, is to pursue a way of thinking about literature as a complex set not just of interrelated texts but also of social activities as well as writerly practices, as a kind of interactive process during many moments of which different evanescent aspects of sexuality occasionally find expression. This involves considering sexuality as an evolving, circulating set of cultural concepts and practices of which, in some ways, sexual identities are themselves an effect. I am considering *The Malady of Death* and its contexts—especially different bits of discourse generated around it—to form together one *interactional* text, whose structures of relevance, especially those structures of relevance having to do with misfit sexualities, are what are under discussion here. As Michael Silverstein puts it, "The problem of informational 'relevance' and the problem of how discourse comes to some kind of segmentable textual 'form' as *effective social interaction* are interrelated and cannot be either productively stated or solved independently."[1] To reinstall a text in one of its earlier contexts is to point out that the links (indexical relations) between a text considered *interactive* (as opposed to a text already segmented, its beginning and ending authoritatively established) and its contexts are always under negotiation, subject to debate and contestation, more or less amenable to revision, that there cannot be a finalized set of things that are *relevant* in the text/context relation, that relevance is attained over interactive time. The "meaning" of a literary text is largely the product of this ongoing process of negotiating structures of relevance.

To repeat some of the main points of previous chapters, by misfit sexualities, I mean those sexualities that often escape dominant, and sometimes even residual or emergent, categories of apprehension.[2] Such sexualities frequently resist representation by the way they fail to conform to the categories that normally enable the apprehension of sexuality. It is often difficult to *refer* to or to *denote* these sexualities, because they do not exactly have a name, or because naming them with an extant name would betray something about them. If they cannot exactly be referred to, if they do not have a strong *semantic* existence, they can nonetheless be gestured at; they can, to varying degrees, exist pragmatically. That is, if they exist at all (which they do), and if they can be perpetuated (which they can), it is usually in practical (as opposed to theoretical or representational) ways that escape both easy representation and easy conceptualization.

Duras's relationship with Yann Andréa—the experience that is arguably at the heart of *The Malady of Death* (and several texts associated with it, including *Blue Eyes, Black Hair*)—involved one of these misfit sexualities. As we saw in the case of Beauvoir's *L'invitée* and the context I reconstructed for it, a sexuality of this kind registers itself not in any particular representation, but in relations between texts, in the pattern of the scattering of its traces across different platforms, different texts, different genres. Let me begin to assemble some of the scattered traces that can be brought to bear upon *The Malady of Death*, that allow something "about" that text to become visible.

Here is something Duras said on June 18, 1981, in Paris in an interview with Suzanne Lamy:

> Men and women. We are irreconcilable, yet still we try, as we have for centuries, to reconcile ourselves to each other. With each love we do this. This is what I call the fabulous richness of heterosexuality. And, on the other hand, the incommensurable poverty of homosexuality. They love themselves in loving the other. Whereas we love our inverted image. We love our opposite, our antidote, our own hell. That is where the immensity of this richness is to be found.[3]
>
> (Nous, l'homme et la femme. Nous sommes irréconciliables, nous essayons toujours, depuis des millénaires de nous réconcilier. Cela à chaque amour. C'est ça que j'appelle la richesse fabuleuse de l'hétérosexualité. Et par contre

l'incommensurable misère de l'homosexualité. Ils s'aiment eux-mêmes en aimant l'autre. Tandis que nous aimons notre image inversée. Nous aimons notre contraire, nous aimons notre antidote, nous aimons notre enfer. Et c'est ça, l'immensité de la richesse.)

My interest is not only in how something like this (a perfectly banal, clichéd, and familiar set of hostile observations about homosexuality) can come to be said by someone like Duras in 1981, but also in what it expresses beyond its apparent direct meaning.[4] My idea is not to excuse this kind of speech but to begin to notice that what is being expressed here is not just what is said—in all its palpable symbolic violence—but also something about a person or persons, about a culture, and about a sexuality that is finding it can enunciate itself only with great difficulty within its world of discourse.

Late in his life, and at roughly the same time that Duras wrote *The Malady of Death* and gave the interview from which I just cited, the American sociologist Erving Goffman wrote an essay called "Felicity's Condition" that was published posthumously in 1983 in the *American Journal of Sociology*. The large topic Goffman addresses in that essay has to do with what he calls the "bases of constraint in formulating utterances," in particular with the phenomenon of "social propriety" that determines, among other things what can be said to whom and when.[5] At one point Goffman frames his question this way: "Given that you have something that you want to utter to a particular other, how do you go about getting into the circumstances that will allow you appropriately to do so?" (32). And he asks us at a certain point in his discussion to "consider some of the circumstances in which individuals may feel that to make a statement they must first establish a state of talk to house it in" (36). I bring Duras and Goffman together in this way because I am curious about how a situation might have occurred in the early 1980s in which Duras assumed or was granted the authority to speak in the way we have just seen her speaking, and to write what she wrote in *The Malady of Death*—a work, as we shall see, that could be said to stand as an exemplification of her comments on homosexuality from the 1981 interview. What different forces contributed to producing a state of talk that could appropriately (or inappropriately?) house utterances such as these? To whom might they have been addressed? How were they received? How are they to be received now?

An ideology of literature, beliefs about what it is and what it is for, and practices related to it, played a role in building that house of discourse for Duras. So to start with we might ask quite large questions, such as: Why would anyone think of literature as a place in which to learn of, to experience something about, or to authorize discourse about sexuality? What mechanisms would create the belief that a literary author could speak or write authoritatively about sexuality, and how might that authority arise in particular out of the makeup of the literary practices and the literary field involved?

Across much of her career, when Duras spoke or wrote, she cultivated a certain attitude, a certain "literary" stance toward language, that she expected her listeners and readers to appreciate and participate in with her. We might call it an *oracular* stance. About the book *Emily L.* that she published in 1987, she said in an interview with Didier Eribon: "I sometimes have the feeling that I didn't write this book. That it passed through me, passed through that space where I found myself. Almost as if I were a spectator at its writing."[6] In 1977, in an interview about her film *Le camion* (*The Truck*), Duras spoke of her "passion to be nothing but a kind of space of total availability to what is out there."[7] These are but two of many expressions she gave to what I call her oracular stance, a stance key to her writing practices as well as to her literary ideology.[8] We could also say that this practice of oracularity was related to the position Duras took up in the French literary field as she gave a particular twist to the writing styles and preoccupations of people such as George Bataille and Maurice Blanchot, as she constructed her affiliation with these other writers. This can help explain what we will observe to be her preoccupation with a Bataille-inflected version of the problem of finitude, that is to say the problem of understanding what kinds of limits exist between different beings, and the problem of dealing with (enjoying, enhancing, expanding, ignoring, repressing) the connection that sexuality does or does not provide between otherwise finite beings.[9]

I pause here briefly to expand on what an oracular stance, as I am calling it, might be. Émile Benveniste famously defined the first person in the following way: "*I* signifies 'the person who is uttering the present instance of discourse containing *I*.'"[10] Yet things can be more complicated, as ethnographic work has the potential to help us see. Alan Rumsey, for instance, in an article drawing on fieldwork done by various people in Polynesia and New Guinea, notes the occurrence of a usage "by chiefs of the first person singular 'I' to refer at once to themselves and to the social collectivity . . . with which they are identified," adding that "the social identity indexed by 'I' (or 'my') is capable of changing in scope according to its anaphoric context." He summarizes:

> It should be clear that we cannot presume a constant reality called "the self" which, everywhere it exists, is directly expressed by the pronoun "I." Rather than indexing a constant self, what each situated use of this pronoun does is to index its speaker in such a way as to entail what Erving Goffman called a

"footing" from which she speaks: in Goffman's terms her current "alignment," "set," or "projected self." . . . Speech-act participants move in and out of footings strategically through an interplay between the direct indexicality of words such as "I" and "you" and their anaphoric relations to other expressions in the surrounding context of discourse.[11]

The "footing" Duras endeavors to produce for herself in her works and via her statements about her works also draws on a way of discussing what happens in literary writing (*écriture*) that was elaborated by Blanchot. Two crucial essays of his in this regard can be found in *The Infinite Conversation*, "Everyday Speech" and "The Narrative Voice (the 'he,' the neutral)." In the first essay, Blanchot writes that "the everyday is the movement by which man, as though without knowing it, holds himself back in human anonymity. In the everyday we have no name, little personal reality, scarcely a figure, just as we have no social determination to sustain or enclose us."[12] As I show in what follows, this experience of *l'anonymat humain* is central to Duras's vision both of politics and of (oracular) writing.

Blanchot actually mentions Duras in "The Narrative Voice," noting in the same paragraph in which he mentions her that narration is the space of "the intrusion of the other. . . . But when the other is speaking, no one speaks because the other . . . is precisely never simply the other. The other is neither the one nor the other, and the neutral that indicates it withdraws it from both, as it does from unity, always establishing it outside the term, the act, or the subject through which it claims to offer itself."[13] Duras's literary first person, we could say, is meant to be a space in which the other (the collectivity, human anonymity) intrudes. For Duras, it is only writing in which this oracular intrusion is palpable that should properly be called writing (*écriture*).

The aura of oracularity that came to surround both Duras's person and her texts was possible because of the state of the cultural field around her. Part of her brilliance as a literary artist was to know with great precision how to exploit the resources of that field to her best advantage. The oracular role was one that she found ready-made in the literary field, and that she stepped into and made her own. That oracular speech could focus on sexuality in particular emerged as a possibility within the French literary field of the mid- to late twentieth century, and such speech was especially salient in certain avant-garde writings of the early 1970s. We could think of this practice of oracularity as a resource that was collectively produced across a number of generations of writers, and one that Duras exploited with unquestionable mastery across several decades.

Alongside Duras in this effort we could, for instance, place a figure such as Pierre Guyotat. Different writers in the 1960s and 1970s (and beyond) would develop this conjuncture between writing and sexuality in different ways, striking a variety of avant-garde postures and developing an array of experimental writing practices. For many such writers, Bataille, Blanchot, Beckett, and a number of surrealists would be claimed as important precursors—although not always in the same ways. Before considering Duras's own relation to Bataille and Blanchot, let us examine briefly the exemplary case of Guyotat and some of the implications that can be drawn from it.[14] The French government's effort to censure Guyotat's 1970 novel *Eden, Eden, Eden* provided the occasion for a number of writers and intellectuals to express themselves at length regarding literature's relationship to sexuality, and the texts that were written in his defense encapsulate rather neatly much of the avant-gardist ideology of the time.[15] Consider some remarks Michel Foucault made in 1970 as part of an effort to protect Guyotat's novel from legal sanctions.[16] Foucault's remarks come from an open letter to Guyotat in support of *Eden, Eden, Eden*, published in the newsweekly *Le Nouvel Observateur*. There Foucault offers a description (in language that seems very much typical of its moment) of Guyotat's theoretical and representational achievement in his novelistic treatment of sexuality, commenting in particular on the ways that Guyotat's text forces us to question a standard intellectual habit of viewing sexuality as a characteristic attached to an individual subjectivity. (The project he assigns to Guyotat was in fact a collective one in which many avant-gardist writers were caught up.)

I have the impression that you thereby connect with what we have known about sexuality for some time, carefully shielding ourselves from this knowledge in order to protect the primacy of the subject, the unity of the individual, and the abstraction of "sex": that sexuality is not, on the level of the body, something like its "sex," nor is it a method of communication from one body to another, nor the fundamental and primary desire of the individual. It is rather that the very framework of its processes is there well before any individual, and the individual is only a precarious, provisory prolongation of it, one that is quickly effaced. The individual is finally only a pale form that surges up for a few instants from a huge, persistent, and repetitive stratum. Individuals are the pseudopodia of sexuality, and quickly retracted. If we wish really to know what we know, we will have to give up what we imagine to be our individuality, our self, our positions as subjects. In your text, it is perhaps the first time that the relations between the individual and sexuality are decisively and forthrightly reversed: we no longer have characters being effaced in favor of elements of a novel, structures, personal pronouns, but rather sexuality which crosses to the other side of the individual and ceases to be "subjugated."[17]

We might note that sexual identity and identity politics (themselves often taken to be social constructs that received new energy and took on new importance in the post-1960s world) seem incidental to the avant-gardist project of understanding sexuality itself as some kind of excessive aspect of human (and not only human, obviously, for any reader of Guyotat) existence.

When sexuality comes up in Duras's oracular speech, her discourse often resonates with a kind of hostility to identity politics that was typical of certain strains of leftist discourse in these years (Guyotat being one instance). "Il n'y a pas de sexualité masculine ou féminine," Duras says in an interview from 1980: "There is no specifically masculine or feminine form of sexuality. There is only one sexuality in which all relations swim. Whatever is particular about homosexuality is not sealed in watertight."[18] This is but one instance of an utterance that hints at a kind of subterranean tension developing in these years between avant-gardist literary ideologies and identity-based social movements.

Avant-gardist writers who took up the subject of sexuality at this time sought out writing practices appropriate to their theoretical viewpoint. In a text Duras wrote in May 1968 as part of her work with the Comité d'action étudiant-écrivains (of which Blanchot was also a member), she emphasized "each person's desire to be interchangeable with everyone else" (la volonté de chacun d'être interchangeable), noting that "this promoting of depersonhood seems the only truly revolutionary kind of promotion. It goes along with the promoting of one's personhood separate from the roles one plays" (cette promotion de la dépersonne nous paraît être la seule révolutionnaire. Elle s'accompagne de la promotion de la personne séparée de son personnage).[19] What kind of writing practice could instantiate an ideological program of this kind? How would people engaged in such writing practices interact with social movements based on identity politics and with the publics and the cultural producers affiliated with those movements?

In these years, a set of meanings beginning to coalesce around the word *écriture* was a key component in the effort to tie together different avant-gardist literary practices and radical sociopolitical agendas (or in the tensions that came into being between them). Given the difficulty of much of this writing, the project of linking it to different leftist political movements posed a number of challenges. Over and over again in these years, writers with an interest in the "subversive" potential of sexually explicit, avant-garde writing felt obliged to note that the public for their writing was, in fact, quite small, and that this fact was linked to the various practices of *écriture* in which they were invested.[20] An interview with Guyotat (in which writers are viewed as researchers pursuing a scientific project through the practices of writing they develop) published in *Tel Quel* in 1970 aptly illustrates the problem:

A question presents itself here, given that you say you are politically engaged alongside the working class. It has to do with the accessibility of your writing. What do you have to say on this subject at the present moment?

. . . it would be indecent either to claim that "workers" are, as things stand, well suited to understand texts like these—that's simply false and poisons the entire contemporary "cultural" process—or to demand that a researcher abdicate his or her role as a researcher for what are claimed to be the immediate needs of social and political efficacy. The consequence of this would be that he or she would have to give up all the recent discoveries in literary language. No, the way for a writer [l'homme d'écriture] to give the working class (excluded from power and therefore from culture) a better idea of what writing might have been in other times is to work away at his research.[21]

Guyotat imagines in this interview and related texts that these avant-garde literary practitioners/researchers are developing an analysis of the past and present functions of writing that could serve somehow to prepare the working class for an understanding—one both materialist and rational—of what is "new" about the present moment.

Other writers, such as Duras, would doubtless put things somewhat differently, but do insist on the political content of their work, however inaccessible it might be. While talking about her film *Le camion*, for instance, she will insist that her political engagement with communism is the central experience of her life, and that one translation for the word "communism" is "love." "In the beginning," Duras says, "I thought that it [the film] told the story of what happened between the truck driver and the woman. In fact, it's a political story. It's also the story of me and politics." She insists that the film places her on an equal footing with everyone. "I would like for *Le camion* to be released in popular cinemas. Not just in cinemas in the 5th arrondissement [where people who like art movies might go see it]." Michelle Porte, interviewing her, seconds her ambition: "The film is made in a way that relates to popular narration, the traditional teller of tales, anyone can relate to it, it relates to everyone."[22] Needless to say, Porte was being a bit optimistic, or even perhaps, indecent, to return to Guyotat's word. Why expect that popular audiences would be well suited to Duras's idiosyncratic, hieratic style of filmmaking? These days it is next to impossible to find a copy of *Le camion* to see.[23]

In any case, the word *écriture* itself in these years became a kind of shibboleth in a debate about what constitutes committed writing (politically efficacious writing), what constitutes avant-gardist writing, and what the relation between those two kinds of writing would be. Duras was one of the rare practitioners of an avant-gardist practice of *écriture* who also occasionally managed, in the 1970s and 1980s, to achieve a kind of popular success that arguably peaked in 1984 with the publication of *The Lover*, which became a best seller. In a television interview shortly after the publication of *The Lover*, Duras rehashed the terms of the debate about *écriture*, commenting: "Sartre didn't write; he didn't know what writing was. He always had other issues he was concerned with. . . . He always drew from social concerns. . . . He wasn't someone about whom I would say, he wrote. Blanchot wrote. Bataille wrote. I'm not making a value judgment here."[24] This way of mobilizing the figures of Sartre, Blanchot, and Bataille turns out to provide important clues for understanding part of what is going on in Duras's own *The Malady of Death*. Her notion of what *écriture* is as a practice is central to the production of that text, just as her sense of how she fits into a tradition that includes Bataille and Blanchot and that understands its project in distinction to the figures of Sartre and Genet is central to what the text might mean.[25]

When Duras comments that Sartre did not know what it was to "write" and links this to the fact that he always had "social" concerns that inhibited his ability to experience what "writing" could be, she disassociates political commitments of a certain kind from the practice of writing with which she aligns herself—but clearly she does so to align that practice of writing with a different experience that could also lay claim to being called "political," a kind of experience often associated in the latter half of the twentieth century not just with writers such as Blanchot, Bataille, and Duras but also with words like "communication," "communion," and "communism"—words to which they give a particular inflection. Their mobilization of these words needs to be understood in opposition to *communautarisme*, the French equivalent of "identity politics," to which there is a normative hostility in many segments of French society, from radical writers and philosophers to mainstream politicians, to dictionaries such as the *Petit Robert*, which defines *communautarisme* as a "system that expands the formation of communities (ethnic, religious, cultural, social . . .), capable of dividing the nation to the detriment of integration."[26] The objection to identity politics put forth by the *Petit Robert* is due to its purported divisive potential, its potential to trouble an always already troubled agenda of integration (in which certain kinds of difference are effaced to stabilize a normative—and obviously neither neutral nor disinterested—national identity).

The other major objection that has frequently recurred in discourse about sexuality in France has been that identity politics limits the radical potential of a given sexuality.[27] Thus Gilles Deleuze could write in 1974 in a preface to a book by the gay activist Guy Hocquenghem that, "for the new kind of homosexual, it's a question first of laying claim to the right to be that way, in

order finally to say: no one is that way, it doesn't exist."[28] The rhetorical gesture
Deleuze makes here is made again nearly a decade later (1983), this time in a
gay magazine, *Masques*, in a review of Patrice Chéreau's first movie, *L'homme
blessé* (*The Wounded Man*) (with a screenplay written by Hervé Guibert). Consider the terms in which the critic Alain Sanzio praised the movie:

> As I see it, *The Wounded Man* is one of the first films that, while representing
> the story of a passion between two people of the same sex, is not a homo-
> sexual film. *The Wounded Man* blows these categories to pieces, demonstrating
> their obsoleteness. The two main characters are not identified as homosexual:
> whether they are or not is a question of no interest. Moreover, the relation
> between them is not coded according to one or the other available registers
> to which we have become accustomed over the last two hundred years. It is
> understood on the order of any other *human* relationship, I would say.[29]

Sanzio seems to take the sexuality the film represents, a sexuality that happens
between men in train station restrooms and other anonymous semipublic locations, as an instance of something new, challenging, and avant-gardist—as
opposed to a centuries old kind of sexuality between men that perhaps often
exists alongside other more organized and identitarian forms. This is a conundrum often encountered in sexuality studies then and now: the impulse
to imagine that there is something necessarily radical or innovative about a
sexuality that happens outside or on the margins of available identity categories, which sometimes leads people to speak as if the participants in these
often quite vulnerable sexualities were self-consciously enacting some kind
of intentional critique of other identitarian social forms of sexuality, as if they
were intentionally challenging identitarian norms.[30] Watching *L'hommé blessé*
today, it is difficult to lend credence to Sanzio's enthusiastic assertions. Rather,
the film seems to represent a quite recognizable sexual culture between men (a
misfit one that draws on a specific set of social forms) with a long history of its
own, perhaps a history that has sometimes closely paralleled the history of the
identitarian "homosexuality" Sanzio seems so interested in disparaging, perhaps in such a close parallel that the histories could sometimes be confused.
Sanzio's anti-identitarian discourse might seem odd in someone writing for
Masques, one of the more significant post-1968 gay and lesbian publications
in France, a product of the gay social movement. Yet it is, in fact, typical. As a
discourse, it might even be taken to be emblematic of a certain way of being
gay in those years.[31] A similar situation can be found a couple of years earlier
in an interview Duras gave to the magazine *Gai pied*.

   Gai pied, along with *Masques* one of the more significant post-1968 "gay"
publications in France (both first appeared in 1979), published this interview

with Duras in one of its earliest issues. Here it is the interviewer who poses the leading question that seemed aimed at provoking her to respond with some version of the discourse we have seen Deleuze and Sanzio voicing. Duras does not fully take the bait:

> *Is it your impression that homosexuality has now been fully co-opted?*
> I don't think it's been fully co-opted yet, but rather that it is becoming organized, that it is trying to organize itself.
>
> *And this is a new thing, isn't it, that homosexuality is becoming organized?*
> All I can say in response is this: however difficult it may be to admit or accept this, it was something that had to happen. Of course there is a lot to worry about, and the greatest fear is related to the power any organization ends up producing. There is no such thing as an innocent organization.
>
> *From the moment homosexuals start to form groups, found journals, attempt to pursue political goals, shouldn't we be worried that homosexuality will be losing something of its specificity?*
> It is always the case that organizing results in the retreat of a certain kind of wildness or innocence or childhood. Yet again surely it was inevitable that you would start organizing yourselves?[32]

When read today, these texts from the 1970s and early 1980s, before the AIDS epidemic and its consequences had entered anyone's awareness, sound odd, somehow naive, indeed, "innocent," to use Duras's word. In one of her last essays, Eve Kosofsky Sedgwick gives an invigorating account of the utopian hopes and theoretical ambitions of this "post-1968 moment," noting how for "Hocquenghem's cohort" there was an impulse to seek out "danger [as] a revolutionary flash point to be sought out and exploited." Sedgwick recalls how "a utopian motive, or a catastrophe-seeking or otherwise revolutionary one, actually could have come to imbue many people's sexual pleasures as well as their theorizing and, perhaps, activism."[33] Within this historical moment, we could say, there was a sense of newness (however justifiable or unjustifiable, however sustainable or unsustainable) that certain people felt in relation to their sexualities, a sense of openness and possibility, a sense of an uncertain and unpredictable future to the shape of sexuality itself in any given individual instance. Such people were seeking out the means to express this supposedly open and unfixable experience of sexuality or this set of beliefs of sexuality. In doing so, they would sometimes denigrate other relations (historical, practical, and discursive) to same-sex sexuality. Deleuze again:

> It's obvious that Hocquenghem doesn't speak like Gide, nor like Proust, even less like Peyrefitte: but style is politics—as it is differences between generations,

ways of saying "I." . . . Based on a new style, homosexuality today produces
statements that have no bearing on, that should have no bearing on, homosexuality itself.[34]

One way to understand what is going on in many of the utterances in this
vein that can be found in these years is to think of them as setting out to perform a kind of discursive clearing, setting out to make space for new ways of
speaking. They also concomitantly perform a kind of discursive maintenance
work, maintaining this newish way of speaking and seeking to make it ever
more authoritative. As Bourdieu notes in "The Production and Reproduction
of Legitimate Language," the perpetuation in time and the extension in space
of legitimate language requires a "process of continuous creation . . . unceasing
struggles between . . . different authorities."[35] In such discursive maintenance
work, people of course make use of older authorities (Bataille and Blanchot
in Duras's case) to contest the discursive positions they oppose and to bolster
the positions they occupy. They may also sometimes find themselves moving
uncomfortably close to, beginning to sound like, voices emanating from positions of a political persuasion they cannot imagine themselves belonging to.
Thus the "revolutionary" anti-identitarianism of a Hocquenghem, or a Duras,
or a Bataille, or a Deleuze can, over time and in specific contexts, come to
sound like the kind of reactionary opposition to claims made by progressive
social movements that characterizes a certain conservative French "republi-
can" discourse that favors integration over specificity or singularity or pecu-
liarity.[36] Duras's *Malady of Death* can serve as a pointed case of these kinds of
anomalies within discursive history. We can understand something of where
this history is coming from by noting how much it relies on resources taken
from Bataille's writings disparaging Jean Genet.

Bataille (and Blanchot) often chose to cast the reading and writing practices
in which they engaged in opposition to the ideology and practices of literature
advocated by Sartre and the team organized around Sartre's journal *Les Temps
Modernes*. (Sartre, of course, would return the favor on occasion.) Doubtless
partly because Genet became so connected to Sartre with the publication of
Sartre's *Saint Genet* in 1952, Genet's name and his work became caught up in
this somewhat obsessive-compulsive way of insisting on an insurmountable
opposition between Sartre and Bataille within the French intellectual field.[37]
For instance, in 1952 Bataille chose to advocate for his own literary ideology
by attacking Genet's novelistic practice; critiques of Genet in precisely the
same terms that Bataille used can be found coming from the pens of Blanchot
and Duras a few years later. The cumulative effect of this stream of Bataille-

school discourse critiquing Genet is part of what enables Duras to insist in 1980 on a certain necessarily nontransgressive element to identity-based same-sex relations, to offer an "avant-gardist" critique of homosexuality that today, several decades later, and perhaps even in 1980 could sound simply homophobic. The discourse of Bataille helps establish the state of discourse in which the homophobic discourse of Duras could occur, in written texts and during spoken occasions.[38] For *The Malady of Death* can be seen as a re-formulation of Bataille's critique of Genet, with its antihomosexual potential fully foregrounded.

Bataille's critique of Genet as a novelist was built around his sense of what is missing from the *experience* of reading Genet. What is missing is "the consciousness of that lightning strike that constitutes authentic communication" (la conscience de la fulguration qu'est la communication authentique). Bataille continues:

> In the depression resulting from these inadequate exchanges, where a glassy barrier is maintained between the reader and the author, I am sure about one thing: humanity is not composed of isolated beings but of communication between them. Never are we revealed, even to ourselves, other than in a network of communications with others. We are swimming in communication, we are reduced to this incessant communication whose absence we feel, even in the depths of solitude, like the suggestion of multiple possibilities, like the expectation of the moment when it is accomplished in a cry heard by others.[39]

Genet, Bataille claims (for no good reason, it has to be said), cannot offer any such experience to his readers.

Remember Duras's text from 1968, extolling "each person's desire to be interchangeable with everyone else." There she strikes a Bataillean stance in support of the political effervescence of that particular moment. Remember one of her statements from the interview in *Gai pied* in 1980: "There is only one sexuality in which all relations swim. Whatever is particular about homosexuality is not sealed in watertight." There she gives a Bataillean spin to one of the currents of radical discourses on sexuality around her that meant simultaneously to advocate *for* freedom of expression of same-sex sexualities but *against* identity politics.

In similar fashion to Bataille, Blanchot opines in 1953 that Genet falls short of an understanding of the most radical experience of literature (of which Samuel Beckett provides an example). To attain that experience, "the work demands that . . . the man who writes it sacrifice himself for the work, become other—not other than the living man he was, the writer with his duties, his satisfactions, and his interests, but he must become no one, the empty and animated space where the call of the work resounds." If Genet fails to meet this demand of the work of literature, it is because his work seems best to fit with "a classical way of describing the literary experience, in which one sees the writer happily deliver himself from the dark part of himself by a work in which that part becomes, as if by a miracle, the happiness and clarity stemming from the work itself, in which the writer finds a refuge and, even better, the flourishing of his lonely self in free communication with the other."[40] For Blanchot, it almost seems that Genet's "failure" as a writer has to do with what Blanchot considers a practice of identity politics. Genet writes about who he is so that others can see him as that, Blanchot seems to be suggesting. Genet does not put himself or his reader at risk.

A few years later, Duras picks up where Blanchot left off, in a short article she wrote on Bataille that appeared in 1958. She concludes the article comparing Genet and Bataille, the comparison being, of course, in Bataille's favor:

> Genet's abjection, so severely criticized by Bataille, expresses the singularity of his characters. It brings them out into themselves, into a royalty that is utterly unique because irreplaceable and "incommunicable." By contrast, Edwarda and Dirty [two of Bataille's characters] are possessed by dispossession. If Dirty still likes and prefers one person in the world, Edwarda likes and prefers no one. Her prostitution has penetrated her heart. Bataille's abjection, unlike that of Genet, delivers his characters from their singularity and brings them out into their indeterminacy. They are no longer caught in the gangue of an individual royalty but are on their way toward dissolution, toward annihilation: we meet them in passing.[41]

The movement from "singularity" to "indeterminacy" resonates both with a Bataillean discourse of self-disruptive communication and with various post-1968 avant-gardist discourses about radically indeterminate forms of sexuality. (Not that sexuality, in Bataille's own writing, ever ventured far from what we might as well call heterosexuality.)

Commentators have had a hard time explaining this odd habit of criticizing Genet for failing to meet a certain set of Bataillean expectations—especially since, to many of these commentators, Bataille's critique makes no sense. It would seem at least as reasonable to claim that Genet, in many of his works, does precisely what Duras, Blanchot, and Bataille accuse him of being unable to do: offer a reading experience that has the potential to shake up any reader's sense of the contours of their own singularity. "Nothing could be more surprising," Yve-Alain Bois notes, "than Bataille's very critical attitude toward Jean Genet, an author whose entire output should, as Jacques Derrida has remarked, have brought these two sensibilities together."[42] Bois here refers to

Derrida's discussion in *Glas* of Bataille's remarks on Genet.[43] Eribon also refers to this same moment in Derrida in his treatment of the question of the relation between Genet and Bataille in *Une morale du minoritaire*, where he points out that "the destabilizing contact with Genet's books" called to the surface of Bataille's writing a disciplinary impulse that had hitherto been hidden within his thought on transgression.[44]

Rather than try to ascertain possible underlying reasons for the seeming oddity of the critique of Genet voiced by Bataille and then recirculated by Blanchot and Duras, I want to pose a different question, on the effects of the use of the "same" discourse in different situations at different times. Obviously, by reusing Bataille's discourse, Blanchot and Duras affiliate themselves with Bataille; they do a kind of intellectual identity work, even if the discourse they revoice is a discourse critiquing identity.[45] But as the contexts in which this discourse is revoiced shift over time, the potential meaning produced by the discourse shifts, and in this case, as we shall see, with the writing of *The Malady of Death*, its homophobic potential becomes ever more palpable. The situation is highly paradoxical. Duras had many gay fans and many gay men among her closest circle of friends and admirers. Within those gay circles, an anti-identitarian discourse circulated as an emblem of a certain kind of radical new gay identity. In Duras's hands, a variant of this anti-identitarian discourse so familiar to them reveals a potential for symbolic violence against people like them that calls into question their own reliance on it in the maintenance of their own identities.[46]

I turn now to that part of Duras's career corresponding roughly to the 1980s, and to the importance in those years of her relation with Yann Andréa, her companion for the last sixteen years of her life. (Duras died in 1996.) In what follows I want to continue to lay out and develop the contexts that seem useful for understanding Duras and Andréa's relation, for understanding how that relationship was caught up in Duras's practices of writing, caught up in its particular claims for an oracular literariness. I want to ask whether, as an effect of that relationship, a certain recalibration happened in Duras's discourse on sexuality, and on male homosexuality in particular, and, if so, how that recalibration itself might be the sign of something inarticulate being expressed about the misfit sexuality that Duras and Andréa shared.

In 1980 Duras was commissioned to write a series of articles for the newspaper *Libération*, to appear during the summer. The first installment appeared on Wednesday, July 16. Sometime that July, a man in his late twenties, named Yann Lemée, knocked on the door of Duras's apartment in Trouville. Around the time Duras's third installment appeared on July 30, Hocquenghem

published a three-part series on gay life in New York City.[47] That summer, the
United States and several other countries were boycotting the Moscow Olym-
pics to protest the Soviet Union's invasion of Afghanistan. The Iranian Revolution was in its second year. There was a huge famine in Uganda. This was
also the summer when labor strikes began in Poland, particularly in Gdansk—
leading to the establishment of the Solidarity movement in September of that
year. For Duras, writing for *Libération* as the events unfolded that summer,
"Gdansk" came to represent a renaissance of the political hopes she had expressed in 1968. In *L'été 80* (Summer 1980) (the volume that reprints the ten
articles Duras published in *Libération* between July 16 and September 17), we
could say that Duras attempts to become Gdansk's oracle. In the installment
published on August 20, she writes:

> Someone from *Libération* telephones to ask how far I've gotten and I reply that
> I've done nothing because I'm anxious about what is going on in Gdansk. [The
> developing situation in Poland is front-page news roughly from August 16
> through the first week of September.] I say that I'll try. I sit in front of the blank
> pages for a long while and then I lock up the house, go up to my room and find
> myself once again confronted by the blank pages of the strike in Gdansk. As for
> Uganda, people can see for themselves. [The famine in the Karamoja region of
> Uganda in 1980 is said to have killed 21 percent of the population. *Libération*
> publishes stories on the famine on August 21 and 27.] But Gdansk, no, almost
> no one can see what Gdansk is. All at once the truth is clear: there is almost no
> one left who can feel the happiness of what is happening in Gdansk. I am alone
> in this happiness. I recognize this solitude in which I find myself, a solitude we
> can distinguish from all others, one henceforth without recourse, irremediable:
> political solitude. It is this happiness which I can tell to no one that prevents
> me from writing. . . . People no longer know how to see the happiness that is
> Gdansk because it is of a revolutionary nature and revolutionary thinking has
> abandoned people.[48]

The room where Duras goes to write, *la chambre noire*, is for her an oracular
space, a space of vision, but also of association, and it seems that in that space
an association is formed between her hopes for Gdansk, her vision of what it
represents, and her sense of the utopian or revolutionary possibilities immanent in the relation that she is establishing with a certain anonymous person
who begins to be referenced as "vous" in the final articles Duras wrote for
Libération.[49] Here is part of the passage in which the association is the clearest.
It appeared on September 10:

> Yes, I think that we saw each other, that I recognized you when I opened the
> door, I think that is what happened. You left after several days, and so, in the

same way, for several days running, the town was gloomier than before and the room was left empty, troubled by your absence, as if punctured by the blow that had been struck against the solitude it had always known. Yes, that is why I went into the room, because they were saying that they were afraid for Gdansk, afraid of the power of arms and of armies. No, I do not associate Gdansk with the fear that it will be destroyed. Nor with the power of arms and of armies. I don't associate it with anything, really; no, that's not right, no, I do, with me. With you. With love for you, for your body. No, Gdansk has nothing to do with the power that would destroy it. . . . You should come with me into the dark and deserted room, you shouldn't be afraid any longer. You were much too afraid. Moscow can no longer understand Gdansk, what do you expect? How could Moscow manage to understand Gdansk? How? This motion of the sea, of the wind? These quiet powers? This love? Moscow, these very things, what do you expect?[50]

This person's arrival is an event that affects the structure of the space in which *écriture* unfolds. Duras recognizes something in him, just as she recognizes something in what is happening in Gdansk, a potential, something undefined, an energy as unruly as the sea or the wind, a kind of hope that can replace a generalized fearfulness. Could we say that for Duras, Gdansk is to Moscow as hope is to fear, as movement is to fixity, as potential is to reality, as love between Duras and this young gay man would be to love between couples who conform to more normative expectations for coupling?

When the articles Duras wrote for *Libération* that summer were collected and published in book form, the book, *L'été 80*, was dedicated to Andréa. In 1999, Andréa published a book about his relationship with Duras, titled *Cet amour-là*. In it, he writes:

> The father's name she does away with. She keeps the first name, Yann, which is John, as in John the Baptist. My saint's day is June 24. And she adds my mother's first name: Andréa. Surely it is because of the repeated vowel, the a, the assonance, that she chose my mother's first name. She said, with this name, you've got nothing to worry about, everyone will remember it, it's unforgettable.
>
> She did away with her father's name, Donnadieu, choosing the name Duras, the village in the Lot-et-Garonne region near her father's house in Pardaillan. We both have assumed names, pen names, fake names that become true because she chose them and she wrote them. It is precisely she who writes them, and who in that manner arranges a spiritual filiation.[51]

This is, among other things, a textual representation of oracular literary authority in action—of the authority of a literary figure extending beyond the literary domain, assigning new names, reshaping kinship, choosing for Yann

Lemée a name more resonant, memorable, markedly feminine, assimilating his pseudonymous status to hers.

Another level of complication was added to this associative naming process in 1992, when Duras published a book called *Yann Andréa Steiner*, a complicated text that in parts recounts and recasts versions of certain moments in her relation to the person she had referred to in yet another of her books as "Y.A., homosexuel."[52] The name Steiner was already familiar to devoted readers of Duras, who wrote three different texts called *Aurélia Steiner*, published in 1979 in a collection of writings called *Le navire Night*. Two of the texts were turned into short films the same year.

About his shifting name, Andréa commented in an interview in *Le Nouvel Observateur* shortly after the publication of *Cet amour-là* in 1999:

> She made up my name from my first name and my mother's first name. She got rid of my father's name. My background is Breton, but she made me Jewish by tagging onto my new surname that of Steiner. I became Yann Andréa Steiner. Less a human being, more a character, a book, a film.[53]

In fact, he became a character in a film quite quickly after meeting her in 1980. Duras had him appear with Bulle Ogier in *Agathe et les lectures illimitées*, a film she made in 1981. With some of the outtakes from that film, Duras constructed another, *L'homme atlantique* (The Atlantic man), also dated 1981, and whose soundtrack was published as a text under the same title in 1982. The second-person pronoun, the *vous* that indicated Andréa's presence in *L'été 80*, serves the same function in *L'homme atlantique* and also in *The Malady of Death* (1983).

Andréa's fascination with Duras began, he tells us in *Cet amour-là*, just after high school, when he came across a copy of an early novel of hers, *Les petits chevaux de Tarquinia* (1953, The little horses of Tarquinia), which he found so captivating that he began to drink the same drinks as the characters in the novel; he also stopped reading all the philosophy books he was supposed to be studying and began reading all of Duras. In 1975, Duras attends a screening of her film *India Song* in Caen, the city where Andréa lives. He asks a question after the film, asks her to sign a copy of one of her books, asks for an address where he can write her. She gives him her home address in Paris. He begins writing her, sometimes several times a day, he says. This continues until 1980, when Duras sends him a copy of her book *L'homme assis dans le couloir* (*The Man Sitting in the Corridor*). It is the first time he reads something by her that he does not care for, or does not understand. Flummoxed, he stops writing her. Not hearing from him, she sends him a second copy. Then she sends him a copy of *Le navire Night*, and even writes him a letter in which she tells him that she reads his letters and that one of the texts called "Aurélia Steiner" was written for him. In July, having read the columns she was writing for *Libération*, he calls her, and then goes to meet her in Trouville, where she is spending the summer. At her death in 1996, one of the articles published in *Libération* put things in this journalistically sensationalist way: "Yann Andréa was Marguerite Duras's final lover. Then for fifteen years behind closed doors he served as her assistant. In the end, she turned him into a fictional character. . . . The first night he sleeps in the next room. The next, they make love."[54]

Across the years, Duras regularly refers to a mysterious communion that seems to mark her relationship to Andréa, to the intimate connection he has to the universe represented in her writing, and to certain particularities of his own identity that apparently foster the connection between them. Already by December 1980, others in Duras's social circles are using the name Yann Andréa. In a diary entry dated December 15, 1980, the writer Dominique Noguez notes: "Last night, a party at the Dupuis'. Marguerite makes an appearance with her new favorite, Yann Andréa."[55]

In general, we could say that Duras's way of introducing Andréa and her relationship with him to her readership in *L'été 80*, her various ways of incorporating him into her life, into her writing practices, and into her literary output, all indicate that her relationship with him was part of what we might call her experimental sociopolitical imaginary, a particularly Durassian form of utopian "communism."

The Malady of Death was published in January 1983. Andréa describes the circumstances of the writing of this text in two different books. The first is *M.D.*, his account, also published in 1983, of Duras's hospitalization in the autumn of 1982 in order to withdraw from her dependency on alcohol. The second is *Cet amour-là*, from 1999. Duras wrote *The Malady of Death* before her hospitalization in November 1982, and corrected the proofs of the text after leaving the hospital. It would seem that her alcoholism was so advanced during the period she was composing the text that she was unable to write clearly by hand, her usual compositional practice, and so she dictated this text to Andréa, who typed it. Here are a few passages from *M.D.* describing the process:

> I await the word, I hear your voice and then it is inscribed on the sheet of paper. I don't comprehend. I simply hear the sound of your voice. I am caught up in the fear that I might stop you, that I might ask you to repeat, that the word might be lost. The fear of mistaking one word for another also rises up, as well as the fear of not being able to follow you. You immediately forget what you have just dictated. You are always caught up in what follows.
>
> You are absent. I have known you forever, I know this gaze that seems to

be gazing at nothing, this fixedness along with the movement that allows the word to appear. Nothing else exists except for the sentence in the making and the one to follow. We are seated at the oval table, but separately.[56]

Note here the studied attempt to refer to certain forms of impersonality in the writing. Duras's voice itself is impersonal; it comes from elsewhere, arising out of her absence. She does not compose the words, so much as they pass through her. The words seem to inscribe themselves on the page. Andréa seems to strive after a certain kind of impersonal absence himself, as if it were out of the absence created by the presences of these particular two people at the oval table that the text arises and then appears on the page.

> Around eleven o'clock you come down from your room, I hear your steps approach. You stop in the room with the television, catching your breath. You move toward the kitchen. A glass of wine calms you down. You don't speak. You just walk up to the worktable and there you sit facing the garden for hours on end. And then suddenly, brutally, you dictate. I am always ready. I type immediately. Sometimes you fall asleep on the pages. I let you sleep. I wait. You pick up right where you left off. The text moves forward. It grows under my eyes. (16)

The writing table itself is experienced as a sacred space, and writing as a ritual act. Andréa's own participation in the process is one of attentive and disciplined self-effacement. Duras sacrifices herself to producing a text of which she appears merely to be a medium. Her abuse of alcohol is part of this ritual process.

These same elements are present when Andréa comes back to this scene of writing in 2001 in *Cet amour-là*:

> We are shut up together and we write. I am there and I type the words, the sentences. I don't try to understand, I simply try to type fast enough that I don't lose a word, so as to follow perfectly that which is in the process of being written. And in that moment, here is how I would put it, there is a third person with us. We no longer exist. There is no name, no author's name, there is only writing that is happening. What an emotion is there, not linked to beauty, or not only, not as I see it. Rather this: an emotion of truth itself. Something true is being said, being written down forever. Some bit of truth. A timeless truth, something she and I recognize immediately, something that is being said to me, that she knows she is able to say to me and only to me.[57]

Duras and Andréa are both absent presences who participate in the transcription of this impersonal writing. The text of *The Malady of Death* is, of course, addressed to a man by a woman, yet it is as if that address were put on hold in the scene of writing (or of dictation and typing). Still, even if in this account Andréa does not seem fully to experience the text he is typing as addressed to him by Duras, he is clear about the fact that despite the impersonality of the writing, it is important to the "truth" of what is being inscribed that this scene be transpiring between these two people. It is the conjunction of these two people specifically that enables the ritual scene to carry itself off felicitously.

How can something be both impersonal ("We no longer exist . . . there is only writing") and intensely personal at the same time ("only to me")? In a book called *Écrire* (*Writing*), published in 1993, Duras describes the impersonal aspect of her writing process this way:

> It's the unknown in oneself, one's head, one's body. Writing is not even a re-flection, but a kind of faculty one has, that exists to one side of oneself, parallel to oneself: another person who appears and comes forward, invisible, gifted with thought and anger, and who sometimes, by their own doing, risks losing their life.[58]

But Duras sometimes also seems to suggest, when she speaks about these kinds of things, that when a person is being spoken through, the voice is somehow shaped by the vessel; the person being spoken through nonetheless gives contours to what is spoken. In the same interview from which I cited at the outset of this chapter, Suzanne Lamy recalls a moment when Duras refers to herself as an echo chamber, and asks:

> S.L.: *So when you say you are an "echo chamber" is it that you experience yourself as a collective memory?*
> M.D.: Yes, for example as in *L'été 80*. No doubt Gdansk is something that is difficult to say, but still I am the one who wrote it.[59]

That is to say, Duras claims that in *L'été 80* she allows a collective reaction to world-historical events to speak through her (in her writing about the birth of the Solidarity movement in Poland), yet the speech is recognizably hers. It could happen because of who she is or who she has made herself into. As she said a bit earlier in that same interview, "After all, the imaginary always belongs to someone, is always lived by someone. But you have to remove it from this personal orbit and treat it from the outside" (58). It is a personal imaginary, spoken from the exterior by an artist with a capacity and a responsibility to do so. Yet as she says elsewhere in this same interview, "As for one's own imaginary, there's nothing that can be done to control it" (67).

Still, we might say that Duras intentionally experiments with her imaginary, testing its limits, exploring what within it is fixed and what malleable.

La chambre noire, the space of writing, is perhaps also an objective correlative of the imaginary and of its potential. It is into that space that Duras invited Andréa in the summer of 1980: "You should come with me into the dark and deserted room, you shouldn't be afraid any longer" (Vous devriez venir avec moi dans la chambre noire et déserte, ne plus avoir peur).[60] Notice the similarity (in the French) between this sentence and the first sentence of *The Malady of Death*, "You wouldn't have known her, you'd have seen her everywhere at once, in a hotel, in a street, in a train, in a bar, in a book, in a film, in yourself, your inmost self, when your sex grew erect in the night, seeking somewhere to put itself, somewhere to shed its load of tears" (Vous devriez ne pas la connaître, l'avoir trouvée partout à la fois dans un hôtel, dans une rue, dans un train, dans un bar, dans un livre, dans un film, en vous-même, en vous, en toi, au hasard de ton sexe dressé dans la nuit qui appelle où se mettre, où se débarrasser des pleurs qui le remplissent).[61] One finds the same modal verb ("vous devriez") employed in a way that is half hypothetical, half a command, encouraging or delineating the moment where something experimental could commence. Yet we will discover that if in *L'été 80*, the experiment's results are as of yet unpredictable, by the time the first sentence of *The Malady of Death* is composed, something will have been foreclosed.

It seems easy, placing *The Malady of Death* alongside other texts such as *L'été 80*, or *L'homme atlantique*, or *M.D.*, all of which invoke *la chambre noire*, all of which invoke a practice and an ideology of writing as an oracular state, all of which use the second person as their dominant form of address, to read it as a text addressed to Yann Andréa, a gay man, spoken in a state of frustrated desire, and giving voice to a certain kind of derogation of the man's sexuality for not having the kind of openness a partner had hoped for. The text either tells of, or else instructs a man, or else imagines a man, finding a woman willing to accept payment for a few nights so that he may try to have sex with her:

> You say that you want to give it a try, to attempt it, to attempt to know that, to get used to that, to that body, to those breasts, to that smell, to beauty, to the risk of childbearing that that body represents, to that hairless form lacking the shape of muscles, lacking strength, to that face, to that naked skin.[62]

Certain moments in the text make little secret of the fact that this is a man sexually experienced with other men, but not with women:

> You say: Yes. I don't know that yet and I want to penetrate there too. And just as vigorously as I'm used to doing. They say it offers more resistance, that it has a velvety softness that offers more resistance than the empty space does. (3–4)

Or later:

> She asks: Haven't you ever desired a woman? You say no, never.
>   She asks: Not once, not for a single moment? You say no, never.
>   She says: Never? Ever? You repeat: Never.
>   She smiles, says: A dead man's a curious thing.
>   She goes on: What about looking, haven't you ever looked at a woman?
> You say no, never.
>   She asks: What do you look at? You say: All the rest. (30–31)

This is the text that Duras dictates to Andréa, that he types, that his own entranced presence at the ritual table enables. Many people have read (and continue to read) this text without noticing that it is "about" homosexuality. Noguez says that Duras told him in September 1982 that she was writing "a text about homosexuality" and that it was called *The Malady of Death*. "Holy cow, what a title!" he notes in his journal.[63] Yet Peter Handke will make a movie out of the text, apparently without noticing it is about homosexuality, and Blanchot will write an article about it, first published in the spring of 1983 in a journal called *Nouveau Commerce*, and incorporated later that year into his book *The Unavowable Community*, in which Duras believes he too fails to notice the text is about homosexuality. When Duras is interviewed in 1985 by some people from the *Cahiers du cinéma*, one of them comments:

> —*I was surprised when I met Handke at Cannes before his movie was shown. I told him that the text was talking about homosexuality. He was flabbergasted.*

Duras replies:

> —Like Blanchot. It just depends, or so it seems. [Comme Blanchot. C'est selon, semblerait-il.][64]

Whether or not Blanchot understood the text to be about homosexuality is a question about which people might disagree. Certainly Blanchot understood that there was a relation between Duras's project in *Malady* and the thinking about May 1968 in which they had been involved together. In *The Unavowable Community*, he writes a description of what was for him the lesson of May 1968 that could also be an account of the hopes Duras had for her relationship with Andréa:

> May '68 has shown that without project, without conjuration, in the suddenness of a happy meeting, like a feast that breached the admitted and expected social norms, *explosive communication* could affirm itself (affirm itself beyond the usual forms of affirmation) as the opening that gave permission to everyone,

without distinction of class, age, sex or culture, to mix with the first comer as if with an already loved being, precisely because he was the unknown familiar.[65]

Of course Andréa, longtime reader and fan of Duras, was not any old "first comer." Their meeting in person in the summer of 1980 was overdetermined by the many social structures in which they were participating as well as by their own past history. But Blanchot's passage does nicely encapsulate the paradox of *The Malady of Death*: whatever the utopian potential of "explosive communication" might have been in certain places and at certain times, it evolves in *Malady* into the highly normalizing assertion that if gay men want to be truly revolutionary, they need not only to be able to sleep with women but to want to.

Commentators in the French gay press generally understood *The Malady of Death* to be about gay sexuality. For instance, when Andréa's *M.D.* appeared later that year, it was reviewed in *Masques* by René de Ceccatty, who wrote:

> Yann Andréa isn't really what you could call a writer, nor does *M.D.* really constitute what you could call a book. Yet for all that, *M.D.* does turn out to be an astonishing book. It was upon finishing *The Malady of Death*, the cruelest and most sincere book a woman could write about male homosexuality to a man she loves—the book revitalized a career that had been in decline, that had become repetitive, it revived her genius—that Marguerite Duras decided not to let herself die of alcoholism. The testimony of Yann Andréa about the private life of someone of her standing who was on the brink of disaster is remarkably valuable. . . . There is no need to add that there can be nothing cynical in Yann Andréa, with his immense Durassian love for a woman forty years his senior: he shows us how it is possible to describe someone's decline, but to do so out of love, and thereby enhance and even save the person in question.[66]

Cecatty performs here the role of a sophisticated gay fan of Duras. (It was well known that she was a favorite author for many gay men, and the practice among them of memorizing certain of her texts was not unheard of.) But it is not very specific about what it means for a text such as *The Malady of Death* to be "cruel" or "sincere," or for Yann's love for Duras to be "Durassian." Cruel, perhaps because the project of Duras's text seems to be to represent a gay man's attempt to confront what we have seen her call elsewhere the "poverty" of his homosexuality, a poverty that seems related to the absence of that capacity for "communication" that Duras, following Blanchot and Bataille, claimed Genet suffered from because of the form of his sexuality. Remember Duras's words from her article contrasting Genet and Bataille: "Bataille's abjection, unlike that of Genet, delivers his characters from their singularity and brings them out into their indeterminacy. They are no longer caught in the gangue of an individual royalty but are on their way toward dissolution, toward annihilation: we meet them in passing." The terms used here are quite similar to those found in *Malady*, which can be understood as a text in which a gay man experiments with sex with a woman as a form of "deliverance" from sameness or narcissism or, in Duras's somewhat fancified language, "the gangue of an individual royalty." Gay sexuality is played out here as a mistaken relation to sovereignty, a fear of the female body as the locus that should force one to confront one's own finitude:

> You look at the malady of your life, the malady of death. It's on her, on her sleeping body, that you look at it. You look at the different places on the body, at the face, the breasts, the odd place of joining that is her sex.
>
> You look at the place where the heart is. The beat seems different, more distant. The word occurs to you: more alien. It's regular, it seems as if it would never stop. You bring yourself close to the object that is her body. It's warm, fresh. She's still alive. While she lives she invites murder. You wonder how to kill her and who will. You don't love anything, anyone, you don't even love the difference that you think you have in your life. The only grace you know is that of the bodies of the dead, the bodies of people like you. Suddenly you become aware of the difference between the grace of the bodies of the dead and the grace that is here present, made of ultimate weakness that a mere gesture could destroy—this royalty.
>
> You realize it's here, in her, that the malady of death is fomenting, that it's this shape stretched out before you that decrees the malady of death.[67]

Homophobic stereotypes abound here. Gay men are in some way dead; they have a murderous intention toward women, who represent for them an abject space of inhuman vitality. Gay men, in their relations with women, exemplify a mistaken experience of sovereignty. Gay men lack the humanizing desire to experiment with difference (which means trying to have sexual relations with a woman) in an effort to correct something that is inherently impolitic in their way of being.

It is one thing to demonstrate that Duras's text is "about" homosexuality and to point to the banal forms of homophobic discourse it invokes when read on this level.[68] This is an aspect of the text's meaning that may or may not be available to, may not be perceived by, this or that particular reader. "C'est selon," was Duras's compact observation. "It depends." It depends on the contexts you know, the information you have, and also the person you are when you read the text, your own sensibility, your own location within culture.

If it is a bit complicated to make and support the claim that *Malady* is a text "about" homosexuality, it is perhaps even a bit more complicated to make the claim, perhaps a related one, that *The Malady of Death* is (also) "about" the sexuality that Duras and Andréa shared—that this sexuality that has no easy name is what the text registers on some level even as it reproduces various canards about the ethical and existential inadequacy of men sexually interested in other men.

One question posed to Duras in her 1980 *Gai pied* interview was the following:

> *How do you explain the interest and the fascination that your books and films exercise over gay men, whereas in your books one finds no trace of male or female homosexuality, or at least it's not explicitly represented?*

To which she replies, in part (including a few sentences I cited earlier):

> There is no specifically masculine or feminine form of sexuality. There is only one sexuality in which all relations swim. Whatever is particular about homosexuality is not sealed in watertight. I see it as a form of violence seeking its scene of confrontation, therefore as nostalgic for a new redistribution of the current structure of violence, but a confrontation that it would construct for itself. I speak without any firsthand knowledge, but I have the right not to know, just as you have the right to ask me the question.

She adds, a bit later on, "All of my erotic fantasies are fantasies of interdiction."[69] Published in November 1980, this interview occurred after Duras had become involved with Andréa. We might therefore take Duras's reply to this question to be an early attempt to speak about her relationship with him. But we can also notice that it turns out to be extremely difficult for *anyone*, including Duras, to find a framework that would allow for talk about the sexuality that the two of them shared. In general, and here perhaps we see "culture" at work, one either talks about Duras's heterosexuality and Andréa's homosexuality, or else one speaks, as Duras does here, of there being only one sexuality that we all share—although it is hard not to notice that that generalized sexuality comes almost inevitably to seem like a heterosexuality that effaces all other particularities.

But perhaps we might also know, or we could imagine, that the sexuality that Duras and Andréa lived and shared is another one of those misfit sexualities with a long history and recognizable features; we kind of know about it, we see it and sort of acknowledge it, but without actually naming it or speaking of it. The violence of Duras's writing is perhaps an index of this particular cultural limitation as much as it could be a sign of how she became trapped in ways of speaking that might have been adequate to past contexts but became increasingly inadequate to her present experience and the experience of many of those around her.

At one point, the interviewer for *Gai pied* asks Duras about something she had said in an earlier interview:

> *In your interviews with Xavière Gauthier, there is a moment when you said that currently the only people you live with are women and gay men. Is that still true?*

Duras replies:

> It's true. You know there are a lot of us who live like that, among gay men and women.

This is an interesting comment, suggesting that in Duras's own view, her experience with Andréa, which is being at least implicitly referred to here, is one she and he share with other people. (Perhaps there is even something ordinary enough about it to suggest that Duras's insistence on its transgressive aspects is misplaced). That it might be a common or ordinary experience on which Duras and Andréa have embarked is, of course, in some ways contradicted by the fact that Duras is about to spend roughly a decade producing literary texts intended to make it seem extraordinary, to insist on the pain and violence involved in what she is going through. But perhaps her extraordinary oracular statements on this experience could also be understood as somehow referring to something general or generalizable, something in which others will recognize a part of their own daily experience.

A few years farther into the experience with Andréa, Duras produces *Blue Eyes, Black Hair*, which redeploys several elements found in *The Malady of Death*. Duras also takes up the same writing practice: dictating to a typing Andréa. She describes the writing of *Blue Eyes, Black Hair* in a short text called *The Slut of the Normandy Coast*:

> It is the summer of 1986. I'm writing the story. Throughout the summer, every day, sometimes in the evening, sometimes at night. It is then that Yann enters a period of cries, of shouts. He spends two hours a day at the typewriter, typing the book. In the book, I'm eighteen. I'm in love with a man who loathes my desire, my body. Yann types as I dictate. While he types, he isn't shouting. That happens afterwards. He shouts at me, he becomes a man demanding something, who doesn't know what that something is. He wants something, but doesn't know what. So he shouts, to say that he doesn't know what he wants. And he also shouts to find out, so that, from the current of his words, the information will come out of him regarding what he wants. He can't manage to separate the detail of what he wants this summer from the whole of what he has always wanted.[70]

Andréa's desire to scream might not be that difficult to understand. Like *The Malady of Death*, *Blue Eyes, Black Hair* is the imagining of a scenario in which a gay man who experiences no desire for women will find himself in a room with a woman and will feel compelled somehow to try to find a way to have sex with her. She, in turn, will make a point of reminding him that he will never have any children.

In general, *Blue Eyes, Black Hair*, together with the interviews, articles, and other bits of text by Duras that accompany it, seems the most ardently homophobic text she ever produced. There may have been confusion in the minds of various readers about whether *The Malady of Death* was a book "about" her relation to homosexuality, but for anyone following the press surrounding the publication of *Blue Eyes, Black Hair*, there could have been little question about the matter. In an article from *Le Matin* of November 14, 1986, Duras would make the following claim:

> "About homosexuality," she tells us, "people speak loads of rubbish, really, without ever having gone to see themselves, gone into the homosexual world [le lieu homosexuel], which I did for six years. It's an utterly terrible place, yet now I know that love can appear there in a form of unbearable reciprocity—but one stronger than any other, so strong you could die from it."

In this interview Duras is quite specific about what makes what she calls "le lieu homosexuel" such a terrible place: it is, as the title of the 1983 volume suggests, the malady of death. "I can also say that there is death in homosexuality," she says, "because, in general, homosexuality can't be spread through the children it has, since it doesn't have any. As if it were trying to hasten death. Just the way death exists in the brains of animals like antelopes or lemmings who go off together to die in groups without in any way realizing what orders they are following."[71] Given that the years around 1986 were also the years in which the seriousness of the AIDS crisis was coming to people's awareness, Duras's language seems, at least in retrospect, especially unseemly here, increasingly out of joint with its time.[72]

Take the issue of *Le Nouvel Observateur* from November 14, 1986. As part of the publicity campaign around the publication of *Blue Eyes, Black Hair*, it included an interview with Duras in which she comments:

> It isn't a book about sex, it's a book about desire. Having sex isn't important, it's having desire. [Ce n'est pas de baiser qui compte, c'est d'avoir du désir.] The number of people having sex without desire, enough is enough. [Le nombre de gens qui baisent sans désir, ça suffit comme ça.] All of these women writers write so badly about this, but it's a whole world coming down on you! I've known since childhood that the world of sexuality was fabulous, enormous. All the rest of my life has only confirmed that fact. I say so in the book.[73]

The cover story for this issue of *Le Nouvel Observateur* was one of those predictable pieces that magazines periodically recycle on topics such as "the sexuality of the French." The issue includes an article called "L'amour sous cellophane" (Love under plastic wrap), about safer-sex practices and the organizations created to disseminate information about these practices, producing advertisements, distributing condoms in bars and nightclubs, and so on. In particular, the article notes, the AIDS services organization AIDES is producing a series of eight video clips that it plans to have shown in nightclubs, in the metro, and in high schools. As the article describes it, these clips are "ads for both straights and gays that are strikingly sex-positive [qui sont presque des incitations à la débauche]. 'The message we are trying to send,' says Dr. Mettetel, president of AIDES, 'is to keep having sex, but less risky sex' [c'est continuez à baiser, mais à moindre risqué]."[74]

There is something odd that happens when you juxtapose Duras's "Ce n'est pas de baiser qui compte, c'est d'avoir du désir" with Mettetel's "continuez à baiser, mais à moindre risque," when you juxtapose the idea that safer-sex campaigns could be "incitations à la débauche," with Duras's insistence that "Le nombre de gens qui baisent sans désir, ça suffit comme ça." Despite Duras's passing insult to women writers of the 1970s and 1980s who were using writing to explore the concept of female desire, it does really seem as if her general accusation were directed specifically at male same-sex sexuality. It is gay sexuality that for her exemplifies a sexual culture in which sex exists without desire. Yann, she tells us in *The Slut of the Normandy Coast*, was both at the center of the writing of *Blue Eyes, Black Hair* and a danger to it. During the summer she was writing it, he spent much of the time he was not yelling at Duras cruising for men: "I hardly ever see him, this man, Yann. He's hardly ever there, in the apartment by the sea where we live together. He goes for walks. . . . He heads to the big hotels, looking for handsome men. He finds a few handsome bartenders. Golf courses, too, he searches" (15–16). What exists between Duras and Yann, it would seem, is "le désir." What happens between Yann and the men he encounters is "la baise." The effort at symbolic domination that Duras makes through the opposition she creates between *la baise* and *le désir* is, of course, painfully easy to deconstruct. Duras's normative logic goes like this: it is a failure of imagination, a failure of their humanity, for gay men not to be able to desire women and not to act on that desire that escapes them. There is an opposing failure, of course, which she does not seem to articulate: her own failure to imagine a sexuality that would be outside heterosexuality.[75]

Duras's status, her symbolic capital, we could say, or her oracular authority, meant that people who might have been positioned to know better, or indeed, who admitted to knowing better, still had difficulty resisting the glamour of her utterances. Hugo Marsan, the editor of *Gai pied* in 1986, wrote that publication's article reviewing *Blue Eyes, Black Hair*. Such was the allure of Duras's writing that the person who in *Gai pied* in October 1986 could be writing editorials pondering the question of whether gay men should be tested for HIV (in a moment when the absence of any effective treatment for HIV infection made it debatable what purpose knowledge of one's serostatus would serve) could, then, in November 1986, in the same magazine, write a review of *Blue Eyes, Black Hair* in which he admitted: "And I, who by all rights should here be outraged, I find myself agreeing with her, accepting the devastating lucidity of her book as it takes the measure of the perdition to which a man in search of other men devotes himself." He notes, a bit later: "The cry that sounds in the pages of *Blue Eyes, Black Hair* was already audible in *The Malady of Death*. But here the writer and the woman have reconciled, completely grasping the grandeur of homosexual destruction."[76] For Marsan, under Duras's spell, she seems to be writing about *his* sexuality rather than about *her own*, rather than about the difficult sexuality that she shared with Andréa. To me, that is the most astonishing feature of the experience of a misfit sexuality to which Duras gave such violent expression: partly because of the status she held within the literary field, but also partly because of the seemingly inherent difficulty in perceiving (or even in conceiving) misfit sexualities in their own right, people took Duras's subject to be homosexuality. And of course, it doubtless was— even to her, but it was not only that.

Duras herself was perhaps not totally unaware of how it was her own misfit sexuality—and Andréa's—that found expression through speech of amazing symbolic violence that took as its ostensible object gay male sexuality. In a book from 1987, *Practicalities* (*La vie materielle*), she seems almost to grapple explicitly with the fact that all this homophobic speech and writing arises from an experience of a misfit sexuality (or of the meeting of two misfit sexualities—hers and Andréa's) that does not have the words or concepts to express itself. In the section of that book called "The Book," she writes:

> The book is about two people who love one another. But who love one another unawares. It happens outside the book. What I'm saying now is something I didn't want to say in the book but which I mustn't forget to say now, even though it's hard to find the words to do so. The essence of this love is that it can't be written. [Cet amour se tient dans l'impossibilité d'être écrit.] It's a love that writing hasn't yet reached. . . . Yes, the book is about an unavowed love between people prevented by an unknown force from saying they love one another. . . . These are people who don't know how to love one another and yet do have a love affair. But the word to express it never crosses their lips, nor

does desire come to their sex, to express it and vent it and then be able to chat and have a drink. Nothing but tears. . . . I've merged into the characters, and what I'm doing is telling of an impossible (just as I'd tell of a possible) affair between a woman and a homosexual, whereas what I really want to tell of is a love affair which is always possible even though it seems impossible to people unfamiliar with writing. For writing isn't supposed to concern itself with that kind of possibility or impossibility.[77]

Of course, "the book" of which she speaks in this passage could be the recently published *Blue Eyes, Black Hair*. But it might also have a less easily locatable referent. Rather than a book existing between two covers, it might gesture toward the interactional space she and Andréa have been inhabiting together and in which so much writing (by them and others) has happened. "The book" would then be less a material object than some kind of record of a process in which their sexuality has sought textual representation, whose written traces cross multiple platforms as well as the interstices between various written artifacts. Writing, *l'écriture*, then would here become not simply the vehicle of a discourse hostile to sexuality between men, not the space of the ridiculous project of producing a general theory of sexuality out of one older woman's experience of the lack of sexual desire a younger gay man feels for her even as they knit complex bonds of intimacy between themselves. Rather it becomes the effort to track a process that eludes finalized representation, that escapes the usual categories of reference; it becomes the effort to record—or to en-register, or to produce the space(s) of—the evolving and obviously painful experience of the misfit sexuality they shared.

Multivariable Social Acrobatics and Misfit Counterpublics: Violette Leduc and Hervé Guibert

The previous two chapters have been engaged with, among other things, a methodological question: what kind of a critical practice is necessary to study the way in which misfit sexualities whose existence is largely pragmatic leave their traces in gaps and interstices between different kinds of texts, in indexical relations between texts, and also between texts and the social worlds and cultural fields of their production? In the present chapter, my interest is slightly different, and has two vectors. The first has to do with what we might call the sociological idiosyncrasy of misfits and a kind of social acrobatics that involves practical (i.e., not fully conscious) ways of playing with multiple social variables and with their interactive effects. The second has to do with the significance of misfit counterpublics, the ways they come into being, and the representation they and their formation receive in a number of different works by Violette Leduc and Hervé Guibert.

I begin with a letter Simone de Beauvoir wrote to her American lover, Nelson Algren, on June 28, 1947 (four years after the publication of *L'invitée*, two years before the publication of *The Second Sex*). In it she recounts having dinner with Violette Leduc, whom she refers to (and I suppose we might consider this in some ways a term of endearment) as "the ugly woman":

> I had a dinner with the ugly woman. We went to a very nice old restaurant in the Palais Royal gardens and we drank champagne. I do not know why we always drink champagne when we have a dinner together. In the same restaurant there was Jean Cocteau, a very well known French poet and pederast; he is sixty years old and he had a dinner with three rather beautiful young homosexuals. He was very friendly and funny and we talked some time together; as the ugly woman is rather a lesbian if she is anything, I was the only heterosexual

one in this meeting and I felt a little vicious, being so. The way these young homosexuals behave always makes me laugh: the way they try to be very manly and tough and yet very womanly too. They are friends with the ugly woman and I think I rather do some good to her, helping her to write good books and to make friends through these books. She is not quite so unhappy as before. She is surely the most interesting woman I know and we spent a good evening.[1]

English not being her first language, there is perhaps a certain clumsiness to be heard in Beauvoir's syntax and word choice here and there. It is clear that she admires her talented protégée, whatever her way of characterizing Leduc's physical appearance.[2] "The most interesting woman I know" is high praise indeed from someone like Beauvoir. She is obviously fascinated that someone from such an underprivileged background, someone with the odd and difficult personality that was Leduc's, could produce such astonishing writing, breaking new ground in the description of women's lives and of female sexuality in particular. Beauvoir was also obviously intrigued by the fact that the writing Leduc produced had earned her the apparently unlikely admiration of a set of fashionable and elite gay male readers. Leduc's first novel, *L'asphyxie*, had appeared in 1946, and thanks to its publication (in which Beauvoir played an important role), Beauvoir now sees Leduc as belonging to a specialized literary subculture (queer, we might call it today) of which Beauvoir does not consider herself to be a part. We might (a bit anachronistically) label Beauvoir as queer-friendly; she seems happy to have queer friends, proud of her liberalism, and proud of Leduc's literary achievement, one that gained for her important readers such as Cocteau and his circle of friends. There would seem to be some implied nuance in Beauvoir's use of sexual categories: referring to Cocteau as a "pederast," but to his three dinner companions as "young homosexuals" perhaps indicates some kind of awareness of the diversity of extant forms of male same-sex sexuality, or their relation to age or to generation. Similarly, referring to Leduc as "rather a lesbian if she is anything" reveals Beauvoir to understand that female same-sex sexuality is itself multifarious, and does not always take on an identitarian caste (as her own past experience would attest, even if that past experience seems to be something totally unavowable in the context of this letter). Beauvoir's *L'invitée* was not a book that was written "to make friends" of the kind Leduc is able to make with her writing. Leduc's writing, as I mentioned in chapter 2, constitutes a kind of appeal to a counterpublic that will only come into being around her writing—a counterpublic that, as this letter attests, includes the sophisticated gay aesthetes of Cocteau's set. We will meet other members of this counterpublic, random alienated teenagers in Normandy as well as young Parisian lesbians, in the pages ahead.

We already saw in chapter 2 that the young Leduc herself read literature as a way of joining a counterpublic of sexual outsiders and misfits. Leduc the writer imagines her own literary work in a similar way. She produces litera- ture, we might think, *in order to* generate her own intimate counterpublic. In this, she might show some similarities with Hervé Guibert, whose work I will be juxtaposing with hers in this chapter. In this regard, we could take there to be a marked difference between the ambitions of her writing and that of either Simone de Beauvoir or Marguerite Duras. Traces of the experience Beauvoir and Duras had of a misfit sexuality can certainly be found in various of their works, as chapters 4 and 5 have endeavored to demonstrate, but it would seem accurate to say that Beauvoir and Duras wrote their works for the world at large (which is to say, that part of the world given to reading certain kinds of highbrow literature). Their form of address was a more general one. They did not intend exactly to speak for, or even explicitly to speak about, an experience of sexual misfittedness. Guibert and Leduc do write, we might say, *for* people seeking both a certain experience of, and a representation of the experience of, misfit intimacy, an intimacy that creates fleeting communities formed of often quite heterogeneous individuals; they write idiosyncratically, let us say; they write in pursuit of this odd form of misfit counterpublic, and, to the extent it is successful, their writing correspondingly produces certain specific circuits of recognition.

Wilted Lettuce: Leduc's Idiosyncrasy

Idio: personal, distinct, private. *Syn*: together, alike. *Krasis*: mixture, combina- tion. Idiosyncrasy is the particular combination of things that, when brought together, make someone distinct, peculiar, eccentric. The word contains within itself the suggestion that something idiosyncratic might be broken down into its component parts, parts that in and of themselves might be quite common, not idiosyncratic in the least. It would just be their particular mixture that is peculiar. In the essay "Understanding" that comes at the end of *The Weight of the World: Social Suffering in Contemporary Society*, Pierre Bourdieu suggests as much in discussing how we might come to a sociological understanding of the idiosyncrasies associated with the utterances made by certain individ- uals: "contrary to what might be believed from a naively personalist view of the uniqueness of social persons, it is the uncovering of immanent structures contained in the contingent statements of a discrete interaction that alone allows one to grasp what is essential in the make up of *idiosyncrasy*."[3] Social structures of various kinds are immanent in, implicit in, everyone's speech; we could say that those structures are indexed by or invoked through what we say. If something of our social world is shared by our interlocutor, if our interlocutor can reconstruct something of the point of view from which we speak, our implicit invocation of various social structures will be part of what makes us intelligible to them, despite whatever implicitness may be involved. The more idiosyncratic our speech, the more risks we take with intelligibility. Yet, heard in a certain way, Bourdieu suggests, certain kinds of idiosyncratic speech are sociologically revelatory; they can reveal something essential about the social context in which they occur and from which they arise. The project of *The Weight of the World* was to hear with sociological ears the idiosyncratic speech of individuals exposed to certain kinds of vulnerability, and by an act of interpretation to make explicit the implicit structures that produce various kinds of social suffering that positional vulnerability might cause. "We are offering here the accounts that men and women have confided to us about their lives and the difficulties they have in living those lives" (1), Bourdieu writes in opening the volume. Anyone who has read much Violette Leduc will of course be aware that much of the power of her writing has to do with the portrait of social suffering it traces. Consider the sentences that open Leduc's *La Bâtarde*:

> My case is not unique: I am afraid of dying and distressed at being in this world. I haven't worked, I haven't studied. I have wept, I have cried out. These tears and cries have taken up a great deal of my time. Whenever I think of it, that lost time tortures me. I am not capable of thinking for a long time at a stretch, but I can take pleasure in a withered lettuce leaf offering me nothing but regrets to chew over. There is no sustenance in the past. I shall depart as I arrived. Intact, loaded down with the defects that have tormented me. I wish I had been born a statue; I am a slug under my dunghill. Virtues, good qualities, courage, meditation, culture. With arms crossed on my breast I have broken myself against those words.[4]

> (Mon cas n'est pas unique: j'ai peur de mourir et je suis navrée d'être au monde. Je n'ai pas travaillé, je n'ai pas étudié. J'ai pleuré, j'ai crié. Les larmes et les cris m'ont pris beaucoup de temps. La torture du temps perdu dès que j'y réfléchis. Je ne peux pas réfléchir longtemps mais je peux me complaire sur une feuille de salade fanée où je n'ai que des regrets à remâcher. Le passé ne nourrit pas. Je m'en irai comme je suis arrivée. Intacte, chargée de mes défauts qui m'ont torturée. J'aurais voulu naître statue, je suis une limace sous mon fumier. Les vertus, les qualités, le courage, la méditation, la culture. Bras croisés, je me suis brisée à ces mots-là.)

Her case is not a unique one, she begins, but there is little doubt she is also tracing a portrait not so much of her typicality, but of her idiosyncratic differences from people closer to some kind of mainstream. What is the nature of her distress, what are its sources? She offers herself somehow as a portrait of exclusion, a portrait of an author who aspires to join the literary world (and, indeed, who has ended up being published by Gallimard), but apparently without wanting to or being able to have any truck with culture. She is someone who seems, in her distress, at times willfully antisocial, knowing the kinds of social and cultural capital she needs to acquire in order to achieve the kind of success she desires, but willfully refusing—or constitutionally unable—to acquire that capital or to hold on to it.

Much of this sense of paradoxical exclusion is encapsulated in the not so implicit comparison she makes in this paragraph between her project in *La Bâtarde* and its sequels (*Mad in Pursuit* [*La folie en tête*] and the untranslated *La chasse à l'amour* [Chasing after love]) and the project of Proust's *In Search of Lost Time*. Proust is invoked, of course, by the three words "du temps perdu" ("that lost time") in her fifth sentence. This might help us to hear the "longtemps" ("for a long time") of the following sentence as an ironic reference to the first word of the famous first sentence of Proust's novel: "Longtemps, je me suis couché de bonne heure" (For a long time, I would go to bed early). It might also help us to notice the rather brilliantly compressed comparison of Proust's famous madeleine—the taste of which, mixed with a spoonful of lime-blossom tea, frees up Proust's narrator's memory of his childhood—to a wilted leaf of lettuce. Proust's narrator, feeling how the memories of his childhood are beginning to reemerge thanks to the oddly familiar taste of tea-infused madeleine, is overcome by "a delicious pleasure," but it requires some effort to allow the memories that are stirring to rise to his consciousness: "Ten times I must begin again, lean down toward it [the memory in question]. And each time, the cowardice that deters us from every difficult task, every work of importance, has counseled me to leave it, to drink my tea and think only about my worries of today, my desires for tomorrow, which can be chewed over again and again [qui se laissent remâcher] quite easily."[5] Leduc seems to have this sentence in particular in the back of her mind in composing her opening paragraph. There is no doubt about her long-standing admiration for Proust. Rather, what is intriguing here is the way her careful invocation of his novel allows her to make a sociological point about people whose childhood experiences are likely to include the taste of a madeleine dipped in lime-blossom tea.[6] Courage and culture are theirs, she seems to say, as is the world of literature. Whereas she, her comparison implies, will never overcome her own "cowardice," will never rise in the aesthetic contemplation of her own life to the level of "a delicious pleasure." She is fated by her social position to find modest contentment in (*me complaire sur*) her wilted leaf of lettuce, never transcending the task of chewing over (*remâcher*, another word she borrows from Proust) her various kinds of troubles, past and present. Leduc will forever envy those who seem comfortable in the trappings of culture. Even when she attains some of those trappings (as she would following upon the huge success of *La Bâtarde* when it was published in 1964[7]), they will remain trappings in which she always experiences a certain sense of discomfort or alienation.

In moments like these, Leduc provides us with an image of herself as what Bourdieu (in a section of *The Weight of the World* written in collaboration with Patrick Champagne) calls a "raté relatif," a relative failure:

> The model of these innumerable *relative failures* found even at the very highest levels of success—with, for example, students at less prestigious schools compared to the students of elite schools, or, within these elite schools, students ranked low in comparison to those who get a top ranking, and so on—is no doubt the musician in Patrick Süskind's play, *The Double Bass*, whose very deep and very real misery comes from the fact that at the very heart of this highly privileged world to which he belongs, everything is as if designed to remind him that the position he occupies in it is a low one. (424)

No matter her success, Leduc understands herself as constitutionally incapable of fitting into the cultural universe in which those she so admires (Proust, Beauvoir, Cocteau) move with ease—in which they are, in fact, at home. Her literary success is, of course, all the more remarkable given the lack of entitlement that characterized her origins and her upbringing: illegitimate daughter of a domestic servant who had an affair with the son of the family she was working for. Raised in straitened circumstances by her mother (who had become a shop assistant) and her grandmother, until her mother married again, and thereby improved their financial situation slightly, Leduc's access to "legitimate" culture was profoundly constrained by her situation. Her way into the literary world, once she had failed the oral portion of her baccalaureate exam, was to take some vocational courses in publishing at the Maison du livre, and then find a clerical position in the Plon publishing house. It is an odd strategy for someone wanting to pursue a literary career—a harebrained one, we might even say, but perhaps as such indicative of the place she occupied in the social world and of the kinds of ways forward she was capable of imagining as open to her. When Bourdieu and Champagne, in the passage from *The Weight of the World* devoted to the *ratés relatifs*, are discussing a moment when the French educational system expanded in a "democratic" fashion so that a university education would be available to a more economically diverse set of students, they note how nonetheless it remained the case that the most socially entitled students ended up following the most socially

successful trajectories, simply because they were well-enough positioned to
know what the wise strategies were:

> After an extended school career, which often entails considerable sacrifice,
> the most culturally disadvantaged run the risk of ending up with a devalued
> degree. . . . Related to streaming and selection procedures that take place at an
> ever younger age, the multiplication of tracks toward different levels and quali-
> fications leads to "gentle" exclusionary practices or, better yet, *insensible* ones—
> taken in the dual sense of continual/gradual and imperceptible/unperceived, as
> much by those who inflict them as by those on whom they are inflicted. (423)

Working in a clerical position at Plon is a fairly good way of ensuring that
you'll be unlikely to make it from the margins to the center of the literary
world, that you will suffer from being in the world you want to be in, but
marginally located within it. Yet despite this unpromising beginning, Leduc's
trajectory will end up being quite an exceptional one. She will eventually give
up the job at Plon due to an illness. Her literary career, her practice of writing
and her eventual publication, will only be launched through a series of fits
and starts, involving practice in odd para-literary genres (fashion journalism,
in particular), and following a rather astonishing path that includes chance
meetings with a series of figures who open various kinds of doors for her:
Alice Cerf, Denise Tual, Maurice Sachs, and finally Simone de Beauvoir.[8] Once
her work does begin to be published (excerpts from her first book, *L'asphyxie*,
along with other articles of hers, were published in *Les Temps Modernes* before
the novel itself appeared in a series edited by Albert Camus), commercial
success will nonetheless entirely elude her until 1964 despite her talent being
recognized by a variety of figures, including Sartre, Beauvoir, Camus, Genet,
Jouhandeau, and Cocteau.

Having your talent recognized by a certain subset of the elite literary figures of your time does not constitute a completely satisfying form of success,
as it turns out, at least not for Leduc, who was, of course, poor and desperate to
earn money from her writing, and who also hungered for wide recognition. To
say that her early books sold poorly would be an understatement. Consider the
passage in the posthumously published *La chasse à l'amour*, in which Leduc
recounts receiving a letter from her publisher informing her that Gallimard is
on the verge of pulping the remaining unsold copies of *L'asphyxie*. The passage
reveals, among other things, her lucidity about the commodity function of the
literary work, and also reveals again the place Proust holds for her as a symbol
of someone fully consecrated within the literary field, someone for whom she
is filled with admiration but also against whom she figures her own ambitions:

A letter from my publisher. Could it be good news? "My publisher." Who are
you kidding. He's Proust's publisher. There's a clear difference between a cathe-
dral of hawthorns and a louse coated with excrement. Let's open the envelope.
My God! . . . They are going to pulp the remaining copies of *L'asphyxie*. My
book is dying. It never even really had a life. No one read it. Today is a day of
mourning. I have lost a child. . . . The editor has run out of storage space. Did
it really take up so much room in his cellars, my scrawny little kid?[9]

What kind of an investment does a publisher make in an author? Different
publishers doubtless have different policies regarding how long they will keep
a book stocked before finding a way to unload it. Gallimard would surely fall,
at least for part of what it publishes, into the category of what Bourdieu, in
The Rules of Art, calls "enterprises with a *long production cycle*," businesses that
keep books available over a longer term, understanding that they may have a
larger public in the future than in the present. And yet, as Bourdieu notes, and
as Leduc's example illustrates, "this production (entirely turned towards the
future) tends to constitute stocks of products which are always in danger of re-
verting to the state of material objects (and valued as such, that is, for example,
by their weight in paper)" (142–43). Leduc has friends and admirers, but those
friends and admirers do not suffice to guarantee the value of what she does.

A bit later on in the same passage from *La chasse à l'amour*, Leduc realizes
that Gallimard is actually offering her the chance to buy the remaining copies
of *L'asphyxie* at a reduced rate, and she imagines what she might do if she were
able to afford to purchase all the copies Gallimard was about to dispose of.[10]

I read the letter again. I hadn't understood it fully. I have the chance to buy all
the unsold copies before they are disposed of. There are 1,727 copies left. What
will I do with them? Inspirational pamphlets. I'll ring doorbells and hand them
out. They'll turn their dogs on me. Who believes in generosity anymore? I'll
sneak them into the bins of the booksellers that line the banks of the Seine
before they even notice I've done it. I will go to the bookstore La Hune and,
fraudulently, I will place a single copy on their shelves for the letter L. I will
sing "Death, where is your sting?" as I leave La Hune. (144)

Her scenarios are intriguing. First, she imagines that, assuming she could
afford to buy the bulk of the remaining copies of her own book, she could
distribute it door-to-door the way people deliver religious tracts. But then
her imagination takes an interesting turn: since people were unlikely to be
receptive to that tactic, she could surreptitiously slip her book in among the
others on the shelves of the booksellers along the banks of the Seine, where
someone might buy it. Even more daring, she could slip into the bookstore

La Hune, located for many years on the boulevard Saint-Germain between the Café de Flore and Les Deux Magots—at the heart of Left Bank literary culture—and put just a single copy of her book on the shelf. Genet became famous for having stolen books. Leduc imagines buying them from her publisher and then sneaking them into places where, if someone should buy them, the profits (at least the financial ones) would not be hers (or her publisher's). If she calls this a form of fraud, it is hardly because she is swindling anyone financially, but rather because she apparently feels her books would not have earned the legitimate right to be on the bookstore shelves where she herself would have placed them.

And yet even though she accepts that, officially speaking, her book's availability for purchase would be fraudulent (unauthorized by the official gatekeepers of the literary field: publishers and booksellers), Leduc nonetheless seems to be claiming a different kind of right (an unofficial one) for her book's continued availability. She does so despite what she recognizes as the officially correct aesthetic failings of her writing: wilted lettuce to Proust's madeleine, a stinking louse to his fragrant hawthorns. It is not, I think, that she has any intention for her work to undermine or undo official culture. Rather, she knows that somewhere there is a public for her perverse, misfit point of view, a public that would appreciate the inappropriateness of what she does, a public that shares some kind of an experience of inappropriateness.

Illegitimacy is, of course, at the heart of Leduc's self-image. When she was in literary company, she often had difficulty fully accepting that she belonged where she was. This self-doubt comes, in her writing, to be intimately tied up with her sense of the unruliness of her sexuality—an unruly sexuality that indeed often provides the material about which she writes. In *La folie en tête* (*Mad in Pursuit*), there is another scene that provides a description of this ongoing experience of inappropriateness structuring Leduc's relation to cultural production. This is a scene in which she describes herself feeling as if she has no right to sleep in the bed she has been given for the night, the bed of the actor Jean Marais, Cocteau's companion. For one result of the odd kinds of recognition Leduc received for her early work (admired by a select segment of the literary elite, but ignored by the general public) was that Leduc found herself invited in July of 1947 to stay for a week or so at Jean Cocteau's country home. It is during this visit that she finishes writing her second book, *L'affamée*.

> My lovely curlers, my lovely lengths of dark and greasy string, shall I dare to use them? Would I dare to inflict them on Jean Marais's hollow cheek on the pillow? If I sacrifice my little curls, tomorrow I shall have to appear before

Cocteau with lank hair. I opted for my frizzers, and felt sorry for the movie actor. He had no idea that a scarecrow was sliding down between his sheets while he faced the camera.[11]

For Leduc, somehow sleeping in Marais's bed involves impinging on his own bodily well-being. Putting her curler-laden head on his pillow is a sacrilege. Yet how could she face Cocteau in the morning without her hair curled? It might seem strange, then, that despite her apparent respect for Marais's bed, pillow, and sheets, she has no problem with rearranging his furniture. Already in bed with the lights out, not feeling particularly at home, suddenly she turns the lights back on to admire the look of her notebooks on Marais's fancy table. She then decides the table is in the wrong place, and gets up and moves it:

> I switched the light back on: not bad, my notebooks . . . not bad at all on the Empire table; but the table in the middle of the room, that wasn't good at all. I wanted it in front of the window, in front of the sky, in front of the kitchen-garden. I got out of bed, I dragged it over, inch by inch, so that no one would know what I was doing, at midnight, in someone else's house. It was where I had imagined it; now I felt a little more at home. I switched off the light before getting back into bed. I wanted to spare that noble bed the spectacle of an ugly woman clambering into it wearing a flannelette nightdress. (190)

Of course, the scene is written for comic effect, but something in it captures both the willfulness and the fragility that characterizes Leduc's relation to culture and to the world of successful writers and other cultural figures: she has no hesitation about dragging a table across the floor in the middle of the night in the room in which she is an invited guest in order to make the room suit her needs as a writer, and yet she turns out the light before making her way back to the bed out of some shame at her physical appearance and her sorry wardrobe. Proust's madeleine, her wilted leaf of lettuce; Proust's elegant hawthorns, her shitty louse; Marais's handsome cheek, her slimy curlers; Marais's noble bed, her cheap nightgown; Marais's fancy table, her simple notebooks—her insistence on the inappropriateness of who she is, what she wears, everything she carries with her, and what she writes about to the surroundings in which she finds herself runs consistently through all these oppositions.[12] Her personal and physical misfittedness are understood as part of the same phenomenon as her writerly misfittedness, the relation of her books to other books, the way that she as reader relates to other books. Her books take up too much space in Gallimard's basement, and then if they manage to avoid being pulped, they attempt to sneak their way onto the shelves of bookstores in the literary heart of Paris, hoping to ensnare an unsuspecting reader before they are found out and evicted.

Leduc obviously enjoys flaunting this inappropriateness, flaunting both her personal and her writerly status as an unseemly misfit. Yet despite all the cultural incongruities she lays out for us, she seems to be happy and productive, almost at home, writing on the table in Jean Marais's bedroom in Jean Cocteau's house, once she has moved that table over to the window:

> I was writing in Jean Marais's sun-flooded room after my walk. Paul Morihen and Georges were playing football outside. They were shouting, they were yelling, they were shrieking their heads off. Poor Cocteau, I said quietly to myself. Writing the end of *L'Affamée* under the roof of a poet was tending to go to my head. It wasn't commercial, but perhaps I was going as far as the Surrealists . . . A small edition for a great inspiration. (199)

She sympathizes with her host regarding loud, inconsiderate guests. She remains overwhelmed by the poetic aura of the place in which she finds herself, and yet she also finds herself capable of meeting the challenge her surroundings represent: she proves herself the equal of the surrealists in what she writes. (Not that they would likely fit in very well in Cocteau's toney digs.) She realizes there is likely no commercial value in what she does, however successful it may be aesthetically. The greater the inspiration, the smaller the print run. It is as if she has read Bourdieu's *The Rules of Art* regarding how profits and aesthetic interest/disinterest relate to each other, and is, at least in this moment, happy to be producing successful writing that will likely earn her nothing much financially—although in the end it seems more that even though she knows that *nothing* is what she *should* want to earn from her published writings (nothing except the acclaim of her literary peers that is), in fact it is not (especially given her financial insecurity) what she does want to earn. Part of what she wants is economic success—along with, as we shall see, various forms of sensual and sexual satisfaction.[13]

The surroundings in which Leduc is granted this briefly satisfying sense of writing high-quality not-for-profit literary works are pretty fancy. Jean Marais is, after all, a movie star. Paul Morihien (whose name Leduc misspells), obnoxiously loud outside the window, helps publish deluxe editions of certain kinds of books (including, eventually, the one she has just finished writing). Jean Cocteau incarnates a certain somewhat ambiguous kind of literary and worldly success. But as she has already made clear, if Leduc finds Marais's room appealing, it is not only because of its symbolic location within the world of cultural production. There are other forms of fascination, less purely literary or aesthetic ones, that are involved for her. Consider the way she rifles through his clothes when she first arrives:

> The sliding door slid open without sound, the interior lit up just as the kitchen garden had lit up at my arrival. Displayed were russet suède shorts, cinnamon suède shorts, beige suède shorts, with fringes, with flaps: Jean Marais's Tyrolean costumes for *L'Aigle à deux têtes*. Silence is sometimes a tempter. I stood for a long time, in the silence of his dressing room, fingering the flap covering the swelling of his sex; I felt the edge of the short suède leg where it was pressed by the hard muscles of his thigh. I touched the suspenders, the horizontal bands that pressed against his athletic torso. I could hear the slightly husky, almost common voice of Jean Marais, I was outlining the profile of a hero with my thumb and forefinger. A fagged-out face, a fagged-out voice, I said to myself as I stroked the suède, which is itself a soft, fagged-out sort of leather. I stroked the russet suède, the beige suède, the cinnamon suède with the steady rhythm of a pendulum; I felt nothing stir inside me, and yet, having Jean Marais's tired face in front of my eyes like that began to exhaust me. (189–90)

This is a display of an intentionally illicit, partly fetishistic, partly onanistic relation to the trappings of the cultural universe into which she has been temporarily admitted. We could say it purposefully debases a certain kind of relationship to culture, representing—of course in highly stylized literary prose—an obsessive, sensual interest in the clothing that has been in touch with Marais's body. It insists on the fundamental sensuality (the feeling of fabric between fingers, an array of colors, the sound of a voice) and sexuality (the way clothes make a body erotic, the imagined relations between a fan and a star) of certain kinds of slightly dubious aesthetic responses.

It is a regular part of Leduc's artistry to pause to insist on inappropriate (often inappropriately sexualized) relations to aesthetic objects or figures (or to their surrogates) but to use sophisticated aesthetic resources in doing so. (We will see in what follows that hers is, off and on throughout her life, a literary sexuality—that is, that literature features in her sexuality, that it is an element of, or a central component of, sexual experience for her.) Here she is, a guest in Cocteau's country house, rifling through Jean Marais's closet, indulging her fascination for the crotch of his costumes before sitting down at his table later during her visit to compose prose that rivals that of the surrealists. She is, and experiences herself to be, a walking contradiction, somewhat of a trespasser we might say, a poacher (yet one supported by Beauvoir and Cocteau) surreptitiously exploring the literary field, waiting to be caught and evicted. She is hypersensitive, it seems, to the social forces that structure this literary field. In the field as Leduc experiences it, there are Gide and Proust, who broached the topic of same-sex sexuality in a way that counted as prestigious, and who exist as nearly sacred figures for her; there is Genet, her contemporary, who challenges the sense of who in the field had the capability of taking up the topic of same-sex sexuality in an aesthetically daring and socially challenging way; there are the surrealists, who create a certain vision of literary avant-gardism linked to new styles and practices of writing meant to explore new regions of the human psyche and certain forms of human sexuality, but not others; there is Cocteau the aesthete and his circle of precious friends who appreciate certain forms of literary finesse and obviously have a carefully delimited interest in the literary exploration of same-sex sexuality; there are Sartre and Beauvoir and their ethos of socially engaged literary practices, and their interest in writers like Genet and Leduc who have the potential to break new ground in their writing. And then there are the readers who don't buy *L'asphyxie*. Leduc, we could say, writes the form of the literary field into her books, explaining to herself and to us the conditions of her own precarity.

One of those conditions is, of course, that she is a woman. However seriously she may be taken by Sartre, Jouhandeau, Cocteau, Genet, and Beauvoir, something about her being a woman means that both the social world and the literary field as such treat her differently than they treat, say, Genet. Leduc registers this aspect of her situation in many ways, including the portrayal of the mental and physical distress she experiences following Gallimard's refusal in 1954 to publish those sections of her novel *Ravages* having to do with the sexual relations of Thèrese and Isabelle at boarding school, the representation of an abortion and its aftermath, and several other passages.[14] If these passages were so important to her, it is because she understood them to be a key part of her attempt to break new ground in literature, just as Genet was doing. One can also trace in her correspondence with Beauvoir from a few years before this episode, her sense that Beauvoir's *The Second Sex* had a similar kind of importance for the evolution of culture. She expresses her support for Beauvoir as she confronted the violently misogynist reactions to her book, and her pride at being cited by Beauvoir in the volume. "I thank you with all my heart for citing me on several occasions," she writes Beauvoir sometime in 1949. "What touched me was the actual moment during which you were writing my name in a serious book."[15]

Leduc's sense that she, Genet, Beauvoir, and Sartre were breaking important new ground in the ways they struggled to represent sexualities that previously had no place in serious writing finds further expression in a letter from the following year. Early in 1950, Leduc makes a comparison between the audacity of Genet in his novels and the audacity of Beauvoir in *The Second Sex*: "Genet's authority appears as strong as ever when you reread him. How salubrious are all the sexual audacities to be found in contemporary literature! I could feel the world-wide barrier of resistances begin to give way as I read volume 2 of *The Second Sex*, as I reread Genet."[16] Clearly she meant for her own writing in these years to contribute to this same project. This helps explain why the frustrations of seeing her work censored, along with the frustration of the poor sales of her books, were almost too much for her to bear.

In the essay called "The Contradictions of Inheritance" that comes about two-thirds of the way into *The Weight of the World*, Bourdieu notes (in a passage I have used as an epigraph for this book) that

> narratives about the most "personal" difficulties, the apparently most strictly subjective tensions and contradictions, frequently articulate the deepest structures of the social world and their contradictions. This is never so obvious as it is for occupants of precarious positions who turn out to be extraordinary "practical analysts": situated at points where social structures "work," and therefore worked over by the contradictions of these structures, these individuals are constrained, in order to live or survive, to practice a kind of self-analysis, which often gives them access to the objective contradictions which have them in their grasp, and to the objective structures expressed in and by these contradictions. (511)

The self-analysis of which Bourdieu speaks is a kind of "socioanalysis" (as opposed to psychoanalysis). It reveals our social being to us. My contention in this chapter is that Violette Leduc and also, in a different way, Hervé Guibert—even though superficially they may sometimes seem to be among the most self-obsessed of writers—count as examples of these "practical analysts" of whom Bourdieu speaks, people whose experience of disequilibrium—experiences that may be linked to a specific period in time or to particular spaces within a given social field—allows them a certain kind of practical insight into the workings of social structures, an insight they then find ways of using their literary craft to express. Many writers might walk through the literary field without much ability to articulate what they are doing and what the field is doing to them. Leduc is hypersensitive, we might say, to the press of the social forces of the literary field upon her and to the way her responses do or do not further her own best interests. She uses her writing to report back to us on both the suffering, and, occasionally, the joy her experience in the field causes her.

Bourdieu's way of understanding idiosyncrasy and the distress that can be associated with it seems well suited to advance our understanding of the sociological acumen sometimes found in writers like Leduc or Guibert. In both cases, their experience of the literary field and their experience of sexuality are inseparable. The kind of acumen they exhibit about sexuality, or about literary sexuality, we might say, depends on no relation—or on a very troubled relation—to typicality, to identity categories, to the most commonly received concepts for rendering sexuality intelligible. Indeed, it is, we could almost say, from their claims to and experience of unintelligibility and atypicality, and from the aesthetic work that goes into the literary representation of the social suffering that goes along with that experience, that their capacity for sociological acumen arises. They demonstrate a capacity to render a point of view that is perhaps only precariously intelligible, and then to demonstrate how the conditions of its precarious intelligibility are produced and reproduced over time through confrontations with other points of view in the social world around them.

Playing with Variables

Leduc is well known as the author of books, fictional and autobiographical to varying degrees (*Ravages, Thérèse et Isabelle, La Bâtarde*), that include scenes recounting in detail sexual relations between women. Her books also include accounts of her unrequited love for a series of gay men (including Maurice Sachs, Jean Genet, and Jacques Guérin); her physical and emotional feelings for Simone de Beauvoir (never reciprocated across the several decades of their friendship, a word that perhaps cannot quite do justice to the odd and unbalanced relation they had); as well as her marriage and another relationship later in life with a construction worker she calls René in her writings. She was fascinated by sexual outsiders of many kinds, and it does not seem that the categories that other people used to talk about her sexuality or sexuality in general had much pertinence for her. Noting the fact that Monique Wittig claimed Leduc as a precursor in the preface to the English language edition of *The Lesbian Body*, Elaine Marks comments: "It is obvious that the scenes in *La bâtarde* and in *Thérèse et Isabelle* in which young girls make love are acceptable to Wittig not merely because females are making love but because the narrator as lesbian is describing her own experience. The lesbian is no longer the object of literary discourse seen from an outside point of view."[17] And yet "lesbian" is a word Leduc applies only to others.[18]

Consider the extraordinary letter she writes to Beauvoir in late summer 1950 about her feelings for Beauvoir and her feelings regarding a couple of women who run the hotel in which she is staying in the village of Montjean:

> That you should not love in the way that I love you is well and good, since that way I will never grow tired of solemnly adoring you. My love for you is a kind of fabulous virginity. And yet I have passed through, and am still in the midst

of, a period of sexual frenzy. . . . I have been obsessed by, hounded by, that couple of women I wrote you about. I have been humiliated, revolted. They have found in this village, they have made real a union, whereas I have for 15 years been consumed by, and am still consumed by solitude. I have often felt as if I were in Charlus's skin as I spied on them, as I envied them, as I imagined them. They never even spend 15 minutes apart, and I often cry with rage and jealousy when I notice this fact. They are mistrustful, they are shut up inside their happiness. One night I told them, after all the people summering here had left, I told them in very nuanced terms that I loved you and about your beautiful friendship for me. It was a one-sided conversation. I gave, but got nothing in return. They are even more extraordinary than Genet's "Maids." The difference in their ages—I have also already told you about this, one is thirty, the other fifty-six—is something I find enchanting and consoling. . . . How simple they are, I keep coming back to this, how unrefined, how sure of themselves. The younger one has the face of a brute. Their fatness is the weight of sensuality. When seated they open their legs wide, like the soldiery, whereas so-called normal women keep them crossed or closed tight. They are a torment to me without even knowing it but they also intensify my love for you because you are a part of the disaster that I am. I often think about lesbians in their cabarets, who exist on another planet, who are nothing but sad puppets.[19]

(Il est bien que vous n'aimiez pas comme je vous aime puisque ainsi je ne me lasserai jamais de vous adorer avec gravité. Mon amour pour vous, c'est de la virginité fabuleuse. Pourtant j'ai traversé et je traverse encore une période de délire sexuel. . . . J'ai été obsédée, traquée par ce couple de femmes dont je vous ai parlé. J'ai été humiliée, révoltée. Elles ont trouvé, réalisé dans un village une union pendant que je me suis consumée quinze ans et que je me consume encore dans la solitude. Je me suis souvent sentie dans la peau du baron de Charlus en les épiant, en les enviant, en les imaginant. Elles ne se quittent pas un quart d'heure et j'ai souvent des larmes de rage, de jalousie en le constatant. Elles sont méfiantes, elles sont enfermées dans leur bonheur. Je leur ai dit un soir, après le départ de tous les estivants, je leur ai dit avec des nuances que je vous aimais et votre belle amitié pour moi. Ce fut un monologue. J'ai donné mais je ne recevrai rien. Comme elles sont beaucoup plus extraordinaires que les "bonnes" de Jean Genet. Cette différence d'âge—je vous l'ai dit aussi: l'une à trente ans, l'autre a cinquante-six ans—m'enchante et me console. . . . Comme elles sont simples, j'y reviens encore, rudes, sûres. La cadette a une tête de brute. Leur grosseur, c'est le poids de sensualité. Elles ouvrent fort leurs jambes quand elles sont assises, à la soudard, tandis que les femmes dites "normales" les croisent, les serrent. Elles me tourmentent sans le savoir mais elles intensifient aussi mon amour pour vous car vous êtes dans ma débâcle. Je songe souvent aux lesbiennes de cabaret qui sont sur une autre planète, qui sont des malheureux pantins.)

The letter is typical of Leduc in all her idiosyncrasy: verging here and there toward the preposterous without ever quite tipping over into it, excessive in its emotivity, self-consciously obsessive, and also profoundly curious about the way sexuality functions (which doesn't mean she can't make the odd homophobic remark), and about the lack of fit between her sexuality and everyone else's (in this case, Beauvoir's, the two women in question, and lesbians who frequent queer bars and cabarets). She is attentive to a number of characteristics, axes of variations in sexualities we might say, that aren't always factored into typical discussions of sexuality: that sexualities have a class or regional component; that age difference is important in some sexualities; that girth can have a relation to gender and to sexuality; that sexualities such as her own and that of this couple apparently are sometimes best understood by way of representations from the world of literature (Genet's two maids), and that the representations chosen can sometimes rely on transgendered forms of identification (her link to Proust's Charlus).

Consider another more condensed example of Leduc's attentiveness to what we might call the multivariable experience of sexuality. *La Bâtarde* recounts several outings taken by the young Leduc and her mother to see different shows while they were living under the same roof in Paris. (They once went, for instance, to see the cross-dressing aerialist Barbette.) As they set out on one such outing, Violette takes her mother's arm:

> "Don't put your arm through mine. You're such a farm boy!" she said.
> Farm boy. The use of the masculine got to me. (127)

> (—Ne me donne pas le bras. Mais que tu es paysan! me disait-elle.
> Paysan. Le masculin m'affligeait. [133])

In one very compact utterance, Leduc's mother registers her impression of her daughter's sexuality, subtly linking together gender, object choice, and that odd mixture of regional identity, class, and race that is contained in the French concept of peasant, *paysan*. It is also a generically interesting utterance, because of the way it indexes a complicated cultural framework for understanding sexuality, a framework that could only belong to someone located socially close enough to the peasants in question to have a detailed awareness of how their social and/or sexual culture operates, but not wanting to be associated with it.

Leduc's representations of her mother's reactions to the sexually dissident forms of behavior she exhibits while growing up (and later) provide consistently interesting evidence of a point of view (her mother's) that is neither exactly approving nor exactly disapproving, but is certainly matter-of-fact about such expressions of dissidence, and that can be perfectly nonchalant about them. When Leduc is expelled from her girls' school because of her sexual relations with one of the teaching staff, she is sent by train to Paris, where her mother is now living. Her mother meets her at the station: "I saw my mother at the front: a brush stroke of elegance. A young girl and a young woman. Her grace, our pact, my pardon. I kissed her and she replied: 'Do you like my dress?' We talked about her clothes in the taxi. My mother's metamorphosis into a Parisienne eclipsed the headmistress and sent the school spinning into limbo. Not the slightest innuendo. Giving me Paris, she gave me her tact" (111). There is a complicity between mother and daughter, a shared choice not to take up the subject of Leduc's behavior or its consequences. We might see behind this complicity a shared set of reference points regarding sexual culture, an understanding that their point of view and that of the headmistress are not the same, a further sense that Parisian sexual culture is a bit different from what they are used to. Clearly, the sexual culture of the countryside, villages, and towns they came from was, while not the same as what they see around them in Paris, already a rich, diverse, and conflicted one. This means that they are already in full possession of a practical understanding of sexual diversity and dissidence that allows them to communicate with and understand each other on all sorts of implicit levels.

This practical understanding of sexual diversity that Leduc shares with her mother is, of course, present in her letter to Beauvoir as well. Her practical understanding tells her that her love for Beauvoir, the relationship between the two women she encounters that summer, and the sexuality of Parisian lesbians are all related and yet different. José Esteban Muñoz at one point uses the phrase "nodes of difference" and at another point the phrase "identity differentials" in describing an intersectional way of thinking about sexuality and identity. Both phrases are suggestive in an effort to understand Leduc's relation to forms of sexuality she finds in the world around her. Nodes of difference and identity differentials would be terms helpful to understanding why it is that Leduc's own sexuality never seems to coincide with the sexuality of the people she meets and enters into intimate relationships with.[20] Among the identity differentials or nodes of difference that count for her might be those between country life, small-town life, and city life, and those between people involved in literary or intellectual pursuits (Beauvoir) and those who are not.

In a number of interesting critical works on Leduc from the late 1990s and early years of this century, it was common to talk about her idiosyncrasy as a form of queerness, and as instantiating "a new and less gender-bound identity," or "the potentially fluid character of gendered and sexual performance," or to speak of "the realm of sexual flexibility and illegitimacy adumbrated in Leduc's life-writings," or to characterize *La Bâtarde* as "a text that not only gives queerness a voice, but also takes a queer delight in challenging normative notions of what gender is and should be." I think that in order to grasp what Leduc is up to, it is probably necessary to qualify these assertions first of all by detailing the ways that for her sexuality is tangled up in more factors than gender and object choice. It can involve age, regional and ethnic identity, class, and cultural or literary affiliations. (That list is not exhaustive.) It is a kind of position-taking in all of these ways. It is also, we might say, sedimentological: it is connected to multiple layers in our personality that have been laid down at different times. Some aspects of it are highly resistant to change, some mercurial. Leduc's sexual engagements, as we shall see in more detail below, involve position-taking of many kinds. If they seem flexible and fluid viewed from one vantage point, from another, the *constraints* that govern those engagements, and that produce such suffering for Leduc, might be more salient.[21]

One strand of Bourdieu's work has to do with how the incorporation of the social world by any given social agent involves incorporating categories that allow us to divide up that world and represent it to ourselves. Since there is, as Bourdieu frequently notes, a plurality of points of view on the "same" social world, both conflict and change can arise from the meeting of different and competing points of view. The misfits I have been studying throughout this project all have points of view on the world that produce different kinds of conflict and suffering because of the way their point of view produces for them an experience of sexuality that is out of the ordinary, incongruous. The strand of Bourdieu's work that I wish to call attention to here has to do specifically with his way of understanding the interaction of different socially pertinent variables within a given social field, especially as it relates to an experience of what we often call identity. Bourdieu's work in *Distinction* (1979) is particularly helpful for that effort.

Any given social variable, Bourdieu explains in *Distinction*, needs to be understood as influencing and as being under the influence of an array of other pertinent social variables. Here is how he expresses this insight, one that led to a particular way of collecting and processing data, and also to a practice of modeling it geometrically:

> The particular relations between a dependent variable (such as political opinion) and so-called independent variables such as sex, age and religion, or even educational level, income and occupation tend to mask the complete system of relationships which constitutes the true principle of the specific strength and form of the effects registered in any particular correlation. The most independent of "independent" variables conceals a whole network of statistical relations which are present, implicitly, in its relationship with any given opinion or practice.[22]

Bourdieu draws attention to how difficult it can be to perceive how different variables are interacting with each other in producing either a sense of social location, of social intelligibility, or of social identity. Leduc's writing in particular, when brought into relation to Bourdieu's thought, has helped me to understand how useful it can be to think of sexuality both as a variable in its own right and as the effect of the interaction of a wide-ranging (and never finalized) set of other sociological variables, and how much the particularities of both the (phenomenological) experience of and the (epistemological) apprehension of sexuality are tied to, indexed to, particular locations within a given social field. Indeed, phenomenological and epistemological considerations may be inseparable, and literary writing, which binds the two together, becomes a particularly useful tool for investigating this conundrum.

Bourdieu's method, in *Distinction*, is meant to work against certain tendencies to imagine, for instance, that it might be possible to understand, to construct, to plot, the relation of two social variables (say sexuality and class, or amount of education and income level) in isolation from others. Should you attempt to do that, you end up, he suggests, simply hiding the effects of other pertinent variables from yourself: "Relationships such as those between educational capital, or age, and income mask the relationship linking the two apparently independent variables. Age determines income to an extent which varies according to educational capital and occupation, which is itself partly determined by educational capital and also by other, more hidden factors such as sex and inherited cultural or social capital" (104). It is perhaps easier to think in terms of a smaller set of variables, or to take one variable at a time, but it limits our ability to grasp what might actually be going on: "When, as often happens, the analysis is conducted variable by variable, there is a danger of attributing to one of the variables (such as sex or age, each of which may express in its own way the whole situation or trend of a class) the effect of the set of variables" (105–6). All of these considerations lead to Bourdieu's compelling description of what social class might be, a description that might also hold for sexuality. Imagine, then, in the following passage, replacing the words "social class" with the word "sexuality":

> Social class is not defined by a property (not even the most determinant one, such as the volume and composition of capital) nor by a collection of properties (of sex, age, social origin, ethnic origin . . . income, educational level etc.), nor even by a chain of properties strung out from a fundamental property . . . in a relation of cause and effect, conditioner and conditioned; but by the structure of relations between all the pertinent properties which gives its specific value to each of them and to the effects they exert on practices. (106)

It strikes me that in a very practical way, this is how Leduc understands her own sexuality, and also a range of sexualities in the world around her. Some of those sexualities take on names (lesbian) that seem to make them a property in their own right, and certainly that is how many people experience those sexualities. For Leduc, the experience of sexuality as a *property* is an alien one: sexuality is, for her, the *effect* exerted on certain *practices* by a shifting structure of relations between a shifting set of "pertinent" properties. It is a summing of multiple vectors, a summing that happens for her almost intuitively. Her frustration and suffering around sexuality frequently arise from the fact that her way of doing these sums is undecipherable to those around her; it somehow makes no sense to them.

Village Life

Leduc's experience in Montjean in the summer of 1950 did not only result in a letter to Simone de Beauvoir, but it also resulted in a quite remarkable short text, little known today, "Au village" (Village life), that was published in *Les Temps Modernes* in March 1951. Leduc spends fifteen pages describing a number of eccentric figures that she met during her vacation, including the couple of women referred to in the letter to Beauvoir and a cross-dressing man she refers to as La Chauplanat. It might be read superficially as belonging to the genre of a sophisticated Parisian recounting droll stories of small-town life—were it not for the fact that Leduc is herself a product of small-town life, and that the intellectually serious *Les Temps Modernes* would seem an unlikely location for that particular literary genre. "Au village" can better be understood as a kind of experimental writing about, among other things, the conjoined perception and experience of sexual culture. If we take Leduc's writing as being, at many points, *sociologically* experimental, we can notice her attunement to problems of categorical division in the experience of sexuality and sexual culture that are simultaneously phenomenological, epistemological, and sociological. She seems attuned as well (although perhaps not consciously—it is more something that is part of her writing practice) to the sense that sexuality is perceived by most of us simultaneously as a pertinent sociological characteristic in its own right and as the effect of the structural relations between a considerable number of other pertinent sociological variables (age, class, education, regional affiliation, race, religion, etc.). Sexuality is a variable and a multivariable effect simultaneously. Leduc seems intent on illustrating how the kinds of excess meaning that can accrue to certain lived experiences of sexuality, excesses that are understood differently by people observing them from different points of view, reveal that there are multiple possible futures in which those meanings might unfold.

In describing La Chauplanat, one of the things that interests Leduc is the difference between the way the villagers react to him and the way summer visitors do:

> Once the summer visitors have left, no one takes any particular notice of La Chauplanat in the village. La Chauplanat is a man. Married to an egg (his bald wife wears a turban day and night), le Chauplanat is a father and a grandfather: three sons, three grandsons. The person whose hair is fixed like Ingrid Bergman's, who balances on top of that hair one of the tall striped caps worn by a New York showgirl on parade, the person who is the bandleader, tailor, organist, and cashier in his son's delicatessen thinks of himself as a woman, and a chaste one. It has been this way for twenty years. No one has heard any stories about him suggestive of particular kinds of tastes. He doesn't cheat on his wife, that's how kind folks put it. The proud village listens to, admires, and absolves its head musician in make-up when he waves his conductor's baton. . . . The farmers whose chests swell when this musician signals the drummers somehow fail to notice that their man is conducting a military march wearing silk stockings. . . . The summer visitors are a little less ingenuous. They are obsessed by la Chauplanat, who is for them a nightmare, a source of fascination. The factory blacksmiths, the hosiery sales reps, the itinerant road workers who insult her and tear her to pieces also dream of her. Hotel dining rooms are the coliseums into which they throw her, trample her, lift her up, throw her down, tear her apart, break her into pieces. The women among the visitors, overshadowed by a man who conducts himself as a woman beyond reproach, egg on these jeering toreadors.[23]

Leduc is, herself, neither an ingenuous villager capable of accepting at face value and without comment the transgendered way of life of La Chauplanat, nor is she, it would appear, the obsessed outsider who seemingly can do nothing but produce an endless stream of derogatory talk about her. Leduc's fascination is different in kind, she suggests, from that of the mostly working-class people who spend their summer vacations in this town. Her description carefully points out how understanding La Chauplanat involves taking into account his or her (Leduc gives us no indication as to a preferred pronoun of address, so I shall alternate) marriage, her family life, the ambiguous sexuality and gender of his wife, her profession, his religiosity, her desire for female celibacy, his musicality, her fashion sense, and so on. All this is implicitly known and in some practical way understood by the entire village, it seems, which is what allows La Chauplanat simply to be a part of the ordinary life of the village. It is the possibility of (and the fragility of) this ordinariness that seems to fascinate Leduc. Her presentation is structured by a movement from the extraordinary to the ordinary, and then back to the extraordinary, before finally concluding in a more ordinary register. She begins the passage referring to La Chauplanat with feminine pronouns:

> La Chauplanat aims to be the woman with the most artistic makeup, the whitest lingerie, the tightest corset, the most painful shoes. She wishes to be the most noticeable, the most frequently pointed out, and the best behaved. She is the great eccentric, she is discretion itself.

> (La Chauplanat se veut la plus artistement maquillée, la plus neigeusement lingée, la plus strictement corsetée, la plus douloureusement chaussée. Elle se veut la plus remarquée, la plus désignée, la plus sage. C'est la grande excentrique et la grande réservée. [1598–99])

In short, La Chauplanat stands out, and makes a point of doing so. It is only a few sentences later that we learn that this eccentric woman who makes a point of simultaneously being noticed and incarnating distance and discretion is not exactly what she seems. "Once the summer visitors have left, no one takes any particular notice of La Chauplanat in the village. La Chauplanat is a man" (La Chauplanat passe inaperçue dans son village quand les estivants sont partis. La Chauplanat est un homme). If this comes across, in part, as a sensationalist revelation of gender nonconformity, Leduc's goal nonetheless appears to be simultaneously to sensationalize and to desensationalize the situation. This woman who dresses so as to stand out is, in fact, somehow unremarkable (as regards her gender nonconformity) to the village for most of the year. Notice that at this point in Leduc's account, once it has been announced that "La Chauplanat is a man," linguistic gender switches back to the masculine for a while; La Chauplanat even becomes Le Chauplanat briefly, as information about his background is provided. Only when the passage turns to consider the obsessive, hostile discourse of the summer visitors is La Chauplanat once again (almost) consistently referred to in the feminine as she is subjected to the discursive violence of the summer visitors, male and female. Then, with the summer visitors gone, the passage gently oscillates back and forth between genders:

> As he sits near the window sewing, assuming the attitude of a young noblewoman from a ruined family embroidering her trousseau with her hair weeping about her, Chauplanat looks younger than his years. Ambition keeps you young. He is a serene sage who would be a woman and thinks no further than that. La Chauplanat has been forgiven because she has never sinned. She is

a moving figure, a stoic. She is the legend accompanying an image from a summer vacation.

(Chauplanat ne paraît pas son âge lorsqu'il coud près de la fenêtre, lorsqu'il a l'attitude épanchée d'une jeune noble ruinée brodant son trousseau, la chevelure éplorée. L'ambition conserve. C'est un sage, un serein qui se veut féminin et qui n'imagine pas plus loin. La Chauplanat a été pardonnée parce qu'elle n'a pas fauté. C'est une émouvante, c'est une stoïque. C'est la légende d'un souvenir de vacance. [1600])

If La Chauplanat is so exemplary, it would seem to be because of the way she can exist in the village with a gender that adjusts according to circumstance, where the use of pronouns in any utterance is indicative both of her or his gender and of the context of the utterance, of the social positioning and the intentions of the interlocutors, of their awareness (or lack of awareness) of all the pertinent sociological variables in play in the situation.

The portrait of La Chauplanat offers a lesson about the complexity of sexuality in situation, and about the practical and somewhat subliminal calculations we are always performing in refining our perceptions of the composition of other people's sexuality in situation. (This is why certain people in the village regularly rehearse the fact that even though it might seem that someone with La Chauplanat's profile would be the kind of person who would be off secretly seeking out sexual encounters with men, that does not, in fact, seem to be the case; and indeed, upon further consideration of all the variables in play, it comes to make some kind of sense to most people that such sexual encounters are not part of what La Chauplanat is seeking.) The portrait that follows it, and that resembles it in some ways, takes these insights a step further. This is the portrait of the Panther and Juno, the couple of women Leduc referred to in her letter to Beauvoir, the Panther being twenty-six years older than Juno, and Juno being, it turns out, married to a farmer named Julien, who visits the couple on Sundays. We can take Leduc's portrait of the couple (like her letter to Beauvoir about them) to be part of an effort to imagine how their sexuality might be understood, what other social variables it is connected with, how its manner of being reported (to her and by her) becomes part of the problem regarding what it is, whether (remembering the way we talked of the timeliness of a given form of sexuality in chapter 1) this kind of sexuality looks historically forward or backward, or whether it might be tied to its location in this village even more tightly than it is tied to any moment in time. The complex utterance that is Leduc's letter to Beauvoir indexes multiple frameworks for understanding sexuality, as does her portrait of these two women in her article. The letter also recounts an interaction between her, the Panther, and

Juno that is not included in "Au village"—Leduc's "monologue" to them about
her love for Beauvoir, about their friendship—in which Leduc attempts (and
apparently fails) to negotiate a shared framework for understanding different
kinds of relations between women that might include both hers and theirs.

As with the portrait of La Chauplanat, the portrait of the Panther and Juno
makes a point of distinguishing between the attitudes of the summer visitors
to the village and the attitudes of the locals. In both cases Leduc's own position
is neither that of the visitors nor that of the locals. She gets information about
the Panther both from the locals and from visitors like a prurient blacksmith
from Paris who caught the two women kissing in the kitchen early one morning. (He is in fact renting a room from the Panther and her partner.) Providing
a social location not only for your own point of view, but for the source of
each piece of information you accumulate about someone seems a key part
of Leduc's procedures for this portrait, which would therefore appear also to
be about how the implicit social calculus of sexuality works, how it interfaces
with other processes of social positioning. One of the pieces of information
Leduc picks up from a local early on is that Juno, the Panther's partner, "is
married" (1602), and much of the rest of the portrait of the two women will
be an effort to present enough pieces of pertinent information to allow an informed reader to arrive at a practical understanding of this village same-sex
sexuality that Leduc finds so fascinating and appealing.

Julien is the name of Juno's husband, and Leduc is there, in the women's
kitchen, one day when Julien comes to visit, bringing fruits and flowers from
the farm where he lives with his mother. After his departure, the Panther asks
Leduc a question, as if wondering what their situation must look like from
a socially distant point of view, that of a sympathetic female summer visitor
from Paris:

> "What kind of a marriage is this anyway? Can you tell me? It was a whim, she
> married him on nothing more than a whim. And he wasn't the first fiancé . . .
> Bouboule, Lulu, L'Aigrefin . . . What kind of fiancés were they all?" . . .
>
> "You aren't telling the whole story," Juno chimed in. "I took him to save
> the house. You know that's true! His property is ours. In fact, our business is
> as much his as it is ours." . . .
>
> "We could have found another way to solve the problem," cried the Panther.
> "He's not the only person around who has property . . . When he shows up here,
> I have to leave. I'll never be able to bear it. It's too much for me."
>
> (—Ça ressemble à quoi ce mariage? Vous pouvez me le dire, vous? C'est par
> caprice, uniquement par caprice, qu'elle l'a épousé. Oh! ce n'est pas le premier
> fiancé . . . Bouboule, Lulu, L'Aigrefin . . . Ça ressemble à quoi ces fiancés? . . .

—Vous ne dites pas tout, a commencé Junon, je l'ai pris pour sauver la maison. Vous le savez! Nous avons son bien. Le commerce est d'ailleurs autant à lui qu'à nous. . . .

—Nous nous serions arrangés autrement, a crié la Panthère. Il n'y a pas que lui qui possède du bien sur la terre . . . Quand il vient ici, il faut que je m'en aille. Je ne le supporterai jamais. C'est plus fort que moi. (1604)

The marriage was, it seems at first glance, a practical financial move. Julien was apparently not Juno's first male suitor, and is willing (at least for the time being) to content himself with brief visits, and to allow the women to use his money to keep their café afloat. Juno seems happy with the arrangement. It drives the Panther a little crazy.

And yet, the Panther has other reasons to go along with a marriage that on some level seems intolerable to her:

> "I'm twenty-six years older than she is," she whispered without glumness. "You have to look ahead. Julien may not be much, but she won't be alone. . . . She'll have my house and his money. I could easily die before her. But what kind of a man is he really?"

> (—J'ai vingt-six ans de plus qu'elle, a-t-elle murmuré sans s'attrister. Il faut être prévoyante, ce n'est rien un Julien, mais elle ne serait pas seule. . . . Elle aura ma maison et son argent. Je pourrai m'en aller avant elle. Mais à quoi ça ressemble un homme comme ça? [1605])

Julien, whatever his inadequacies (none too handsome? none too bright?), seems at least like a good insurance policy. And, as Juno makes a point of adding at this juncture, he doesn't really take up that much room: "He only comes by on Sunday nights and often, admit it, he doesn't spend the night" (1605). Which means, of course, that on some Sundays he does stay overnight and the Panther, enraged, goes and stays somewhere else.

Leduc is intrigued, wanting to know where and how far away he lives. The Panther supplies her response: "He lives with his mother, of course. . . . On his farm with his animals. That's only natural. He has to tend to his riches. Can you see him living around here? He's a bit dim, really" (1605). We see the category of the unsophisticated peasant functioning again here, intersecting with, deflecting in various ways, pathways that might otherwise on their own seem fully to constitute a given sexuality.

Leduc will add a few more variables for us to take into account, having to do with the way this marriage functions and the way gender operates in this complex familial system. The two women think fondly back to the way they spent the night before Juno's marriage to Julien:

"The day before the wedding," the Panther informed me, "we ended the day, her and me, watching a boxing match. It was a crazy thing to do. Eight hundred francs a seat . . . She's crazy about wrestling," she admitted.

(—La veille de son mariage, m'a détaillé la Panthère, nous avons fini la journée, elle et moi, dans une salle de boxe. C'était une folie. Huit cents francs la place . . . Le catch la passionne, a-t-elle avoué. [1605])

Female masculinity at its finest, we might say, this couple of women making a point of reminding Julien where he stands by their extravagant expenditure on a particular form of spectatorship the night before his marriage to Juno. In the paragraphs following this piece of information, Leduc carefully provides a few more for us to factor into our sense of these women, and the context in which they live out their sexuality. We learn, for instance, from the Panther's mother, that "the Panther had recently turned down three marriage proposals" (1606). We also learn that not everything is smooth sailing in this situation when Juno expresses her unhappiness with the way the Panther reacts when Julien does in fact spend a night with his wife:

"But really, there's something you need to stop doing," she added, "and that is to go back to your mother's and smash up everything in the bedroom you grew up in on the nights he's staying here."

(—Mais ce que vous ne devriez pas, a-t-elle ajouté, c'est vous retirer chez votre mère, tout casser dans votre belle chambre de jeune fille, quand il reste ici la nuit. [1606])

Whatever unresolved tensions there may be in their situation, these women live their situation openly. "Que dit le pays?" Leduc queries. "What do people round here say about you?" "'They can all just mind their own business,' the Panther replied. Juno nodded her approval." The mailman says hello to the two women as they walk down the street arm in arm, and Leduc concludes the portrait with the following moral, "People who are sure of themselves don't bother others" (Ceux qui s'imposent n'indisposent pas les autres) (1606). This might recall for us a comment made by Colin R. Johnson about sexuality in small-town America:

Rural and small-town Americans have a long history of accounting for various forms of difference in terms of eccentricity, idiosyncrasy, or simply the predictable weirdness of neighbors, friends, and family members whom they may not always love, or even particularly like, but whom they also realize they are going to live with whether they want to or not. In some cases, rural and small-town residents have even been known to demonstrate a certain kind of protectiveness toward social outliers, especially when criticisms of these individuals are seen as coming from outside the community.[24]

All in all, the example of Juno and the Panther, as given to us in Leduc's prose, provides further evidence that Leduc's way of understanding sexuality, and of offering that practical understanding to us, conforms to the model Bourdieu offers. Sexuality, for Leduc, seems to be intelligible as a structure built up of multiple properties; it is "the structure of relations between all the pertinent properties which gives its specific value to each of them and to the effects they exert on practices" (*Distinction*, 106). Leduc's writing constantly suggests that in every situation in which she enacts her own sexuality, or offers a portrait of someone else's, there will always be a complex operative set of features in play that are partially determinative of that sexuality. The particular set of features may involve a sense of social position (class) and a sense of a peculiar and somewhat fragile point of view on the social field, a sense of ethnic positioning (taking *paysan* to be a kind of ethnic category), in Leduc's case a sense of literariness (I will be coming back to this), and a sense of necessary sexual illegitimacy. All these are braided together in unpredictable ways that perhaps produce something that is not a recognizable sexual identity as such. What seems to be produced is some kind of intersectional or multivariable pattern that feels meaningful to her and whose meaning and value it is her goal to transmit to us. Leduc's sexuality and her understanding of other misfit sexualities are patterned. Sometimes the pattern is such that those who enact that misfit sexuality find a way of fitting into their social world (La Chauplanat, Juno and the Panther); sometimes the pattern is such that the person caught up in it cannot fit into the social fabric as a whole, thereby producing a situation of what Bourdieu calls suffering and Leduc calls "les larmes et les cris."

Writing Schoolboys

On a number of occasions in the late 1940s and early 1950s, Leduc uses the words "chastity" or "virginity" or "fidelity" or "purity" to describe her understanding of her unreciprocated desire for Beauvoir.[25] What she renounces for Beauvoir, she says at one point, is her love for inaccessible gay men (Jean Genet and the industrialist and literary philanthropist Jacques Guérin) and for a trio of male high school students who begin writing her in the spring of 1948. In a letter to one of those three young men, Leduc describes what writing is for her:

> Yes, when you are writing you have to write for someone, but not write for a
> public. And yet true writing involves letting go, without going so far as auto-

matic writing; it involves following behind the pen you are holding even as you keep it under control. (*Correspondance*, 84)

Not a public, but someone. Not automatic writing, but a kind of controlled free writing that allows something implicit to emerge. Receiving letters from "someone" who has read you, who has identified with something implicit in your writing, and who has felt compelled to make contact with you—this experience was obviously immensely important to Leduc, and, as one might expect, given her constant association of literary fervor with sexual impulses, her relationship with two of the three high school students rapidly becomes sexualized.

"Please understand I'm not trying to draw you into some kind of unpleasant trap," Leduc writes to the first of these fellows, all of them schoolmates in Rennes, preparing for the baccalaureate examination, encouraging him to economize on the expense of a hotel during his upcoming trip to Paris, and sleep on her sofa. A few days after his visit, she will be writing to one of his friends: "I wasn't being honest when I invited him. My friendship had become clouded with something else, and what he wrote me was moving me deeply even in my lower regions. I didn't have the strength to stop him from coming, even though I knew the sordid tricks I would get up to" (j'ai triché avec lui lorsque je l'ai invité. Mon amitié était devenue trouble et ses phrases bouleversaient aussi mon ventre. Je n'ai pas eu la force de l'empêcher de venir alors que je savais déjà ma saleté à venir) (*Correspondance*, 81, 90). When she comes to describe this episode from her life in *Mad in Pursuit*, it produces some astonishing writing, including the following passage:

> Cock, ring my doorbell tomorrow and I will let you in. Open your fly for the fireworks display, open up, open up . . . I will curl it; rollers, curlers, clips, pins, a hairdresser on the rue de Charonne is what I must have. You'll find one a hundred yards along the street. Thank you. Don't mention it. What am I when I write? Quickly. Quickly, before you open the door of the hairdresser's. I am a forger making a bad copy of her neighbor's work. And who is my neighbor? The sky, the stars. Rollers, curlers, hairspray, comb. What am I when I write? A release, a deliverance, but I am not there. Always me in what I write. Always. But I give to this terrible sheet of paper without holding back. What am I when I write? This time I've got you by the throat, my copyist. What am I when I write . . . a peasant, a peasant who desists and gives way at the Angelus; the page is so vast to be filled. (229–30)

> (Bite, sonnez à ma porte demain, je vous ouvrirai. Ouvrez votre braguette pour le feu d'artifice, ouvrez, ouvrez . . . je vais la friser, bouclettes, frisettes, pinces, épingles, un coiffeur rue de Charonne se laisse désirer. Vous en avez un à cent

mètres. Merci. De rien. Qu'est-ce que je suis quand j'écris? Vite. Vite avant d'ouvrir la porte du coiffeur. Je suis un faussaire qui copie mal sur sa voisine. Qui est-ce, ma voisine? Le ciel, les étoiles. Bouclettes, frisettes, laque, peigne. Qu'est-ce que je suis quand j'écris? Une délivrance, mais je suis absente. Toujours moi dans ce que j'écris. Toujours. Mais je donne sans compter à ce terrible papier. Qu'est-ce que je suis quand j'écris, cette fois je te serre à la gorge, copiste. Qu'est-ce que je suis quand j'écris . . . un paysan, il cède à l'angélus, la page est vaste à remplir. [360–61])

So many elements we have encountered previously reappear here: an immense sense of sexual frustration; Leduc's obsession with her hair and different ways of wearing it; her intermingling of sex, reading, and writing; her fascination with the forms of freedom from identity that writing can produce—a division within the self that allows for freedom from it, even as writing seems simultaneously and relentlessly to bring her back to her obsession with herself and her sense of illegitimacy; and finally, perhaps with a glancing evocation of Millet's painting, *The Angelus*, a deep-rooted identification between herself and a peasant whose religiosity is brought out by the sound of bells rolling across a landscape, whose toil in an enormous field resembles for her the never-ending task of literary devotion, a self-exploration that goes on page after page.

Here we come to the crisscrossing of the two major themes of this chapter: the theme of the multivariable and idiosyncratic experience of sexuality that is Leduc's (and Guibert's), on the one hand, and the theme of the search for a reader who might share an experience of, and have acquired a practical understanding of, that experience of some such misfit sexuality. The discovery of that reader, the formation of that public will not necessarily occur around an identification with a particular social form of sexuality. (Indeed, we might say that both Guibert and Leduc demonstrate for us that particular sex acts themselves are not always the rituals that produce adhesion to a mainstream sexual identity.) Often the formation of that misfit community seems to happen around the shared affective experience of misfittedness itself, of living on a sociological fault line, of being, in one of Bourdieu's favorite terms, *en porte-à-faux*, misaligned, out of kilter, off balance, caught in an experience of a state of precarious social (un)intelligibility. For Leduc, that state is a durable one. For a frustrated teenager, faced with an exam that bears heavy consequences for the future, it might be more temporary.

It is the third of the three young men (called Robert in the correspondence, and Flavien in *Mad in Pursuit*) in whom Leduc ends up investing the most energy, and with the most disastrous consequences. Very early in their exchange of letters she feels inspired to send him the typescript of her second novel, *L'affamée*, a gesture she recognizes as excessive in a letter she sends to his two friends, informing them of her action: "Yes, it's just as I told you and Alain, I gave the typed manuscript of *L'Affamée* to Robert. I sent it in an inspired moment. It hadn't crossed my mind even five minutes earlier. . . . I'm really nothing but an insane woman, but organized in her instability" (95). The justification comes in a letter from a few weeks later: "He [Robert] occupies a huge place in my universe, a space of reality in the irreality of it" (99). The gift of a typescript is a prelude to an effort at even greater intimacy: Leduc goes to Rennes, and the two meet up in her hotel room. The editor of Leduc's correspondence, Carlo Jansiti, describes the weekend in the following terms:

> Locked up in her hotel room with Robert, under age at the time, V. Leduc lived through, in Alain's words, "three days of orgies and of violence." The school-boy's mother took the occasion to hand over V. Leduc's letters to the police, but she refused to press charges. The police nonetheless went to the hotel and escorted, manu militari, V. Leduc to the train station. The version of her stay in Rennes given in *Mad in Pursuit* is quite different. (102n2)

Leduc's major frustration after this debacle will be that she almost immediately loses contact with Robert. He joins the military, is sent to Africa, and stops writing to her. As she puts it in a letter to Alain (the one of the three she didn't try to engage in sexual relations) in September 1948, "when I was in Rennes and that family delivered my letters to the police, Robert was on my side and was offended for both of us. Afterwards he humiliated me by refusing to see me again. . . . Soon I will be forced to think that Robert was just playacting. . . . He would have needed the personality of a genius to take me and keep me" (103). This dream of an intimate literary community involving herself and three young men will have lasted all of eight months, and yet will have marked her for much longer. Sexualized misfit literary counterpublics are fragile, it would seem, and often implode in ways that are hard to recover from.[26] Yet clearly they are part of the experience of literary idiosyncrasy that I have been tracing here. We can find a similar situation in the work of Hervé Guibert, to which I now turn.

The Failure of Certain Maps

Part of my reason for bringing Leduc and Guibert together is that their experience of idiosyncrasy (an idiosyncrasy in which their literary and their sexual practices are closely intertwined) seems to make them consistently refractory to certain forms of social integration, and it is thanks to this refractory situation that their works end up being so sociologically powerful. It is not exactly that they are off the social map; it is that they seem to see, experience, and use the map differently, or perhaps they use a different map to cover the same terrain. They seem to inhabit a social space that is out of kilter with the space occupied by most of their fellows. In his piece called "Of Other Spaces," on what he calls heterotopias, Michel Foucault describes one way that such other spaces can function: "their role is to create a space of illusion that exposes every real space, all the sites inside of which human life is partitioned, as still more illusory."[27] The fact of being out of kilter, to the extent that it can be used to make explicit divisions in the social field that we often experience unconsciously, can, for all the suffering often associated with it, also operate as a prompt toward some kind of critical relation to social experience. In Guibert's case, I will be interested in his resistance to certain identity categories, in the production of various misfit communities in and around his work, and in the way the idiosyncratic situation of being out of kilter was aggravated by his infection with HIV and his battle with AIDS-related illness. Guibert's AIDS novels demonstrate how the spreading of the epidemic in places like France in the 1980s and 1990s caused the social map to be redrawn in a way that changed how HIV-infected people could exist in the social world. As social space is reconfigured, so is the ability of certain people to interface with it.

Let me digress for a moment here and introduce a passage from Annie Ernaux's brilliant 2008 novel *Les années* (The years), a compelling example of a literary project that sets out to experiment with the kind of socioanalysis Bourdieu discusses. Leduc and Guibert are resolutely first-person writers, of course, and Ernaux has been as well, for much of her writing career. In *Les années*, the choice to employ the third person in a somewhat idiosyncratic manner is at the center of the novel's sociological ambitions:

> What is important for her is . . . to get a hold on that span of time that constitutes her passage on this earth at a given period, this time that ran through her, this world that she recorded by the simple fact of being alive. There was another feeling in which she found the intuition of what the form of her book would be, a sensation in which she finds herself submerged when, starting from a fixed image in her memory—of being in a hospital bed alongside other children who had had their tonsils removed after the war ended or of being in a bus crossing Paris in July 1968—she has the sense of melting into an indistinct totality, from which, by an effort of critical consciousness, she manages to isolate one by one those elements that make it up, customs, gestures, words, and so on. . . . In moments like these she rediscovers . . . a kind of vast collective feeling, in which her consciousness, indeed all her being, is *caught up*—in a similar fashion to when alone in her car on the freeway, she feels caught up in the indefinable totality of the world of the present, from near at hand to far away.[28]

Each of these three examples offers a different sense of how partaking in an experience that is in some way typical allows for a feeling that one belongs somehow to a totality, and moreover allows for the sense that this relation between typicality and totality offers comfort of a kind, or perhaps meaningfulness, forms of comfort and meaningfulness that other peoples' experience sometimes denies them (Leduc throughout long portions of her life, and Guibert for crucial periods during his). Having a tonsillectomy as a child in the mid-twentieth century could be experienced (perhaps more retrospectively than in the moment itself) as part of a set of experiences establishing a typical, normal relation to the medical system and to your own body. Perceived in a certain way, it could be said to take you out of your specificity and into your typicality. The history of your own body is experienced as running in parallel to the experience of other similar bodies around you. Being on a bus in Paris in July 1968, you may feel that you are part of a shared experience of an ambiguous political moment. De Gaulle's party, the Union for the Defense of the Republic, may just have won a parliamentary majority in June, and police violence against protestors may have been a regular fact of daily life, yet it could still feel as if the events of May represented a watershed, a turning point, and that the collective social body was absorbing this experience, even if different people might react to it and absorb it differently. You could think of these two examples as in some ways properly social experiences, with co-presence being a key feature, essential to the production of a sense of belonging to a collectivity. The third example Ernaux provides seems more abstract, almost metaphoric. Alone, in a car, on a freeway, you experience yourself as caught up in the freeway system, or as participating in a particular culture of transportation, or as following paths that have been laid out for you.[29] That is, your own route, where you enter the freeway, where you exit, what turnings you take to get to the freeway, what turnings you take once you leave the freeway to find your destination, are perhaps specific to you, but you are on a shared map, following paths that have been laid out and that others too have followed with varying degrees of frequency. And there is perhaps something for you to understand about "yourself" in the way your routes and the frequency with which you follow them map onto the routes and frequencies followed by other travelers within the same transportation system. Yet for people such as Leduc or Guibert, the maps they are handed seem often to be of no use. Here is an example.

The example comes from an exchange that took place between Hervé Guibert and Christophe Donner, in an interview from February 1991, around the time of the publication of Guibert's *The Compassion Protocol*, the second of his books dealing with his experience of AIDS-related illness. Guibert's work, with such an intense investment in expression in the first person, raises certain questions that should by now seem familiar based on what we have seen of Leduc's writing. Donner poses what may seem like an annoying question to Guibert. First, he comments that "I learned just recently that Narcissus, Freud's hero, did not drown as a result of spending so much time gazing at his own reflection in the water: he was transformed into a flower." This might seem a way of critically preparing the ground for a question about what it means for a gay man to be so engaged in a project of first-person literary production, and, indeed, that is how Guibert seems to understand the question Donner finally asks: "Have you ever had dealings with the sin of narcissism?" Here is part of Guibert's response:

> I really don't know. That's part of a vocabulary that's mostly used by idiots. When people talk about narcissism, "that's narcissistic, that's a kind of navel-gazing, that's perverse, that's unhealthy . . . ," in general it's a dubious discourse, coming from people who are sloppy thinkers or who don't know how to think, don't know how to read, who have misunderstood, who don't have what it takes, who settle for this kind of observation because they don't have the means, the intellectual means, or aren't sensitive enough, to understand what is going on. In general, these words are manipulated in really stupid ways. At the same time, I suppose I could speak about narcissism, about perversity, but these aren't really words that are part of my world, just like the word homosexuality. That's a word that for me has never felt like it had any relationship to me, which seems strange because obviously it does, but that's just not how I see things, that's not the way I live, that's not how I feel about myself, I have the impression that I am to be found somewhere else than in these. . . .[30]

This exchange is, we might say, packed with implicitness. What is at stake for Donner in the fact that the details of Ovid's version of the Narcissus story, in which Narcissus was turned into a flower, do not coincide with a version familiar to him in which Narcissus drowns while trying to reach his own image? Is it that self-absorption results in a beautiful flower instead of a watery death? And what would this have to do with Freud's concept of narcissism? Guibert himself doesn't seem all too clear as to what the question is about either. First, he takes it as a question having to do with the kind of writing he does, which some might take to be egotistical, a perception he considers mistaken—understanding, as he clearly did, that the kind of idiosyncratic experimentations in self-exposure that he engaged in revealed a good deal more than simply "himself." Then he takes it to be a question regarding sexuality, perversity, homosexuality. This seems a reasonable assumption given that Donner has mentioned Freud, and that it is reasonably well known that in his essay "On Narcissism," Freud writes: "We have found, especially in persons

whose libidinal development has suffered some disturbance, as in perverts
and homosexuals, that in the choice of their love-object they have taken as
their model not the mother but their own selves. They are plainly seeking
themselves as a love-object and their type of object-choice may be termed
narcissistic."[31] This would seem to be part of the context Donner meant to
invoke in asking the question. Perhaps we could surmise that he imagines his
discovery that in the *Metamorphoses* Narcissus was turned into a narcissus and
didn't drown in pursuit of his own image (although he did of course starve
himself to death) contains the seed of a critique of Freud's theory of homosexual narcissism. This whole possible thread of the conversation, Guibert
dismisses with his interesting comment about "the word homosexuality," to
which he expresses an intriguing kind of ambivalence. It both applies to him
and it does not; it's "a word that for me has never felt like it had any relationship to me, which seems strange because obviously it does." Or perhaps we
could say that he understands there is a category of people who might choose
to use the word to talk about him, and perhaps he is acknowledging that they
would be right to do so from their point of view. It's just that from his point
of view they would be wrong: "that's just not how I see things, that's not the
way I live, that's not how I feel about myself, I have the impression that I am
to be found somewhere else than in these . . ." He trails off there for a moment,
before closing the interview with a few disjointed remarks about what beauty
is for him. The three dots represent not just a pause, one imagines, but also an
effect of intonation, and also, perhaps, a physical gesture, a raising of a hand
and a little wave perhaps, as if to ward off an intrusion of the categories of the
normative world into the space of his own existence, a space organized differently, a heterotopia, we might hazard, where sexual acts and sexual identities
do not line up in the way people in the ordinary world often take them to.

Perhaps this is for reasons similar to those we have found in Leduc's case,
that for Guibert, as for Leduc, the experience of sexuality involves the experience of (again in Bourdieu's terms) a structure of relations between a range of
pertinent social properties, but a range of properties that is wider than what is
normally included in most people's way of talking about sexuality and sexual
identity. Guibert's correspondence with the Belgian writer Eugène Savitzkaya,
along with a few associated texts, are one place we can find evidence of his
effort to give literary expression to his idiosyncratic and misfit point of view.
In AIDS novels such as *To the Friend Who Did Not Save My Life* and *The Compassion Protocol*, he continues this same project, but finds himself willy-nilly
caught up in another one, in the project Ross Chambers has called "a community autobiography . . . emphasizing the pluralized experience of a community
undergoing diminishment." Chambers suggests that in such situations, the

community itself becomes "the true subjective source of the writing and the agency of its haunting effect, of which the writer is only the agencer."[32] In fact, the collective project Chambers describes for us, arising out of an attempt to account for the disaster of the AIDS epidemic as experienced in places like Paris in the 1980s and 1990s, when taken up by Guibert, will make use of the kinds of tools and strategies we have observed Guibert and Leduc using in their earlier projects of idiosyncratic and implicitly sociological literary experimentation around sexuality. The tale Guibert tells of a trip to Casablanca near the end of *The Compassion Protocol* proves to be a compelling locus where all of these elements come together to remarkable effect, and it is toward a reading of that episode from *The Compassion Protocol* that I am heading.

Guibert and Savitzkaya

"Je t'aime à travers ce que tu écris. Je t'aime en train d'écrire," Guibert writes to Savitzkaya in "Lettre à un frère d'écriture" (Letter to a brother in writing), an open letter first published in 1982.[33] "I love you through what you write. I love you as you sit there writing." He continues a bit later, sounding more than a little like Leduc, "I would like, at the moment your body is caught up in writing, to weave around it an entire network of servile acts of attention, rolling up the legs of your trousers to bathe your feet and your ankles in lukewarm water in which I will melt herb bennet twigs . . ." (65). As his fantasy continues, he imagines what he might do to prepare the body of his brother in writing for his work:

> But before that, before you even sit down to work and in preparation for it, to polish your implement, I would wash your fingers and your nails, get the grit out, or rather I would leave the blackness there that seems to drip like ink onto the paper, and I would wash your hair, knead the muscles of your back with delicate massages so that they are better prepared for your sitting. You would wear a white shirt, collarless, with a notched neckline. You'd be in your underwear, and I would never see your sex, and it would please me to think that you didn't have a sex, that it was indefinite, that perhaps it is a cleft. (65)

Enough things are braided together in Guibert's imagination that we could begin to see how in his world a sexual encounter could happen between two men that would not be related to homosexuality (or not primarily so), but rather would be literary, tied to sensual bodily practices that are not exclusively sexual, tied to a body that is itself ambiguously sexed, tied to the idea of writing. This is an attitude or a way of being Guibert seems to share with Savitzkaya. In Guibert's "Entretien avec Eugène Savitzkaya" (Conversation with Eugène

Savitzkaya), to which "Lettre à un frère d'écriture" served as a kind of preface, Guibert comments to Savitzkaya that in his writing, "You don't have a sex, you aren't holding onto a sex . . . you pass from one to another, and beyond the fact that your writing is quite erotic (due as much to the variegated surface of the language as to its images), that creates an additional kind of trouble" (tu ne tiens pas un sexe, tu ne tiens pas à un sexe . . . tu passes de l'un à l'autre, et outre que ton écriture est très érotique [par la moire de la langue, autant que par ses images], cela crée un trouble supplémentaire). Savitzkaya responds: "I think it is related to my own existence, my way of life. I can't stand anything that is definitive; I think that sex has no gender" (Je crois que ça tient à ma propre existence, à ma manière de vivre. J'ai horreur de ce qui est définitif, je pense que le sexe n'a pas de genre).[34] The eroticism of a writer's language is to be found in the oscillating patterns on its surface, fluctuating shades of light and dark, not in any particular imagery. Guibert and Savitzkaya seem erotically linked by the shared ability to write and read in that way. What relationship this kind of erotic sharing has to sexuality itself remains a bit unclear.

There was indeed some kind of sexual encounter that took place between Guibert and Savitzkaya a few years later, sometime around New Year's Day 1984. Its traces can be found both in a short story Guibert wrote called "Papier magique" where Savitzkaya is called Fernand and in the correspondence between the two writers that was published in 2013. In both texts, it is the idiosyncrasy of the encounter that is emphasized. Here is an excerpt from "Papier magique":

> I went down into the small area under the stairs where Fernand had made up a bed for himself; I had hesitated about going down, now I hesitated to stay. There was a risk, through sex, of falling into common territory. We spent hours kissing without taking any interest in our genitals. His wide-open eye had reopened mine and now wouldn't release it: we had become insects. (69)

Here is the related passage from the correspondence:

> This morning: only a week ago I had just spent the night with you. . . . Now I have some regrets. I think about saying to myself: I wasn't as animated with you as I should have been, I didn't make as much as I should have, with you and for you, of your presence. I should have licked your ass and gotten really deep inside you using lotion and my spit, and made you have a huge orgasm. But I had the impression that with these, our first caresses—and we were kissing the way my sister and I used to kiss when we were little: with our tongues sticking out of our mouths—that by engaging in sex we would fall back onto common, banal, ordinary territory, whereas we had seemed to be flying with joy during

that walk towards the mountain, clinging together on the way out, hand in hand on the way back. It was so beautiful.[35]

On January 22, 1984, Guibert writes to Savitzkaya,

> My dear Eugène
>   I am in a state of absent sensuality that could be confused with the absences of news from you. I pick up one of your books: there is sensuality. Imagining how crazy I must be to allow myself to consider the book as a series of letters that you addressed to me keeps me amused. I am no conventional admirer: I am a disastrous lover. (68)

That lovely last sentence could have been pronounced by any number of the misfits we have encountered in these pages, "Je ne suis pas un admirateur conventionnel: je suis un amoureux désastreux." Deprived of physical or epistolary contact, Guibert has returned to the sensual surface of the writing itself in search of some form of engagement. Their passage through some kind of physical expression, some kind of sexual encounter, seems to have both succeeded and failed. In one moment of retrospection, Guibert decides he should have been more traditionally sexual during that encounter, and given Savitzkaya a more mainstream kind of gay sexual experience. In other moments, he leaves human sexuality behind altogether, and imagines that the two of them had entered the realm of insect sexuality, where there seems to be almost no motion or activity, just two eyes open and directed at each other. That this disastrous misfit counterpublic of two is a fragile one, bolstered by no attachments to recognizable sexual identities, can be felt throughout the correspondence of the two writers. The physical encounter fades into the past, quite quickly, it seems, for Savitzkaya, who had already written back to Guibert on January 10, 1984, "Don't be unhappy, Hervé: weren't we happy together? and wasn't our joy powerful enough to remain intact for a long time before seeing each other again? I haven't burned your shirt, I will wear it often" (58). Throughout Guibert's work and his life, it seems, men have sex together without managing to have any durable relationship to the word "homosexuality," any sense that it fits their experience, as if their sexualities required some other form of mapping to account for them, as if their sexualities weren't just about sexuality. (The virus we know as HIV would only be isolated and identified later in 1984; but safer-sex advice for men being sexual together had been developed a few years earlier. We might then wonder to what an extent concerns about AIDS played a role in the practical determination of ways of being sexual together that different men arrived at around this time. We might also wonder if for different men at different times there exist different ways of "being sexual" with other men that do not carry the meaning of "being homosexual.")

Serostatus, Biopolitics, and Oddly Intimate Publics

Widespread recognition came late to Leduc, with the publication of *La Bâtarde* in 1964 when she was fifty-seven years old. Until 1964, she had to endure what was for her the extremely painful task of contenting herself with the admiration of a very small set of readers. (She died of breast cancer in 1972.) Guibert was also a writer admired by a small set of often quite distinguished readers for much of his career. In early 1990, at the age of thirty-four, he published *To the Friend Who Did Not Save My Life*, a book dealing with, among other things, his AIDS-related illness. That book found a much wider reading public, as did its 1991 sequel, *The Compassion Protocol*, and subsequent publications of his. Guibert died in December 1991.

The history of the AIDS epidemic in the 1980s in countries such as the US or France made painfully apparent how easy it had always been to relegate gay men and other affected populations to a different, inferior, social status. Novels such as *To the Friend Who Did Not Save My Life* and *The Compassion Protocol* offered detailed accounts of individual attempts to survive, including negotiating with medical institutions, their personnel and procedures.[36] Guibert's novels do more than provide compelling witness to this difficult period. They continue to address questions of publics, forms of intimacy, and the work of categories in enabling or disabling social intelligibility. With the onset of the AIDS epidemic and early efforts to combat it, new social categories came into existence: HIV positive and HIV negative, for instance. Guibert's novels give a remarkable and phenomenologically rich account of what it feels like to encounter these novel serostatus categories, ones that might suddenly be applied to select sets of people in very consequential ways. It is a cruel irony that a misfit writer such as Guibert, so attuned to the way categories inevitably leave certain people (or parts of certain people) out, should suddenly find a huge public when his work turns to studying this particular vulnerability (both a sociological and a medical one), this particular, highly visible kind of *porte-à-faux* situation, of being infected with HIV, a situation that was, in Guibert's moment, frequently a fatal one.

Guibert's success arrived in the moment between the publication of *To the Friend Who Did Not Save My Life* and that of *The Compassion Protocol*. "Now he had to face the thorny question of his relationship with a mainstream audience," David Caron notes. "Was a kind of community possible with them at all?"[37] It will come as no surprise that *The Compassion Protocol* has as a central concern Guibert's newfound public and his way of being in touch—corresponding—with them. What kind of commonality or intimacy could there be between them and him? How would idiosyncrasy and unconventionality figure in this new situation?

Serostatus as a ritually produced social identity lies at the heart of *To the Friend Who Did Not Save My Life*. Section 49 of that novel—more or less the midpoint of its carefully structured, one hundred sections—tells of the narrator and his companion Jules deciding to undergo, and then going through, with an HIV antibody test at an anonymous testing site in Paris. He addresses the protocol of the test itself with something approaching scorn: have your blood drawn, wait two weeks, come back and receive your results from the anonymous voice of science, with a bit of counseling thrown in. Or, as he puts it:

> A doctor was going to open an envelope . . . containing the verdict, and it was his job to pass on this verdict using the appropriate psychological recipe. A daily newspaper published a study showing that about 10 percent of the people taking the test in this center were seropositive, but that this figure wasn't symptomatic for the general population, given that the center was geared precisely to the fringe populations that were labelled "at risk." I didn't like the doctor who gave me my results, and of course I greeted the news coldly so that I could escape as soon as possible from this man who did his work on the assembly line, thirty seconds and a smile plus a brochure for the seronegative, a five- to fifteen-minute "personalized" interview for the seropositives: asking me if I lived alone, showering me with ads for Dr. Nacier's new association, and advising me (to deaden the blow) to come back the following week, time enough for them to do a follow-up test that might contradict the first one (there was one chance in a hundred, he said).[38]

Of course, the doctor is antipathetic and seemingly unaware of the sociological power with which his voice is invested as he conducts this ritual assigning people to these new categories. Yet Guibert has constructed his narrative in a way that oddly undercuts the power of the ritual in which his novelistic self is caught up. By adding a slight narrative quirk to this scene, Guibert underscores the extent to which the identity in question is in fact becoming part of the fabric of the ordinary life of many individuals, the extent to which the assignment of the identity comes to be rehearsed in the most ordinary and offhand of interactions.[39] The quirk has to do with the fact that he already "knows" his result.

That is to say, he has already had other blood work done: "Suspecting that our results would be bad, and wishing to speed up the process because of my approaching return to Rome, Dr. Chandi had already sent us to the Institut

Alfred-Fournier for the blood analyses that are done after a seropositive result, specifically to ascertain the progress of the HIV virus in the body" (130–31). The results of the blood work (probably a T4 cell count, a measure that drops in those with an active HIV infection, rendering them more liable to opportunistic infections) will be ready sooner than the results at the anonymous test site. If the results of the blood work are not good, the results revealed at the test site would then almost be redundant.

Guibert's telling of this episode brings in another consideration as well. Both he and his friend Jules do this testing together, and yet everything about the testing somehow works to separate them, as if their individual confrontations with medical professionals somehow interfered with the friendship between them. First, there is the appointment for the blood work:

> Jules, who'd promised to take the same tests at the same time as I did, was forced to postpone this one, to his fury, because he hadn't followed the instruction to fast before having the test. He waited while they finished with me. Looking over my lab slip, the nurse asked me, "How long have you known that you're seropositive?" I was so surprised I couldn't answer her. (131)

Just a bit of innocent conversation, of course. For normally anyone having these tests done would already know he or she is seropositive. Guibert, separated from his friend, confronts a voice of supposition that itself has a kind of ritual effect, assuming his place in an identity category to which he does not yet quite belong, at least officially.

Constantly, the two friends find themselves both united and divided by the slow process of being assigned to this new social category: "since I couldn't have the blood analysis lab report sent to my apartment, because my mail there was being automatically forwarded to Rome, I'd given Jules's address as my own, and he kept the results of my analysis (which he'd poured over attentively) to himself until the morning we went to find out about the seropositivity tests. It was in the taxi in which I picked him up at home, on our way to the dispensary run by Médecins du Monde on the Rue du Jura that he announced to me that our analyses were bad, that you could already see the fateful news there without knowing the results of the test" (131). Jules may say "our analyses," but of course the results are only those of Hervé, Jules not having been able to have the T4 count done. Jules thus "knows" Hervé's serostatus, while maybe still being able to entertain doubts about his own. This explains, perhaps, the differing reactions of Hervé and Jules to the news they receive of their status, news received separately of course, but news that reminds them of their shared situation.

I don't know what happened in the cubicle where Jules was, however, and in fact I didn't want to find out, but I'd finished with my interview and watched the door as it opened and shut several times while people rushed in and out, so I could see that Jules's presence in that little room was creating a huge disturbance in the center, as the receptionist called for a second doctor, and then a social worker. I think that Jules, who seemed so strong, fainted dead away when he heard a stranger tell him what he already knew, that when this certainty became official, even though it remained anonymous, it became intolerable. That was probably the hardest thing to bear in this new era of misfortune that awaited us: to feel one's friend, one's brother, so broken by what was happening to him—that was physically revolting. (133)

They are separated as they submit to this experience, undergoing a symmetrical ritual experience that seems to threaten to divide them as much as to bring them together.[40]

Perhaps part of what was so gripping about *To the Friend Who Did Not Save My Life* for its first readers was the visceral sense, not just of illness, but of a social identity undergoing such a brutal reconstruction. The newly inhabited social identity of being seropositive would involve an intimate experience of a particular relationship to power that people such as Guibert might never have experienced previously. Foucault's elaboration of the form of power that he calls biopolitical is now well known. Guibert's novels implicitly offer an account of what it means abruptly to become a subject of that regime of power. A compact description of biopolitics sufficient for our purposes can be found in the lecture Foucault gave on March 17, 1976, as part of his seminar called "Society Must Be Defended":

Unlike discipline, which is addressed to bodies, the new nondisciplinary power is applied not to man-as-body but to the living man, to man-as-living-being; ultimately, if you like, to man-as-species. To be more specific, I would say that discipline tries to rule a multiplicity of men to the extent that their multiplicity can and must be dissolved into individual bodies that can be kept under surveillance, trained, used, and, if need be, punished. And that the new technology that is being established is addressed to a multiplicity of men, not to the extent that they are nothing more than their individual bodies, but to the extent that they form, on the contrary, a global mass that is affected by overall processes characteristic of birth, death, production, illness, and so on.[41]

What does it mean to be addressed not as an individual body, but as a global mass caught up in a process of illness? Guibert traces this experience in the way he describes himself, his body, as a container for blood, blood in which the medical establishment has a certain kind of interest that is separate from any interest it might have in Guibert. The thematics is already present in *Friend*, although it will become more explicit in *The Compassion Protocol*.

> Long before my positive test results confirmed that I had the disease, I'd felt my blood suddenly stripped naked, laid bare, as though it had always been clothed or covered until then without my noticing this, since it was only natural, but now something—I didn't know what—had removed this protection. From that moment on, I would have to live with this exposed and denuded blood, like an unclothed body that must make its way through a nightmare. My blood, unmasked, everywhere and forever (except in the unlikely event of miracle-working transfusions), naked around the clock, when I'm walking in the street, taking public transportation, the constant target of an arrow aimed at me wherever I go. (*Friend*, 6)[42]

> I myself carried the plastic pouch with all my blood in it to the lab . . . Nowadays I like carrying my blood whereas before I'd have passed out, I'd have felt my knees giving way. I like there to be a direct line between my thought and yours, so that style doesn't get in the way of the transfusion. Can you stand a story with so much blood in it?[43]

> At the Broussais Hospital . . . they lost the tubes from two weeks before, I have to go back and have the tests done again tomorrow morning though I still haven't taken off the bandage from the blood draw done this morning by a fat oaf who was so scared he spilled blood everywhere. But one can't refuse Claudette Dumouchel anything. I asked her: "Doesn't it tire the body out to draw all this blood? Sometimes it feels like I'm dealing with a gang of vampires . . ." She replied, "I assure you we aren't using it to make blood sausage." (*Compassion*, 191–92)[44]

All three passages are interested in circulation, we could say, in the social bonds blood enables or undoes. The simple observation "nowadays I like carrying my blood" is a wonderfully compact statement about a change that has occurred in the relation between an individual psyche, the body it inhabits, and what we might call the sociobiological field in which it exists. Of course, the passages demonstrate that there is humor to be found in the experience of expropriation, in which you and the blood that is in no simple way yours, or part of your body, are treated as part of a species rather than as belonging to a person. It also points out that this experience of expropriation disrupts our more common everyday experience of the bonds that knit us to a given social world.

That this challenge to one's experience of the social world entails a reimagining of the kinds of social bonds that are possible is also hinted at in the way Guibert slides from writing about bags of blood moving around a hospital to comparing his own writing to an act of transfusion between himself and his reader. The necessity of this reimagining arises in part from a misfit relation to a social world. For both Leduc and Guibert, as the passages we have been looking at make clear, literature and the patterns of circulation of literary works play multiple functions within this misfit experience of the social world. One of the functions of writing in these situations of vulnerability is to further the development of that network of misfit circulation, to produce what Lauren Berlant has characterized as "intimate publics." For Berlant, intimate publics are "laboratories for imagining and cobbling together alternative construals about how life has appeared and how legitimately it could be better shaped not merely in small modifications of normativity."[45] In her book *The Female Complaint*, she notes that "an intimate public is an achievement. Whether linked to women or other nondominant people, it flourishes as a porous, affective scene of identification among strangers that promises a certain experience of belonging and provides a complex of consolation, confirmation, discipline, and discussion about how to live as an x."[46] Now for people like Leduc and Guibert, there is no easy word to fill in that "x." There might be a cumbersome phrase we could put in there, like "someone who experiences their misfit sexuality as an effect exerted on certain practices by a shifting structure of relations between a shifting set of other pertinent sociological properties." But this idea of an effort to achieve an intimate public helps us to understand something about the way many of Guibert's and Leduc's books are interactive with earlier ones they have written, and interactive with their readership. Thinking about the role intimate publics play in literature dealing with misfit sexualities might help us understand the strange story that comes near the end of *The Compassion Protocol* and takes up a fifth of the volume, the story of Guibert's trip to visit a healer in Casablanca. The recounting of this trip, its planning and its execution, highlights the practice of constructing intimate publics as a resource against the kinds of suffering caused not only by illness, but by an experience of social idiosyncrasy. It also highlights the particular use of literature that has been at the heart of this chapter—literature that consists in detailing idiosyncratic suffering as a form both of sociologically inclined maieutics and as a form of communication that can provoke an experience of belonging that is based not on shared identity categories but on a shared experience of misfit in regard to those categories.[47]

To recall the episode in question briefly: even though it comes toward the end of the volume, it describes events that seem to have taken place quite early in the period the volume covers. After writing *To the Friend Who Did Not Save*

My Life, Guibert made an appearance on Bernard Pivot's television program, *Apostrophes*. The interview was broadcast on March 16, 1990.[48] In the course of the interview, Guibert, quite ill, announced that he didn't expect to write any more books. The result was that he began receiving a large number of letters from people who had seen the interview and/or had read *To the Friend* and who begged him to keep writing. In a certain way, *The Compassion Protocol* is a response to the effect of *To the Friend*. It is dedicated "To all those women and men who wrote me about *À l'ami qui ne m'a pas sauvé la vie*. Each of your letters overwhelmed me." In it, Guibert comments that "in fact, I wrote a letter that was directly faxed into the hearts of 100,000 people, it's something extra-ordinary. I'm now writing them another letter. I'm writing to you" (104). He meets readers while riding the bus. Readers send him cassettes, records, cash-mere sweaters, perfume, books, and endless letters. "People were encouraging me to keep writing. The fervor of these strangers was beautiful" (154). Some of the letters seem crazy. There is one letter, one that he admits would probably seem among the craziest to any objective reader, that he nonetheless keeps on top of the pile, rereads, and eventually follows up on:

> It was the only one among the masses of mail I had received after the publi-cation of my book to offer a proposition, however far-out, that really tempted me above and beyond the renewal of hope, because it had the makings of a novel. It gave glimpses of a possible story as much as of possible hope. The man who had written it ended with: "The perusal of the least of my works would convince you that I am not, if you'll excuse my saying it so frankly, either a madman or a crook." (152)

The letter's author is neither crazy nor a crook, nor a reader of Guibert. He is looking for readers himself. He is a writer no one reads who, along with his wife, saw Guibert on *Apostrophes* (a show they watch apparently as a form of self-flagellation—a weekly dose of resentment at the authors who have been invited to appear), and invites him to come to Casablanca to be treated by a healer:

> He told me he was an athletic person, who had done some boxing. This detail pleased me immensely: a boxer, retired industrialist, performing miracles in Casablanca, it was what I needed to feel an increasing desire to meet him. (158)

If Guibert understands that *The Compassion Protocol* is a letter that he sends back to all those who have written him, he does admit that, "overwhelmed by the avalanche of mail, I hadn't replied to any of the letters" (153). Why then, does this one, from Casablanca, capture his attention? Why does the story of this letter and the trip it causes him to undertake, to Casablanca—two sessions

with the healer—with a side trip to Tangier, occupy such an important place
in the book?

> Of all the letters I had received, that one was the only one I thought of following
> up, possibly because it came from Casablanca, which had a fabulous ring to
> it, and because it called to mind the face of that other, the Tunisian as he was
> known, a retired manufacturer who continued to practise his mysterious art
> for the love of it. (153)

Guibert's choice, we could say, is an idiosyncratic one. He ties it to his sense of
who he is in a few different, haphazard, fragmentary ways. The image of the
healer doing his work has captured his imagination, and when he describes
the sessions with the healer they seem vaguely like sexual encounters:

> The Tunisian has stood up in front of me, holding his hands above my head.
> I hear him whispering:
>> "My son, I am penetrating you . . . In the name of Our Saviour Jesus Christ,
> I cure you." (185)

Sexuality lurks in the background of the whole trip, in fact: "Because
Casablanca still evoked transsexuals' clandestine operations, I had told all
and sundry, as a joke, that I was going there for surgery, in order finally to
please Vincent" (152). (Vincent is a young man with whom Guibert has had a
fascination, a friendship, a dysfunctional sexual relationship for a number of
years, another misfit relation, we could say. He fictionalized their relationship
in *Fou de Vincent*.)[49] Yet despite time spent watching boys and men on the
beach in Casablanca and also during a side trip he takes to Tangier, Guibert's
sexual energy is quite diminished during his time there. At one point, lying on
the beach, he finds himself unable even to come up with the strength required
to stand up:

> I wanted to feel the contact of sand on the soles of my bare feet. I sat down to
> take off my shoes and my socks. Then I realized that I could not get up. There
> was no support to get hold of, nothing I could cling to in order to hoist myself
> up on legs that had lost all their power. That emptiness, the immense stretch
> of emptiness facing the ocean, and me struggling like a crab trying to get back
> on its feet, intriguing the youths who were bracing their bodies in complex
> balancing acts, who didn't understand why a man who seemed to be thirty
> years old was moving like that, like an old man. . . . When I started to put on
> my socks, I noticed that my feet were covered with oil. (188)

Everything about the trip seems wretched or piteous, from the banal orien-
talism of the underlying narrative genre to which Guibert is subscribing ("My
story was titled *Miracle at Casablanca*" [149]), to the unpleasantness of his

relations with the testy and resentful writer who is his host, to the exhausting
effort of being a tourist while ill, to the idea of finding an efficacious cure at the
hands of the healer. It is linked to Guibert's writerly curiosity, to what remains
of his sexuality and its mismatches and failures, to his illness. It is an impossible trip, a fiasco even. Yet it is nonetheless a trip that operates as an image of
a dreamed of heterotopic displacement of the kind that could perhaps never
really happen. This is not to say that there may not be some necessity for
pursuing the dream—one that holds open the possibility, in Berlant's words,
of "alternative construals about how life has appeared and how legitimately
it could be better shaped," a search, both hopeful and hopeless, not only for a
cure, or for a good story, but for a form of connection, for an intimate public.
It is a wager on a meeting among strangers that might provide (again recall-
ing Berlant's words) "a certain experience of belonging and . . . a complex of
consolation, confirmation, discipline, and discussion about how to live as an
x," even if "x" seems in these circumstances undefinable. Certainly, the trip is
linked to a writer's need for correspondence with his readers, even if here that
desire is carried to an absurdist extreme. Of all the letters he received, Guibert
chooses to answer the one written by someone who hasn't yet bothered to read
him, and yet feels some form of connection despite all that.

What brings Leduc and Guibert together in my mind, and why I have been
discussing them together here, has to do with the intensity of their experience
of a misfittedness that is inseparably social, sexual, and literary, and with their
investment in telling of the fiascoes to which their particular misfittedness
gives rise. They not only recount their fiascoes. In doing so, the provide us
with the results of a careful investigation of what it means and feels like to
occupy a misfit position, an idiosyncratic one, sociologically telling in its failures of typicality, in its fraught relation to any widely shared way of mapping
the social world. They write about this situation as a way of understanding it
and compensating for it, making literature a potential prompter of an intimate community that fails to respect categories of sexual and social identity.
Guibert's trip to Casablanca (and perhaps in key ways Leduc's trip to Rennes
resembles it) functions within his novel as one of many tales of heterotopic
misfittedness. The telling of such tales by Leduc or Guibert or writers with
similar concerns can rarely count on the success of any project they undertake. The best that they can do is to undertake to address an unknown misfit
counterpublic from whom some recognition might someday come.[50]

7

The Talk of the Town: Sexuality in Three Pinget Novels

To a certain degree, one can speak by means of intonations alone, making the verbally expressed part of speech relative and replaceable, almost indifferent. How often we use words whose meaning is unnecessary, or repeat the same word or phrase, just in order to have a material bearer for some necessary intonation.

M. M. BAKHTIN, "Towards a Methodology for the Human Sciences"

One could hear in his books more intonations and more accent than in his speech. . . . It is an accent marked by no sign on the page, indicated by nothing in the text; and yet it clings to the sentences, which cannot be spoken in any other way; it was the most ephemeral but the most profound thing in the writer, the thing which will bear definitive witness to his nature.

MARCEL PROUST, *In the Shadow of Young Girls in Flower*

The only thing that interests me is to capture a tone of voice, and this tone of voice is always a component of my own voice that I isolate and objectify. There's always a little bit of myself in each of my characters, but that bit is objectified until it becomes a character all on its own. . . . Our ears are recording devices just as powerful as our eyes. I think it is correct to say that the tone we habitually use, with ourselves or those close to us, is made up of a variety of tones that, along with inherited ones, and ones heard in books, we have recorded since our childhood. It can be interesting, when writing a letter for instance, to become aware after the fact of this natural tone. But it is even more interesting to analyze its make-up and to construct a book out of each component.

(La seule chose qui m'intéresse c'est de capter un ton de voix; ce ton de voix est toujours une des composantes de ma propre voix que j'isole, que j'objective. Il y a toujours un peu de moi-même dans chacun de mes personnages, mais qui est objectivé jusqu'à devenir un personnage lui-même. . . . Notre oreille est un appareil enregistreur bien aussi puissant que notre oeil. Or je crois pouvoir dire que notre ton habituel, celui que l'on a par exemple avec soi-même ou avec ses proches, est une sorte de composé de divers tons, outre les héréditaires et ceux des livres, enregistrés par nous depuis notre enfance. S'il est intéressant, dans une lettre par exemple, de prendre connaissance soi-même et après coup de ce ton naturel, combien plus intéressant d'en analyser les composantes et de chacune tour à tour faire un livre.)

ROBERT PINGET, interviewed by Bettina L. Knapp

Throughout this book, I have been interested in a set of features of language that go by different names—connotation, implication, register, effects of intonation, nonreferential and/or social indexicality—and I have been interested in the way these features of language link up with a predicament of certain kinds of sexuality that exist in culture and in language mainly pragmatically (as opposed to semantically or by explicit representation), and thus only outside of normative nomenclature.[1] I have also been tracing the way certain twentieth-century French authors (Colette, Genet, Leduc, Guibert, and now Pinget) explore in their works the pragmatics of these misfit sexualities, and the way certain works by these and other authors (Beauvoir, Duras) themselves have a pragmatic function both within and beyond their contexts of origin involving the circulation of knowledge about the practice of these misfit sexualities. Among the most compelling examples I know of literary works that not only express and investigate the experience of sexual misfittedness that has been one of the central topics of this book, but that also explore with immense virtuosity those features of language-in-use I have just mentioned, are three novels by Robert Pinget, *The Inquisitory* (1962), *Someone* (1965), and *The Libera Me Domine* (1968).[2] Pinget performed in his novels a good deal of implicit theorizing about the way sexuality exists in spoken language— and in culture more generally. As we saw toward the end of chapter 2, when speakers respond to what Pinget calls tone—the aspect of language use that lies at the heart of his novelistic project—they often demonstrate a practical awareness of how different features of social life (including sexuality in its multiple relations with other social variables) express themselves verbally, particularly through nonreferential aspects of language. Moreover, for Pinget, being a competent user of these nonreferential features of language (and different people are competent to different degrees) involves having a practical awareness of how to manipulate the various meanings different "tones" might take on within a given sociolinguistic universe of language users, a practical awareness that should be more or less shared by other language users in that universe. In the "Author's Note" at the end of *The Libera Me Domine*, Pinget describes the work (often unconscious) that for him goes into finding a tone in which to cast the voice that will enable a book to unfold. "It has started off as something more like a tonality, which becomes more specific as it is worked on, in the course of the book, that is, and which finally becomes a tone, maybe only on the last page." The tone, he indicates, determines the content of the book: "I never know at the outset what I am going to say. . . . People have spoken of the plots of my books. Rather than plot, I would prefer situation, and this is imposed on me by the chosen tone."[3] A tone, it would seem, implies content, implies a whole world of talk, and one voice's place within it. We could say that Pinget, in waiting to hear a tone that will then unfold as a situation, is waiting to hear a voice in which multiple pertinent social variables interact to produce some kind of a vocal signature that is the correlate of a sociologically situated story. A sensitivity to the audibility of sexuality's place in the social world (with sexuality understood in all its multivariable complexity) is what we've been tracking throughout *Someone*. It can be found in authors and their works; but it must also manifest itself in the acts of reading or in the counterpublics that some of those works hope to find. Pinget is aware that readers who are not sensitive to the tonal features that interest him will have the impression of reading a somewhat disjointed story, where much remains confusing and unexplained. This is a price he is willing to pay for the ability "to insinuate between the lines, in the winding course of a sentence, things that I prefer not to formulate clearly, either because it would take too much attention to formulate them, which would disrupt the general rhythm, or else because it seems to me more effective to suggest them than to say them."[4]

Here is one way of describing Pinget's *The Inquisitory*. It is a five-hundred-page fictional transcript of the interrogation of an elderly, retired, nearly deaf male domestic servant by an official of some kind.[5] Questions are handed to the man on slips of paper. His replies are captured by a typist. The novel prints the questions and the answers. Together, they slowly reveal things about the questioner, the respondent, and the social universe in which the respondent has lived most of his life. The questioner is interested in the goings-on of the servant's former employers, a pair of gentlemen, and their friends and associates. The employers seem to be gay men, with a wide-ranging network of gay and lesbian acquaintances, or at least gay-friendly ones, sometimes from widely different social circles. They throw lavish dinners, and wild parties of various kinds. There may also be drugs, pornography, marriages of convenience, male prostitution, real-estate swindles, tax evasion, occult practices, trafficking in art objects, and other suspicious activities, including unexplained deaths, associated with them and their acquaintances. The questioner's goal seems to be to get the servant to avow in so many words the truth about the various illicit practices he must have been witness to. He is urged to call things by their names. Yet perhaps he doesn't know the names in question; perhaps he has other interests and loyalties; perhaps he has other ways of understanding and communicating information about social and sexual practices and identities. Perhaps he understands (at least practically) that different kinds of information can have different kinds of existences within language, different ways of being housed within the talk that transpires in the world around him. "Tout se sait dans un petit pays," he comments at one point, "everything gets known in a small place," but the kind of knowledge he speaks of is not always easily expressible in words themselves.[6] I offer one slightly comic example, and then a more serious one:

Was Hallinger married
　I don't think so no
　Why don't you think so
　Because Marthe said dress-designers never marry
　Have you any idea why
　It must be because they've got too much work with all their collections,
Marthe said she'd actually read about Hallinger that he used to work night and
day and when he takes some time off he's probably not short of women he's got
six mannequins it seems (171)

Do people like Marthe and the servant know more than what they say explicitly? Is the servant being crafty and knowing in the amount of information
he gives his interlocutor access to? Is he capable of putting up verbal smoke
screens? Who is playing off the ignorance of the other here?[7] Our retired
servant claims that his fellow servant, Marthe, is the source of much of his
"knowledge," but it is possible that much of what he "knows," he is careful to
communicate only by implication, or only to those with ears to hear. Consider
this longer passage in which the person interrogating him is trying to understand why he is more forthcoming with details about some people (someone
named d'Eterville in this case) than with details about his employers:

　You were a lot more reticent about such questions with regard to your em-
ployers, why
　　Because by going on so you pushed me into it but anyway with my
gentlemen it's not the same
　　Why
　　Because
　　Answer
　　Because it's not the same people don't understand anything yet you're
meant to tell the truth and it's not easy so it's better to say nothing
　　Why not
　　Because things of that sort I realise they're this way or that way even if it's
difficult to talk about them they're true and only concern the people who do
them, and you've got them mixed up with morality that's what's really dirty and
I don't want to discuss it with you because I don't know you
　　Does it matter to you so much all of a sudden the good opinion we might
have of your employers
　　It's not that it's because of the truth I've just told you it's too difficult, if I've
seemed prudish or let's say if I *am* I can't do anything about it now we've got
all these barriers in our head and your questions don't help me to get rid of
them, it all needs a lot of thought and you won't get me on that subject again
　　In other words the details you're giving about d'Eterville you refuse to give
about your employers

I repeat you pushed me into it and I repeat if people can't understand one
another it's because of folk like you who don't want to understand and who get
their morality all mixed up in things where it's no business to be (228)

The servant "slipped up" and told the interrogator something he had wit-
nessed that revealed the sexual proclivities of his previous employer, d'Eterville. Overall, he gives the impression of being familiar with many aspects
of human sexuality. He also seems, perhaps only implicitly, to be trying to
explain something about how human communication works to his interrogator: because of who you are and who I am, because of the extent of our
acquaintance, it will turn out to be the case that I may slip up and tell you
certain kinds of things about certain people, but I will not tell you the same
kinds of things about other people, even if I know those things. You should
understand that patterns of information circulation like this are part of what
defines my relationship to you and my relationship to the people I am (or am
not) telling you about. I might pass a certain kind of moral judgment on one
person's behavior that I would not on another's. This is evidence of the difference of my social standing and my history in relation to those people; it is
part of the way talk works within my world that I would pass on to you certain
kinds of information about some people, but not others. It is not at all clear to
me how you fit into the world of talk that constitutes my daily life. This might
be why I sometimes slip up and say things to you I wish I hadn't. My patterns
of communication, like my relative social position, would normally be intelligible to people who share my social world. They should understand the kinds
of strategic decisions I make without needing to have them explained. Don't
count on me to tell you explicitly everything I know about the way sexuality
works in the world around me. I will tell you only the kinds of things someone like me is likely to say to someone like you, and more and more I don't
think we are well suited to understanding each other. Nor do I think that you
are linguistically (pragmatically) well equipped to function at a high level of
understanding within the sociolinguistic world that I live in.

Yet across the five hundred odd pages of *The Inquisitory* we do learn an in-
credible amount of detail about the geography of the region where the servant
lives, about the history of the region and its inhabitants, about the habits and
characters of many of those inhabitants, and ultimately about the tragedies
that mark the life of our informant. It is as if Pinget has another fact he wants
to drive home: that we are not just producers of talk; we are all inhabited by
talk and its structures. When we talk, what we do is not only provide information, or reveal things about ourselves; we also expose the structures of the
social world as it and they exist in talk; we reveal that within our ability to

talk is an ability to produce a representation of the social world that will be calibrated to our own position in it and to the relationship we imagine ourselves as having with our interlocutor. We are a node in a structured world of talk, it would seem, and as we function within the world of talk, we both act on and are acted upon by the structures of talk that we have been absorbing since our earliest years.

Pinget's talkers are, in general, marked by various forms of unhappiness, and that unhappiness is often reflected in their longing for an interlocutor who could somehow understand something that is deeply implicit in their speech, someone who could understand something about them no one else has ever grasped. That longing for an unspoken understanding seems frequently to have some kind of a relationship to intimacy, sometimes to sexual intimacy, often to intimacy between people of the same sex. The narrator of *The Inquisitory* is a widower who lost a son when the child was young. And yet his own sexual and family history does not prevent him from experiencing fondness for and loyalty toward his queer employers and an apparently open-minded attitude toward all the wild goings-on associated with them. One of the oddest features of the book is the revelation toward the end that he has somehow managed to answer more than four hundred pages worth of questions without mentioning one entire wing of the Château de Broy (where he was employed) and the person who lived there: Monsieur Pierre. It would seem that he willfully kept this information back, and only through an inadvertent slip does he signal to his questioner the presence of this strange live-in friend of the two gentlemen who were his main employers:

> Tell the truth, was someone living in one of those towers
> > Why are you laying another trap for me
> > Answer
> > He'd never have wanted me to say
> > Who
> > Monsieur Pierre he only wanted one thing to be left in peace
> > Who was Monsieur Pierre
> > A friend of my gentlemen's they're very fond of him though he never mixed
> with anyone he lives all alone in the south-west tower lonely as a hermit, he's
> an expert in astronomy he's got a big telescope up at the top there to observe
> the stars and he's forever writing things for astronogical societies and all those
> books in his library, yes an expert but as for coming to the house it was as if it
> was the end of the world still my gentlemen went on pressing him he refused
> except very occasionally, he only liked a few of my gentlemen's friends who
> used rather to go to his place to see him just as I did although he preferred not
> to be disturbed but there was always one advantage, I'd go and see him and he'd

show me the sky through his telescope and the moon explaining it to me as best
he could, if I'd been able to I'd have gone every evening it was such peace being
up there alone with him, five minutes at noon even once a day wasn't enough
I used to take him his luncheon (366–67)

Accompanying the unhappiness of many of the men whose voices populate
Pinget's novels is an inarticulate longing for unspecified forms of intimacy
with other men. Often the partners who are imagined for these intimate scenarios will differ across many other social axes: class, education, abilities of
various kinds, age, ethnicity, religious beliefs, styles of masculinity, and so on.
The intimacy sought after may or may not even be sexualized. In *Celibacies:
American Modernism and Sexual Life*, Benjamin Kahan considers the possibility that celibacy itself could be understood "primarily as a coherent sexual
identity rather than as a 'closeting' screen for another identity."[8] Kahan offers a
number of paradigms for thinking about celibacy. While certainly, as we shall
see, there are plenty of men who have sex with men, women who have sex with
women, and men and women having sex together in Pinget's novels, celibacy
also seems to offer itself as an important way of living out one's sexuality, in
either the short or the long term. Kahan comments that "celibacy outplays,
outsmarts, parries, and fakes out the hetero/homo binary by occupying neither term and both terms simultaneously." It "exceeds the boundaries of the
hetero/homo binary, requiring a rethinking of sexual categories and the concept of sex as such" (145). The moment I have just cited from *The Inquisitory*
may be an example of celibacy doing precisely this. Monsieur Pierre seems, by
his living arrangements and his close friendship with the two gentlemen who
employed the servant, to be gay affiliated, and yet he is like a solitary hermit,
holding himself apart from the various shenanigans his friends orchestrate.
Our elderly, deaf servant, who longs to spend time in Monsieur Pierre's company, had a heterosexual past and is not, unlike some of their other servants,
privy to many of the activities of his gentlemen employers.[9] He is uneducated,
and makes regular mistakes ("astronogy") with spoken vocabulary. And yet
he seeks out the company of the solitary hermit as much as he dares, and the
hermit reciprocates his attention to a certain degree. They represent at least
the ghost of a couple of celibate misfits, the special status they hold for each
other (or at least that Monsieur Pierre holds for the servant) hinted at, implied
by what is not said as much as by what is.[10]

For five hundred pages, the questioner tries to drag knowledge out of the
servant, mainly the kind of knowledge we saw Michael Silverstein refer to
in chapter 1 as "-onomic," or lexically explicit knowledge. The servant is full
of knowledge about his world and the people in it, and clearly he has needs,

desires, longings, allegiances related to the world he lives in. And yet all of these forms of attachment to his world he communicates in aspects of language that refuse or fail at lexical explicitness.

Someone and *The Libera Me Domine*, following the line of investigation begun in *The Inquisitory*, become even more sophisticated in their investigation of talk and of tone, of sexuality's place in talk, and of the way that talk and its tonal features can house both a social world and a particular point of view on that social world. In *Someone*, we hear the voice of an older man, who, along with a partner, runs a suburban boarding house while apparently also working away on a manuscript as an amateur botanist. Or perhaps what he actually does each night is to pen an account of a day at the boarding house. It might seem at first that he is engaged in describing for us one particular day of his life at the boarding house, yet by the end of the book it seems almost as if he is describing any and every day in a highly routinized life: days, weeks, and even years resemble each other in ways that feel frighteningly monotonous. People endlessly repeat themselves in word and deed. Time passes slowly. Perhaps the Christmas holiday occasionally stands out as an event that breaks the routine (except that many Christmases turn out to resemble each other), or perhaps summer vacations break the routine, when various boarders visit family for a few weeks and the house feels deserted (except that the same people seem to leave at the same time each summer to visit the same relatives). In any case, these proprietors and boarders don't seem to have much in the way of family. A few of the boarders are married. The proprietors certainly are not. Family members to visit are few, and what relations there are with those cousins, nieces, and nephews seem often to be strained. Everyone's finances are also fragile. Their social world is constricted in every possible way; even new subjects of conversation are hard to come by. Most—whether or not to try a different butcher shop, or buy a washing machine or a refrigerator—are endlessly recycled. It is rare that anyone says anything that hasn't already been said many times before. The atmosphere is stifling.

One thing our narrator does to try to break the monotony is to imagine visiting a neighbor whom he has never met. In one such flight of imagination, one of Pinget's own central preoccupations seems to rise to the surface of the novel. Our narrator wonders if Fonfon, one of the occupants of the boarding house, might be known to the neighbor. (Fonfon is "a simple-minded lad we took in to do the odd jobs.")[11] If so, their acquaintance might provide a good opening gambit for a conversation:

> If Fonfon knows the neighbor that's a good opening remark. Say to the neighbor for example I hope our poor lad doesn't importune you. Say importune,

that sounds cultured. So he doesn't take me for just anyone, so he's aware of the distance. The stupid fool. It's so true, when you're all the time trying to abolish distances you don't do yourself any more good than you do the others. They think you're one of them for five minutes but you can't keep it up any longer than that and then, well, you're up shit creek. The other realizes he's made a mistake, he changes his tone, he closes up, he starts blathering, and for our part we don't know how to get out of it, we despise ourselves, we tell ourselves that we shouldn't have started that way, it was dishonest, we try to patch it up while we go on talking but all the time thinking we mustn't use this or that word so as not to disconcert him, in no time at all you've lost all track of what you were saying, you've wrecked the whole thing, it's intolerable. Mark out the distances right from the start. Say importune. Doesn't our poor child importune you? Not in the least, Monsieur, he says Monsieur, not in the least, he plays with the cat, ah, you have a cat? That's it, the conversation has started, has got off to a good start, on the appropriate level. The tone is there. The tone. The most difficult thing to capture. Your whole life can be messed up by a wrong tone. It's terrifying when you come to think of it. (39)

(Si Fonfon connaît le voisin c'est une bonne entrée en matière. Dire au voisin par exemple j'espère que notre pauvre petit ne vous importune pas. Dire importuner, ça fait cultivé. Qu'il ne me prenne pas pour n'importe qui, qu'il sente la distance. Ce con. C'est vrai ça, à tout le temps vouloir effacer les distances on ne se rend pas plus service qu'aux autres. Ils vous prennent pour un des leurs l'espace de cinq minutes mais on ne tient pas le coup plus longtemps et là alors c'est le merdier. L'autre se rend compte qu'il s'est trompé, il change de ton, il se ferme, il bafouille et nous on ne sait plus comment s'en sortir, on se méprise, on se dit qu'on n'aurait pas dû commencer comme ça c'était malhonnête, on essaie de rafistoler tout en continuant à parler et en pensant tout le temps ne pas employer tel mot pour ne pas le dérouter, très vite on ne sait plus ce qu'on dit, on a tout gâché, c'est intenable. Marquer les distances dès l'abord. Dire importuner. Notre pauvre enfant ne vous importune pas? Pas du tout, monsieur, il dit monsieur, pas du tout, il joue avec le chat, ah vous avez un chat? Ça y est la conversation est partie, bien partie, sur le plan qui convient. Le ton y est. Le ton. Ce qu'il y a de plus difficile à attraper. Un ton faux peut vous amocher toute une vie. C'est effrayant quand on y pense. [67])

Meeting someone new might be a distraction from the monotony of day-to-day life, but it also means negotiating a new social relation—a prospect that seems painful and anxiety provoking. Your speech will be listened to, sized up, used to put you in your place. You will have to recalibrate your sense of tone and register. Could Fonfon, with his intellectual disability, serve as a kind of sacrificial offering, potentially furnishing the possibility of engaging in a conversation that has fewer risks, the possibility of a kind of mutually acceptable condescension: "Doesn't our poor child importune you? Not in the least, Monsieur, he says Monsieur." If that pitiful exchange counts as conversational success, surely it must be because the narrator is used to conversational disasters. In fact, he seems to harbor a fair amount of pent-up rage at all the interlocutors who have ever treated him badly: "So he doesn't take me for just anyone, so long as he's aware of the distance. The stupid fool." One has the impression that tone has indeed made a mess of the narrator's life.

If tone has made his life into such a mess, it is doubtless in part because he has never been able to speak in such a way as to cease being "n'importe qui," any old body, and to become "quelqu'un," someone. How does the tone with which you speak help you to be or become someone, not just anyone? There are a number of ways of being someone, the book seems to suggest. One is to occupy a social role that carries with it symbolic power, authority, or wealth. That avenue seems foreclosed to the namby-pamby fifty-something unmarried man who depends on a sorry lot of boarders and an equally inconsequential business partner to sustain his life. Another option would be to achieve some meaningful form of intimacy. As he says at one point: "I would like there to be someone, at least someone, who understood the state I'm in but I know very well that that's impossible. Let's forget about it" (90) (Je voudrais que quelqu'un, au moins quelqu'un se rende compte de mon état mais je sais bien que c'est impossible. N'y pensons plus [151]). There is no one who could hear what he is saying about who he is through the tone in which he speaks. A few pages later, he adds, "I tell myself that this is one of the things that I regret, not that I regret, since I don't regret anything, but which still makes me suffer at my age, not to have had anyone, or so rarely, in any case not to have anyone any more who watches me sleep" (98) (je me dis que c'est une des choses que je regrette, pas que je regrette puisque je ne regrette rien, qui me fait encore souffrir à mon âge, de n'avoir eu personne ou si rarement, en tout cas de n'avoir plus personne qui me regarde dormir [164]). So it is both a problem of being seen, heard, and understood, and a problem of intimacy.

The narrator's difficulties with intimacy are implied throughout the book: one gets the impression that while he may have had a few sexual relations in his distant past, he has not had any for some time. He seems to disapprove of, or at least to avoid, masturbation: "I have nothing against lust. It suits a lot of people and they're lucky. But not me. It depresses me and what's more I lose my head" (25) (Je n'ai rien contre la luxure. Elle convient à beaucoup et ils ont de la chance. Moi pas. Elle me flanque le cafard et surtout je perds la tête" [45]). He seems not particularly interested in women. Nor does he seem to have any active sexual interest in men.[12] His closest attachment in fact seems to be to Fonfon: "I've become attached to this Fonfon" (23), he notes at one point (Je m'y suis attaché à ce Fonfon [41]). Later he observes, "If I had to be frank about what really keeps me in the guest house apart from the obligation of staying there, I would say Fonfon" (75) (Si je devais dire franchement ce qui me retient le plus à la pension à part l'obligation d'y rester, je dirais Fonfon [127]). Here is what we know about Fonfon himself:

> A simple-minded lad we took in to do the odd jobs. He only does them by halves but we keep him on just the same. We can't send him back to the carpentry shop we rescued him from at his mother's request. She was afraid he'd lose a finger or get his foot or his head crushed or everything at the same time. I've become attached to this Fonfon. That's a nickname, incidentally. His name is Gilles Fontaine. (23)

> (Un garçon demeuré qu'on a pris chez nous pour les petits travaux. Il ne les fait qu'à moitié mais on le garde quand même. On ne peut pas le renvoyer à la menuiserie où on l'a cueilli à la demande de sa mère. Elle avait peur qu'il se fasse couper un doigt ou écraser le pied ou la tête ou tout à la fois. Je m'y suis attaché à ce Fonfon. C'est un surnom, par parenthèse. Il s'appelle Fontaine Gilles. [41])

The relationship between the narrator and Fonfon is difficult to characterize. It is a patchwork quilt made up of pieces that seem paternal, fraternal, avuncular, and sometimes a bit romantic; perhaps celibacy or asexuality is also part of the mix. It is a misfit assemblage. The narrator protects Fonfon against the bullying other members of the boarding house would inflict on him. He tries to educate him, and to improve his manners. He takes him botanizing:

> Yes, Fonfon's bunches of flowers. I had to insist on him being allowed to put them in a vase and on the table himself. The guests have had to resign themselves to it but they snicker. And my Fonfon must realize it in spite of everything because I took him out herborizing with me once and he picked me some flowers. He ran ahead to a spot he knew and brought them back to me saying I've picked you some companialas in order cause you're the only one who loves me.
> Some companialas. (63–64)

> (Oui les bouquets de Fonfon. Il a fallu que j'exige qu'on lui permette de les mettre lui-même dans un vase et sur la table. Les pensionnaires ont dû se soumettre mais ils ricanent. Et mon Fonfon doit malgré tout s'en rendre compte parce qu'une fois, je l'avais pris avec moi pour herboriser, il m'a cueilli des fleurs. Il a couru en avant où il connaissait le coin et il me les a rapportées en me disant je vous ai cueilli des companiules pour que personne ne m'aime sauf vous.
> Des companiules. [107–8])

Campanulas can be given, in the traditional language of flowers, as a sign of gratitude or a declaration of love. Fonfon not only mispronounces the name of the flower (weaving in suggestions of companion, buddy), he seems to make an interesting grammatical error, "pour que" for "parce que." I picked you these flowers so that no one but you would love me. I picked you these flowers because you are the only one who loves me. Is it possible to decide between the meanings? And what is the tonal effect of the narrator repeating Fonfon's pronunciation error: "Des companiules"? Perhaps the index of an imagined companionate community of two.

Also tonally interesting here is the "mon" in "mon Fonfon." Here is a brief digression meant to suggest how delicate a tonal effect can be achieved simply by the use of a small word like *mon*. At several points in his correspondence with Eugène Savitzkaya, Hervé Guibert worries over his use of "mon" in his salutation to his friend, "Mon Eugène." He starts using the "mon" in his letters to Savitzkaya in April 1983. On January 7, 1984, he wonders (based, one assumes, on the tone and frequency of Savitzkaya's replies to his letters) if he will soon have to resolve to "abandon this *mon*." It comes and goes for a while in his salutations. In January 1984, he wishes "if only it were the case that you were touched that I still addressed you like that" (si seulement cela pouvait t'être doux que je t'appelle encore comme ça). In July 1984, he is still worried:

Mon Eugène
—this "mon" is perhaps still wrongfully assumed, or has always been: you see how difficult it is for me to stop using it.

(—ce "mon" n'est-il pas encore ou pas toujours usurpé: tu vois, j'ai du mal à le laisser tomber.)[13]

There are only two letters in the correspondence, letters dated December 6, 1985, and February 27, 1986, when Savitzkaya addresses Guibert as "Mon cher Hervé" and "Mon beau." Expressions of intimacy, we can imagine, are delicate things. They depend on knowledge of cultural norms, personality, and the sensitivity of your ear. Guibert's insistence on opening his letters "Mon Eugène" absent steady reciprocation by Savitzkaya means something, or a number of things, but it might be hard to say precisely what. Savitzkaya's stinginess with the same mark of affection similarly communicates something, although even he may not be able to clarify what. Clearly, it means something when the narrator of *Someone* says "mon Fonfon," just as it means something that Fonfon gives him a bouquet of campanulas. It means something that, having reported Fonfon's speech on presenting him with the flowers, he places on a new line a repetition of the mispronounced name of those flowers. No new information, except on the level of tone.

Another example of a richness of tone attached to a single line of words comes at the end of the remarkable episode recounting Fonfon and the narrator's brief experience of a television. One summer, it turns out that all the other inhabitants of the boarding house except for the narrator and Fonfon are away. The two of them have the house to themselves. It is something that had never happened before, and it seems never to have happened again. It is a landmark, an oasis in which the monotony of passing time seems for a moment to be interrupted. During this unprecedented summer month, they get along swimmingly. Fonfon wakes the narrator up each morning. They have breakfast, go for walks around town and in the woods; they eat a wider and more appetizing variety of food than is normally served at the boarding house; and then, out of the blue, the narrator has the idea of using some of his savings to rent a television for a month. Each evening they find themselves in front of the rented television watching an episode from an adaptation of *Les Aventures du Capitaine Corcoran*, a novel originally published by Alfred Assollant in 1867:

> And in the evening, I shall remember this for the rest of my life. When we switched it on and there was a serial, Captain Corcoran! Yes, for the rest of my life. I can't even describe it exactly any more, it moves me so deeply. Fonfon's eyes were popping out of his head, he clapped his hands, he was unrecognizable. I thanked heaven for having given me the idea. Maybe I was going to be able to save Fonfon that way, with the television. But I was saving myself too, I might perhaps have been able to save myself. We spoke of nothing other than Captain Corcoran, we spent the whole day imagining what he was going to do that evening after dinner. . . . And after that it was spectacle, amazement, paradise. Corcoran saved the princess, she was in love with him, he set fire to towns, he went horse riding in the bush, he took command of armies, and there was that tamed tiger, everything, everything, we held our breath, we were the captain's friends. . . . Fonfon remembered from one time to the next, I didn't, in the end he was the one who was telling me. We were coming back to life. (131–32)

> (Et le soir, ça je m'en souviendrai toute ma vie. Quand on a ouvert le poste et c'était un roman-feuilleton, le capitaine Corcoran! Oui, toute ma vie. Je ne peux même plus dire exactement, tellement ça me remue. Fonfon avait les yeux exorbités, il battait des mains, il était méconnaissable. Je remerciais le ciel de m'avoir donné cette idée. J'allais peut-être sauver Fonfon comme ça, avec la télévision. Mais moi aussi je me sauvais, j'aurais pu me sauver peut-être. On ne parlait plus que du capitaine Corcoran, on imaginait toute la journée ce qu'il allait faire le

soir après dîner. . . . Et ensuite c'était le spectacle, l'éblouissement, le paradis. Corcoran sauvait la princesse, elle était amoureuse de lui, il brûlait des villes, il chevauchait dans la brousse, il prenait le commandement des armées, et il y avait ce tigre apprivoisé, tout, tout, on retenait notre souffle, on était les amis du capitaine. . . . Fonfon se souvenait d'une fois à l'autre, moi pas, c'était lui qui finissait par me raconter. On ressuscitait. [219–20])

They form a community of viewers. Fonfon reveals capacities and forms of attention and memory that were previously unsuspected. Imaginations expand. Joy enters the boarding house.

But all good things must end. Toward the end of the month, the narrator's partner, Gaston, returns home. He arrives a day early, the day before the television is returned to the shop, and is annoyed at the narrator's gratuitous expenditure. The adaptation of *Corcoran* apparently comes to an end at the same time. Fonfon is distraught. The narrator takes to sitting with him beside his bed each night, having placed an old crate at the end of the bed, pretending the crate is a television and then narrating invented episodes of Corcoran's ongoing adventures:

> And every evening I went up to his room to tell him the next episode, and every evening he got all red in the face, he clapped his hands. But I gradually made it less frequent, I only went up one evening out of two, then once a week, and then not at all. We had forgotten. Life went on as before with the guests, the slaps, the evenings that destroyed you. We had nearly been saved.
>
> Where are you, my Corcoran. (133)
>
> (Et tous les soirs je remontais dans sa chambre lui raconter la suite, et tous les soirs il était tout rouge, il battait des mains. Mais peu à peu j'ai espacé, je ne montais plus qu'un soir sur deux, ensuite une fois par semaine, et ensuite plus. On avait oublié. La vie comme avant continuait avec les pensionnaires, les gifles, les soirées à se détruire. On avait failli être sauvé.
>
> Où es-tu mon Corcoran. [221])

It is that final sentence that is so tonally powerful. Most likely it is a citation from the serial they were watching, and most likely the words were spoken by a woman. It had almost seemed that Fonfon and the narrator could find salvation together, each one a kind of Corcoran for the other, each one a damsel in distress. And yet circumstances are such, and they themselves are such, that the couple they form cannot withstand the pressures of life's routines. When our narrator utters that phrase, "Où es-tu mon Corcoran" (and it is hard not to notice the similarities between "mon Fonfon" and "mon Corcoran"), how might we characterize the inarticulate wish for intimacy that it registers? How might we understand the degree to which the relation between the narrator and Fonfon both moves toward fulfilling and yet remains unable to fulfill what the narrator (and perhaps also Fonfon) longs for?

Both *The Inquisitory* and *Someone* thus register in remarkable ways a half-met and profoundly uncharacterizable longing for intimacy between mismatched men. *The Libera Me Domine*, often considered Pinget's most complex and remarkable achievement, does something related and yet different. *The Inquisitory* extracts the representation of a social universe as it is registered in one person's mind, and in doing so reveals that a great deal of knowledge about that universe is conveyed pragmatically, nonreferentially. It reveals to what a degree our social knowledge includes nonlexicalizable (or not-yet-lexicalized) forms of knowing. *Someone* paints the social and linguistic universe of a miserable suburban boarding house through the eyes of a single resident. In that boarding house, seemingly impossible longings for intimacy struggle to find meaningful expression, blighted by an environment as oppressive linguistically as it is socially.[14] *The Libera Me Domine* works with similar materials, but in a wider arena. We could say that it takes *talk* as its object, and that in fact, in the novel, people are sometimes understood primarily as the support for talk. *The Libera Me Domine* studies talk as it circulates about a small town; it studies what happens to events as they are stored in talk, as they are reverbalized time and again, as their representation in talk is passed from person to person over the years (rather like an extended game of telephone). To some readers it has seemed as if there is a single first-person voice that speaks throughout the novel; to others it has seemed that the first person in question might belong to different members of the town at different times, or might occasionally become simply an abstract instance supporting a given state of talk.[15]

"In each epoch, in each social circle, in each small world of family, friends, acquaintances, and comrades in which a human being grows and lives," Bakhtin wrote in his essay on speech genres, "there are always authoritative utterances that set the tone."[16] In "Intellectual Field and Creative Project," Bourdieu notes that

> whatever the form, a plurality of social forces almost always exists in all societies, sometimes in competition, sometimes coordinated, which by reason of their political or economic power or the institutional guarantees they dispose of, are in a position to impose their cultural norms on a larger or smaller area of the intellectual field and which claim, *ipso facto*, cultural legitimacy whether for the cultural products they manufacture, for the opinions they pronounce on cultural products manufactured by others, or for the works and cultural attitudes they transmit. (106)

Pinget's novel understands something of all of this, and carefully represents how not all talk—not all opinions—within a given sociolinguistic universe are equal. There are centers of gravity within a given state of talk. There may be, within a town, different worlds of talk covering the same geographical territory—people who speak "the same language," of course, but who speak it differently and who police the borders of certain social groups, certain worlds of talk, through everyday acts of language use. Within each of the competing (or at least geographically proximate but sociologically distinct) worlds of talk found in Pinget's novel, there are places (and speakers) of (differing degrees of) authority: for the common folk whose voice is preponderant in the novel, the pharmacy and the pharmacist represent one locale with a certain weight. The parish priest and the church are another. The parish priest might, in fact, be a kind of switch point between the common world of talk and more elevated worlds. There are certain epicenters of talk that have a commanding presence—even across the invisible orders of different worlds of talk—because of the social capital of the people who control and reside in those places. The dining-room table of Ariane de Bonne-Mesure, head of one of the notable landed families in the region, is one such epicenter, as is the dining-room table at the Château de Broy, which also belongs to important personages (distant cousins of Ariane's, it seems, who claim to be of an older aristocratic family than hers), though perhaps ones of dubious morals. Perhaps the drawing room of the boarding house run by Mortin (a boarding house considerably more sophisticated, and with a much greater amount of cultural capital associated with it, than the one we got to know in *Someone*) would be another such epicenter.[17] Certain of these elevated epicenters (Mortin's boarding house, the Château) are clearly thought of by some residents of the town as a little off-kilter, as straying from certain of the norms that govern other regions of the social space in question. (There is, regarding both those locations, a certain amount of suspicion that may exist regarding the lifestyles and morals of various people found there.) This has an impact on the kind of authority they hold, but does not fully dismantle that authority. The school and the schoolteacher (a person with authority over children but little cultural capital otherwise, and apparently unable to command much respect around town) have their own particular place in the distribution of verbal importance. There is one final space in the novel notably different from the others: the odd, geographically unsituated mental asylum, where speech may apparently either be incoherent and untrustworthy, or perhaps may contain some kind of wild truthfulness certain auditors would rather not take into account.

Michael Silverstein has studied the phenomenon he calls *emanation*: "privileged ritual sites of usage," he notes, "anchor . . . a multiplex social formation; their emanations constitute power—frequently politicoeconomic—to warrant or license usage of particular verbal forms . . . with particular meanings germane to certain interested ends of self- and other-alignment."[18] There is a good deal of frustration at various points in the novel on the part of speakers who understand that their own speech and the speech of others belonging to their particular world of talk, which is certainly marked by—identifiable through—the usage of particular verbal forms, is likely to be ineffectual, lacking in what we might call emanatory force. In fact, we could almost say that the novel is most interested in speech that happens outside privileged ritual sites and knows itself to be on the outside, speech (often gossip of various degrees of maliciousness) that can apparently do little to alter the various kinds of social alignments that exist in the world around it. Consider, in this regard, the way Mortin and his boarding house are spoken of:

> Monsieur Mortin she said my goodness that takes you back doesn't it, Alexandre his christian name was, you remember the guest house he started after his wife died, she was against it while she was alive, may her ashes rest in peace, such a refined guest house, no one but aristocrats or at least people out of our class, educated people . . . (147)

> (Monsieur Mortin qu'elle disait mon Dieu c'est bien vieux tout ça, Alexandre de son prénom, vous rappelez-vous la pension qu'il avait fondée après la mort de sa femme, elle s'y opposait de son vivant, paix à ses cendres, une pension tellement distinguée, il n'y avait que des aristos ou du moins des personnes pas de notre milieu, de l'éducation . . . [141])

If what we see here is the novel's speaker reporting the speech of one of the townsfolk, it would seem that the novel's speaker must in fact belong to the same milieu, the same world of talk, as the woman whose speech is being reported. Mortin, not being of their milieu, can endure without worry the fact of being associated in the talk of the village with a visiting priest who became entangled in a sex scandal with a boy just before leaving town:

> the Father, he was an old acquaintance of his, he had stayed there for nothing during the Mission, that relieved the curé who only just had the wherewithal, the scandal in question had rubbed off on to Mortin, tell me who your friends are . . . but his life was so remote from all our tittle-tattle that it probably didn't worry him, his guests took his side, educated people don't take the slightest notice of the opinion of the vulgar masses and in any case the preacher's conversation was so exquisite . . . (149)

([le] R. P., une vieille connaissance à lui [Mortin], il l'avait logé gratuitement le temps de la mission, ça déchargeait le curé qui avait juste de quoi, le scandale en question avait éclaboussé Mortin, dis-moi qui tu hantes, mais lui vivant loin de nos commérages n'a pas dû en souffrir, ses pensionnaires tenaient son parti, les gens éduqués ne font aucun cas de l'opinion du vulgaire et d'ailleurs le prédicateur avait une conversation exquise . . . [143])

(One can't help noticing that abbreviation for the naughty Révérend Père's title is the same as Robert Pinget's initials.)[19] Mortin and his circle may be geographically close to the villagers whose gossip forms most of the book, but they are apparently socially far apart; correspondingly, their feelings about certain sexual behaviors seem to differ. If Mortin has queer friends, he must be a queer himself, the village seems to think. How should a reader evaluate such information? We see posited here two geographically proximate and yet radically different worlds of talk, in which understandings and ways of communicating about sexuality are incompatible with each other—a good deal of this being due to tonal features the worlds of talk perhaps do not share.

The voice that speaks in the novel also suggests that belonging to one world of talk rather than another has certain kinds of consequences for behavior. Here is how that insight is expressed:

Which more or less came to the same thing as saying that the whole of the psycho psychi life of our little society might well rest on one or two very vague phrases, a few remarks about anybody or anything invented by two or three people at the outside which may well unconsciously have set the general tone for years to come of the conversations or rather of the behavior of our compatriots, yes it certainly was odd, this network of gossip and absurd remarks had conditioned our existence to such an extent that no stranger coming to live in our midst could have resisted it for long and that if he had come to follow the trade of let's say baker he would inevitably have branched off into that of child killer for instance, without his having been in the least responsible . . . (151–52)

(Ce qui reviendrait à dire que toute la vie psycho psychi de notre petite société reposerait sur une ou deux phrases en l'air, quelques affirmations controuvées à propos de n'importe qui et de n'importe quoi émanant de deux ou trois personnes au plus lesquelles auraient donné le ton généralement sans le savoir aux conversations depuis des années ou mieux au comportement de nos compatriotes, décidément oui c'était drôle, ce réseau de bavardage et de propos absurdes avait conditionné notre existence si bien qu'un étranger s'installant parmi nous n'y aurait pas résisté longtemps et que venu pour exercer la profession disons de boulanger il aurait infailliblement bifurqué sur celle de tueur d'enfants par exemple, sa responsabilité n'y étant pour rien . . . [145])

We notice Pinget's central preoccupation with tone here again, along with the idea that part of what circulates through language is a set of tones, perhaps we could say registers, that bring with them consequences for our identities and for our behaviors. Conversations and comportments are both marked by tone, the passage insists. Would your sexual comportment be the same if you lived in Mortin's world of talk or this one?

There is also a good deal of implicit self-understanding on display in this description of a group of people linked in a world of talk. They know on some level that much of what they say is untrue. They know that even though they are, in the larger picture, an uninfluential group of people whose talk does not have much capacity to impact those outside their group, nonetheless, among them there are a few who set the tone. And they know that as a group they are obsessed with gossip about sex and violence, particularly violence (and perhaps sexual violence) against children. The novel, after all, opens with the reaction of the narrator to the news that the schoolteacher, La Lorpailleur, has recently accused him of having been involved in the unsolved murder of a four-year-old boy some ten years earlier.[20]

I want to concentrate here, not on the novel's opening preoccupation with that unsolved murder,[21] but rather on the manner in which the illicit sexual life of the village is shown throughout the novel to exist in language and, in particular, in its tone. In each world of talk, tonal features work differently, which means that talk about sexuality will not always be the same. Certain people in the novel will seem to find themselves caught between registers, between worlds of talk, because of their sexuality. Sometimes they will do their best to escape from, to leave behind a certain world of talk because, whatever their sexuality is, it cannot exist happily in that given state of talk. In order to appreciate how sexuality exists in the common talk of the village, let us consider the strange ways the word *parfaitement* (quite so) comes to be used across the novel. (The list of examples I give here is not complete.) Consider what it must sound like, and how it must function, in this particular world of talk:

> that old Lorpailleur's mother apparently quite so with the doctor when she was young, filthy things like that. (49)

> (que la mère à la Lorpailleur aurait parfaitement avec le docteur dans sa jeunesse, des saletés de ce genre. [50])

> Jean-Claude . . . had apparently quite so with the youngest Moignon girl, which would explain her hasty departure to the Argentine . . . (69)

> (Jean-Claude . . . aurait parfaitement avec la cadette des Moignon, ce qui expliquerait le départ précipité de celle-ci en Argentine . . . [68])

the lady's maid had been dismissed on account of quite so that she was supposed to have, I'm not making it up, with Maurice the butler . . . (87)

(la femme de chambre avait été renvoyé rapport à parfaitement qu'elle aurait,
je n'invente rien, avec Maurice le maître d'hôtel . . . [85])

by the way Passavoine is still a fine figure of a man and I've heard that when it
comes to quite so he's very much in evidence, isn't it admirable so many qualities combined in one man, not like that poor Magnin not to mention anyone
else it seems he's no bigger than that . . . (114)

(. . . par parenthèse Passavoine est toujours bel homme et j'ai entendu dire que
pour ce qui est du parfaitement il est un peu là, c'est quand même admirable
toutes les qualités réunies en un seul, pas comme ce pauvre Magnin pour ne
citer que lui qui paraît-il n'est pas plus gros que ça . . . [109])

Madame Moineau was going home very late from the sewing-bee and she
heard someone panting in a hedge, she was frightened but she suddenly recognized in the clear night the Father in the act of quite so young Tourniquet . . .
(137)

(madame Moineau revenant fort tard de l'ouvroir avait perçu un bruit d'essouf-
flement dans une haie, elle avait eu peur mais soudain reconnaissait dans la
nuit claire le R. P. en train de parfaitement le petit Tourniquet . . . [132])

Lorduz the gendarme whom Monsieur Monnard had surprised one day in the
station urinal in the act of quite so with a railway employee, Monnard hadn't
said anything about it until ten years later when Lorduz had been moved to
another region, in any case he had got married in the meantime, do you realize.
(138)

(le gendarme Lorduz que monsieur Monnard avait surpris un jour dans
l'urinoir de la gare en train de se parfaitement en compagnie d'un cheminot,
Monnard n'en avait parlé que dix ans après, Lorduz ayant été affecté à une autre région, il s'était d'ailleurs marié entre-temps, est-ce que vous vous rendez
compte. [133])

Monette after her religious mania had I don't know how to put it with the
Doudin girl who was so ugly you recollect her don't you, well yes quite so, and
they even used for their thises and thats so it seems an instrument with so it
seems, isn't it terrible, can you imagine, it looks as if everything happens in
our region even though it is so pure, so close to the good Lord with its lovely
country and soft sky . . . (138–39)

(Monette après sa crise religieuse s'était je ne sais comment dire avec la fille
Doudin qui était tellement laide vous la remettez, eh bien parfaitement, même
qu'elles employaient pour leurs ébats un instrument parait-il avec parait-il,

quelle horreur, vous imaginez, on aura tout vu dans notre région pourtant si
pure, si près du bon Dieu par la douceur du paysage et la suavité du ciel . . .
[133])

Parfaitement, you could say, is a word that allows you (assuming you are one
of the group of townsfolk who are involved in this world of talk) to display
how much you know about sexuality without having to have the words to
describe all the things you obviously know about: extramarital sex, premarital
sex, penis size, some kind of sex between visiting priests and altar boys, men
who have sex with men in railway station restrooms (but later get married),
women who use sex toys together. *Parfaitement* also usually involves talking
about sex in a scandalized tone, despite the fact that you have always been
perfectly aware that these kinds of behaviors exist all around you.

This idiosyncratic use of *parfaitement* has another function as well: it indicates your membership in the group of townsfolk who talk in this way. "Sometimes, a speaker uses special linguistic expressions of a particular language as
identity markers," notes Michael Silverstein.[22] Clearly not everyone in town
would claim this *parfaitement*-user form of identity. The parish priest probably wouldn't, nor, obviously, would the R. P., nor Mortin and his friends, nor
the residents of the Château de Broy, nor Ariane de Bonne-Mesure. The article
by Silverstein from which I just quoted is concerned with how different kinds
of institutional forces contribute to "shaping the way people's ethnolinguistic
identities are being asserted and contested." He suggests thinking about the
existence of a "social space-time" as a "multidimensional framework in which
mutual locating can be accomplished." It is "a kind of pulsating, changing
intersection of many competing principles of structuring," and it contains
"points and intervals" that "groups of people arrogate to themselves . . . as 'inside' identity, from which and in terms of which they wish radially to project
an 'outside'" (533). This strikes me as a helpful description of what we encounter in *The Libera Me Domine*, a dynamic representation of worlds of talk in
the process of interacting with each other, and sometimes assigning people
to places they do not want to be. Those interactions can certainly happen
around specific kinds of events, such as the arrival in town of a stranger (e.g.,
the R. P.), an outsider whose relation to the different worlds of talk in town is
something that will have to be established after his arrival, and whose alleged
sexual proclivities, discovered only after he has been assimilated to village
life, will then be taken up in talk with all sorts of effects, and for all sorts of
reasons. Here is a snippet from one of the scenes in which the parish priest
is at Ariane de Bonne-Mesure's estate for their weekly lunch and the topic of
the R. P. is raised:

Sitting on the terrace with the curé and Mademoiselle Francine, they were all
waiting for the luncheon bell, just a finger of port in each glass, on a beautiful
July day, during the first week, they were discussing the previous Sunday's sermon given by the Reverend Father, the Mission preacher, its tone had somehow
displeased Mademoiselle Ariane, was it a little unctuous, Mademoiselle her
niece was yawning with her mouth shut, it was nearly one o'clock and the curé
was weighing his words before replying but couldn't find anything to say other
than he's an excellent man the children love him. (41)

(Assise sur la terrasse en compagnie du curé et de mademoiselle Francine, ils
attendaient tous trois la cloche du déjeuner, un doigt de porto dans chaque
verre, par une belle journée de juillet, première huitaine, ils en étaient au sermon du dimanche précédent par le R. P. prédicateur de la mission, quelque
chose dans le ton qui déplaisait à mademoiselle Ariane, était-ce l'onction, mademoiselle sa nièce bâillait bouche fermée, il était presque une heure et le curé
pesant ses paroles avant de répondre mais ne trouvant rien à dire que c'est un
·excellent homme il se fait aimer des enfants. [42])

Francine is bored by the conversation; her aunt has decided for unspecified
reasons that the R. P. is not to her liking; the local priest tries to say something
diplomatic that might smooth things over, hoping to prevent a potentially
difficult rift among his more distinguished parishioners. His choice of words,
we will learn ninety pages later, is unfortunate.

What Ariane has against the R. P. we will never really learn. In the world
of talk the novel provides us with, her initial dislike is always recounted in
proximity to some reference to the scandal that blows up around him, even
though Ariane doesn't seem exactly like the kind of person who would care
deeply about the sexual habits of priests. Here is an interesting example from
quite late in the novel:

It was the year of the Mission, the Father had just appeared in the parish,
everyone thought him so distinguished except perhaps Mademoiselle Ariane
who detected in him an air of how could she describe it, would it be affectation,
would it be haughtiness, in short an ambiguous air, what they call a funny
look, which she repeated to her niece who didn't agree with her but didn't
contradict her, it was of such minimal importance in comparison with the
interest that the preacher had immediately shown in the children, the good
Lord's own creatures, little allotments in which the good seed must be sown,
a magnificent sermon on the future of humanity which depended on each
and every one of us, we were all responsible et cetera, and he took the trouble,
he cut short his private prayer time to take the trouble to go for walks in the
village and approach the young people with so much kindness, getting their

confidence . . . he's a man who is really with it, he's a saint, a whatever you liked to call him. (198)

(C'était l'année de la mission, le R. P. venait de faire son apparition dans la paroisse, on le trouvait si distingué, sauf peut-être mademoiselle Ariane qui lui voyait un air comment dire, serait-ce affecté serait-ce hautain, bref à deux airs, ce qu'elle répétait à sa nièce qui n'était pas de son avis mais la laissait dire, c'était de si peu d'importance au prix de l'intérêt que le prédicateur avait tout de suite manifesté pour les enfants, ces créatures du bon Dieu, ces petits lopins de terreau qu'il fallait ensemencer de la bonne graine, un sermon magnifique sur l'avenir de l'humanité qui dépendait de chacun de nous, nous étions tous responsables et caetera, et il prenait la peine, il prenait sur son temps de prière la peine de se promener dans le village et d'aborder les jeunes avec tant de douceur, les mettant en confiance . . . voilà un homme à la page et bon, voilà un saint, un comme on en voudrait. [190])

At least at the outset, the R. P. had winning ways. He and his talk seemed to fit right in; some of it seems to have been easily taken up into the talk of the town. (Conceivably this passage is traversed by multiple tones, a couple of them cruelly comical regarding the naïveté of the villagers and the tastelessness of the R. P.) Ariane seemed a lone exception. How could we understand this? The novel doesn't really offer an explanation, leaving it up to us as readers to extrapolate from our own social knowledge. Ariane seems to like priests well enough. She invites the parish priest to lunch once a week. We can easily imagine that she has friendly relations with many of the queerer folk among the upper set around town: she is, perhaps, a rich countrywoman, more sophisticated than her surroundings, with plenty of gay friends, socially adept and also aware of the duties of someone in her position. This wouldn't mean that she couldn't take a profound dislike to a new arrival, an affected and perhaps patronizing, condescending priest whose manner works wonders on many in the village, but rubs her the wrong way, provoking, perhaps, some latent hostility to him linked to what she perceives to be his sexuality, a hostile impulse she could perhaps never exactly acknowledge, but that could cause her to act in unexpected ways. (Note that here I am performing something I wrote about earlier, in the chapter on Genet's *Querelle*; I am activating my own pragmatic cultural knowledge of different kinds of people's attitudes toward sexuality—attitudes that may never have been explicitly expressed, but may nonetheless have been registered in their tone—in order to understand the lesson *The Libera Me Domine* is offering me regarding how the pragmatic features of language, and in particular the nonreferential aspects related to sexual culture, act upon us as we read, or, indeed, in social interactions more generally.)

The Libera Me Domine obsessively recounts one particular luncheon of Ariane's to which she has invited not only her niece and the local priest (the usual guests), but also, in an unheard of social move, the schoolteacher, La Lorpailleur, one of the worst of the town's gossips. There must be a reason why La Lorpailleur would have been graced by such an invitation. Talking about the lunch over and over again serves as the novel's way of trying to establish what that reason must have been: could it be part of the campaign Ariane has undertaken against the R. P.?

> Ariane . . . would have added apropos of the Father I told you so I told you so, meaning by that that the way of speaking she hadn't liked had made her smell what you might call an unconscious rat which justified her ten years later in giving them to understand that she had not been so wrong in mistrusting the preacher. (137)

> (Ariane . . . aurait ajouté à propos du R. P. j'avais bien dit j'avais bien dit, signi-fiant par là que le ton qu'elle n'avait pas aimé lui avait mis pour ainsi dire une puce inconsciente à l'oreille qui la justifiait dix ans plus tard à faire entendre qu'elle n'avait pas eu tort de se méfier du prédicateur. [131–32])

It seems, as best one can decipher all the confusion that marks this novel, that the R. P., who had left the town when his mission ended shortly after having been sighted in the bushes with Tourniquet, returns ten years later—for a short visit to friends like Mortin and the proprietors of Broy perhaps? Is it his return that sends a set of ripples through the social field of the town, causing all sorts of conversations to take place for all sorts of reasons? At about the point in time corresponding to his return, La Lorpailleur seems to be invited to lunch with Ariane, to an event at Mortin's boarding house, and to lunch at the Château de Broy, lone woman at table with a group of handsome men of various ages. These inexplicable turns of events do have one clear consequence: they introduce into the novel the topic of young men like Tourniquet and a fellow named Pinson (all well known to La Lorpailleur as former students), born into the suffocating world of talk in which the novel has immersed us, and somehow needing to escape from it. Here is the scene when La Lorpailleur is invited to lunch at Broy and finds herself uncomfortably seated at the same table as (indeed, right next to) the R. P., newly returned to town.[23]

> And one thing leading to another still according to the butler apropos of some-thing quite different from the presence of the Father at table, perhaps apropos of the young people who left the district the moment they had finished their

schooling, someone tactlessly brought up the name of Tourniquet or was it on purpose, in short old Lorpailleur blushed to the roots of her hair and didn't dare look at the preacher any more but he very calmly said that he remembered the child and asked what had become of him, no one had any answer, but without a shade of embarrassment. (164)

(Et de fil en aiguille toujours selon le maître d'hôtel à propos de tout autre chose que la présence à table du R. P., peut-être à celui de la jeunesse du pays qui s'exilait sitôt ses classes terminées, quelqu'un a maladroitement prononcé le nom de Tourniquet ou était-ce volontaire, bref la Lorpailleur s'est mise à rougir violemment et n'osait plus regarder le prédicateur qui très posément disait se souvenir de cet enfant et demandait ce qu'il était devenu, personne ne pouvait répondre, mais sans l'ombre d'une gêne. [157–58])

Certain of her former students, or perhaps we should say a certain kind of former student, tend, it seems, to leave town as soon as they are able. There must be a list of them in everyone's mind. In fact, a bit later in the novel, we learn that currently another name occupies the place in the talk of the town that Tourniquet's used to hold:

As to the Tourniquet affair it had long since given place to that of young Pinson, the lad of rural extraction who frequented the aristocrats, he had broken with his family and didn't live in our midst any more, a room in town paid for by you know whom, talk about immorality and it kept turning the knife in the wounds as you might say of our bog-trotters, they hadn't forgotten the dreadful scandal ten years before of little Frédéric who had been violated in the woods by a sex-maniac who they thought one thing leading to another might have had some dealings with you know whom, it had upset the whole district that business but the child had got over it all right, at least that's what the poor mother said even though no one went to see, when he'd finished his apprenticeship the young man went to live in Paris where they lost sight of him. (187)

(Quant à l'histoire Tourniquet elle avait depuis longtemps fait place à celle du fils Pinson, ce garçon d'extraction rurale qui fréquentait les aristos, il avait rompu avec sa famille et ne vivait plus chez nous, une chambre en ville payée par qui vous savez, tout ça d'une immoralité et qui remettais constamment le doigt dans la plaie si j'ose dire à nos culs-terreux, ils n'avaient pas oublié l'affreux scandale il y avait dix ans du petit Frédéric violé en plein bois par un satyre dont on se demandait de fil en aiguille s'il n'avait pas eu à l'époque des accointances avec qui vous savez, cette affaire avait bouleversé le pays mais l'enfant s'en était bien remis, c'est du moins ce qu'affirmait la pauvre mère encore que personne n'y soit allé voir, son apprentissage une fois terminé le jeune homme s'est installé à Paris où on l'a perdu de vue. [179–80])

Ariane de Bonne-Mesure's high-toned homophobia is not the only kind that exists in town, it now seems clear. In the world of talk the novel presents to us, there is an awareness of young men whose sexual interests (and perhaps their looks) might give them a leg up the social ladder ("frequented the aristocrats"), or produce the desire to get out of town as soon as possible ("the young people who left the district the moment they had finished their schooling"). Some kind of a connection with the R. P., or with Monsieur de Broy, or maybe with Mortin, might be a stage in this kind of trajectory. For some of the people whose talk we are experiencing throughout much of the novel (the particular subset referred to here as the "culs-terreux," rustics, we might say, in a polite tone), there seems to be a confusion (cognitive or discursive) between, on the one hand, men who have sex with men and youth with similar inclinations, and, on the other, men who commit certain acts of sexual violence. Within a world of talk, structured in this way, what is somebody like the young Tourniquet or the young Pinson to do?

Here is how the young Pinson is talked about a bit later on in the novel:

> Or that they knew next to nothing about young Pinson except that he was very reserved with the ladies, that his behavior had never given rise to any gossip and that the good people really wondered why he had not taken Holy Orders, he could only be attracted by higher things, there weren't a hundred and one different sorts of men, he must be unhappy to have got on the wrong track like that, they did say that his anticlerical background must have put a spoke in the wheel at the age when a vocation is normally determined, and what would become of him in his old age all by himself such an affectionate person without a good wife to mend his socks and wash his underwear and cook for him, he was much to be pitied, that sort of thing. (209)

> (Ou qu'on savait fort peu de chose du fils Pinson sinon qu'il était très réservé avec les dames, que sa conduite n'avait jamais donné prise à aucun commérage et que les bonnes gens se demandaient vraiment pourquoi il n'était pas entré dans les ordres, il ne pouvait être attiré que par les choses d'en-haut, il n'y avait pas trente-six sortes d'hommes, qu'il devait être malheureux d'avoir ainsi fait fausse route, on disait bien que son milieu anticlérical avait dû mettre des bâtons dans les roues à l'âge où se décide normalement une vocation, et qu'allait-il devenir dans sa vieillesse tout seul lui si tendre sans une bonne épouse qui lui reprise ses chaussettes et lui lave son petit linge et lui prépare sa cuisine, il était bien à plaindre, ces sortes de choses. [200–201])

Pinson, along with Mortin (the widower who now runs what might be a somewhat queer boarding house) and Lorduz (the policeman caught having sex with another man in the railway station men's room who has left the region and gotten married) will be our last examples of misfits for this book. We don't know anything like the truth of their sexualities, just that, within the talk of the town, something is registered regarding the fact that they are not normal. There is no possibility within that space of talk for them to elaborate upon themselves. As far as the talk of the town is concerned, there is nothing new under the sun, and men apparently either get married, become priests, or end up alone, with holes in their socks, and generally unhappy. In this world of talk, there seems also to be a notable division between believers and nonbelievers, a division that corresponds to the opposition between tradition and modernity. New forms of sexuality are apparently understood as being linked to, even caused by, a loss of tradition.[24]

One way it might be possible to think about these novels by Pinget, *The Libera Me Domine* in particular, is that they represent the situation of a variety of gay men doing the best they can to survive in small-town France at a time when a modern gay identity was difficult to sustain anywhere but in a big city (or in isolated cultural bubbles such as the Château de Broy). I don't think this would be wrong, but I also don't think it would fully account for Pinget's interest in characters like the servant in *The Inquisitory* or the narrator of *Someone*—or even a few of the characters in *The Libera Me Domine*. It might be tempting to think that from our point of view, we know all that needs to be known about the sexuality of, say, the R. P. or of the young Pinson, or of Lorduz, or of Mortin. But who is to say we might not be mistaken about them, or that we might not have missed something. There may, for instance, be (as we saw in *Querelle*) men having sex with other men in Pinget's novel without exactly sharing a sexuality. Perhaps, just as what the talk in the village is capable of saying about certain sexualities is limited, so what we can know about a Tourniquet, a Pinson, a Lorduz, a Mortin, or someone like the narrator of *Someone* or the person being interrogated in *The Inquisitory*, is somehow limited by our own state of talk. Remember the passage from Foucault's *Archaeology of Knowledge*, cited in chapter 3:

> Instead of studying the sexual behavior of men at a given period . . . instead of describing what men thought of sexuality . . . one would ask oneself whether, in this behavior, as in these representations, a whole discursive practice is not at work; whether sexuality . . . is not a group of objects that can be talked about . . . a field of possible enunciations . . . a group of concepts . . . a set of choices. Such an archaeology . . . would reveal, not of course as the ultimate truth of sexuality, but as one of the dimensions in accordance with which one can describe it, a certain "way of speaking." (193)

Or, we now see, not *a way* of speaking, but rather *competing ways* of speaking that represent distinctive worlds of talk within a single social space-time.

Someone like the young Pinson, for instance, clearly moves from one way of talking about sexuality to another when he switches social spheres. If we were to talk to him, what would we ask, and what would he say that would accurately identify all there is to identify about his sexuality (assuming he has just one as he moves across social space and social time)? In what tone would he speak?

Maybe Pinson, or Tourniquet, or Mortin, or Lorduz, or the narrators of the other novels would turn out to be a bit like Leduc, for whom I argued that the experience of sexuality as a simple property of our social being is an alien one. The idea I elaborated in chapter 6, based on Bourdieu's work, seems more promising: sexuality could be experienced by such people as the summing of multiple vectors, the effect exerted on certain practices by a shifting structure of relations between a shifting set of other pertinent social properties. Pinget may have found a sophisticated way of presenting such a vision of sexuality in his universe of exquisitely calibrated voices, where the exploration of tone allows for a sense of the ways different social features of a self are necessarily overlapping. Silverstein asks at one point if what he is calling "ethnolinguistic identities" (and I think we could take sexuality to be one of those) might not in some sense "come and go, providing a transient or punctuated sense of catego-rizable selfhood."[25] That, too, seems relevant to Pinget, to the sense his novels convey that when you leave one world of talk for another, or that as the world of talk you are in evolves, you may find that different aspects of your selfhood, including your sexuality, recombine into new formations. Pinget is, in short, the most linguistico-anthropological of the writers we have read, perhaps the most technically challenging to read as well. With only rare exceptions, he is not mentioned in recent discussions of French literary writing about same-sex sexualities, nor has sexuality come up in many treatments of his work. Perhaps the conditions have yet to be met for him to find the necessary set of counterpublic readers.

Manners and Melodies

So who might be the someone who would read *Someone*? Who would read *The Inquisitory* or *The Libera Me Domine*? Another, more abstract version of the question might be: Why do we end up becoming attached to one book rather than another? Or, why do we end up *liking* one book and not another? I want to approach this question a bit sociologically, although it might not seem so at first. I start my approach with a look at a moment in *Swann's Way* in which Proust's narrator discovers an author who will rapidly become an obsession of his, and later something of a friend: Bergotte. The narrator starts reading

Bergotte on the recommendation of his pretentious schoolmate Bloch, who, on one occasion when the two of them are talking, scoffs at the narrator's expressed admiration for Musset, admits he has himself never read Bergotte, but suggests the narrator do so because some older person whose opinion he admires has recommended him:

> I had heard Bergotte mentioned for the first time by a friend of mine older than I whom I greatly admired, Bloch. When he heard me admit how much I admired "La Nuit d'Octobre," he had exploded in laughter as noisy as a trumpet and said to me: "Beware this rather low fondness of yours for the Honorable de Musset. He's an extremely pernicious individual and a rather sinister brute. . . . Here's a book I don't have time to read right now, which is recommended by that colossal fellow [Leconte, a critic Bloch admires]. I've been told he considers the author, the Honorable Bergotte, to be a most subtle individual. (92)

This is a painful kind of scene some among us might recall, when our naive expression of admiration for an author or a work we deem valuable is taken up as a subject of ridicule by someone we imagine to incarnate a degree of sophistication to which we as of yet only aspire, even though we perhaps secretly already see through the pose of our pseudo-sophisticated friend and know there are surer guides to sophistication to be found, perhaps even within ourselves. The exchange between the narrator and Bloch of course offers an illustration of the phenomenon by which the name of some newly discovered author, read or unread, quickly becomes a token of exchange, an emblem of group belonging functioning within a delimited social sphere. Yet neither Proust nor his narrator have much interest in this kind of bland brandishing of emblems of group identity. The novel moves quickly to a more substantive (and more substantively sociological) investigation of why someone might find themselves liking this or that writer's body of work.

As it turns out, the narrator, upon reading the book Bloch loans him, rapidly becomes a fervent admirer of Bergotte, and his reflections on the reasons for this admiration offer an intriguing set of terms for understanding why he and, at this point in time, only a few others, are so taken with the author:

> In the first few days, like a melody with which one will become infatuated but which one cannot yet make out, what I was to love so much in his style was not apparent to me. I could not put down the novel of his that I was reading, but thought I was interested only in the subject, as during that first period of love when you go to meet a woman every day at some gathering, some entertainment, thinking you are drawn to it by its pleasures. Then I noticed the rare, almost archaic expressions he liked to use at certain moments, when a hidden wave of harmony, an inner prelude, would heighten his style; and it

was also at these moments . . . that he expressed an entire philosophy, new to
me, through marvelous images which seemed themselves to have awakened
this harp song which then arose and to whose accompaniment they gave a
sublime quality. (96)

The narrator is taken by style, not by subject. Style here involves the mobilization of an archaic lexicon; it is further related to melody and harmony. The
expression of "an entire new philosophy" seems to happen not through any set
of propositional statements, but rather through an experience of a particular
array of elements of discourse, in whose combination that philosophical position is somehow experienced as immanent. Proust's narrator suggests that we
are drawn to books because there is something immanent in them, something
we experience through the way they allow us to orient ourselves within discursive or literary space. We feel an affinity to them because somehow they
seem to offer us access to a position in discursive or literary space where we
feel we might be at home. The narrator's experience reading Bergotte is one of
"joy," and it is not related simply to this or that moment in this or that book by
Bergotte: "I no longer had the impression I was in the presence of a particular
passage from a certain book by Bergotte, tracing on the surface of my mind a
purely linear figure, but rather of the 'ideal passage' by Bergotte, common to all
his books, to which all the analogous passages that merged with it had added a
sort of thickness, a sort of volume, by which my mind seemed enlarged" (96).
We could offer a slight translation of the terms of the narrator's analysis: as he
reads Bergotte's works, he comes to an understanding of where Bergotte fits
within the intellectual and cultural universe of which the narrator is a novice
explorer. By gaining a detailed sense of all of the elements that constitute Bergotte's position in that universe, that cultural field, the narrator implicitly understands the whole field better, and understands where his own dispositions
are encouraging him to settle. It is an experience of a certain kind of kinship.
    Others experience this kinship as well, as the narrator soon learns:

I was not quite Bergotte's only admirer; he was also the favorite writer of a
friend of my mother's, a very well read woman, while Dr. du Boulbon would
keep his patients waiting as he read Bergotte's most recent book; and it was
from his consulting room, and from a park near Combray, that some of the
first seeds of that predilection for Bergotte took flight, a rare species then,
now universally wide-spread, so that all through Europe, all through America,
even in the smallest village, one can find its ideal and common flower. What
my mother's friend, and, it seems, Dr. du Boulbon liked above all in Bergotte's
books, as I did, was that same melodic flow, those old-fashioned expressions,
a few others which were very simple and familiar, but which enjoyed, to judge
from the places in which he focused attention on them, a particular preference

on his part; lastly, in the sad passages, a certain brusqueness, a tone that was almost harsh. (96–97)

Proust is here drawing our attention to a level of experience of reading that he suggests is, on the one hand, intensely personal and, on the other, somehow sociological—about the way people sort into groups around sound—or, in this case, around the sound imputed to a written text, or the mental image of sound (of the tone and timbre of the voice that is "speaking") that is induced in us as we read.[26] The mutual fondness the narrator, his mother's friend, and Dr. du Boulbon feel for Bergotte's writing turns out to be an index of some element of a social profile that they share.

Here is how Bourdieu, in *The Rules of Art*, describes what is perhaps the same phenomenon—when we discover how a functional map of the social distribution of certain categories of speech sounds has somehow been inscribed in our own being, enabling us to respond sociologically to what we might call the nonpropositional content of what we are reading: its manner, not its matter. Bourdieu is speaking about Flaubert's intense formal work on language in *Sentimental Education*, and about how the sociological force built into that novel is not to be found, to recall Proust's terms, solely or even primarily in its "subject," but more in the "hidden wave of harmony" that carries the writing forward:

> Finally, to make of writing an investigatory practice [une recherche] that is inextricably formal and material and that aims to use words which best evoke, by their very form, the intensified experience of the real that they have helped to produce in the very mind of the writer, is to oblige the reader to linger over the perceptible form of the text, with its visible and sonorous material, full of correspondences with a real that is situated simultaneously in the order of meaning and in the order of the perceptible, instead of traversing it as if it were a transparent sign, read and yet unseen, in order to proceed directly to the meaning. It means thereby to constrain the reader to discover there the intensified vision of the real that has been inscribed through the incantatory evocation involved in the work of writing. (109)

What kind of critical work would be involved, we might ask, in mapping the social real that is inscribed in language in this way, in attempting to perceive not simply how the sonorous real of language, in all of its sociological implications, exists in what we read, but how, in certain literary (novelistic) contexts, it is manipulated in an effort to produce certain kinds of meaning? To do this kind of mapping was part of Bourdieu's project in *Distinction*, published some twelve years prior to *The Rules of Art*. Let me recall briefly one of Bourdieu's findings in *Distinction* that seems germane to Proust's narrator's experience of practical kinship with Bergotte, and that will allow me then to bring this discussion back to Pinget's novels. Bourdieu is writing here about "the distributional properties acquired by . . . works in their relationship (perceived with varying clarity depending on the case) with different classes or class fractions" (19). He does not exactly mean that only one kind of reader reads a certain book, but that one kind of reader is likely to read a certain book *in a certain way*:

> The opposition found at the level of distributional properties is generally homologous to that found at the level of stylistic characteristics. This is because homology between the positions of the producers (or the works) in the field of production and the positions of the consumers in social space (i.e., in the overall class structure or in the structure of the dominant class) seems to be the most frequent case. Roughly speaking, the amateur of Mallarmé is likely to be to the amateur of Zola as Mallarmé was to Zola. Differences between works are predisposed to express differences between authors, partly because, in both style and content, they bear the mark of their authors' socially constituted dispositions. (20)

We might say, then, that if Proust's narrator finds joy in the sounds he experiences in Bergotte's writing, it is because he finds in that sound a confirmation of his sense of his own differential position in social space—a position that can be discovered by using sound-based coordinates as much as by propositional content, by the experience of nonsemantic features of language that produce what linguistic anthropologists like Silverstein refer to as social indexicality. It may even be that the joy comes from having pertinent differences that structure the cultural field and that were below the threshold of awareness rendered palpable to you, even if perhaps they are not brought to the level of awareness that would make it possible to articulate them propositionally.

Being able to "hear" in what you read something that produces a joyful impulse of recognition turns out to be, for Proust's narrator, what makes you affiliate with a work's life-world; it turns you into a node in its circulatory pattern. Proust's novel itself is a bit more complicated. Doubtless the experience Proust's narrator has with Bergotte's works is an experience readers can and do have with Proust, but Proust's novel also *studies* that experience extensively. That is, both Proust and his narrator have ears attuned to the sounds of social indexicality—tone, melody, harmony, frequency patterns in lexical usages, accent even. And the novel understands itself to be engaged in that very kind of writerly "investigatory practice" that Bourdieu found in Flaubert, a practice that is "inextricably formal and material and that aims to use words which best evoke, by their very form, the intensified experience of the real that they have helped to produce in the very mind of the writer."[27] I have been suggesting for most of the earlier parts of this chapter that Robert Pinget is another writer who does this, having doubtless learned a lot from Proust. Remember what he wrote in the "Author's Note" at the end of *The Libera Me Domine*: "It is not what can be said or *meant* that interests me, but the *way in which it is said*." Remember the way he used the word "tone" to describe *manner*, all those features of language that don't have to do with the *matter* at hand. It would be a tone of voice, a manner of speaking that he needed to discover, to hear in his ears, in order to begin writing: "And once I have chosen this *way*—which is a major and painful part of the work, and which must therefore come first—it imposes both composition and subject-matter on me. And once again, I am indifferent to this subject matter" (234). And yet the manner arguably *is* the subject matter for Pinget, and again in a sociological way. A novel such as *The Inquisitory*, for instance, almost reads as the representation of a linguistic anthropological experiment: a five-hundred-page transcript of the interrogation of a hearing-impaired, retired, domestic servant who spent most of his life working in a number of queer, more-or-less aristocratic households in provincial France.[28] Pinget understands that once he has found a tone, he has found a point of view on the social universe in question, and the five hundred pages of *The Inquisitory* relentlessly drag the immanent knowledge of the social, as well as the geographic, topology of the unnamed servant's world out of him. The servant's interrogator may or may not have the ears to hear what is in the tone of the servant's voice, but Pinget does, and that is what he seems to ask of his readers.

But if I turn to Pinget to end with, it is partly because his novels are really not novels of the *joy* of discovery of literary kinship, of a shared social identity, of a common set of social characteristics as instantiated in the melodies of one's speech. Rather they are voices of social misery. Pinget's voices, at least in the novels I have looked at here, *The Inquisitory, Someone*, and *The Libera Me Domine*, are the voices of misfits, people articulate or inarticulate in various ways, troubled in various ways. They are failures, the downtrodden, people with various kinds of disabilities, and often people whose experience of sexuality is destabilizing.

When people find themselves "performing an identity-defining move in *social space*," and here I borrow some more language from Michael Silverstein, they also "create the very social-spatial framework in which this can be discerned." Literary works do this as well. We occasionally hear them do it. When the "projected cultural framework" of a work is one we somehow manage to step right into, we may be overjoyed.[29] Pinget's novels function differently (as has been the case for most of the writing I have examined in this book, from Colette to Hervé Guibert). They deal with identities that cannot quite be performed, with identity-defining moves that might misfire a bit unless they encounter exactly the right set of participants, with social-spatial frameworks that cannot quite be discerned; the projection of a cultural framework by their speakers ends up blurred. If we become readers of books like these, if we affiliate with them and become nodes in their circulatory patterns, as I have done here, if we resonate with what we imagine their life-worlds to be, and invite them into ours, this perhaps does not (or not only) arise out of the kind of joyous experience that Proust's narrator recounts for us, but from a different if related one: a recognition of an experience of unintelligibility, of occupying an unlocatable position, or of the untenability of any position-taking one attempts. In the introduction to *Someone*, we saw Judith Butler speak of the "nonplaces where recognition, including self-recognition, proves precarious if not elusive, in spite of one's best efforts to be a subject in some recognizable sense."[30] Colette wrote of the "impossible balancing pose" held by some of the figures she wanted to recall for her readers, whose effort to exist in all their idiosyncrasy represented for Colette "a kind of poetry."[31] Colette's own poetic mastery of the implicit as a resource for those whose intelligibility is precarious set a high bar for later writers like Leduc or Pinget. The acrobatic poetry of the misfit that Colette aimed both to witness and to enact requires a sympathetic public, a counterpublic really, in order to be noticed. As I mentioned at the end of chapter 2, the word "someone" has been, throughout these pages, a kind of talisman, a symbol of hope (or despair) for an interlocutor capable of hearing the implicit content of a misfit utterance. The semiotic predicament of misfits within spoken interactions becomes the semiotic predicament of misfit texts as they circulate among publics and counterpublics over time and over both social and geographic space. Who can read and understand what *Querelle* "says" about sexuality, and how and why (and where) is it possible for them to do so? How many different (counter)publics did Beauvoir's *L'invitée* have in Paris upon its publication, hearing different things as they read it? How has the ability to read it in different ways changed as time has passed? What did people hear in *The Malady of Death* when it was first published, and why? Did it sound the same everywhere? How might it sound today? When the weight of the world falls on you, as it did on Violette Leduc and Hervé Guibert, what kind of understanding might it bring, and how might you write about (or write out of) that understanding? If it is an understanding that exists and endures on a practical, nearly unspoken level, an understanding that arises, as Bourdieu wrote, in "occupants of precarious positions ... [who are] situated at points where social structures 'work,' and [are] therefore worked over by the contradictions of these structures,"[32] then it will likely resonate with people who share some version of that vulnerable experience and implicitly understand the kinds of verbal resources that can be marshalled against it. Literature was one such resource for people like Leduc and Guibert, but literature written and read somehow obliquely, as if aimed at the construction of a fragile, evanescent, intimate, heterodox, and misfit community. The joy of discovering some such community (for those lucky enough to do so) would necessarily be tempered by the sense of its vulnerability and impermanence. Understandably, given that evanescence, that vulnerability and impermanence, many of the misfits of these pages have for the most part felt socially, sexually, and semiotically forlorn.[33] "Try to understand me," laments the narrator of Pinget's novel *Someone*, "try to put yourself in my place. I wonder if there's someone who would. Someone."

Acknowledgments

Books are objects in the world that can be used in a variety of ways. One of the cats who lived with me while I was working on my book *The Misfit of the Family* (we called him Buster) taught me this lesson repeatedly as I worked on that project. On any number of occasions when an exciting new book would arrive from France, glowing (at least to my eyes) with an aura of prestige and intellectual sophistication (Bourdieu's *Méditations pascaliennes* is the example that stands out in my mind), he would find a secret moment when the book was lying around unattended to leave some tooth marks in the cover, or even to take away a bite of it. Cats have uses for books too, silly humans. Remember that and me the next time you consult that volume. Another feline companion, Maggie, may have mostly disdained books, but she surely had a bit of Colette in her, and so *Never Say I*, whose production she helped oversee, was her book in some ways. *Someone* was written during what I think of as the Rascal years. That glorious creature left us just as this volume was making its way toward publication, so I will never have the joy of seeing him make use of it. Mainly he liked to lie on top of books, using them to prop up one or the other of his shoulders. In any case, given how assiduously he accompanied the writing process of *Someone*, I know he inhabits its pages somehow, and I wish he could still be here to form part of its misfit public.

Somewhere near the heart of *Someone* is the question of how and why people offer to be publics to and for each other—how and why people afford others a space in which to be, to act, to speak in public, even if the public is a public of one. This book took shape little by little over more than a decade, and I'm especially grateful to the many people who offered occasions for parts of it to find a public, and thereby to grow in response to that public's reactions. Extenders of invitations and kind hosts over the years I worked on *Someone*, and

who enabled me to hear how bits of it sounded, included, in roughly chrono-
logical order, James Schultz, Yopie Prins, Robert Tobin, Richard Dellamora,
Susan Bernstein, Elliott Colla, William Burgwinkle, Andrew Counter, Emma
Wilson, Nick White, Judith Lyon-Caen, the GRIHL (Groupe de recherches
interdisciplinaires en histoire du littéraire) at the École des Hautes Études en
Sciences Sociales (EHESS) in Paris, Katherine Ibbett, Tavia Nyong'o (for a
conference in honor of Henry Abelove, a key teacher from my undergraduate years), Michael Sheringham, Michael Allan, Tobias Warner, and Elisabeth
Ladenson. Thanks to all these friends and colleagues for their interest and
support, and to the audiences that listened so patiently. Thanks as well to
Randy Petilos, Mark Reschke, and Alan Thomas at the University of Chicago
Press, and the Press's two anonymous readers, for their roles in helping turn
the manuscript into a book.

I was fortunate enough to be named the Bernie H. Williams Professor of
Comparative Literature at Berkeley from 2011 to 2015, and the research funds
that came with that professorship both enabled many crucial trips to work at
the Bibliothèque nationale in Paris and supported the publication of this book.
A Berkeley Humanities Research Fellowship in 2008 was also of enormous
assistance, as was an invitation to spend a month at the EHESS in January
2010. A generous grant from the Andrew W. Mellon Foundation to offer a
summer dissertation seminar in 2011 provided a wonderful occasion for rich
methodological discussions with a sharp group of Berkeley graduate students.

Intellectual and emotional support from Berkeley colleagues, including
Karl Britto, Tim Hampton, Leslie Kurke, Celeste Langan, Debarati Sanyal,
and Ann Smock has meant a lot. Judith Butler has been this book's guardian
angel. Thanks, too, to the many Berkeley undergraduate and graduate students
who over the years gamely put up with my fascination for Leduc and Pinget,
Colette and Beauvoir, Genet, Guibert, and Duras (not to mention Bourdieu,
Goffman, Silverstein, and company), and through their own reactions to these
authors and thinkers prodded me to express my thoughts more clearly. Sharon
Marcus commented helpfully on some of these pages, and conversations with
her over the years have kept me on my toes. It was Didier Eribon who insisted
on my reading Pinget. (I think I still have a few books to return to him.) Conversations with Didier and Geoffroy de Lagasnerie during research jaunts to
Paris are a memorable part of the history of this book's making for me. Tom
McEnaney and Tristram Wolff quickly became collaborators in linguistic anthropological explorations. Their ongoing companionship has meant a lot as
have all the conversations with participants in our American Comparative
Literature Association seminars and Modern Language Association panels

over the years. A special thanks to Michael Silverstein for being so welcoming of our explorations and so generous with his insights.

Losing interlocutors has been a painful part of the process of writing *Someone*. My sadness at not being able to offer a bound copy of these pages to Eve Kosofsky Sedgwick, Ted Rex, Michael Sheringham, and Ross Chambers runs deep. Eve's work remains a constant inspiration to me, and her interest in what I had to say was an immense gift to me; Ted's musical and intellectual companionship enriched my life from my very first days at Berkeley, and is sorely missed; Michael's collegiality, his endless and willingly shared erudition, his infectious intellectual enthusiasm, along with a shared fascination with Violette Leduc, made him very dear to me; Ross read almost all of these pages in earlier form, often multiple times, and through encouraging phone calls, letters, and conversation, not only did a lot to influence the shape this project took, but kept reminding me it was important.

That I can no longer send a copy of these pages to my mother, Nancy Therese Brozovich Lucey, is another kind of loss altogether.

This book is for Gerry Gomez—and for misfits, as well as their friends and companions (human or animal).

✱

Earlier versions of some material from these chapters, which I'm grateful to be able to reprint, appeared as follows: an afterword to Violette Leduc, *Thérèse and Isabelle*, trans. Sophie Lewis (New York: Feminist Press, 2015), 215–43; "When? Where? What?," in *After Sex? On Writing since Queer Theory*, ed. Janet Halley and Andrew Parker (Durham, NC: Duke University Press, 2011), 221–44; "Simone de Beauvoir and Sexuality in the Third Person," *Representations* 109 (Winter 2010): 95–121; "The Contexts of Marguerite Duras's Homophobia," *GLQ: A Journal of Lesbian and Gay Studies* 19, no. 3 (2013): 341–79, reprinted by permission of the publisher; and "Playing with Variables: Leduc au village," *Romantic Review* 107, nos. 1–4 (2016): 199–213 (copyright of the original by the Trustees of Columbia University in the City of New York).

Notes

Introduction

1. See, for example, Lucey, "A Literary Object's Contextual Life" and "When? Where? What?" as well as two previous books: *Never Say I* and *The Misfit of the Family*.

2. Eng, Halberstam, and Muñoz, "Introduction: What's Queer about Queer Studies Now?," 4.

3. Butler, "Critically Queer," 228.

4. Muñoz, *Cruising Utopia*, 189.

5. Butler, "Is Kinship Always Already Heterosexual?," 108.

6. Butler, 108.

7. Bourdieu, *Distinction*, 102.

8. Lucey, *Misfit*.

Chapter One

1. Lucey, *Never Say I*, 257.

2. Colette, *The Pure and the Impure*, 138–39.

3. See Colette, *Oeuvres*, 3:1566. See also Latimer, *Women Together, Women Apart*, 23–26, 152n19. On Colette's relation to physical culture in a slightly earlier period (1900–1914), see chapter 5 of Tilburg, *Colette's Republic*.

4. On the development of transgender identities see, for example, Valentine, *Imagining Transgender*. For instance, Valentine poses the questions: "how is it possible to extract certain actors from the categorical embrace of 'homosexuality' and into 'transgender'? What has this historical reorganization *done*?" (31). On Proust, Colette, and lesbianism, see Ladenson, *Proust's Lesbianism*, esp. chapter 2, and "Colette for Export Only." See also Huffer, *Another Colette*, 89–100.

5. Kadji Amin suggests that "*The Pure and the Impure* demonstrates that, in some cases, historical vernaculars are insufficient to the emergent practices of gender and sexuality that they might seek to describe." See Amin's perspicacious article "Ghosting Transgender," 115.

6. "Il agite de vieilles choses d'amour, se mêle des amours unisexuelles,—enfin il fait ce qu'il peut . . ." Colette, *Lettres à Hélène Picard*, 374.

7. Agha, *Language and Social Relations*, 148.

8. Silverstein, "'Direct' and 'Indirect' Communicative Acts in Semiotic Perspective," 340.

9. Agha, "Voice, Footing, Enregisterment," 38.

10. Agha notes in "Voice, Footing, Enregisterment" that "a register grows in social domain when more and more people align their self-images with the social personae represented in such messages. The stereotypic social range of the register may change during the process of its demographic expansion when those exposed to it seek to formulate additional, partly independent, or even counter-valued images of what its usage entails" (56). That seems like a good description of part of what is at stake in Colette's *Ces plaisirs* . . . .

11. The *Trésor de la langue française informatisé* in its entry on "bisexuel" provides an example from 1906 from Alain-Fournier, in a letter to Jacques Rivière (both men would become members of the literary circle around André Gide and the *Nouvelle Revue Française*): "Scheffer—a slender chap, rosy complexion, bright-eyed—somewhere between 32 and 42. Prematurely grey— bisexual. I'll be taking him some books this evening. Maybe he'll get us invited to Rachilde's Tuesdays." Consulted online at http://atilf.atilf.fr/.

12. San Francisco Human Rights Commission LGBT Advisory Committee, *Bisexual Invisibility*. For similar documents from the French context, see the site of the organization Bi'Cause, in particular the series of manifestos they publish there, for example, the 2007 version of the "Manifeste français des bisexuelles et des bisexuels": http://bicause.fr/wordpress/wp-content/uploads /2013/01/manifeste-francais-des-bisexuels-sept2007.pdf. On attention in the popular press to the ever-vexing question of terminology in relation to sexual identity, see the article, "Generation LGBTQIA," published in the *New York Times* on January 9, 2013: http://www.nytimes.com/2013 /01/10/fashion/generation-lgbtqia.html.

13. I am thinking of genre here in terms of what Bakhtin calls a "speech genre," a relatively stable and recognizable type of utterance specific to a particular sphere of communication. See Bakhtin, "The Problem of Speech Genres." Bakhtin notes: "Utterances and their types, that is, speech genres, are the drive belts from the history of society to the history of language. There is not a single new phenomenon (phonetic, lexical, or grammatical) that can enter the system of language without having traversed the long and complicated path of generic-stylistic testing and modification" (65).

14. A question posed by Michael Silverstein is germane here: "Precisely which communicative events count as, in effect, ritual centers of authority in which usage is licensed, warranted, and endowed with its cultural dimensionalities of locally understood autonomy? These will determine how the denotational norm is informed by specific genres, voicings, registers, and indexicalities interdiscursively licensed by such contexts, so as to orient people's senses of good vs bad usage and the limits thereto over a population of even part-time and perhaps only partly knowledgeable users of forms encompassed under it." (Silverstein, "Contemporary Transformations of Local Linguistic Communities," 405–6.)

15. Silverstein, "'Cultural' Concepts," 634. For a valiant attempt regarding same-sex sexualities, see Sinfield, "Lesbian and Gay Taxonomies."

16. Silverstein notes in a slightly different context that there are instances in which "it is extremely difficult, if not impossible, to make a native speaker take account of those readily-discernible facts of speech in action that (s)he has no ability to describe for us in his or her own language." Silverstein, "The Limits of Awareness," 382. In the specific realm of sexuality, we could remember here part of Eve Kosofsky Sedgwick's discussion of her first axiom, "People are different from each other," in the "Introduction: Axiomatic" to *Epistemology of the Closet*. Sedgwick notes the "rather amazing fact" that "of the very many dimensions along which the genital activity of one person can be differentiated from that of another (dimensions that include preferences for certain acts, certain zones or sensations, certain physical types, a certain frequency, certain symbolic investments, certain relations of age or power, a certain species, a certain number of

participants, etc. etc. etc), precisely one, the gender of object choice, emerged from the turn of the century, and has remained, as *the* dimension denoted by the now ubiquitous category of 'sexual orientation'" (8). A few pages later, she offers a list of things "most of us know" that can "differentiate even people of identical gender, race, nationality, class, and 'sexual orientation'—each one of which, however, if taken seriously as pure *difference*, retains the unaccounted-for potential to disrupt many forms of the available thinking about sexuality" (24–25). Another way of putting this would be to say we all "know" things about sexuality that disrupt the taxonomies that we use to refer to it. Among the items on Sedgwick's list: "Even identical genital acts mean very different things to different people," and, "To some people, the nimbus of 'the sexual' seems scarcely to extend beyond the boundaries of discrete genital acts; to others, it enfolds them loosely or floats virtually free of them." Much of Colette's *Ces plaisirs . . .* could be taken as an exploration of this very axiom of Sedgwick's.

17. Work on transnational sexualities and queer of color critique has driven home the point that time and place need to be brought into our accounts of sexuality, and that part of doing so will involve recognizing that understandings of sexuality are, often on the most practical level, always intertwined with understandings of other aspects of cultural identity, including class, race, religion, ethnicity, ableness, and senses of regional belonging. See, for instance, Jafari S. Allen's compelling statement in ¡*Venceremos?* (12) regarding his effort to account for "the ineluctable situatedness of desire" in his ethnographic work in Cuba.

18. Colette, *The Pure and the Impure*, 118–19; *Oeuvres*, 3:617.

19. On Solidor, see Latimer, *Women Together, Women Apart*, 105–14, and Carbonel, *Suzy Solidor*, 79–90. Latimer notes that many "lesbian cultural leaders" shunned Solidor and her cabaret. Colette, Latimer indicates, was an exception (107).

20. See Love, *Feeling Backward*. "A shared feeling of backwardness in relation to the coming of modern homosexual identity is what draws me to these authors," she writes (8). A number of the authors she discusses are near contemporaries of Colette: Willa Cather, Radclyffe Hall, Sylvia Townsend Warner.

21. I owe my knowledge of these articles in *Fantasio* to Nicole Albert's helpful "Présentation" to a reprinting of *Dames seules*, a magazine article from *Le Rire* in 1932 by Maryse Choisy with illustrations by Marcel Vertès. See 28n4. On Colette's relation to *Fantasio* in a slightly earlier period, see Lucey, *Never Say I*, 123–34.

22. "Les propos de Fantasio," *Fantasio*, no. 483, March 15, 1927, 423.

23. Choisy, *Un mois chez les filles*, 171. Choisy and Colette seem to have been sufficiently acquainted around this time for Choisy to have asked Colette to serve as godmother to her daughter (named Colette). The socialite whom Choisy convinced to serve as godfather, André de Fouquière, makes an amusing mention of this fact in his memoirs, *Cinquante ans de panache*, 428.

24. See Boucharenc, *L'Écrivain-reporter au coeur des années trente*, 106. See also Albert, "Présentation," 28n3.

25. A few years earlier, Colette herself, in an article called "Breasts" written for *Le Matin* in 1924, had noted the fashion trend toward smaller breasts, but insisted fuller busts were coming back into fashion: "You thought that no more of them were to be found, that they were over and done with, finished, their name forgotten, their turgescence, welcome or unwelcome, a thing of the past, a bubble burst? If you spoke of them at all, it was to curse them as some kind of past folly, some kind of collective hysteria, an epidemic lost in the depths of time, isn't it so? Dear Madame, let's get our facts up to date. They still exist; they persist, however hunted and despised. There is, within them, a sly kind of vitality, which gives them hope." (Vous croyiez qu'il n'y en avait plus, que leur compte était réglé, bien réglé, leur nom banni, leur turgescence, aimable ou

indiscrète, morte et dégonflée ainsi que le cochon de baudruche? Si vous parliez d'eux, c'était pour les maudire comme un errement du passé, une sorte d'hystérie collective, une épidémie des âges tombés dans la nuit, n'est-ce pas? Remettons, s'il vous plaît, Madame, la chose au point. Ils existent et persistent, pour condamnés et traqués qu'ils soient. Une vitalité sournoise est en eux, qui espèrent.) (Colette, *Oeuvres*, 2:1152.) See the helpful article by Anne Freadman, "Breasts Are Back! Colette's Critique of Flapper Fashion."

26. Edmond Tourgis, "Vous gênent-ils?," *Fantasio*, no. 533, April 15, 1929, 434.

27. "Les propos de Fantasio," *Fantasio*, no. 557, April 15, 1930, 480.

28. Amin writes that "Eleanor's imagined amputation of her breasts in the 1930s is positioned as the extreme sign of a fall into history and a capitulation to the subcultural trend of a cross-gender masculinity synonymous with modernity." See "Ghosting Transgender Historicity," 119.

29. Love, *Feeling Backward*, 31–32.

30. See chapter 3 of Lucey, *Never Say I*. See also Colette, *Lettres à Missy*. In fact, as Frédéric Maget points out, in the version of *Ces plaisirs . . .* published by *Gringoire*, Colette didn't even avail herself of the flimsy disguise of calling Missy "La Chevalière." In *Gringoire*, Colette wrote "La Marquise." Maget suggests that Colette substituted "La Chevalière" in subsequent versions because Missy wrote to complain and offers the interesting hypothesis that Missy's complaint may have had something to do with the decision by the editors of *Gringoire* not to publish the whole of Colette's text. (I doubt that Maget's hypothesis can fully explain that editorial decision, since the editors did so much more than just cut out the sections devoted to Missy.) See Maget, "De Missy à 'La Chevalière,'" 251–52. See also, Colette, *Lettres à Missy*, 239.

31. Colette, *The Pure and the Impure*, 70–77; *Ces plaisirs . . .* , 64–68.

32. Boellstorff, *A Coincidence of Desire*, 192, 190, 210.

33. Elizabeth Freeman, "Introduction," 163.

34. Carolyn Dinshaw et al., "Theorizing Queer Temporalities," 190.

35. See Thurman, *Secrets of the Flesh*, 386–89, for information on Colette's relations with different lesbian circles in Paris in the 1920s and 1930s. See also Colette, *Oeuvres*, 3:1506n7.

36. Colette, *The Pure and the Impure*, 57; *Ces plaisirs . . .* , 53.

37. "The most resolutely objectivist theory must take account of agents' representation of the social world and, more precisely, of the contribution they make to the construction of the vision of this world, and, thereby to the very construction of this world, via the *labour of representation* (in all senses of the term) that they continually perform in order to impose their own vision of the world or the vision of their own position in this world, that is, their social identity." Bourdieu, "Social Space and the Genesis of 'Classes,'" 234.

38. Bourdieu, *The Weight of the World*, 511.

39. Here is how Bakhtin describes what it means for a register to become recognizable: "When one begins to hear voices in languages, jargons, and styles, these cease to be potential means of expression and become actual realized expression; the voice that has mastered them has entered into them. They are called upon to play their own unique and unrepeatable role in speech (creative) communication." (Bakhtin, "The Problem of the Text," 121.) Despite having constructed a recognizable style for herself, the voice Colette inhabits in speaking about sexuality in *Ces plaisirs . . .* seems hard to hear, hard to recognize, hard to respond to.

40. The phrase is Henry Abelove's. See "Some Speculations on the History of Sexual Intercourse during the Long Eighteenth Century in England," in *Deep Gossip*, 21–28.

41. "Metapragmatic function serves to regiment indexicals into interpretable events of such-and-such type that the use of language in interaction constitutes (consists of). Understanding

discursive interaction as events of such-and-such type is precisely having a model of interactional text." Silverstein, "Metapragmatic Discourse and Metapragmatic Function," 37.

42. Colette, *The Pure and the Impure*, 77–78; *Ces plaisirs . . .* , 68–69.

43. See Lucey, "A Literary Object's Contextual Life."

44. Povinelli and Chauncey, "Thinking Sexuality Transnationally: An Introduction," 446.

45. Colette, *The Pure and the Impure*, 139.

46. Examples (more of which will be cited in the second part of this chapter) might include Jeanne Galzy, *Les Démons de la solitude* (1931) and *Jeunes filles en serre chaude* (1934); Francis Carco, *Prisons de femmes* (1931); Rosamund Lehmann, *Dusty Answer* (1927); Jacques de Lacretelle, *La Bonifas* (1925); Maryse Choisy, *Le vache à l'âme* (1930), and so on.

47. Lee and LiPuma, "Cultures of Circulation: The Imaginations of Modernity," 192.

48. Amin asks a pertinent and pointed related question regarding Colette's interlocutor's social existence: "What if, regardless of whether or not s/he had any surgeries, we take the historical evidence at face value and allow that Mathilde/Max may have experienced hir gender *contextually*, becoming Monsieur le Marquis with servants and staff, Missy with long-standing intimates, Oncle Max with more recent, younger friends, and Mathilde de Morny in the press and with high society?" See Amin, "Ghosting Transgender Historicity," 127.

49. Michael Silverstein, "What Goes Around," 65.

50. Silverstein, 65–69.

51. For instance, in her introduction to the NYRB Classics edition of *The Pure and the Impure*, Judith Thurman writes, "After only four of nine projected installments had run—and apparently in response to the outrage of certain conservative readers—the publisher of *Gringoire*, a Corsican named Horace de Carbuccia, abruptly cut off Colette's text in mid-sentence with the word '*Fin*'" (xiii).

52. Goudeket, *Près de Colette*, 85 (Il avait commencé de paraître, dans l'hebdomadaire *Gringoire*, mais son directeur en arrêta la publication après le deuxième feuilleton, par une lettre à Colette rédigée à peu près en ces termes: "Chère amie, cette fois-ci, c'en est trop. De toutes parts je reçois des protestations. Je me vois forcé . . .").

In their biography of Colette, Claude Francis and Fernande Gontier seem not to notice that Goudeket indicates he is quoting the letter from memory and not citing a document. They also don't notice his mistake about the number of installments that appeared in *Gringoire*: "*Ces plaisirs . . .* first appeared in the weekly *Gringoire*. The editor stopped the publication with the second installment: 'My dear friend, I'm afraid this time it's gone too far. I'm hearing objections from all sides. I am thus obliged . . .'" Francis and Gontier, *Colette*, 331–32.

53. Harris, *L'approfondissement de la sensualité dans l'oeuvre romanesque de Colette*, 9. What is the origin of the habit of believing that "we" are more sexually liberated than those who came before us? The so-called sexual revolution of the 1960s is doubtless partly responsible for this way of thinking. Yet that revolution—however real it surely was—doesn't justify a claim that in any given time and place prior to the 1960s prudishness was the norm.

54. Colette, *Lettres à Hélène Picard*, 389.

55. Colette, *Lettres à ses pairs*, 399, 304.

56. Colette, "*Ces plaisirs . . .* ," *Gringoire*, December 25, 1931, 5.

57. I have been citing, and will continue to cite, from an illustrated edition of the book that was published in 1934 with a different pagination from the 1932 edition: Colette, *Ces plaisirs . . .* (Paris, Le livre moderne illustré, J. Ferenczi et fils, 1934), 142.

58. On the considerable amount of work Colette did on these passages, see Dupont, "Faire

une fin: remarques sur *Le Pur et l'impur* de Colette." In the notes to the Pléiade edition of *Le pur et l'impur*, we can see that Colette's fascination for the sonorities of the word "pure" and the image of a crystal that she associates with this word in the book's final paragraphs also figured in earlier drafts of the passage in question here. See Colette, *Oeuvres* 3:1572.

59. Colette, *Ces plaisirs . . .* , 142.

60. The published English version of *The Pure and the Impure* translates the parallel passages perfectly competently, quite elegantly, even, but in a way that de-emphasizes the sexual connotations. Thus "Pénétration, don voluptueux de blesser!" becomes "Insight—the titillating knack for hurting!" (164) and "le plaisir défendu de pénétrer ce qui est jeune" becomes "the forbidden pleasure of penetrating the world of the young" (163).

61. See Herbert R. Lottman, *The Left Bank*, 71.

62. Emmanuel Berl, *Interrogatoire*, 65–66.

63. Querlin had an odd connection with Colette. As a girl, she attended for three years the same school in Saint-Sauveur-en-Puisaye that Colette had attended and then made famous (or infamous) in her *Claudine* novels. She also had the same schoolmistress, who had not forgotten—nor, it seems, forgiven—her treatment in Colette's novels. See Querlin's article, "L'Enfance de 'Claudine': Mademoiselle Sergent et son secret," on the back page of the first issue of the short-lived weekly *Artaban*, April 12, 1957.

64. Marise Querlin, "Drogués: IV. Soirs d'Opium," *Gringoire*, April 5, 1929, 2.

65. "À l'étalage," *Gringoire*, March 13, 1931, 4.

66. Querlin, *Femmes sans hommes*, 205.

67. See Colette, *Oeuvres*, 3:1512 and 1553–55.

68. "À l'étalage," *Gringoire*, April 8, 1932, 4. It seems that the publicity *Gringoire* provided for Colette's book may have been part of a deal to convince her not to take legal action against the journal for cutting off the publication of her book. See Maget, "De Missy à 'La Chevalière,'" 250.

69. Books and articles by authors such as Louis-Charles Royer or Marise Querlin obviously belonged to a similar genre, reportage about sexual cultures, but also were affiliated with a much less sophisticated register. After cutting off the publication of *Ces plaisirs . . .* , *Gringoire* started printing in its place a book by Francis Carco, *Traduit de l'argot*, that the weekly would describe as a "reportage about the secret lives of gangsters." Even Kessel's adventure novel *Fortune carrée* was linked to the reportage genre. In early 1930, Kessel undertook what was apparently one of the most publicized expeditions in the history of French journalism, to investigate the slave trade in East Africa. The series that resulted was published on a daily basis in *Le Matin* from late May to mid-June 1930, and improved the newspaper's circulation figures enormously. It became a nonfiction book, *Slave Markets*, twinned with the fictional *Fortune carrée*. See Boucharenc, *L'Écrivain-reporter*, 183–200.

70. Benjamin Crémieux, "*1900*, par Paul Morand (Éditions de France)," *La Nouvelle Revue Française*, July 1931, 152. For interesting work on Colette and genre that discusses Colette's 1936 *Mes apprentissages* (which also remembers the belle epoque), comparing it to Cocteau's 1935 *Portraits-souvenirs*, see chapter 2 of Anne Freadman, *The Livres-Souvenirs of Colette*.

71. Fernand Vandérem, "La comédie littéraire," *Candide*, February 11, 1932, 3.

72. Berl, *Interrogatoire*, 65–66.

73. On the relations between Gide, the *NRF*, and Colette, see Lucey, *Never Say I*, 75–86 and 252–53. See also André, *Les Mécanismes de classicisation*, 29–34.

74. On this point, see André, *Les Mécanismes de classicisation*, 16–138, and Anne Poskin, "Colette et 'l'Argus de la presse.'"

75. Jean de Pierrefeu, "La vie littéraire," *Journal des débats*, October 13, 1920, 4.

76. Auguste Bailly, "Colette, *Sido*," *Candide*, August 14, 1930, 4.

77. Benjamin Crémieux, *"Chéri*, par Colette (Fayard)," *La Nouvelle Revue Française*, December 1920, 60. He does, it should be noted, express a specific masculinist reservation he has only one page later: "Enclosed inside her femininity, Colette of course does not know everything there is to know about everything, but rather she knows everything about those things she writes about."

78. Pierre Bourdieu, "Intellectual Field and Creative Project," 97.

79. *Ces plaisirs . . .* , 156–57.

80. It was rewritten in striking ways that also seem to make it a bit easier to understand for *The Pure and the Impure*.

81. The letter is unpublished, although passages from it have been cited, for instance, by Claude Pichois and Alain Brunet in their biography *Colette*, 384–85. It is held in Paris in the Bibliothèque nationale's Département des manuscrits, n. a. fr. 18707, ff. 209–10.

82. There's no evidence that Colette ever read Virginia Woolf's *Orlando* (1928), but it is another contemporary text that can quite intriguingly be placed alongside *Ces plaisirs . . . .* On various ways of relating Colette, Woolf, and a number of their works, see Helen Southworth, *The Intersecting Realities and Fictions of Virginia Woolf and Colette*.

83. On Colette, Hall, Troubridge, and their overlapping interests and circles of friends, see Richard Dellamora, *Radclyffe Hall: A Life in the Writing*.

84. Colette, *The Pure and the Impure*, 121. See *Oeuvres*, 3:618 and 1563.

85. Martha Vicinus, *Intimate Friends*, 15.

86. The exchange of books and letters between Troubridge, Hall, and Colette is an earlier instance of a topic much studied by anthropologists and ethnographers today in relation to new media. Colette is fascinated by printed text and images and the uses she can make of them. In *Out in the Country: Youth, Media, and Queer Visibility in Rural America*, Mary L. Gray works to "understand how media matter to [the] queer-identity work" of the rural youths she writes about. Discussing a documentary on transsexuality that aired on the Discovery Channel, "What Sex Am I?," and the way different people take it up for their own ends, their own identity work, Gray asks, "How do youth and others put media engagements to use in their everyday lives? How might we theorize the dialectic between the significance of some media genres over others and the social realities and inequalities they index?" (164). The aristocratic appeal of the Ladies is interesting to think about in this light. The apprehension associated by Colette with the "democratic" car their imaginary descendants might possess, a car that enables wider and faster circulation of people and of information, is thus perhaps an important index of the role class and social standing play in the sexual imaginary of Colette and many of her interlocutors.

87. Elizabeth Mavor, *The Ladies of Llangollen*, xvi–xvii. For the romantic friendship hypothesis, see also Lillian Faderman, *Surpassing the Love of Men*, 120–25.

88. Mavor, *The Ladies of Llangollen*, 206.

89. Castle, *The Apparitional Lesbian*, 93–94.

90. Colette, *The Pure and the Impure*, 124–25.

91. Abelove, *Deep Gossip*, xii.

92. Colette, *The Pure and the Impure*, 132–33. "Je ne découvre, sauf erreur, qu'une seule fois les mots 'la chambre,' et 'notre lit.' Libre aux lecteurs anglais, plus âpres et plus pervertis que moi, d'y voir une preuve, mais une preuve de quoi? Jaloux d'une si imperturbable tendresse, ils voudront que ces deux filles fidèles aient failli à la pureté—mais qu'entendent-ils par pureté? Je cherche querelle à ceux qui estiment que l'on ne manque pas aux convenances en flattant de la main une jeune joue, chaude et fraîche comme la pêche sous son velours; mais si la paume

épouse, presse et soupèse légèrement le sein rose à l'égal de la pêche, comme elle ombiliqué, il faut rougir, crier d'alarme, flétrir l'assaillante . . . Que les honnêtes gens ont donc de peine à croire à l'innocence! . . . Je sais bien, je sais bien que la joue reste froide, tandis que le sein s'irrite. Eh, tant pis pour le sein! Ne peux-tu, petit sein indiscret, nous laisser au-dessus de toi rêver en égoïstes, évoquer les pulpes, les aurores, les monts, divaguer entre les planètes,—ou ne penser à rien? Que n'es-tu de marbre tiède, anonyme, respectueux de la paume caressante et sans desseins? Nous ne te demandions pas ton avis, mais tout de suite te voilà sans mystère, quémandeur, et viril que c'en est une honte" (*Ces plaisirs . . .* , 115).

It is interesting to juxtapose this passage with one Colette wrote several decades earlier, "Nuit blanche" ("Sleepless Night"), about the place in the country she shared with Missy: "In our house there is only one bed, too big for you, a little narrow for us both. It is chaste, white, completely exposed; no drapery veils its honest candor in the light of day. People who come to see us survey it calmly and do not avert their gaze in a complicitous manner, for it is marked, in the middle, with but one soft valley, like the bed of a young girl who sleeps alone." ("Sleepless Night," in *The Collected Stories of Colette*, 91). I discuss this passage in *Never Say I*, 154–55.

93. Nealon, *Foundlings*, 8.

94. Cf. these remarks by Michel Foucault: "Instead of studying the sexual behavior of men at a given period . . . instead of describing what men thought of sexuality . . . one would ask oneself whether, in this behaviour, as in these representations, a whole discursive practice is not at work; whether sexuality . . . is not a group of objects that can be talked about . . . a field of possible enunciations . . . a group of concepts . . . a set of choices" (*The Archaeology of Knowledge*, 193).

95. Pierre Bourdieu, *Pascalian Meditations*, 9.

Chapter Two

1. For an interesting exploration of Bourdieu's concept of the field and potential limitations in the deployment of that concept, see Lagasnerie, *Sur la science des oeuvres*.

2. Bourdieu, "The Genesis of the Concepts of Habitus and of Field," 23n.

3. Bourdieu, "Intellectual Field and Creative Project," 100.

4. See Sapiro, "Pour une approche sociologique des relations entre littérature et idéologie." See also Lucey, *Never Say I*, 12–14.

5. Boschetti, *La poésie partout*, 309.

6. Bourdieu, "Legitimation and Structured Interests in Weber's Sociology of Religion," 127. Bourdieu adds: "The prophet's charismatic action basically achieves its effects by way of the prophetic word, which is exceptional and discontinuous, whilst the action of the priesthood follows a 'religious method of a rational type,' which owes its most important characteristics to the fact that it is practised on a continuous basis, every day."

7. Bourdieu, *The Rules of Art*, 62.

8. See Bourdieu, 60–68 and 132–34. On this topic, see also Lagasnerie, *Logique de la creation* and *Sur la science des oeuvres*.

9. Boschetti, *La poésie partout*, 263n.

10. On *Les vrilles de la vigne*, see Lucey, *Never Say I*, chapter 3. On *L'envers du music-hall*, see Gray, "Cross-Undressing in Colette." On *Dans la foule*, see Anne Freadman, "Being There: Colette in the Crowd."

11. See Montfort, *Apollinaire travesti*, 9–13.

12. See Montfort, 16.

13. See Antonioli, "Colette Responds to Louise Lalanne." The editors of Colette's *Lettres à*

Missy, for instance, include Apollinaire's article in a list of laudatory critical responses to *Les vrilles*. See *Lettres à Missy*, 54n4.

14. Louise Lalanne, "Littérature féminine. Colette Willy.—Lucie Delarue-Mardrus," *Les Marges* 3 (1909): 126–31.

15. Boschetti herself has discussed the kind of shortcomings I am signaling here in a recent article, noting that when a study concentrates too much on canonical literature "we risk falling into a normative attitude by taking canons, which are the products of past struggles, for value judgements. We could also end up treating legitimate literature as if it were a totally autonomous reality." See Boschetti, "How Field Theory Can Contribute to Knowledge of World Literary Space."

16. See Dichy and Fouché, Jean Genet: *Essai de chronologie 1910–1944*, 191–237; White, *Genet: A Biography*, 163–214; Héron, *Genet et Cocteau*, 8–24; Sentein, *Nouvelles minutes d'un libertin (1942–1943)*, 270–390.

17. White, *Genet*, 232–33.

18. Sentein, *Nouvelles minutes d'un libertin*, 367.

19. Genet, *Our Lady of the Flowers*, 51; *Notre-Dame-des-Fleurs*, 7.

20. On the fascination with Weidmann, see Walker, "Literature, History and Factidiversiality." For a helpful reading of the opening sentences of *Our Lady of the Flowers*, see Durham, *Phantom Communities*, 138–47.

21. On Jouhandeau and Genet, see Eribon, *Une morale du minoritaire*, 117–36.

22. On the use of different forms of the second person by Genet, see Lucey, "Genet's *Notre-Dame-des-Fleurs*: Fantasy and Sexual Identity"; Eribon, *Une morale du minoritaire*, 42–46; Durham, *Phantom Communities*, 142–45.

23. Eribon, *Une morale du minoritaire*, 46; Warner, *Publics and Counterpublics*, 72.

24. Genet, *The Thief's Journal*, 214.

25. Genet, *Querelle*, 4. See Eribon, *Une morale du minoritaire*, 30.

26. Genet, *The Thief's Journal*, 110. Eribon, *Une morale du minoritaire*, 27.

27. See White, *Genet*, 249, 255.

28. Lindon, "Genet régénéré," 26.

29. Bernard Frechtman, "Genet Censored?" *New Statesman*, April 3, 1964, 520.

30. For more on this, see Lucey, "Genet's *Notre-Dame-des-Fleurs*," and Lindon, "Genet régénéré."

31. On Duras, Bataille, Blanchot, and Genet, see chapter 5 below.

32. Bourdieu, "Legitimation and Structured Interests," 131.

33. Schütz, *On Phenomenology and Social Relations*, 84–85.

34. Warner, *Publics and Counterpublics*, 12.

35. See, for example, Bataille's statement that "in fact there is no communication between Genet and the reader" in *Literature and Evil*, 161.

36. See Eribon, *Une morale du minoritaire*, 31, who cites the exchange.

37. Amin's *Disturbing Attachments: Genet, Modern Pederasty, and Queer History* is a recent effort to contribute to the metapragmatic frames around (counter)public discourse about Genet in queer academic circles. When Sartre says "it's because I am not homosexual that I like them [Genet's novels]," he continues: "les pédérastes ont peur de cette oeuvre violente et cérémonieuse, où Genet, dans de longues, belles phrases parées, va jusqu'au bout de son 'vice,' en fait un instrument pour explorer le monde . . ." (see Eribon, *Une morale du minoritaire*, 31). It's a difficult sentence to translate for a variety of reasons. His usage would seem to imply that for him *pédérastes* and homosexuals would be words designating the same group. Whoever they are (shall we call them well-heeled French gay men of the postwar years?), they are scared of Genet's

writing because of both its style and its subject matter: it is violent and ceremonious, it is made up of heavily adorned beautiful sentences (de longues, belles phrases parées), and Genet delves deep into his "vice" (his set of sexual practices?) in order to take his experience of a particular minority sexual culture and turn it into an instrument for exploring and understanding the world—apparently in a way those gay men would not find agreeable. (There are some interesting tensions and relations between the way Sartre is positioning Genet and the way Colette found herself positioned vis-à-vis the readers of Gringoire.) In Disturbing Attachments, Amin notes that "from his first sexual experience in the boys' reformatory of Mettray through his last significant relationship with Mohammad El Katrani, Genet's sexuality could never adequately be described as merely 'same-sex'; for it to spark, it also required a meaningfully eroticized difference of age or status" (110). This is why Amin refers to it as pederastic: "His pederastic eroticization of 'normal' men may have acted as a solvent of any identitarian or communitarian bond based on a shared sexual identity" (111). Amin's suggestion is that "we have misread [Genet] as a gay man rather than a pederast" (28), where pederasty is taken to be "a nonegalitarian, nonreciprocal sexualization of social hierarchy, an exercise of phallic prowess by a dominant over a subordinate partner" (37). That very statement, "we have misread [Genet] as a gay man rather than a pederast," does a lot of indexical work. The "we" includes, excludes, and accuses. The "a gay man rather than a pederast" implies a shared set of cultural concepts and maybe a shared historical and geopolitical point of view in which "gay man" and "pederast" can be held each to be conceptually coherent in its own right, and the opposition between them to be durably meaningful. If I am not always convinced by or drawn to Disturbing Attachments's categorical claims (it's worth noting that Sartre and Amin probably don't mean the same thing by "pederast," for instance), I appreciated its many illuminating moments, its "attending to . . . multiplicities" (177), and its canny attentiveness to "the genealogical connection between modern and premodern sexualities as well as the charged interrelation of European and Arab-Islamic sexualities" (29).

38. See Eribon, Une morale du minoritaire, 32–44 on this topic. Eribon's book could be taken as marking one of the moments at which now well-developed counterpublic uses of Genet's writing insist on being taken seriously in public.

39. Bourdieu, Chartier, and Darnton, "Dialogue à propos de l'histoire culturelle," 93.

40. Le Bitoux and Barbedette, "Sartre et les homosexuels," 13–14.

41. See, for example, the long philosophical comparison of Genet to Gide and Jouhandeau in Sartre's Saint Genet, 204–49.

42. Leduc, La Bâtarde, trans. Derek Coltman, 51–52.

43. As Elizabeth Locey notes, "Violette couches her discussion of her relationship with literature in the vocabulary of a sexualized seduction." See Locey, The Pleasures of the Text, 36.

44. On Jules Romains, see Boschetti, La poésie partout, 100–106, 113–17, 120–22. On Les nourritures terrestres, see the introduction to Lucey, Gide's Bent: Sexuality, Politics, and Lucey, Never Say I, 190–92.

45. An interesting testimony to this situation is that, at least until recently, almost none of Leduc's works were available in the open stack collection of Salle V, the French literature room, of the Bibliothèque nationale. The collection in those open stacks is intended to provide scholars easy access to the major canonical works of French literature.

46. Leduc, Mad in Pursuit, 72.

47. Boschetti, La poésie partout, 19–20.

48. The following comments by Bourdieu could be taken as relevant to Leduc's case: "The question of the limits of the field is a very difficult one, if only because it is always at stake in the field itself and therefore admits of no a priori answer. . . . There are many agents—I think for

instance of Gustave Flaubert—for whom to exist in a given field consists *eo ipso* in differing, in being different, in asserting one's difference, oftentimes because they are endowed with properties such that they should not be there, they should have been eliminated at the entrance to the field. . . . The limits of the field are situated at the point where the effects of the field cease" (Bourdieu and Wacquant, *An Invitation to Reflexive Sociology*, 100).

49. Leduc, *Mad in Pursuit*, 71–72.

50. Schütz, "The Stranger," 504.

51. Leduc, *Mad in Pursuit*, 74.

52. See chapter 1 of Weiner's *Enfants terribles* for one view of this problem and period.

53. Bourdieu, "Intellectual Field," 100.

54. Jansiti, *Violette Leduc*, 210.

55. See Jansiti, 210–14.

56. Silverstein, "Metapragmatic Discourse and Metapragmatic Function," 37.

57. Silverstein, "'Cultural' Concepts and the Language-Culture Nexus," 638.

58. Silverstein, 634.

59. Pinget, *Le Libera*, 225; *The Libera Me Domine*, 234. The "Author's Note," even though dated 1968 (in the French edition), seems to have been added to the published French edition of the novel only in 1984. Much of the text of the note had already been published by Pinget in a number of previous contexts, including a 1969 interview with Bettina L. Knapp, "Une Interview avec Robert Pinget."

60. He made these remarks in an interview from around the time of the publication of *L'Inquisitoire*: "Pierre Fisson mène l'enquête sur le roman," *Figaro littéraire*, September 29, 1962, 3.

61. *Robert Pinget à la lettre*, 172.

62. See Robert Kanters, "Métamorphoses du roman judiciaire," *Figaro littéraire*, October 27, 1962, 2, and Luc Estang, "'Le Libera' de Robert Pinget," *Figaro littéraire*, February 12, 1968, 20–21.

63. Madeleine Chapsal, "Faux témoignage sous les tilleuls," *L'Express*, no. 869, February 12–18, 1968, 57.

Chapter Three

1. Michael Silverstein, "Languages/Cultures Are Dead!," 114.

2. Roman Jakobson, "The Speech Event and the Functions of Language," 75.

3. Genet, *Notre-Dame-des-Fleurs*, 14; *Our Lady of the Flowers*, 59.

4. Silverstein, "Language and the Culture of Gender," 222.

5. Jakobson, "Shifters and Verbal Categories," 387.

6. Silverstein, "Shifters, Linguistic Categories, and Cultural Description," 52.

7. Peirce, "Pragmatism (1907)," 404–5.

8. Hanks, *Language and Communicative Practices*, 42–43.

9. Silverstein, "'Cultural' Concepts and the Language-Culture Nexus," 622.

10. Silverstein, 632.

11. Genet, *Querelle*, 79; *Querelle de Brest*, 312.

12. Silverstein, "Shifters," 39.

13. "If strategy requires purposive manipulation of pragmatic rules, then it may also require an overt conceptualization of speech events and constituent speech acts. Such characterization of the pragmatic structure of language is *metapragmatics*. . . . The metapragmatic characterization of speech must constitute a referential event, in which pragmatic norms are the objects of description" (Silverstein, "Shifters," 48).

14. In an article on Genet that includes a discussion of this passage, Elizabeth Stephens comments, "the representations of same-sex desire and relationships found in Genet's novels often emphasize the extent to which their characters' perspectives on and understanding of their sexuality involve a constant and complex negotiation through cultural and representational signifying systems that are at once theirs and not theirs." The overarching point of Stephens's article is to demonstrate that "what Genet's fiction thus shows is that if men's understanding of homosexuality and homoerotic desire is constrained by an absence of a language with which to articulate it—the lack of words with which to formulate their thoughts—then, ironically, it is perhaps homophobia itself which provides the language through which they can find the necessary vocabulary." See Stephens, "The Bad Homosexual: Genet's Perverse Homo-Politics," citations from 31 and 38. I certainly don't disagree with Stephens's observations, but I think Genet might also be working on another level, studying how you can enact your sexuality in language and in acts without having the words to *name* precisely what you are or what you do. The social forms of sexuality, both mainstream forms and misfit forms, are continually and continuously emerging from, are innovated, invented, and renovated by means of the stream of social and linguistic practice. Genet's work strikes me as theoretically so sophisticated and historically so specific because he is working so precisely and in such detail on a particular moment in the social and linguistic practice of sexuality.

15. "*Interactionally relevant concepts indexed* (cued) *by words and expressions in text are cultural concepts* that have a special status among the several components of meaningfulness of language. . . . Any time one uses a word or expression it indexes specific values or nodes within such knowledge schemata. . . . What type of person, with what social characteristics, deploys such knowledge. . . . to whom is authoritative knowledge ascribed, and who can achieve at least a conversationally local state of authority with respect to it . . . the variability of linguistic usage presumes upon—and points to (indexes)—the *nonuniformity* of knowledge within a community" (Silverstein, "'Cultural' Concepts," 631–32).

16. Foucault, *The Archaeology of Knowledge*, 193.

17. I am citing Saussure from Patrice Maniglier's remarkably helpful book *La vie énigmatique des signes*, 143, my translation. Here and in the following passages, Maniglier is quoting from the critical edition of Saussure's *Cours de linguistique générale* edited by Rudolf Engler, which provides many alternative versions of what Saussure said in his lectures, taken from the notebooks of different listeners.

18. Cited in Maniglier, *Vie énigmatique*, 150.

19. Bourdieu, "Principles for a Sociology of Cultural Works," 179.

20. Silverstein, "'Cultural' Concepts," 622.

21. As he says in another, related article, "the limits to pragmatic awareness of social action are also definable, constrained, and semiotically-based." Silverstein, "The Limits of Awareness," 401.

22. Mairéad Hanrahan comments interestingly on this passage as part of her extended analysis of *Querelle* in *Lire Genet*. See 159–60. Sometimes, however, Hanrahan seems to view words people use to categorize sexuality as primarily having semantic content rather than fully appreciating the pragmatic force of their use. Thus she writes at one point, "Le roman raconte ainsi la transformation de Querelle en pédéraste" (The novel tells the story of Querelle's transformation into a pederast) (165).

23. Silverstein, "'Cultural' Concepts," 638.

24. Ross Chambers suggested thinking about nonlexical concepts in terms of presuppositions and reminded me of the wonderful title of a book by Raymonde Carroll, *Evidences in-*

visibles, translated into English as *Cultural Misunderstandings: The French-American Experience*, but which might also be rendered "things so obvious as to be invisible."

25. Goffman, "Where the Action Is," 185.

26. Goffman, 169.

27. Goffman, 194.

28. Humphreys, *Tearoom Trade*, 48, 50, 51.

29. Silverstein, "Languages/Cultures Are Dead!," 110.

30. Silverstein, "'Cultural' Concepts," 634.

31. Silverstein, 622.

32. Silverstein and Urban, "The Natural History of Discourse," 5.

33. Foucault, *The Archaeology of Knowledge*, 28.

34. Bourdieu, *The Logic of Practice*, 73.

35. Bourdieu, 73.

36. On this passage, see also Hanrahan, *Lire Genet*, 150–51. Loren Ringer also comments on this passage in *"Saint Genet" Decanonized*, 116–17.

37. This is Ross Chambers's name for it, and I paraphrase his perspicacious characterization of it in the next few sentences (personal correspondence).

38. Silverstein, "'Cultural' Concepts," 629, 632.

39. Ross Chambers suggested to me the possibility that various scenes in the novel, such as this one, be thought of as forms of *mise en abyme* of the project of the novel as a whole—a *mise en abyme* of the act of using a genre in order to call the function of that very genre into question, and to make it do something different, or to make it work on a different level.

40. Genet, *Lettres au petit Franz*, 55.

41. See Sentein, *Nouvelles minutes d'un libertin (1942–1943)*, 239–40.

42. Sentein, 240–41.

43. Sentein, 367.

44. Here is Silverstein's recent characterization of the conundrum we are dealing with: "Most people think synchronically within a framework for understanding the effectiveness or efficaciousness—or, as it has been called, the 'performativity'—of social action, its telic or goal-realizing character. For the Saussure of the *Cour de linguistique générale*, the shape of such a performative event looks merely to be the 'execution [i.e., actualization] of the system of valences,' human teleological or purposive conceptualization of such acts notwithstanding. In such execution, for Saussure, the linear or serial syntagmatic relations of the abstract units of *langue* are transparently instantiated in the time-bound way in which we experience stretches of discourse in *parole* as having duration. . . . And yet, paradoxically, all effective change of the system in diachronic time, he recognized, originates in such social action; all change of *langue*, in his terms, originates in the realm of *parole*. But how does innovation within *parole* come to be a cause with effects in the order of the diachrony of *langue*? Strictly within Saussurean structuralism, there is a real problem of disjuncture here, along several dimensions." (Silverstein, "Postscript: Thinking about the 'Teleologies of Structuralism,'" 82.)

45. Cited in Maniglier, *Vie énigmatique*, 150.

46. On this same sentence, see Hanrahan, *Lire Genet*, 223–24; Ringer, *"Saint Genet,"* 174.

47. Warner, "Publics and Counterpublics," 114.

48. For an account of Genet's literary posterity, see chapter 2 of Provencher, *Queer French*, 53–81.

Chapter Four

1. Beauvoir, *The Prime of Life*, 113.

2. The term "style indirect libre" and the term "represented speech" were both in circulation as of the 1920s. Ann Banfield updated "represented speech" to "represented speech and thought." See her article "Where Epistemology, Style, and Grammar Meet Literary History: The Development of Represented Speech and Thought." Discussions of this narrative technique frequently dwell on its perceived ability to reveal the social construction of individual psyches. Writing in "Jane Austen, *Emma*, and the Impact of Form," Frances Ferguson comments, "I do not mean that consciousness is merely an individual project. Nor does Austen. The brilliance of her deployment of free indirect style is that it recognizes what we might want to think of as a communal contribution to individuals" (164). One of the classic articles on free indirect discourse draws all of its examples from Dos Passos's fiction: McHale, "Free Indirect Discourse: A Survey of Recent Accounts."

3. This passage also comes up in a relevant way in Jameson, *Brecht and Method*, 56–57.

4. Whether free indirect discourse/represented speech and thought can accurately be taken as a representation of "polyvocality" has been a serious bone of contention among certain critics. I'm not particularly interested in any resolution there might be to this debate; rather, my interest is in the functioning of the metalanguage people produce in order to describe/regulate the apprehension of this device. But for examples of the contention in question, see Ducrot, "Charles Bally and Pragmatics"; Banfield, "L'écriture et le non-dit"; Fludernik, "The Linguistic Illusion of Alterity"; Aczel, "Hearing Voices in Narrative Texts"; Banfield, "A Grammatical Definition of the Genre 'Novel.'"

5. Sartre, "John Dos Passos and *1919*," 95.

6. A number of useful previous discussions of Sartre and Beauvoir's narrative techniques focus on the relation between those techniques and certain debates in metaphysics. See, for instance, Prince, *Métaphysique et technique dans l'oeuvre romanesque de Sartre*, and Philippe, *Le discours en soi: la representation du discours interieur dans les romans de Sartre*. My concern here has to do with relations between Beauvoir's narrative practice and her understanding and experience of—and her ability to be articulate about—sexuality.

7. Sartre, *The War Diaries of Jean-Paul Sartre, November 1939–March 1940*, 10–11. A fuller version of Sartre's diary has been published in French since the English translation was done: *Carnets de la drôle de guerre, Septembre 1939–Mars 1940*, 132. For an interesting account of Sartre's attempt at an "ethnography of himself" in these *Carnets*, see Davies, "Sartre and the Mobilization of Lévi-Bruhl," 422–31.

8. McHale, "Free Indirect Discourse," 264.

9. Besnier, "Language and Affect," 429.

10. Vološinov, *Marxism and the Philosophy of Language*, 117.

11. McHale, "Free Indirect Discourse," 270.

12. McHale, 273.

13. For an intense discussion of which sorts of our pragmatic uses of language we are able, as native speakers, to speak about cogently through metapragmatic discourse, see Silverstein, "The Limits of Awareness." Silverstein notes, for instance, that "other functions of language are always being assimilated to reference in terms of native speaker awareness, and are in fact subject to conscious metapragmatic testimony only to the extent that they *are* assimilable to reference, or 'ride along on' referential structure. Thus, how vastly more complicated are the testimonies of native participants in a society, how fraught with danger is our taking at face value any statements by participants about various pragmatically-meaningful action" (401).

14. Beauvoir, *The Prime of Life*, 113.

15. Sartre, "John Dos Passos and *1919*," 95–96.

16. Sartre, "Une idée fondamentale de la phénoménologie de Husserl: l'intentionnalité," 32.

17. Sartre, "Introducing *Les Temps Modernes*," 258–59. For an interesting recent discussion of this passage, see Eribon, *Échapper à la psychanalyse*, 32–37.

18. Merleau-Ponty, *Phenomenology of Perception*, 168.

19. The investigation that followed Madame Sorokine's complaint did not manage to establish the veracity of her claims regarding the relations between Beauvoir and her daughter, but Beauvoir was nonetheless discharged, partly on the grounds that she had her students read Proust and Gide, and involved them in other kinds of activities that were not conducive to the maintenance of France's "family values." See two articles by Ingrid Galster, "Juin 43: Beauvoir est exclue de l'Université," and "'Une femme machiste et mesquine.' La réception des écrits posthumes de Simone de Beauvoir dans la presse parisienne." Some of the police documents from the Sorokine affair are reproduced in chapter 11 of Gilbert Joseph, *Une si douce Occupation*. Joseph is unsympathetic to Beauvoir and Sartre, to put it mildly. The reliability of much of what he reports in his book is questionable (see the review of the book by Michel Contat, "Une si navrante occupation," in *Le monde*, October 11, 1991), but the documents he cites are interesting. Previous accounts of Beauvoir's relationships with her girlfriends include Hawthorne, "Leçon de Philo/Lesson in Love," and chapter 5 of Hazel Rowley, *Tête-à-Tête: Simone de Beauvoir and Jean-Paul Sartre*.

20. Beauvoir, *Lettres à Sartre*, 1:368–69.

21. In *Le discours en soi*, Gilles Philippe gives a helpful and detailed description of what he calls the pragmatics of bad faith in Sartre's novelistic prose. He writes, for instance, "Sartre's point of departure is the opposition between a spontaneous, impersonal consciousness and the *ego* as an object, a pseudo-mirror that consciousness offers itself to fend off the anxiety of being nothing. The major function of interior discourse is to establish this *ego*. It provides the basis for its existence, gives it content; it is the fundamental locus for the life of this *ego*. If this phenomenon is generally a reflex of consciousness, it can also be partially or fully voluntary; whence the possibility of distinguishing between an immediate form of discourse, supple and mostly uncontrolled, and a more thoughtful discourse, more formal, whose form and whose stakes are under control. Behind all of this we can see the notion of *bad faith* being hinted at, something the novel describes as primarily a linguistic phenomenon. In this juxtaposition of novelistic practices and philosophical theory we can see that novelistic technique is in fact a response to a problem of representation" (78). See also, on this topic, 163–82.

22. Beauvoir, *Lettres à Sartre*, 1:255.

23. The claim seems to be that Beauvoir can somehow own her words in the company of Sartre but not in the company of her girlfriends. She is somehow constrained or scripted with her girlfriends, but her talk with Sartre is fresh or honest. The distinction of course seems unlikely to be sustainable. Compare this passage from Erving Goffman's essay, "Footing": "Plainly, *reciting* a full memorized text or *reading aloud* from a prepared script allows us to animate words we had no hand in formulating, and to express opinions, beliefs, and sentiments we do not hold. . . . Often when we do engage in 'fresh talk,' that is, the extemporaneous, ongoing formulation of a text under the exigency of immediate response to our current situation, it is not true to say that we always speak our own words and ourself take the position to which these words attest" (145–46). Resonances between Goffman, Beauvoir, and Sartre have often been noted. Goffman himself makes regular references to Beauvoir and Sartre in *The Presentation of Self in Everyday Life*. See also Rawls, "Interaction as a Resource for Epistemological Critique: A Comparison of Goffman and Sartre." On "fresh talk," see Lucey, "On Proust and Talking to Yourself."

272	NOTES TO PAGES 119–125

24. Beauvoir, *The Prime of Life*, 269.

25. The category of WSW (women who have sex with women), like the category of MSM (men who have sex with men), came out of the recognition in AIDS prevention work that there were many communities in which women had sex with women (or men with men) while having no relation to the identity category of lesbian (gay). See, for example, the fact sheet for WSW produced by the Center for AIDS Prevention Studies at the University of California, San Francisco: "It is important to remember that sexual identity and sexual behavior are not always similar; for example, women who identify as lesbian can also have sex with men, and not all WSW identify as lesbian or bisexual. In this fact sheet, the term 'WSW' will cover all these categories, unless a more specific term or definition is offered." See https://prevention.ucsf.edu/library/women-who -have-sex-with-women-lesbians/.

26. Richard Moran, *Authority and Estrangement*, 32.

27. Such rules of use could be taken to be culturally specific examples of "language ideologies"; see, for instance, Kroskrity, "Regimenting Languages: Language Ideological Perspectives," 8: "Language ideologies represent the perception of language and discourse that is constructed in the interest of a specific social or cultural group."

28. Beauvoir, *Lettres à Sartre*, 1:169.

29. Beauvoir, *The Prime of Life*, 107.

30. Goffman, *The Presentation of Self in Everyday Life*, 252–53.

31. Green, *Journal, 1928–1934*, 73.

32. Beauvoir, *Lettres à Sartre*, 2:41–42.

33. Wayne H. Brekhus's Goffman-inspired comments are helpful here: "Sites and times are *identity settings* for how to feel, how to act, and even for who to 'be.' Individuals have a package of multiple identity characteristics and they may foreground different parts of that package depending on the site or time in which they are situated. They may engage in microtemporal shifts of identity from one setting to the next, playing up different facets of their self to match different temporal and spatial contexts. I refer to this identity variability across time and space as *the microecology of identity*" (*Peacocks, Chameleons, Centaurs*, 17). As for the differences between Beauvoir's letters and her journal (not to mention her memoir) concerning the events of these months, see Hawthorne, "Leçon de Philo/Lesson in Love," and also Simons, "Lesbian Connections: Simone de Beauvoir and Feminism," esp. 149–55.

34. Green, *Journal, 1928–1934*, 23–24.

35. Beauvoir, *She Came to Stay*, 218.

36. Brekhus comments in another context: "Some people have mobile identities that shift from context to context and . . . they are not necessarily bothered by these dual or multiple shifting identities. . . . Some people do not feel deeply conflicted about bracketing different selves. They are able to move between different identities foregrounding different aspects of their self at different time periods and in different settings" ("Commuting to Homosexuality," 67–68). Beauvoir's sexuality and her identity clearly shifted from location to location, from person to person, from genre to genre, and it seems she was sometimes aware of this and sometimes not, sometimes comfortable with it and sometimes not. In any case, this general social phenomenon that she so clearly instantiates is one of the energizing principles of her writing across genres.

Andrew Parker, in "Foucault's Tongues," suggests that a certain kind of "ventriloquism" (83) that can be found in Foucault's writing on sexuality is a form of indirect discourse that might be a typically queer discursive predicament. Lynne Huffer, in "Foucault and Sedgwick," writes of "Foucault's use of free indirect discourse" as related to "a desubjectivating, reparative ethics" (23). "Through free indirect discourse," Huffer claims, "Foucault's self-splitting utterances destabilize repressive dualism through a de-dialectizing movement of aporetic irresolution and fracture" (28). Irresolution seems like a good description of what is happening in Beauvoir's novel, although that irresolution may not have precisely the same resistant relation to repression that Parker and Huffer find in Foucault's writing.

37. Ethnographic work on sexuality can be helpful in this regard. Consider some of the insights to be found in Gloria Wekker's *The Politics of Passion*. Wekker finds in Suriname practices of "a self that is multilayered, complex, integrating various instantiations of 'I'" (2). The women she considers have "a plethora of terms to make statements about 'I,' pointing to the multiplicity and malleability of self" (103). In the same-sex relations between women known as mati work, "no real, authentic, fixed self is claimed, but one particularly strong, masculine instance of the multiplicitous 'I,' who loves to lie down with women, is foregrounded" (193). "Mati work," Wekker insists, "is seen by the actors in terms of behavior; no 'true, authentic' homosexual self is claimed" (71).

38. See, for example, Michael Silverstein and Greg Urban, "The Natural History of Discourse," where they write: "Does . . . a denotational text preserve in any sense the durational contingency, the interactional 'real time,' of its originary entextualization? . . . We seek the durational event of the laying-down process, insofar as traces of the original co(n)text in which a discourse fragment was configured are available to us. So what we are looking for is not the denotational text directly or simply, but rather indications of more originary interactional text(s) of inscription. We seek the residue of past social interaction carried along with the sign vehicle encoding the semantic, or denotational, meaning in denotational text" (5). But see also Bauman and Briggs, "Poetics and Performance as Critical Perspectives on Language and Social Life," where they note, "In simple terms, though it is far from simple, [entextualization] is the process of rendering discourse extractable, of making a stretch of linguistic production into a unit—a *text*—that can be lifted out of its interactional setting. A text, then, from this vantage point, is discourse rendered decontextualizable. Entextualization may well incorporate aspects of context, such that the resultant text carries elements of its history of use within it" (243). I hope what I am achieving in this chapter and the next bears a family resemblance both to what Silverstein and Urban describe and to what Bauman and Briggs describe.

39. Meryl Altman has described the novel as "a lesbian novel only in the way that *To the Lighthouse* and *Mrs. Dalloway* are. They don't signal themselves as such; they aren't *The Well of Loneliness* or *Riverfinger Woman* [sic]; they do not say 'as a lesbian, I' or 'as lesbians, we.' Such works are quite unconcerned about 'lesbian identity,' about drawing a line of demarcation between heterosexuality and homosexuality." See Altman, "Simone de Beauvoir and Lesbian Lived Experience," 227.

40. Beauvoir, *She Came to Stay*, 38.

41. Compare Beauvoir, *The Prime of Life*, 194.

42. Bair, *Simone de Beauvoir*, 231.

43. Silverstein, "'Cultural' Concepts and the Language-Culture Nexus," 629.

44. Bair's biography was written before either Beauvoir's *Journal de guerre* or her *Lettres à Sartre* had been published. The journal and the letters provide much material regarding the writing of *L'invitée* that makes it necessary to revise Bair's (as well as Beauvoir's) account of the novel's composition.

45. Sartre, *The Imaginary*, 139.

46. Dorrit Cohn wrote influentially about the irony she saw built into Sartre's narrative practice in his short story "L'enfance d'un chef." See her article "Narrated Monologue: Definition of a Fictional Style." Martha Noël Evans discusses "style indirect libre" in *L'invitée*, and its occasional use of the first person in "Murdering *L'Invitée*: Gender and Fictional Narrative."

47. Beauvoir, *Journal de guerre*, 264.

48. Descriptions of evenings spent at the Bal Nègre can be found in Philippe Soupault, *Terpsichore*, 77–83; Marcel Duhamel, *Raconte pas ta vie*, 365–66; and the remarkable short story by Joseph Zobel, "Rue Blomet ou Paris by Night." (Thanks to Karl Britto for pointing me to this last reference.) There's also a fair amount of interesting critical writing with information about the place. See Jody Blake, *Le Tumulte Noir*, or chapter 8 of Brett A. Berliner, *Ambivalent Desire*.

49. Sartre, *Lettres au Castor et à quelques autres*, 2:207.

50. Edwards, *The Practice of Diaspora*, 173. On *doudouisme*, see 158–86.

51. Burton, "'Maman-France Doudou': Family Images in French West Indian Colonial Discourse," 81.

52. Brooks, *Bodies in Dissent*, 7.

53. Beauvoir, *Lettres à Sartre*, 2:111.

54. This scene from *L'invitée* contains a number of echoes of Baudelaire's poetry as well as this explicit reference to him. On Baudelaire and blackness, see chapter 2 of Miller, *Blank Darkness*, 69–138. On Baudelaire's interest in lesbians, see Leakey, "*Les lesbiennes*: A Verse Novel?," and also Schultz, "Baudelaire's Lesbian Connections."

55. Holland, *The Erotic Life of Racism*, 46–47.

56. "The fact is that stereotypic meanings—cultural concepts—attached to words and expressions exist in a complex space between authorizing and authorized discursive engagements of the people in a population, and such stereotypes are not uniformly distributed across the population. Cultural knowledge is, in part, intuitive knowledge of such biases of distribution, essentialized as 'kinds of people.'" (Silverstein, "'Cultural' Concepts," 638.)

57. See Berliner, *Ambivalent Desire*, 205–16; Edwards, *The Practice of Diaspora*, 173–75; and Crespelle, *La vie quotidienne à Montparnasse à la Grande Époque 1905–1930*, 131–33.

58. One of the band leaders at the Bal Nègre comments that he stayed for barely two years, and notes that the club was "a victim of its own success, becoming little by little the preferred meeting-place for the queer fauna [*la faune interlope*] of Paris and receiving regular visits from minor thugs lying in wait for some golden opportunity or other," and also notes that he had contracts with a number of tourist agencies to bring in sometimes up to twenty busloads of tourists a night for a thirty-minute stay, including a "folkloric" dance to a beguine by the club's dancers. See Meunier and Léardée, *La Biguine de l'Oncle Ben's*, 171–82.

59. In an earlier note, I cited Gloria Wekker's ethnographic work on female same-sex sexuality in Suriname as potentially having relevance to questions Beauvoir's novel seems to be posing about sexuality's relation to pronoun usage and concepts of selfhood by the way it uses free indirect discourse in order to suggest that sexuality can be linked to parts of our self that we do not integrate into spoken representations of our own identity. Omise'eke Natasha Tinsley, in *Thiefing Sugar: Eroticism between Women in Caribbean Literature*, builds on Wekker's work in one chapter of a book that is in part intended to point out that "*queer* is only one construction of nonheteronormative sexuality among many—and that listening to other languages, and others' historically specific sexual self-understandings, is crucial to broadening the field [of gender and sexuality studies]" (6). In her chapter on Surinamese women's oral poetry, Tinsley reminds us that "what European epistemologies conceive as a single individual is a collective proposition in Sranan" and that a certain speech convention within this poetry "reflects that what in Europe would be understood as *the* consciousness is internally multiple" (64). So perhaps listening to other languages and working to understand epistemologies associated with them can in fact teach us that there may be more epistemologies operative around us in our own worlds than we easily

recognize and more constructions of nonheteronormative sexuality in which we may be caught up than we even know how to say.

60. Other readers of the time were in fact capable of doing so as well. François Sentein records his own, as well as Cocteau's, reactions to the novel (which he had difficulty finishing), in *Nouvelles minutes d'un libertin (1942–1943)*, 402–3. Both Sentein and Cocteau compared Beauvoir's novel unfavorably to Colette's *Claudine* novels (with their piquant same-sex dalliances between schoolgirls and between married women) and to the willfully scandalous public life of Colette, her husband Willy, and various other women. Cocteau and Sentein both seem to have preferred the popular entertainment (Colette) to the tight-laced philosophical lesson (Beauvoir). Violette Leduc apparently commented to an acquaintance after reading the novel (this was before she met Simone de Beauvoir), "I am certain that Simone de Beauvoir loves women." (See Jansiti, *Violette Leduc*, 137.)

61. Frustration and violence (both symbolic and physical) seem often to accompany the experience of this enunciatory difficulty, at least in many of the examples we will encounter in this book. It bears mentioning in this light that Françoise murders Xavière at the end of the novel, an ending nearly no one has found satisfactory (including Beauvoir herself, when she wrote about it later). See, for instance, Evans ("Murdering *L'Invitée*," 83), who calls it "unreal, a cheat and a lie"; or Toril Moi, who refers to it in *Simone de Beauvoir: The Making of an Intellectual Woman*, as "illogical, unrealistic . . . excessive" (97). Perhaps the murder is there in part to make good on the portentous epigraph from Hegel that Beauvoir chose for her novel ("Each conscience seeks the death of the other"); perhaps it represents the fulfillment of the sense of negative affect or hatred Sartre or Beauvoir experienced in relation to the "Dos Passos" way of writing and experiencing subjectivity; perhaps it is a trace, as well, of the enunciatory difficulty of the misfit sexuality that the novel uneasily registers.

62. Many of the documents concerning the initial reception of *The Second Sex* have been assembled in one place in the helpful volume edited by Ingrid Galster, *"Le Deuxième Sexe" de Simone de Beauvoir*.

63. Barnes, "La Lesbienne," 315. Toril Moi writes that "the theoretical and rhetorical confusion of this chapter is indicative of deeper difficulties: it is as if the very subject of lesbianism makes Beauvoir incapable of organizing her thought." See Moi, *Simone de Beauvoir*, 200.

64. On Colette and Beauvoir, see Lecarme-Tabone, "D'une rencontre à l'autre: Colette et Simone de Beauvoir."

65. One of the most compelling and brilliant cases for Beauvoir's ongoing relevance has been made, of course, by Judith Butler in "Sex and Gender in Simone de Beauvoir's *Second Sex*."

66. It seems generically related to other texts, such as Gide's *Corydon*, or Colette's *Ces plaisirs . . .* , or the essay on "Men-Women" that Proust places at the beginning of *Sodom and Gomorrah*. These are all hybrid texts, complexly voiced mixtures of ethnography, conceptual analysis, and social commentary. On *Corydon*, see chapter 3 of Lucey, *Gide's Bent*. On the opening of Proust's *Sodom and Gomorrah*, see chapter 6 of Lucey, *Never Say I*.

67. Beauvoir, *Le deuxième sexe*, 2:191–92. There are two English translations of *The Second Sex*, one (an abridged version) published in 1953, and a more recent unabridged one, published in 2011. It is, in fact, the earlier translation that does a better job with the passage in question here, but, in any case, I provide my own translation of it. For commentary on the two translations of *Le deuxième sexe*, see part 2, chapter 4, "Keywords 4: 'Sex' and 'Gender,'" in Apter, *Against World Literature*, esp. 166–67.

68. Gunther, *The Elastic Closet*, 2–3.

69. Berlant, *The Female Complaint*, 4.

70. "It is a commonplace of communication theory that there is no message without 'noise': since there must always be a channel of communication, there is also a degree of interference between the message's transmission and its reception. . . . to be in touch with 'noise' is to be in touch, not with some accidental happenstance, but with something fundamental, and indeed a message in its own right." Thus writes the brilliant thinker of noise, Ross Chambers, in *Story and Situation*, 181. Elsewhere, Chambers writes: "Modern information theory . . . treats noise as an impediment to communication. . . . But Baudelaire . . . does not present noise as an impediment to communication so much as he sees noise-traversed communication as the only mode available to modern poetic speech; and the problem for him is not to exclude noise from poetic beauty but to find a means of producing poetry which incorporates noise into its texture." See Chambers, "Baudelaire's Street Poetry," 253. On the topic of this chapter and of this book, see also his "Strategic Constructivism? Sedgwick's Ethics of Inversion."

Chapter Five

1. Silverstein, "'Cultural' Concepts," 623–25.

2. On the idea of residual and emergent categories of apprehension, see Williams, *Marxism and Literature*, 121–28.

3. Lamy and Roy, eds., *Marguerite Duras à Montréal*, 69–70.

4. In "'Cultural' Concepts and the Language-Culture Nexus," Silverstein reminds us that people tell us something of how they imagine who they are by the kinds of things they say in certain circumstances: "'Who'—what kind of person in a social partition made relevant in this genred mode of entextualization—can inhabit a particular kind of interlocutory role using such-and-such expression forms?" (638).

5. Goffman, "Felicity's Condition," 27.

6. Didier Eribon, "Comme une messe de mariage," *Le Nouvel Observateur*, October 16–22, 1987, 140–41.

7. Duras, *Le camion*, 125.

8. Let me offer one more fabulous example of her taking that oracular stance. In the early 1990s, Duras, having written a new book, *L'amant de la Chine du nord*, switched publishers from Minuit to Gallimard, and let it be known in the French press that she had done so because she did not care for the way the editor at Minuit, Jérôme Lindon, had treated her manuscript. She denounced him in memorable terms in the newspaper *Libération* in June 1991: "Perhaps Lindon thought: 'She must be getting old, and since she's been sick she won't even notice.' There's only one thing I have to say to him: it's that he will never be a writer. And he had better get used to having lost Duras, because she's not coming back. It's over, from now to death and even beyond. He will get nothing after I die. Even dead, I can still write." (Marianne Alphant, "Duras dans le parc à amants," *Libération*, June 13, 1991, 26.)

9. On Duras and Bataille, see Crowley, *Duras, Writing, and the Ethical*, 1–8; and also the first two chapters of Hill, *Marguerite Duras: Apocalyptic Desires*. In a fascinating book, *Aesopic Conversations: Popular Tradition, Cultural Dialogue, and the Invention of Greek Prose*, Leslie Kurke shows how the textual materials related to Aesop reveal him as a figure that could be called upon for "local, civic resistance" to "elitist practices and privileges" associated with oracularity as institutionalized at Delphi (59). Perhaps what I am attempting here could be thought of as an Aesopian response to Duras and much of the critical tradition that has grown up around her.

10. Benveniste, "The Nature of Pronouns," 218.

11. Alan Rumsey, "Agency, Personhood and the 'I' of Discourse in the Pacific and Beyond," 103, 106, 107.

12. Blanchot, "Everyday Speech," 242.

13. Blanchot, "The Narrative Voice (the 'he,' the neutral)," 385.

14. Guyotat can be associated with the review *Tel Quel* and the version of Bataille that reigned there. On the appropriation of Bataille by *Tel Quel*, see Guerlac, *Literary Polemics: Bataille, Sartre, Valéry, Breton*, 9–37. See also Kaufmann, *Poétique des groupes littéraires*, 148–55.

15. Although *Eden, Eden, Eden* was not banned outright, a ruling was made that it could not be advertised, nor could it be sold to minors. These legal restrictions would be lifted in 1981.

16. Foucault of course was not part of the *Tel Quel* group, although he had a loose affiliation with it in the early 1960s, and some of his writings were extremely important within the group. See Marx-Scouras, *The Cultural Politics of "Tel Quel,"* 30–69. Foucault and Duras could also be seen as closely positioned within the literary/intellectual field in France around 1970, although (as with Foucault and *Tel Quel*) many divergences between them would be apparent as time passed. Cf. the conversation between Foucault and Hélène Cixous, "A propos de Marguerite Duras," from 1975, reprinted in Foucault, *Dits et écrits, 1954–1988*, 2:762–71.

17. Michel Foucault, "Il y aura scandale, mais . . .", reprinted in *Dits et écrits*, 2:75. (J'ai l'impression que vous rejoignez par là ce qu'on sait de la sexualité depuis bien longtemps, mais qu'on tient soigneusement à l'écart pour mieux protéger le primat du sujet, l'unité de l'individu et l'abstraction du "sexe": qu'elle n'est point à la limite du corps quelque chose comme le "sexe," qu'elle n'est pas non plus, de l'un à l'autre, un moyen de communication, qu'elle n'est pas même le désir fondamental ni primitif de l'individu, mais la trame même de ses processus lui est largement antérieure; et l'individu, lui, n'en est qu'un prolongement précaire, provisoire, vite effacé; il n'est, en fin de compte, qu'une forme pâle qui surgit pour quelques instants d'une grande souche obstinée, répétitive. Les individus, des pseudopodes vite rétractés de la sexualité. Si nous voulions savoir ce que nous savons, il faudrait renoncer à ce que nous imaginons de notre individualité, de notre moi, de notre position de sujet. Dans votre texte, c'est peut-être la première fois que les rapports de l'individu et de la sexualité sont franchement et décidément renversés: ce ne sont plus les personnages qui s'effacent au profit des éléments, des structures, des pronoms personnels, mais la sexualité qui passe de l'autre côté de l'individu et cesse d'être "assujettie.")

18. Marguerite Duras, "Duras: The Thing. Un entretien avec Rolland Thélu," 16.

19. Duras, *Les yeux verts*, 82. See, on this text, Hill, *Marguerite Duras: Apocalyptic Desires*, 8–9.

20. One interesting text that takes up this issue and is also something like a manifesto for a certain kind of avant-gardist writing in these years is the essay Tony Duvert wrote to inaugurate the new review *Minuit* that the Minuit publishing house started putting out in November 1972: Tony Duvert, "La lecture introvable," *Minuit*, no. 1 (November 1972): 2–21. On Duvert, see Gilles Sebhan, *Tony Duvert: L'enfant silencieux*, esp. 57–79. Roland Barthes's essays and interviews during these years are also quite revealing. See, for instance, two interviews from the early 1970s, "Fatalité de la culture, limites de la contre-culture" and "Roland Barthes contre les idées reçues," both in *Oeuvres complètes*, 4:193–98 and 4:564–69.

21. Pierre Guyotat, "Réponses: Entretien réalisé avec Thérèse Réveillé," in *Littérature interdite*, 36–37.

22. Duras, *Le camion*, 112, 120, 129–30.

23. Pauline Kael, when she reviewed *Le camion* (admiringly) for the *New Yorker*, described its reception at Cannes: "When 'The Truck' opens at the New York Film Festival this week, there's likely to be a repetition of the scene in May at Cannes. After the showing, Marguerite Duras stood

at the head of the stairs in the Palais des Festivals facing the crowd in evening clothes, which was yelling insults up at her. People who had walked out were milling around; they'd waited to bait her. . . . Faced with the audience's impatience, Duras fights back by going further, defiant, single-minded. There's something of the punitive disciplinarian in her conception of film art; 'The Truck' is a position paper made into a movie. It's accessible, but it's accessible to a piece of yourself that you never take to the movies. Let's put it this way: if you were studying for a college exam and knocked off to go see 'The Truck,' you wouldn't feel you were playing hooky." Pauline Kael, "The Current Cinema," *New Yorker*, September 26, 1977, 123–27. Kael reviews Duras's film alongside one other movie: *Star Wars*.

24. *Marguerite Duras: Les grands entretiens de Bernard Pivot* (dir. Jean-Luc Léridon; 1984; Bry-sur-Marne: INA, 2004), DVD.

25. Duras's notion of *écriture*, linking her to figures like Blanchot and Bataille, and perhaps beyond them to other figures such as Beckett or the surrealists who are sometimes claimed as part of this genealogy, is thus not quite the same as the notion of *écriture féminine* that would also be developed in these same years by writers such as Hélène Cixous, even if there are themes that echo between the two currents, and certain figures who might be claimed for both traditions. In "The Laugh of the Medusa," which lays out one version of *écriture féminine*, for instance, Cixous writes that "Woman must write her self: must write about women and bring women to writing, from which they have been driven away as violently as from their bodies. . . . Woman must put herself into the text—as into the world and into history—by her own movement." For Cixous, an act of collective self-expression is thus at stake, and this is a bit different, it seems to me, than the oracular impersonality Duras claims to be seeking in her writing. Nonetheless, Cixous does, in one footnote, name three writers whose works have something "pervasively feminine in their significance." They are "Colette, Marguerite Duras, . . . and Jean Genet." See Cixous, "The Laugh of the Medusa," 245, 248–49n.

26. "Système qui développe la formation de communautés (ethniques, religieuses, culturelles, sociales . . .), pouvant diviser la nation au détriment de l'intégration." (*Le nouveau Petit Robert de la langue française 2010*, electronic version, s.v. "communautarisme.")

27. The work of Joan Wallach Scott is particularly useful in offering a historical analysis of the debate between "communautarisme" and "universalisme" as it has occurred around several issues. See, for instance, Scott's *Parité! Sexual Equality and the Crisis of French Universalism*, 70–73, 104–8; and Scott, *Politics of the Veil*, 11–16. See also David Caron, *My Father and I: The Marais and the Queerness of Community*. Caron notes that "the French concept of universal citizenship made it nearly impossible for gay men to feel collectively concerned by AIDS *as gay men* because, for the most part, they didn't think of themselves that way" (135). See Antoine Idier, *Les alinéas au placard: L'abrogation du délit d'homosexualité (1977–1982)*, on how forms of gay activism shifted in relation to this question just at the turn of the 1980s.

28. "Il s'agit pour le nouvel homosexuel de réclamer d'être ainsi, pour pouvoir dire enfin: Personne ne l'est, ça n'existe pas." (Gilles Deleuze, preface to *L'après-mai des faunes*, by Guy Hocquenghem, 16.) For an earlier attempt of mine to deal with some of these issues in relation to a different literary work, see Lucey, "Sexuality, Politicization, May 1968: Situating Christiane Rochefort's *Printemps au parking.*"

29. Alain Sanzio, "*L'Homme blessé*: Un nouveau désordre amoureux," 119.

30. For an interesting recent discussion of the situation of "men who engage in sex with other men but do not identify as gay or even bisexual," see Caron, *My Father and I*, 126–37. Caron notes that "the category 'men who have sex with men' exists outside the gay-straight binary and, more important, may provide a much-needed alternative to it and to the cultural dilemma of identity

and universalism. Naming the category 'men who have sex with men' *acknowledges* the existence of a community where there was no articulated awareness of it as such" (136).

31. Of course, this discourse still exists. See, on this topic, Scott Gunther, *The Elastic Closet*. An example from 2012 can be found in the interview of Chantal Akerman by Gildas Le Dem in an issue of the French gay magazine *Têtu:* "For years I would get furious with people in the United States who wanted to program my films in feminist or gay and lesbian film festivals. They were forgetting that before being women's films, feminist or lesbian, my films were first of all *films!* Perhaps I had made 'feminist' films, but when . . . in *Je, tu, il, elle*, I had filmed myself making love to another woman, I didn't tell myself I was making a lesbian film. I simply made the film. Still today I would say that I don't make feminist films. I make art out of women who are washing the dishes—or making love. [She laughs.] Of course, if someone asks me to attend a women's film festival somewhere in Latin America, I'm happy to do it, given how much work still needs to be done there. And of course, at the time when so many people were dying of AIDS, it was absolutely necessary to build upon the kind of work Act Up was doing. In crucial moments like those, that was what was needed, like chanting in May 68: 'We are all German Jews'" (Gildas Le Dem, "La folie Akerman," *Têtu*, March 2012, 106-7).

32. Duras, "Duras: The Thing," 16.

33. Sedgwick, "Anality: News from the Front," 169.

34. Deleuze, preface to *L'après-mai des faunes*, 10-11.

35. Bourdieu, "The Production and Reproduction of Legitimate Language," 58.

36. The two books by Scott mentioned earlier provide interesting analyses of this kind of situation. See also Didier Eribon, *Une morale du minoritaire* and *Papiers d'identité*.

37. A fairly recent example testifying to the ongoing force of this compulsion would be an essay by Jean-Luc Nancy, "Concealed Thinking."

38. The term "homophobia" itself was coming into usage only slowly in the 1970s and 1980s. See Wickberg, "Homophobia: On the Cultural History of an Idea." I am not much invested in homophobia as a psychological question, but rather as a convenient term to designate derogatory discourse and acts directed at people who practice same-sex sexualities. On Duras's homophobia, see Eribon, "Duras et la maladie de la mort," in *Papiers d'identité*, 134-38.

39. Georges Bataille, *Literature and Evil*, 170; *La littérature et le mal*, 148.

40. Blanchot, *The Book to Come*, 215-16. The article on Beckett from which these citations are drawn first appeared in the *Nouvelle Revue Française* in 1953.

41. Duras, "On George Bataille," 18-19.

42. Yve-Alain Bois, "Water Closet," in Bois and Krauss, *Formless*, 204.

43. See Derrida, *Glas*, 216-22, where he writes of Bataille "get[ting] on his high horse" (216) and with "sententious academicism" (221) somehow writing the opposite of what one might have expected from him, "despite . . . what should have, following the general logic of his thought (the simulacrum, sovereignty as an untenable limit, transgression, loss, and so on), led him to another reading" (220-21).

44. Eribon, *Une morale du minoritaire*, 48. Eribon's extended discussion of Bataille, Genet, and also Foucault (45-68) is quite germane to my topic here. See also Bizet, *Une communication sans échange*, 14-15. Bizet notes that Bataille shifted from an initial positive reaction to Genet in the late 1940s, to the negative one of the 1950s. Bizet also recapitulates other critiques (by figures such as Tony Duvert and Françoise d'Eaubonne) that have been offered of Bataille for his derogatory treatment of Genet, and therefore, by implication, of same-sex sexuality between men (*Une communication sans échange*, 207-9, 234, 244-45).

45. Cf. Stanton Wortham, "Accomplishing Identity in Participant-Denoting Discourse," 190-

91: "Culture takes material form as it circulates, getting communicated from one individual or group to another through sign vehicles, like oral or written speech, visual representations, or physical artifacts. The material vehicles disappear or cease to communicate, but culture continues as it circulates farther through other vehicles and into other spaces. Through inertia, culture tends to stay in motion—people will often continue to circulate an idea or pattern just because it is there, or out of habit."

46. It might be tempting to claim, based on certain of her works (including *The Lover* perhaps, or *Destroy, She Said*), that Duras had a more friendly inclination toward same-sex sexualities involving women. People wishing to make that claim will need to account for statements such as the following: "I don't see women who are truly separated from maternity. I don't perceive them. As for one's own imaginary, there's nothing that can be done to control it. I see women with children. I don't see—in the sense of seeing, in the sense of translating into writing—I don't see women without children" (Lamy and Roy, *Marguerite Duras à Montréal*, 67). I don't mean to imply that women cannot have children together or that all women without children are lesbian, but rather that Duras was capable of suggesting that a woman's reproductive role was the necessary core of her identity or her social role.

47. Hocquenghem's first article was devoted to the importance of churches to American gay life. It began: "Gay churches are, for Europeans, the most paradoxical phenomenon found in the American gay community. But it's not a question of small groups of bizarre crackpots, the way they are usually presented in the French press. . . . Given the thousands of people making up the congregations, the hundreds of gay 'marriages,' gay Christians are a real social force, a way of life, and probably the premier institution of the American gay community." ("Un ciel pour tous les 'clones,'" *Libération*, July 28, 1980, 20.)

48. Duras, *L'été 80*, 59–60.

49. Cf. Dominique Denes, "Un lieu à l'oeuvre: 'La chambre noire' de Marguerite Duras," *Voix plurielles* 5, no. 1 (2008), www.brocku.ca/brockreview/index.php/voixplurielles/article/view/477.

50. Duras, *L'été 80*, 86–88.

51. Andréa, *Cet amour-là*, 25. Accounts of the Duras-Andréa relationship can be found in Adler, *Marguerite Duras*; Armel, *Marguerite Duras et l'autobiographie*; and on the website constructed by Thomas C. Spear, http://thomasspear.com/duras. See also Williams, "A Beast of a Closet: The Sexual Difference of Literary Collaboration in the Work of Marguerite Duras and Yann Andréa."

52. "The affair that started when I was sixty-five, with Y.A., who's a homosexual" (Duras, *Practicalities*, 69). (Il m'est arrivé cette histoire à soixante-cinq ans avec Y.A., homosexuel [*La vie matérielle*, 89].)

53. Jean-François Josselin, "Un entretien avec Yann Andréa: 'Elle était d'une jalousie atroce,'" *Le Nouvel Observateur*, August 26–September 1, 1999, 12.

54. Philippe Lançon, "Le survivant," *Libération*, March 18, 1996, 44.

55. Noguez, *Duras, Marguerite*, 131. As the tone of this entry and others in Noguez's book makes clear, the circles around Duras were filled with rivalrous impulses.

56. Andréa, *M.D.*, 8.

57. Andréa, *Cet amour-là*, 35–36.

58. Duras, *Writing*, 33.

59. Lamy and Roy, *Marguerite Duras à Montréal*, 61.

60. Duras, *L'été 80*, 87.

61. Duras, *The Malady of Death*, 1; *La maladie de la mort*, 7.

62. Duras, *The Malady of Death*, 2.

63. Noguez, *Duras, Marguerite*, 145.

64. Duras, *Les yeux verts*, 232.

65. Blanchot, *The Unavowable Community*, 29–30.

66. René de Ceccatty, "Yann Andréa, *M.D.*," *Masques*, no. 20 (Winter 1983): 139. (For those interested in more coverage in the gay press of the time, Renaud Camus can be found commenting on Duras's *Malady of Death* in *Gai pied*, no. 55, February 5, 1983.)

67. Duras, *The Malady of Death*, 32–34.

68. See Didier Eribon's concise "Duras et la maladie de la mort" on this point. See also James Creech, "Life and Death upon the Page: Marguerite Duras and Roland Barthes."

69. Duras, "Duras: The Thing," 16.

70. Duras, *The Slut of the Normandy Coast*, 14–15.

71. Gilles Costaz, "Marguerite Duras: 'La littérature est illégale ou elle n'est pas,'" *Le Matin*, November 14, 1986, 1, 24.

72. I have come across only one instance of Duras mentioning AIDS in print. It was in 1990. The passage in which she does so is another remarkable instance of the kind of associative thinking she does in her *chambre noire*. A bit of background to the passage: In 1985, Duras published her book *La douleur*, translated into English as *The War*. Her husband during World War II, Robert Antelme, had been sent to a German camp as a political prisoner, and almost died there of starvation. In *The War* Duras published an account of the miraculous rescue of Antelme by friends of his, who drove him back to Paris. She tells of the difficult task of nourishing someone so close to death—where eating too much could itself be fatal. And her account recalls the spectacle of the wasted bodies of camp survivors who slowly reappeared in Paris after the war was over. Forty years later, that spectacle was being called to mind in Paris again by the sight of the emaciated bodies of people suffering and dying from various AIDS-related conditions. In 1990, an interviewer for *Libération* asks Duras, "What are you afraid of?" She replies: "Of Hitler. Yes, still, of that. Of that vile thing that became a man named Hitler. I'm afraid of Germany. I'm afraid of the German youth who have not been taught the truth about their own country, the practices that became the golden rule of Hitler's political power, the camps, murder, mutilation, medical experimentation, six million Jews gassed and killed. . . . And by way of an effect of refraction, of the Russian gulag, Stalin and all the sick Stalinists, this AIDS, Marchais, Brezhnev, Ceausescu, etc." (*Libération,* January 11, 1990, 19). The oddity of the context in which she does mention AIDS is striking. It perhaps reveals that the incongruous associations that happen in her *chambre noire* can sometimes constitute important challenges that push us toward politicizing forms of reflection, understanding the AIDS crisis as a form of political violence, a violence in which the state may be complicit.

73. Pierre Bénichou and Hervé le Masson, "Duras tout entière . . . ," *Le Nouvel Observateur*, November 14–20, 1986, 117.

74. Chantal de Rudder, "L'amour sous cellophane," *Le Nouvel Observateur*, November 14–20, 1986, 93.

75. Cf. her interview with Denis Belloc in *Libération* the following year, which ends with the following aphorism criticizing gay men yet again: "Le sexe qui est le désir, ne jamais y penser" (Never to think of that sex that is desire). Marguerite Duras, "L'exacte exactitude de Denis Belloc," *Libération*, September 19–20, 1987, 33.

76. Hugo Marson, "La maladie de l'amour," *Gai pied*, no. 246, November 29, 1986, 40–41.

77. Duras, *Practicalities*, 76–79.

Chapter Six

1. Beauvoir, *A Transatlantic Love Affair: Letters to Nelson Algren*, 37.

2. Indeed Beauvoir's steadfast support of Leduc (both professionally and financially) across several decades is a remarkably moving feature of their relationship. See Carlo Jansiti's comments on the complexity of the effects of Beauvoir's support for Leduc in the "Avant-propos" to his biography, *Violette Leduc*, 13. The 2013 film by Martin Prevost, *Violette*, dwells on this relationship, as does the 2013 documentary by Esther Hoffenberg, *Violette Leduc: La chasse à l'amour*.

3. Bourdieu, *The Weight of the World*, 618.

4. Leduc, *La Bâtarde*, 3 (in English) and 19 (in French).

5. Proust, *Swann's Way*, 45, 47.

6. Note that in one of Proust's earlier drafts, the madeleine was a perhaps less symbolically rich "petite biscotte"—a piece of Melba toast. See Proust, *À la recherche du temps perdu*, 1:696. The decision to replace it with a more shapely, tasty, and symbolically dense madeleine also enhanced a certain sociological specificity to the mythical scene—as Leduc's passage reveals to us.

7. See Jansiti, *Violette Leduc*, 371–88.

8. See Jansiti, 79–146.

9. Leduc, *La chasse à l'amour*, 142–43.

10. Gallimard would once again return *L'asphyxie* to print after Leduc's 1964 success with *La Bâtarde*. It remains in print today. Leduc would also receive a similar letter from Gallimard regarding the fate of the 1473 remaining copies of her second book, *L'affamée*. At the bottom of the letter she wrote, in response, "Pulp them! Pulp them!" Her biographer, Carlo Jansiti, displays and reads from this letter in Hoffenberg's 2013 documentary.

11. Leduc, *Mad in Pursuit*, 190; *La folie en tête*, 309.

12. Illegitimacy as a concept that crosses into many levels of Leduc's experience, from family life to her literary pursuits, has often been commented on in the critical literature about her. See, for instance, one of the earliest book-length critical studies of Leduc, Isabelle de Courtivron, *Violette Leduc*. Courtivron mentions the "shame of illegitimacy" on the first page of her study, and a few pages later has sections subtitled "Legitimation through Literature" and "Literary Illegitimacy" (1, 8, 9).

13. As Bourdieu would put it, Leduc belongs to "the pole of pure production, where the producers tend to have as clients only other producers (who are also rivals)" (*Rules*, 121). Cocteau understood her situation as well. In a letter from October 1948 he wrote to an acquaintance: "Violette Leduc is a wonder and everything that comes out of her should find its way into the hands of anyone who knows how to read with their heart. *L'affamée* needs no defense but times are hard. We have to help it along however we can." (The letter is cited in Violette Leduc, *Correspondance 1945–1972*, 78n.)

14. For details on this history, see Jansiti, *Violette Leduc*, 216–20, 252–56, 262–80.

15. Leduc, *Correspondance*, 130. In an earlier letter, she had noted a preference among certain chapters of the book: "I prefer 'Abortion' and 'Maternity' to 'The Lesbian'" (120).

16. Leduc, *Correspondance*, 142. A scene in the 2013 biopic *Violette* develops this commonality, by showing Beauvoir defending Leduc against her censors at Gallimard, accusing them of being unable to bear the idea of a woman speaking openly about sex between women, and insisting on the urgency for abortion (at the time illegal in France) to be a topic that could be written about in both literary and philosophical contexts.

17. Marks, "Lesbian Intertextuality," 373.

18. See the dissection of this problem in Brioude, "Violette Leduc écrivaine et lesbienne: Du

mythe à la mystification." See, also, the details Jansiti provides regarding Leduc's relations with Michelle Causse and her lesbian friends and partners: *Violette Leduc*, 328–30, 342–44, 355–56.

19. Leduc, *Correspondance*, 174–75.

20. "Intersectionality insists on critical hermeneutics that register the copresence of sexuality, race, class, gender, and other identity differentials as particular components that exist simultaneously with one another," writes Muñoz at one point. "Intersectionality is primarily concerned with the *relations* between different minoritarian coordinates (which . . . also allow for nodes of difference that cannot be anticipated)," he states later. See Muñoz, *Disidentifications*, 99 and 167.

21. The first citation is from Alison S. Fell, "Literary Trafficking: Performing Identity in Violette Leduc's *La Bâtarde*," 870. The next three are from Alex Hughes, *Heterographies*, 139, 142, 146. Nina Bouraoui takes this position to an extreme, commenting about Leduc that "here there is no homosexuality. We find relations, stories, sexuality, nothing else, because literature erases sexual identity . . . A great author is all sexes; a great author is no sex in particular" (Ici, il n'y a pas d'homosexualité. Il s'agit de liens, d'histoires, de sexualité, c'est tout. Parce que la littérature efface l'identité sexuelle. . . . Un grand auteur a tous les sexes, un grand auteur n'a aucun sexe) (Nina Bouraoui, "Violette Leduc, l'écriture comme pratique amoureuse," *Magazine Littéraire*, December 2003, 47). René de Ceccatty's *Violette Leduc: Éloge de la Bâtarde* provides another intriguing account of love and sexuality in Leduc, relating her to many other twentieth-century French writers. See esp. chapters 3, 4, and 9. See also Hughes, "Commodifying Queer: Violette Leduc's Autobiographical Homotextualities."

22. Bourdieu, *Distinction*, 103.

23. Leduc, "Au village," 1599–1600. (La Chauplanat passe inaperçue dans son village quand les estivants sont partis. La Chauplanat est un homme. Marié à un oeuf [son épouse chauve porte turban nuit et jour], le Chauplanat est père et grand-père: trois fils, trois petits-fils. Celui qui se coiffe comme Ingrid Bergman, qui équilibre sur cette coiffure la haute casquette galonnée des girls de défilé new-yorkais, celui qui est chef de fanfare, tailleur, organiste, caissier chez son fils charcutier se veut femme et femme chaste. Il l'a voulu pendant vingt ans. On ne lui connaît aucune aventure, aucune intrigue dites particulières. Il ne trompe pas sa moitié, chuchotent les bonnes âmes. Le village vaniteux écoute, admire, absout son chef de musique fardé quand il remue le bâton de chef d'orchestre. . . . Les agriculteurs qui bombent le torse lorsque ce musicien donne des orders aux tambours ne voient pas que leur homme dirige une marche militaire en bas de soie. . . . Les estivants sont moins candides. La Chauplanat en été est leur obsession, leur cauchemar, leur attraction. Les forgerons des grandes usines, les représentants en bonneterie, les cantonniers ambulants qui la déchirent rêvent d'elle. Les salles à manger des hôtels sont des arènes dans laquelle ils la précipitent, la piétinent, la relèvent, la rejettent, l'écartèlent, la disloquent. Les estivantes qui sont éclipsées par celui qui se veut femme irréprochable, excitent ces toréadors du quolibet.)

24. Johnson, *Just Queer Folks*, 110. The novels of Pinget that I will be considering in the next chapter add to the sense we get from Leduc's writing that the phenomena Johnson is pointing to in the United States exist in France as well.

25. See, e.g., Leduc, *Correspondance*, 121, 150–51, 175, 178–79.

26. A number of passages in *La chasse à l'amour*, the third, posthumously published volume of her memoirs, recount receiving fan mail from a young lesbian reader (called Hortense in the book; in real life, the radical lesbian theorist Michèle Causse), and then detail the attempt to establish a friendly relationship with Hortense and a few of her friends. See *La chasse à l'amour*, 318–26, 351–72. For Causse's version of the story, see Armengaud and Causse, "Violette Leduc: 'La plus démesurément vraie.'" See also the set of remarks Michèle Causse made in 2007

at a colloquium devoted to Leduc in Arras, where she comments on "the lesbophobia of the sometimes homosexual woman" (la lesbophobie de l'homosexuelle occasionnelle), remembering Leduc's comment in *La chasse à l'amour*, "might it by chance be the case that I detest lesbians? They make me sad. They aren't cheerful" (est-ce que, par hasard, je détesterais les lesbiennes? Elles m'attristent. Elles ne sont pas gaies) (326–37). Causse's remarks are available at http://violetteleduc.files.wordpress.com/2013/10/journc3a9e-d_c3a9tudes-c3a0-arras.pdf.

27. Michel Foucault, "Of Other Spaces," 27.

28. Ernaux, *Les années*, 250.

29. See the intriguing reflections on the figure of the automobile, the construction of a network of highways, and the evolution of genres of self-writing in Garreta, "Autofiction: La Ford intérieure et le self roman."

30. Guibert and Donner, "Pour répondre aux quelques questions qui se posent . . . ," 157. (Je ne sais pas trop. Ça fait partie de tout ce vocabulaire qui est en général manié par des abrutis. Quand les gens parlent de narcissisme, 'c'est narcissique, c'est nombrilaire, c'est pervers, c'est malsain . . . ,' en général c'est louche, c'est toujours des gens un peu déficients, qui pensent mal, qui ont mal lu, qui ont mal compris, qui sont insuffisants, qui s'arrêtent à ces formules parce qu'ils n'ont pas les moyens, intellectuels sans doute, ou les moyens de l'ordre de la sensibilité, de comprendre de quoi il est question. En général, c'est toujours plein de bêtise la façon dont ces mots sont manipulés. En même temps je pourrais parler du narcissisme, de la perversité, mais pour moi ce ne sont pas des mots de mon monde, c'est comme le mot homosexualité, pour moi c'est un mot qui n'a jamais eu vraiment un rapport avec moi, bizarrement, alors qu'il en a évidemment un, mais je ne vois pas les choses comme ça, ce n'est pas la façon dont je vis, c'est pas la façon dont je me sens, j'ai l'impression que je suis ailleurs que dans ces . . .)

31. Freud, "On Narcissism: An Introduction," 69.

32. Chambers, *Untimely Interventions*, 297.

33. The first publication was in the journal *Minuit*, no. 49, edited by Mathieu Lindon, from May 1982. It was reprinted in Guibert's *La piqûre d'amour et autres textes*, from which I will cite.

34. Hervé Guibert, "Entretien avec Eugène Savitzkaya," *Minuit*, no. 49 (1982): 11.

35. Guibert and Savitzkaya, *Lettres à Eugène*, 56–57.

36. There is a large critical literature on Guibert's novels. Starting places might be Jean-Pierre Boulé, *Hervé Guibert: Voices of the Self*, or Ralph Sarkonak, *Angelic Echoes: Hervé Guibert and Company*. I have found particularly suggestive an article by Vincent Kaufmann, "Geminga ou qu'est-ce qu'un événement littéraire?," and also the work of David Caron, especially *The Nearness of Others: Searching for Tact and Contact in the Age of HIV*.

37. Caron, *Nearness*, 296. In Vincent Kaufmann's pithy formulation, throughout 1990 and 1991, Guibert was "devoured by his illness and by his readers" ("Geminga," 18).

38. Guibert, *To the Friend Who Did Not Save My Life*, 132.

39. Caron writes brilliantly (and often in dialogue with Guibert) about the kinds of interactions pertaining to a seropositive social identity today in the US and France throughout *The Nearness of Others*. Cf. 3–6, 34–37, 44–46, 55, 111–13, 119–26, 148–63, etc.

40. During the early years of the AIDS epidemic, once an antibody test for HIV became available (1985), there was a great deal of debate as to whether or not people should be tested. When testing first became available, there was no medical reason to be tested, since there were no medical interventions for AIDS-related illnesses before symptoms became apparent. That situation, of course, changed dramatically with the discovery of effective antiretrovirals. Guibert's novels take place in the period of time when the first experimental drugs against HIV (AZT and ddI) were coming into use, but before effective treatment regimens to control infection had

been found. Useful documents from this period include Patton, *Inventing AIDS*, and Pollak, *Les homosexuels et le sida: Sociologie d'une épidémie*.

41. Foucault, *"Society Must Be Defended,"* 242–43.

42. This striking passage is often cited in studies of Guibert. See, for example, Caron, *Nearness*, 36, and Chambers, *Untimely*, 181.

43. Hervé Guibert, *The Compassion Protocol*, 88–89.

44. In 1969, the gay French body artist Michel Journiac, who died of AIDS-related causes in 1995, included a "recipe for blood sausage made from human blood" as part of his conceptual art piece *Messe pour un corps*, in which he performed a mass using *boudin* made from his own blood as part of the eucharist. See *Michel Journiac* [exhibition catalog], 22–29.

45. Berlant and Prosser, "Life Writing and Intimate Publics: A Conversation with Lauren Berlant," 182. One of the resources Berlant draws on in elaborating this notion is Foucault's own notion of heterotopias. See "Life Writing," 181.

46. Berlant, *The Female Complaint*, viii.

47. Berlant: "Distinct social populations, made so by law, science, religion, social conventions, and intellectuals, do not function at a level of theoretical coherence, even if a violent, simplifying force shaped their historical formation. Fantasies and practices of social belonging operate imprecisely, in interaction with complicated and contradictory environments of living" (*The Female Complaint*, 9).

48. Part of the interview can be seen at http://www.ina.fr/art-et-culture/litterature/video /I07290571/herve-guibert-a-l-ami-qui-ne-m-a-pas-sauve-la-vie.fr.html.

49. Guibert wonders early in that volume: "What was it? Passion? Love? Erotic obsession? Another of my inventions?" (*Fou de Vincent*, 8).

50. In the "Roadmap" with which I began this volume, I suggested that utopian longings are only "weakly present in the figures and texts I write about," and perhaps these are such moments, about the strength or weakness of whose utopian longings there might be some debate. I recall here some of the sentences from the opening of José Muñoz's *Cruising Utopia*: "Queerness is not yet here. . . . Queerness is a structuring and educated mode of desiring that allows us to see and feel beyond the quagmire of the present. . . . Queerness is that thing that lets us feel that this world is not enough, that indeed something is missing. Often we can glimpse the worlds proposed and promised by queerness in the realm of the aesthetic. Queerness is essentially about the rejection of a here and now and an insistence on potentiality or concrete possibility for another world" (1). It also strikes me that the misfit experiences we have seen in Leduc and Guibert might be examples of what Muñoz theorized so influentially as *disidentification*. He writes in *Disidentifications* that "counterpublics are not magically and automatically realized through disidentifications, but they are suggested, rehearsed, and articulated. Disidentifications are strategies that are called on by minoritarian subjects throughout their everyday life" (179).

Chapter Seven

1. Here is an image by Sonia Katyal describing a related phenomenon: "The seductive power of categorization—the notion of gay personhood—tethers the very premise of liberation to the same categories as those that originated in order to oppress. These categories—quite . strategically—either erase or overlook the rich and complicated tapestry of human sexuality and identity, potentially excluding vast numbers of individuals whose self-perception may fall outside of the interstices of gay, lesbian, bisexual, or heterosexual identity categories." ("Sexuality and Sovereignty," 1439.)

2. For a helpful recent overview of sexuality in Pinget's work, see Ruffel, "Pinget Queer."

3. Pinget, *The Libera Me Domine*, 236–37. See also his "Pseudo-principes d'esthétique."

4. Pinget, "Pseudo-principes," 316–17.

5. Domestic servants play an important role in many of Pinget's novels. For a thorough treatment of this topic, see Nathalie Piégay-Gros, "Domesticité et subalterns."

6. Pinget, *The Inquisitory*, 150; *L'inquisitoire*, 182.

7. Piégay-Gros reminds us of Jean-Claude Liéber's point in the essay of his that appears at the end of the French edition of *The Inquisitory*, to the effect that, while it may seem that the person asking the questions in the novel is the one controlling the discourse, he is certainly nothing but the servant's straw man. See "Domesticité et subalternes," 133.

8. Kahan, *Celibacies*, 2.

9. In an unpublished text, *Le Livre de Johann*, cited by Piégay-Gros, Pinget has the domestic servant Johann write that he met his gentleman employer "in one of those places frequented by men with little inclination to pay court to women. We got along well quite quickly, yet our physical relations didn't last all that long. . . . Given our different backgrounds, I naturally offered to become his domestic servant, and he was not at all opposed to the idea." Piégay-Gros speculates that *Le Livre de Johann* was, in the end, too explicit for Pinget to publish it. See "Domesticité et subalternes," 138–39.

10. For a different take on the interrogation of the servant and on his relation to Monsieur Pierre, see Longuet, "*L'Inquisitoire*: Feux d'artifice et constellations."

11. Pinget, *Someone*, 23; *Quelqu'un*, 41.

12. Piégay-Gros nonetheless refers to the relationship between Gaston and the narrator as an "avatar of a homosexual relation." See "Domesticité et subalternes," 139.

13. Guibert and Savitzkaya, *Lettres à Eugène*, 55, 70, 91.

14. See the stimulating article by Ruth Amossy, "L'inflexion de la parole commune ou les enjeux de l'écriture dans *Quelqu'un*." Amossy demonstrates how a literary work's sociological ambitions can be revealed in the way the writing itself has been crafted. She studies the striking intertextual relations between Pinget's *Someone* and Balzac's *Le père Goriot*. She also makes the interesting claim that the situation of the narrator in *Someone* reproduces certain features of the situation of the avant-garde writer in France in the 1960s.

15. Cf. Auchlin and Perrin, "Approche expérientielle et texte littéraire," 66, where they claim that Pinget's text "orchestrates a plurality of enunciative voices." In the same volume, Maingueneau and Philippe refer to "the fundamental enunciative undecidability" of *The Libera Me Domine*. See their "Les conditions d'exercice du discours littéraire," 366. The entire volume in which these essays appear is filled with detailed technical analyses of the first few pages of Pinget's novel in which, somewhat astonishingly, gender and sexuality in their relations to language-in-use receive next to no mention.

16. Bakhtin, "The Problem of Speech Genres," 88.

17. There are obvious overlaps in personal names, place names, and locations between the three novels I am discussing here, even if there might also be radical differences between the boarding house we encounter in *Someone* and the one in *The Libera Me Domine*, or between the Château de Broy as it occurs in *The Inquisitory* and as it occurs in *The Libera Me Domine*. Still, it turns out that one of the earlier versions of *The Libera Me Domine* contained a brief description of the start of a gay orgy at the Château. See Renouard and Liéber, "*L'Inquisitoire, Le Libera*: (pré)histoire(s) du texte," 36–39. Elements of these novels would also be recycled in other of Pinget's works in later years. Cf. the short play called *Le bifteck* or the television play *L'affaire Ducreux*, both collected in *L'affaire Ducreux et autres pièces*. See also Pinget's screenplay *15 Rue des*

Lilas, written in collaboration with a few other people, whose English translation was published in 2013 in a volume devoted to Pinget's English translator, Barbara Wright: Renouard and Kelly, eds., *Barbara Wright: Translation as Art*.

18. Silverstein, "'Cultural' Concepts," 621.

19. Ruffel suggests that "in *Le Libera* and *L'Inquisitoire*, the writer is evidently speaking about his own situation as a gay writer. To believe otherwise is to fall into the trap of the book, which is precisely to make us believe that homosexuality is a trap" (132). There are many possible avatars of the author throughout Pinget's writing. Character names recur from work to work, even though it seems that the people bearing those names are not always the same. Jean-Claude Liéber and Madeleine Renouard have noted that there is an unpublished set of works about Mortin, who is already a prominent character in many of Pinget's books. One could be justified, they suggest, in considering Mortin "the author's double." See Liéber and Renouard, "Le Chantier Robert Pinget: L'oeuvre dans tous ses états," 14. See also Brun, "Le propre et le neutre: Le drame des noms dans quelques fictions de Robert Pinget."

20. Or perhaps the boy drowned, or was hit by a truck. The novel produces on-going variations on its thematic material. Pinget was known to use formal principles from music in his writing. Laurent Adert, in an interesting reading of *The Libera Me Domine*, points to its fugal, polyphonic structure. See *Les mots des autres: Flaubert, Sarraute, Pinget*, 252–65.

21. On the continual presence of the motif of murdered children in Pinget's writing, see Piégay-Gros, "La folie, la faute et le secret."

22. Silverstein, "The Whens and Wheres—as Well as Hows—of Ethnolinguistic Recognition," 539.

23. We might hypothesize that it is Ariane's rivalry with her "cher cousin" de Broy over whose family has more status that causes her to take a dislike to the R.P., more closely connected to the de Broy set than to her.

24. The R.P. poses a bit of a problem for this worldview (as might Robert Pinget himself). Ruffel suggests that "Pinget's love of country life means that from the beginning he subverts the simplified opposition that would set the sexuality of a progressive urban environment against retrograde country folk. He in fact joins his two passions, sexuality and the country, in his fictional queer countryside" (144).

25. Silverstein, "The Whens and Wheres," 534.

26. There remains an interesting question regarding what happens when those nonsemantic features of a literary work (here referred to as melodic flow or as tone, and understood as involving frequency patterns in lexical choices as well) that all contribute to producing the sense of social kinship shared by early adopters of Bergotte, then move out through time and through space to locations and readers who do not inhabit the literary field or the cultural space shared by Bergotte and his early readers: Are they still *legible* (or should I say *audible*) in the same way?

27. For more on Proust and language-in-use, see Lucey, "Proust and Language-in-Use." For more on the relations between Proust and Bourdieu in this regard, see Lucey, "'La recherche que l'on peut dire formelle': Proust with Bourdieu."

28. The novel seems to instantiate the point of view memorably stated by Erving Goffman in his 1982 essay, "Felicity's Condition": "conversationally speaking, we are all information storage drums, and for every possible interrogator, there will be an access sequence that allows for entrée to the files" (47).

29. Silverstein, "The Voice of Jacob," 513–14.

30. Butler, "Is Kinship Always Already Heterosexual?," 108.

31. Colette, *The Pure and the Impure*, 57; *Ces plaisirs . . .* , 53.

32. Bourdieu, *The Weight of the World*, 511.

33. Ross Chambers helpfully pointed out to me a number of times in correspondence that the misfit position I have been describing resembles in some ways the "anxiogenic and spectral character of witnessing" under certain kinds of circumstances that he describes and analyzes in *Untimely Interventions*. In that book, he develops a way of thinking about what witnessing involves in circumstances he labels *obscene*: "Since the obscene is wholly or partially excluded from the set of genres that constitutes a given culture, and so liminalized, witnessing writing is obliged to exercise its indexing function through the performance of an act of generic catachresis: in the same discursive act whereby the attention of its readers is turned in an unwonted direction, it turns a conventional genre to new purposes" (32, 36). Misfits, Chambers suggested to me, speak from an "obscene" position without necessarily having undergone any of the causal traumas that mark the writing he investigated in *Untimely Interventions*. This book benefited enormously from Ross Chambers's attention to it.

Bibliography

Abelove, Henry. *Deep Gossip*. Minneapolis: University of Minnesota Press, 2003

Aczel, Richard. "Hearing Voices in Narrative Texts." *New Literary History* 29, no. 3 (1998): 467–500.

Adert, Laurent. *Les mots des autres: Flaubert, Sarraute, Pinget*. [Villeneuve d'Ascq]: Presses Universitaires du Septentrion, 1996.

Adler, Laure. *Marguerite Duras*. Paris: Gallimard, 1998.

Agha, Asif. *Language and Social Relations*. Cambridge: Cambridge University Press, 2007.

Agha, Asif. "Voice, Footing, Enregisterment." *Journal of Linguistic Anthropology* 15, no. 1 (2005): 38–59.

Albert, Nicole. Présentation of *Dames seules*, by Maryse Choisy and Marcel Vertès, 5–53. 1932. Lille: Cahiers Gai-Kitsch-Camp, 1993.

Allen, Jafari S. *¡Venceremos? The Erotics of Black Self-Making in Cuba*. Durham, NC: Duke University Press, 2011.

Altman, Meryl. "Simone de Beauvoir and Lesbian Lived Experience." *Feminist Studies* 33, no. 1 (2007): 207–32.

Amin, Kadji. *Disturbing Attachments: Genet, Modern Pederasty, and Queer History*. Durham, NC: Duke University Press, 2017.

Amin, Kadji. "Ghosting Transgender Historicity in Colette's *The Pure and the Impure*." *L'Esprit Créateur* 35, no. 1 (2013): 114–30.

Amossy, Ruth. "L'inflexion de la parole commune ou les enjeux de l'écriture dans *Quelqu'un*." In *Le Chantier Robert Pinget*, edited by Jean-Claude Liéber and Madeleine Renouard, 129–44. Paris: Jean-Michel Place, 2000.

André, Marie-Odile. *Les mécanismes de classicisation d'un écrivain: Le cas de Colette*. Metz: Université de Metz, 2000.

Andréa, Yann. *Cet amour-là*. Paris: Librairie générale française, 2002.

Andréa, Yann. *M.D.* Paris: Minuit, 1983.

Antonioli, Kathleen. "Colette Responds to Louise Lalanne: Guillaume Apollinaire's 'Bienveillante Rosserie.'" *French Studies Bulletin* 121 (Winter 2011): 83–86.

Apter, Emily. *Against World Literature: On the Politics of Untranslatability*. London: Verso, 2013.

Armel, Aliette. *Marguerite Duras et l'autobiographie*. [Pantin]: Le Castor Astral, 1990.

Armengaud, Françoise, and Michèle Causse. "Violette Leduc: 'La plus démesurément vraie.'" *Roman 20/50*, no. 28 (1999): 47–54.

Auchlin, A., and L. Perrin. "Approche expérientielle et texte littéraire." In *Les modèles du discours au défi d'un "dialogue romanesque": L'incipit du roman de R. Pinget "Le Libera,"* edited by Eddy Roulet and Marcel Burger, 55–81. Nancy: Presses Universitaires de Nancy, 2002.

Bair, Deirdre. *Simone de Beauvoir: A Biography.* New York: Simon and Schuster, 1990.

Bakhtin, M. M. "The Problem of Speech Genres." In *Speech Genres and Other Late Essays*, edited by Caryl Emerson and Michael Holquist and translated by Vern W. McGee, 60–102. Austin: University of Texas Press, 1986.

Bakhtin, M. M. "The Problem of the Text in Linguistics, Philology, and the Human Sciences: An Experiment in Philosophical Analysis." In *Speech Genres and Other Late Essays*, edited by Caryl Emerson and Michael Holquist and translated by Vern W. McGee, 103–31. Austin: University of Texas Press, 1986.

Banfield, Ann. "L'écriture et le non-dit." *diacritics* 21, no. 4 (1991): 20–31.

Banfield, Ann. "A Grammatical Definition of the Genre 'Novel.'" *Polyphonie* 4 (April 2002), http://www.hum.au.dk/romansk/polyfoni/Polyphonie_IV/Banfield_IV.htm.

Banfield, Ann. "Where Epistemology, Style, and Grammar Meet Literary History: The Development of Represented Speech and Thought." *New Literary History* 9, no. 3 (1978): 415–54.

Barnes, Hazel E. "La Lesbienne." In *Simone de Beauvoir: "Le Deuxième Sexe." Livre fondateur du féminisme moderne en situation*, edited by Ingrid Galster, 315–36. Paris: Honoré Champion, 2004.

Barthes, Roland. *Oeuvres complètes, Tome IV, 1972–1976.* Edited by Éric Marty. Paris: Seuil, 2002.

Bataille, Georges. *Literature and Evil.* Translated by Alastair Hamilton. London: Calder & Boyars, 1973.

Bataille, Georges. *La littérature et le mal.* Paris: Gallimard (Folio), 1957.

Bauman, Richard, and Charles Briggs. "Poetics and Performance as Critical Perspectives on Language and Social Life." In *Creativity in Performance*, edited by R. Keith Sawyer, 227–64. Greenwich, CT: Ablex, 1997.

Beauvoir, Simone de. *Le deuxième sexe.* 2 vols. Paris: Gallimard (Idées), 1949.

Beauvoir, Simone de. *La force de l'âge.* Paris: Gallimard (Folio), 1986.

Beauvoir, Simone de. *L'invitée.* Paris: Gallimard (Folio), 1972.

Beauvoir, Simone de. *Journal de guerre, septembre 1939–janvier 1941.* Edited by Sylvie Le Bon de Beauvoir. Paris: Gallimard, 1990.

Beauvoir, Simone de. *Lettres à Sartre.* Edited by Sylvie Le Bon de Beauvoir. 2 vols. Paris: Gallimard, 1990.

Beauvoir, Simone de. "Littérature et métaphysique." *Les Temps Modernes* 7 (1946): 1153–63.

Beauvoir, Simone de. *The Prime of Life.* Translated by Peter Green. New York: Harper & Row, 1976.

Beauvoir, Simone de. *She Came to Stay.* Translated by Yvonne Moyse and Roger Senhouse. New York: Norton, 1990.

Beauvoir, Simone de. *A Transatlantic Love Affair: Letters to Nelson Algren.* New York: New Press, 1998.

Benveniste, Émile. "The Nature of Pronouns." In *Problems in General Linguistics*, translated by Mary Elizabeth Meek, 217–22. Coral Gables, FL: University of Miami Press, 1971.

Berl, Emmanuel. *Interrogatoire par Patrick Modiano suivi de Il fait beau allons au cimetière.* Paris: Gallimard, 1976.

Berlant, Lauren. *The Female Complaint: The Unfinished Business of Sentimentality in American Culture*. Durham, NC: Duke University Press, 2008.

Berlant, Lauren, and Jay Prosser. "Life Writing and Intimate Publics: A Conversation with Lauren Berlant." *Biography* 34, no. 1 (2011): 180–87.

Berliner, Brett A. *Ambivalent Desire: The Exotic Black Other in Jazz-Age France*. Amherst: University of Massachusetts Press, 2002.

Besnier, Niko. "Language and Affect." *Annual Review of Anthropology* 19 (1990): 419–51.

Bizet, François. *Une communication sans échange: Georges Bataille critique de Jean Genet*. Geneva: Droz, 2007.

Blake, Jody. *Le Tumulte Noir: Modernist Art and Popular Entertainment in Jazz-Age Paris, 1900–1930*. University Park: Pennsylvania State University Press, 1999.

Blanchot, Maurice. *The Book to Come*. Translated by Charlotte Mandell. Stanford, CA: Stanford University Press, 2003.

Blanchot, Maurice. *Le livre à venir*. Paris: Gallimard (Idées), 1971.

Blanchot, Maurice. "Everyday Speech." In *The Infinite Conversation*, translated by Susan Hanson, 238–45. Minneapolis: University of Minnesota Press, 1993.

Blanchot, Maurice. "The Narrative Voice (the 'he,' the neutral)." In *The Infinite Conversation*, translated by Susan Hanson, 379–87. Minneapolis: University of Minnesota Press, 1993.

Blanchot, Maurice. *The Unavowable Community*. Translated by Pierre Joris. Barrytown, NY: Station Hill Press, 1988.

Boellstorff, Tom. *A Coincidence of Desire: Anthropology, Queer Studies, Indonesia*. Durham, NC: Duke University Press, 2007.

Bois, Yve-Alain, and Rosalind E. Krauss. *Formless: A User's Guide*. New York: Zone Books, 1997.

Boschetti, Anna. "How Field Theory Can Contribute to Knowledge of World Literary Space." *Paragraph* 35, no. 1 (2012): 10–29.

Boschetti, Anna. *La poésie partout: Apollinaire, homme-époque (1898–1918)*. Paris: Seuil, 2001.

Boucharenc, Myriam. *L'Écrivain-reporter au coeur des années trent*. Villeneuve d'Ascq: Presses Universitaires du Septentrion, 2004.

Bourdieu, Pierre. *Distinction: A Social Critique of the Judgment of Taste*. Translated by Richard Nice. Cambridge, MA: Harvard University Press, 1984.

Bourdieu, Pierre. "The Genesis of the Concepts of Habitus and of Field." Translated by Channa Newman. *Sociocriticism* 2 (1985): 11–24.

Bourdieu, Pierre. "Intellectual Field and Creative Project." Translated by Sian France. *Social Science Information* 8, no. 2 (1969): 89–119.

Bourdieu, Pierre. *Language and Symbolic Power*. Translated by Gino Raymond and Matthew Adamson. Cambridge, MA: Harvard University Press, 1991.

Bourdieu, Pierre. "Legitimation and Structured Interests in Weber's Sociology of Religion." Translated by Chris Turner. In *Max Weber, Rationality and Modernity*, edited by Scott Lash and Sam Whimster, 119–36. London: Allen & Unwin, 1987.

Bourdieu, Pierre. *The Logic of Practice*. Translated by Richard Nice. Stanford, CA: Stanford University Press, 1990.

Bourdieu, Pierre. *Pascalian Meditations*. Translated by Richard Nice. Stanford, CA: Stanford University Press, 2000.

Bourdieu, Pierre. "Principles for a Sociology of Cultural Works." Translated by Claud DuVerliee. In *The Field of Cultural Production: Essays on Art and Literature*, 176–91. New York: Columbia University Press, 1993.

Bourdieu, Pierre. "The Production and Reproduction of Legitimate Language." In *Language and Symbolic Power*, 43–65.

Bourdieu, Pierre. *The Rules of Art: Genesis and Structure of the Literary Field*. Translated by Susan Emanuel. Stanford, CA: Stanford University Press, 1995.

Bourdieu, Pierre. "Social Space and the Genesis of 'Classes.'" In *Language and Symbolic Power*, 229–51.

Bourdieu, Pierre, et al. *The Weight of the World: Social Suffering in Contemporary Society*. Translated by Priscilla Parkhurst Ferguson et al. Stanford, CA: Stanford University Press, 1999.

Bourdieu, Pierre, Roger Chartier, and Robert Darnton. "Dialogue à propos de l'histoire culturelle." *Actes de la recherche en sciences sociales* 59 (1985): 86–93.

Bourdieu, Pierre, and Loïc J. D. Wacquant. *An Invitation to Reflexive Sociology*. Chicago: University of Chicago Press, 199.

Boulé, Jean-Pierre. *Hervé Guibert: Voices of the Self*. Liverpool: Liverpool University Press, 1999.

Brekhus, Wayne H. "Commuting to Homosexuality: Laud Humphreys' Unheralded Theoretical Contribution to the Sociology of Identity." *International Journal of Sociology and Social Policy* 24, nos. 3–5 (2004): 58–72.

Brekhus, Wayne H. *Peacocks, Chameleons, Centaurs: Gay Suburbia and the Grammar of Social Identity*. Chicago: University of Chicago Press, 2003.

Brioude, Mireille. "Violette Leduc écrivaine et lesbienne: Du mythe à la mystification." In *Lesbian Inscriptions in Francophone Society and Culture*, edited by Renate Günther and Wendy Michallat, 103–21. Durham, UK: Durham Modern Language Series, 2007.

Brooks, Daphne A. *Bodies in Dissent: Spectacular Performances of Race and Freedom, 1850–1910*. Durham, NC: Duke University Press, 2006.

Brun, Catherine. "Le propre et le neutre: Le drame des noms dans quelques fictions de Robert Pinget." *Europe* 82, no. 897–98 (2004): 114–21.

Burton, Richard D. E. "'Maman-France Doudou': Family Images in French West Indian Colonial Discourse." *diacritics* 23, no. 3 (1993): 69–90.

Butler, Judith. "Critically Queer." In *Bodies That Matter: On the Discursive Limits of "Sex,"* 223–42. New York: Routledge, 1993.

Butler, Judith. "Is Kinship Always Already Heterosexual?" In *Undoing Gender*, 102–30. New York: Routledge, 2004.

Butler, Judith. "Sex and Gender in Simone de Beauvoir's *Second Sex*." *Yale French Studies* 72 (1986): 35–49.

Carbonel, Marie-Hélène. *Suzy Solidor: Une vie d'amours*. Gémenos: Autre Temps, 2006.

Caron, David. *My Father and I: The Marais and the Queerness of Community*. Ithaca, NY: Cornell University Press, 2009.

Caron, David. *The Nearness of Others: Searching for Tact and Contact in the Age of HIV*. Minneapolis: University of Minnesota Press, 2014.

Carroll, Raymonde. *Cultural Misunderstandings: The French-American Experience*. Translated by Carol Volk. Chicago: University of Chicago Press, 1990.

Castle, Terry. *The Apparitional Lesbian: Female Homosexuality and Modern Culture*. New York: Columbia University Press, 1993.

Ceccatty, René de. *Violette Leduc: Éloge de la Bâtarde*. Paris: Stock, 1994.

Chambers, Ross. "Baudelaire's Street Poetry." *Nineteenth-Century French Studies* 13, no. 4 (1985): 244–59.

Chambers, Ross. *Story and Situation: Narrative Seduction and the Power of Fiction*. Minneapolis: University of Minnesota Press, 1984.

Chambers, Ross. "Strategic Constructivism? Sedgwick's Ethics of Inversion." In *Regarding Sedgwick: Essays on Queer Culture and Critical Theory*, edited by Stephen M. Barber and David L. Clark, 165–80. New York: Routledge, 2002.

Chambers, Ross. *Untimely Interventions: AIDS Writing, Testimonial, and the Rhetoric of Haunting.* Ann Arbor: University of Michigan Press, 2004.

Choisy, Maryse. *Un mois chez les filles.* Paris: Montaigne, 1928.

Cixous, Hélène. "The Laugh of the Medusa." Translated by Keith Cohen and Paula Cohen. In *New French Feminisms*, edited by Elaine Marks and Isabelle de Courtivron, 245–64. New York: Schocken, 1981.

Cohn, Dorrit. "Narrated Monologue: Definition of a Fictional Style." *Comparative Literature* 18, no. 2 (1966): 97–112.

Colette. *Ces plaisirs . . . .* Paris: Le Livre Moderne Illustré, 1934.

Colette. *The Collected Stories of Colette.* Edited by Robert Phelps and translated by Matthew Ward, Antonia White, Anne-Marie Callimachi, and others. New York: Farrar, Straus and Giroux, 1983.

Colette. *Lettres à Hélène Picard.* In *Oeuvres complètes de Colette.* Volume 15, edited by Claude Pichois and Roberte Forbin. Paris: Flammarion, 1973.

Colette. *Lettres à Missy.* Edited by Samia Bordji and Frédéric Maget. Paris: Flammarion, 2009.

Colette. *Lettres à ses pairs.* In *Oeuvres complètes de Colette.* Volume 16, edited by Claude Pichois and Roberte Forbin. Paris: Flammarion, 1973.

Colette. *Oeuvres.* Edited by Claude Pichois et al. 4 vols. Paris: Gallimard (Pléiade), 1984–2001.

Colette. *The Pure and the Impure.* Translated by Herma Briffault. Introduction by Judith Thurman. New York: New York Review Books, 2000.

Courtivron, Isabelle de. *Violette Leduc.* Boston: Twayne, 1985.

Creech, James. "Life and Death upon the Page: Marguerite Duras and Roland Barthes." In *Revisioning Duras: Film, Race, Sex*, edited by James S. Williams, 171–89. Liverpool: Liverpool University Press, 2000.

Crespelle, Jean-Paul. *La vie quotidienne à Montparnasse à la Grande Époque 1905–1930.* Paris: Hachette, 1976.

Crowley, Martin. *Duras, Writing, and the Ethical: Making the Broken Whole.* Oxford: Oxford University Press, 2000.

Davies, Howard. "Sartre and the Mobilization of Lévi-Bruhl." *French Studies* 51, no. 4 (1997): 422–31.

Deleuze, Gilles. Preface to *L'après-mai des faunes* by Guy Hocquenghem, 7–17. Paris: Grasset, 1974.

Dellamora, Richard, *Radclyffe Hall: A Life in the Writing.* Philadelphia: University of Pennsylvania Press, 2011.

Denes, Dominique. "Un lieu à l'oeuvre: 'La chambre noire' de Marguerite Duras." *Voix plurielles* 5, no. 1 (2008). http://www.brocku.ca/brockreview/index.php/voixplurielles/article/view/47.

Derrida, Jacques. *Glas.* Translated by John P. Leavey Jr. and Richard Rand. Lincoln: University of Nebraska Press, 1986.

Dichy, Albert, and Pascal Fouché. *Jean Genet: Essai de chronologie 1910–1944.* Paris: Bibliothèque de Littérature française contemporaine de l'Université Paris 7, 1988.

Dinshaw, Carolyn, Lee Edelman, Roderick A. Ferguson, Carla Freccero, Elizabeth Freeman, Judith Halberstam, Annamarie Jagose, Christopher Nealon, and Nguyen Tan Hoang. "Theorizing Queer Temporalities: A Roundtable Discussion." In "Queer Temporalities." Special issue, *GLQ: A Journal of Lesbian and Gay Studies* 13, no. 2–3 (2007): 177–95.

Ducrot, Oswald. "Charles Bally and Pragmatics." Translated by Catherine Porter, Kara Rabbitt, and Linda Waugh. *diacritics* 21, no. 4 (1991): 2–19.

Duhamel, Marcel. *Raconte pas ta vie*. Paris: Mercure de France, 1972.

Dupont, Jacques. "Faire une fin: Remarques sur *Le Pur et l'impur* de Colette." *Revue d'Histoire Littéraire de la France* 105, no. 4 (2005): 929–38.

Duras, Marguerite. *L'amant*. Paris: Minuit, 1984.

Duras, Marguerite. *Le camion suivi de Entretien avec Michelle Porte*. Paris: Minuit, 1977.

Duras, Marguerite. "Duras: The Thing. Un entretien avec Rolland Thélu." *Gai pied*, no. 20 (November 1980): 16.

Duras, Marguerite. *Ecrire*. Paris: Gallimard, 1993.

Duras, Marguerite. *L'été 80*. Paris: Minuit, 1980.

Duras, Marguerite. *La maladie de la mort*. Paris: Minuit, 1982.

Duras, Marguerite. *The Malady of Death*. Translated by Barbara Bray. New York: Grove Press, 1986.

Duras, Marguerite. "On George Bataille." In *Outside: Selected Writings*, translated by Arthur Goldhammer, 17–19. Boston: Beacon Press, 1986.

Duras, Marguerite. *Practicalities*. Translated by Barbara Bray. New York: Grove Weidenfeld, 1990.

Duras, Marguerite. *La pute de la côte normande*. Paris: Minuit, 1986.

Duras, Marguerite. *The Slut of the Normandy Coast*. In *Two by Duras*. Translated by Alberto Manguel. Toronto: Coach House Press, 1993.

Duras, Marguerite. *La vie materielle*. 1987. Paris: Gallimard (Folio), 1994.

Duras, Marguerite. *Writing*. Translated by Mark Polizzotti. Cambridge, MA: Lumen, 1998.

Duras, Marguerite. *Les yeux verts*. Paris: Cahiers du cinéma, 1987.

Durham, Scott. *Phantom Communities: The Simulacrum and the Limits of Postmodernism*. Stanford, CA: Stanford University Press, 1998.

Duvert, Tony. "La lecture introuvable." *Minuit*, no. 1 (November 1972): 2–21.

Edwards, Brent Hayes. *The Practice of Diaspora: Literature, Translation, and the Rise of Black Internationalism*. Cambridge, MA: Harvard University Press, 2003.

Eng, David L., Judith Halberstam, and José Esteban Muñoz, "Introduction: What's Queer about Queer Studies Now?" *Social Text* 23 (2005): 1–17.

Eribon, Didier. *Échapper à la psychanalyse*. Paris: Léo Scheer, 2005.

Eribon, Didier. *Papiers d'identité: Interventions sur la question gay*. Paris: Fayard, 2000.

Eribon, Didier. *Une morale du minoritaire: Variations sur un thème de Jean Genet*. Paris: Fayard, 2001.

Ernaux, Annie. *Les années*. Paris: Gallimard (Folio), 2009.

Evans, Martha Noël. "Murdering *L'Invitée*: Gender and Fictional Narrative." *Yale French Studies* 72 (1986): 67–86.

Faderman, Lillian. *Surpassing the Love of Men: Romantic Friendship and Love between Women from the Renaissance to the Present*. New York: William Morrow, 1981.

Fell, Alison S. "Literary Trafficking: Performing Identity in Violette Leduc's *La Bâtarde*." *Modern Language Review* 98, no. 4 (2003): 870–80.

Ferguson, Frances. "Jane Austen, *Emma*, and the Impact of Form." *Modern Language Quarterly* 61, no. 1 (2000): 157–80.

Fludernik, Monika. "The Linguistic Illusion of Alterity: The Free Indirect as Paradigm of Discourse Representation." *diacritics* 25, no. 4 (1995): 89–115.

Foucault, Michel. *The Archaeology of Knowledge*. Translated by A. M. Sheridan Smith. New York: Pantheon, 1972.

Foucault, Michel. "Il y aura scandale, mais . . ." In *Dits et écrits, 1954–1988*, edited by Daniel Defert and François Ewald, 4 vols., 2:74–75. Paris: Gallimard, 1994.

Foucault, Michel. "Of Other Spaces." Translated by Jay Miskowiec. *diacritics* 16, no. 1 (1986): 22–27.

Foucault, Michel. *"Society Must Be Defended": Lectures at the Collège de France, 1975–1976.* Translated by David Macey. New York: Picador, 2003.

Foucault, Michel, and Hélène Cixous. "A propos de Marguerite Duras." In Michel Foucault, *Dits et écrits, 1954–1988*, edited by Daniel Defert and François Ewald, 4 vols., 2:762–71. Paris: Gallimard, 1994.

Fouquière, André de. *Cinquante ans de panache.* Paris: Pierre Horay, 1951.

Francis, Claude, and Fernande Gontier. *Colette.* Paris, Perrin, 1997.

Freadman, Anne. "Being There: Colette in the Crowd." *French Cultural Studies* 19, no. 1 (2008): 5–16.

Freadman, Anne. "Breasts Are Back! Colette's Critique of Flapper Fashion." *French Studies* 60, no. 3 (2006): 335–46.

Freadman, Anne. *The Livres-Souvenirs of Colette: Genre and the Telling of Time.* London: Legenda, 2012.

Freeman, Elizabeth. "Introduction." In "Queer Temporalities." Special issue, *GLQ: A Journal of Lesbian and Gay Studies* 13, no. 2–3 (2007): 159–76.

Freud, Sigmund. "On Narcissism: An Introduction." Translated by Cecil M. Baines. In *General Psychological Theory: Papers on Metapsychology*, edited by Philip Rieff, 56–82. New York: Collier, 1963.

Friedrich, Paul. "Social Context and Semantic Feature: The Russian Pronominal Usage." In *Directions in Sociolinguistics*, edited by John J. Gumperz and Dell Hymes, 270–300. New York: Holt, Rinehart and Winston.

Galster, Ingrid, ed. *"Le Deuxième Sexe" de Simone de Beauvoir.* Paris: Presses de l'Université Paris-Sorbonne, 2004.

Galster, Ingrid. "Juin 43: Beauvoir est exclue de l'Université. Retour sur une affaire classée." *Contemporary French Civilization* 25, no. 1 (2001): 139–50.

Galster, Ingrid. "'Une femme machiste et mesquine.' La réception des écrits posthumes de Simone de Beauvoir dans la presse parisienne." *Lendemains* 61 (1991): 53–62.

Garreta, Anne F. "Autofiction: La Ford intérieure et le self roman." In *Genèse et autofiction*, edited by Catherine Viollet and Jean-Louis Jeanelle, 229–39. Louvain-la-Neuve: Academia Bruylant, 2007.

Genet, Jean. *Lettres au petit Franz (1943–44).* Edited by Claire Degans and François Sentein. Paris: Le Cabinet des lettrés, 2000.

Genet, Jean. *Notre-Dame-des-Fleurs.* [n.p.]: Barbezat-L'Arbalète, 1986.

Genet, Jean. *Our Lady of the Flowers.* Translated by Bernard Frechtman. New York: Grove Press, 1991.

Genet, Jean. *Querelle.* Translated by Anselm Hollo. New York: Grove Press, 1974.

Genet, Jean. *Querelle de Brest.* In *Journal du voleur, Querelle de Brest, Pompes funèbres.* Paris: Gallimard (Biblos), 1993.

Genet, Jean. *The Thief's Journal.* Translated by Bernard Frechtman. New York: Grove Press, 1964.

Goffman, Erving. "Felicity's Condition." *American Journal of Sociology* 89, no. 1 (1983): 1–53.

Goffman, Erving. "Footing." In *Forms of Talk*, 124–59. Philadelphia: University of Pennsylvania Press, 1981.

Goffman, Erving. *The Presentation of Self in Everyday Life.* New York: Anchor, 1959.

Goffman, Erving. "Where the Action Is." In *Interaction Ritual: Essays on Face-to-Face Behavior*, 149–270. New York: Pantheon, 1967.

Goudeket, Maurice. *Près de Colette*. Paris: Flammarion, 1956.

Gray, Margaret E. "Cross-Undressing in Colette: Performance, Gender and Music-Hall Labour Practice." *French Cultural Studies* 23, no. 3 (2012): 202–14.

Gray, Mary L. *Out in the Country: Youth, Media, and Queer Visibility in Rural America*. New York: New York University Press, 2009.

Green, Julien. *Journal, 1928–1934*. Paris: Plon, 1938.

Guerlac, Suzanne. *Literary Polemics: Bataille, Sartre, Valéry, Breton*. Stanford, CA: Stanford University Press, 1997.

Guibert, Hervé. *À l'ami qui ne m'a pas sauvé la vie*. Paris: Gallimard (Folio), 1990.

Guibert, Hervé. *The Compassion Protocol*. Translated by James Kirkup. New York: George Braziller, 1994.

Guibert, Hervé. "Entretien avec Eugène Savitzkaya." *Minuit*, no. 49 (1982): 5–12.

Guibert, Hervé. *Fou de Vincent*. Paris: Minuit, 1989.

Guibert, Hervé. "Papier magique." In *Mauve le vierge: Nouvelles*, 61–82. Paris: Gallimard, 1988.

Guibert, Hervé. *La piqûre d'amour et autres textes, suivi de La chair fraîche*. Paris: Gallimard, 1994.

Guibert, Hervé. *Le protocole compassionnel*. Paris: Gallimard (Folio), 1993.

Guibert, Hervé. *To the Friend Who Did Not Save My Life*. Translated by Linda Coverdale. New York: High Risk, 1994.

Guibert, Hervé, and Christophe Donner. "Pour répondre aux quelques questions qui se posent . . ." *La règle du jeu* 3, no. 7 (1992): 135–57.

Guibert, Hervé, and Eugène Savitzkaya. *Lettres à Eugène. Correspondance, 1977–1987*. Paris: Gallimard, 2013.

Gunther, Scott. *The Elastic Closet: A History of Homosexuality in France, 1942–Present*. New York: Palgrave Macmillan, 2009.

Guyotat, Pierre. "Réponses: Entretien réalisé avec Thérèse Réveillé." In *Littérature interdite*, 25–37. Paris: Gallimard, 1972.

Hanks, William F. *Language and Communicative Practices*. Boulder, CO: Westview Press, 1996.

Hanrahan, Mairéad. *Lire Genet: Une poétique de la différence*. Montreal: Les Presses de l'Université de Montréal, 1997.

Harris, Elaine. *L'approfondissement de la sensualité dans l'oeuvre romanesque de Colette*. Paris: Nizet, 1973.

Hawthorne, Melanie C. "Leçon de Philo/Lesson in Love: Simone de Beauvoir's Intellectual passion and the Mobilization of Desire." In *Contingent Loves: Simone de Beauvoir and Sexuality*, edited by Melanie C. Hawthorne, 55–83. Charlottesville: University Press of Virginia, 2000.

Héron, Pierre-Marie, ed. *Genet et Cocteau. Cahiers Jean Cocteau*, novelle série no. 1 (2002).

Hill, Leslie. *Marguerite Duras: Apocalyptic Desires*. London: Routledge, 1993.

Holland, Sharon Patricia. *The Erotic Life of Racism*. Durham, NC: Duke University Press, 2012.

Huffer, Lynne. *Another Colette: The Question of Gendered Writing*. Ann Arbor: University of Michigan Press, 1992.

Huffer, Lynne. "Foucault and Sedgwick: The Repressive Hypothesis Revisited." *Foucault Studies* 14 (2012): 20–40.

Hughes, Alex. "Commodifying Queer: Violette Leduc's Autobiographical Homotextualities." In *Gay Signatures: Gay and Lesbian Theory, Fiction and Film in France, 1945–1995*, edited by Owen Heathcote, Alex Hughes, and James S. Williams, 113–29. Oxford: Berg, 1998.

Hughes, Alex. *Heterographies*. Oxford: Berg, 2000.

Humphreys, Laud. *Tearoom Trade: Impersonal Sex in Public Places*. Enlarged edition. New Brunswick, NJ: AldineTransaction, 2007.

Idier, Antoine. *Les alinéas au placard: L'abrogation du délit d'homosexualité (1977–1982)*. Paris: Cartouche, 2013.

Jakobson, Roman. "Shifters and Verbal Categories." In *On Language*, edited by Linda R. Waugh and Monique Monville-Burston, 386–92. Cambridge, MA: Harvard University Press, 1990.

Jakobson, Roman. "The Speech Event and the Functions of Language." In *On Language*, edited by Linda R. Waugh and Monique Monville-Burston, 69–79. Cambridge, MA: Harvard University Press, 1990.

Jameson, Fredric. *Brecht and Method*. London: Verso, 1998.

Jansiti, Carlo. *Violette Leduc*. Paris: Grasset, 1999.

Johnson, Colin R. *Just Queer Folks: Gender and Sexuality in Rural America*. Philadelphia: Temple University Press, 2013.

Joseph, Gilbert. *Une si douce Occupation. Simone de Beauvoir et Jean-Paul Sartre 1940–1944*. Paris: Albin Michel, 1991.

Kahan, Benjamin. *Celibacies: American Modernism and Sexual Life*. Durham, NC: Duke University Press, 2013.

Katyal, Sonya. "Sexuality and Sovereignty: The Global Limits and Possibilities of *Lawrence*." *William & Mary Bill of Rights Journal* 14, no. 4 (2006): 1429–92.

Kaufmann, Vincent. "Geminga ou qu'est-ce qu'un événement littéraire?" *Furor* 28 (1997): 3–24.

Kaufmann, Vincent. *Poétique des groupes littéraires (Avant-gardes 1920–1970)*. Paris: Presses Universitaires de France, 1997.

Knapp, Bettina L. "Une Interview avec Robert Pinget." *French Review* 42, no. 4 (1969): 548–54.

Kroskrity, Paul V. "Regimenting Languages: Language Ideological Perspectives." In *Regimes of Language: Ideologies, Polities, and Identities*, edited by Paul V. Kroskrity, 1–34. Santa Fe, NM: School of American Research Press, 2000.

Kurke, Leslie. *Aesopic Conversations: Popular Tradition, Cultural Dialogue, and the Invention of Greek Prose*. Princeton, NJ: Princeton University Press, 2011.

Ladenson, Elisabeth. "Colette for Export Only." *Yale French Studies* 90 (1996): 25–46.

Ladenson, Elisabeth. *Proust's Lesbianism*. Ithaca, NY: Cornell University Press, 1999.

Lagasnerie, Geoffroy de. *Logique de la creation*. Paris: Fayard, 2011.

Lagasnerie, Geoffroy de. *Sur la science des oeuvres. Questions à Pierre Bourdieu (et à quelques autres)*. Paris: Cartouche, 2011.

Lamy, Suzanne, and André Roy, eds. *Marguerite Duras à Montréal*. Montréal: Spirale, 1981.

Latimer, Tirza True. *Women Together, Women Apart: Portraits of Lesbian Paris*. New Brunswick, NJ: Rutgers University Press, 2005.

Le Bitoux, Jean, and Gilles Barbedette. "Sartre et les homosexuels." *Gai pied*, no. 13 (April 1980): 1, 11–14.

Leakey, F. W. "*Les Lesbiennes*: A Verse Novel?" In *Baudelaire: Collected Essays, 1953–1988*, edited by Eva Jacobs, 29–47. Cambridge: Cambridge University Press, 1990.

Lecarme-Tabone, Éliane. "D'une rencontre à l'autre: Colette et Simone de Beauvoir." In *Colette*, edited by Gérard Bonal and Frédéric Maget. *Cahiers de l'Herne* 97 (2011): 177–85.

Leduc, Violette. "Au village." *Les Temps Modernes* 65 (March 1951): 1592–606.

Leduc, Violette. *La bâtarde*. 1964. Paris: Gallimard (L'imaginaire), 1996.

Leduc, Violette. *La Bâtarde*. Translated by Derek Coltman. [Normal, IL]: Dalkey Archive Press, 2003.

Leduc, Violette. *La chasse à l'amour*. 1973. Paris: Gallimard (L'imaginaire), 1994.

Leduc, Violette. *Correspondance 1945–1972.* Edited by Carlo Jansiti. Paris: Gallimard, 2007.

Leduc, Violette. *La folie en tête.* 1970. Paris: Gallimard (L'imaginaire), 1994.

Leduc, Violette. *Mad in Pursuit.* Translated by Derek Coltman. New York: Riverhead Books, 1999.

Lee, Benjamin, and Edward LiPuma. "Cultures of Circulation: The Imaginations of Modernity." *Public Culture* 14, no. 1 (2002): 191–213.

Léridon, Jean-Luc, director. *Marguerite Duras: Les grands entretiens de Bernard Pivot.* 1984. Bry-sur-Marne: INA, 2004. DVD.

Liéber, Jean-Claude, and Madeleine Renouard, eds. *Le chantier Robert Pinget.* Paris: Jean-Michel Place, 2000.

Liéber, Jean-Claude, and Madeleine Renouard. "Le chantier Robert Pinget: L'oeuvre dans tous ses états." In *Le chantier Robert Pinget*, edited by Jean-Claude Liéber and Madeleine Renouard, 11–36. Paris: Jean-Michel Place, 2000.

Lindon, Mathieu. "Genet régénéré." *Libération*, September 30, 1993, 26.

Locey, Elizabeth. *The Pleasures of the Text: Violette Leduc and Reader Seduction.* Lanham, MD: Rowman & Littlefield, 2002.

Longuet, Patrick. "*L'inquisitoire*: Feux d'artifice et constellations." *Roman 20-50* 30 (2000): 45–63.

Lottman, Herbert R. *The Left Bank: Writers, Artists, and Politics from the Popular Front to the Cold War.* Boston: Houghton Mifflin, 1982.

Love, Heather. *Feeling Backward: Loss and the Politics of Queer History.* Cambridge, MA: Harvard University Press, 2007.

Lucey, Michael. "Genet's *Notre-Dame-des-Fleurs*: Fantasy and Sexual Identity." *Yale French Studies* 91 (1997): 80–102.

Lucey, Michael. *Gide's Bent: Sexuality, Politics, Writing.* New York: Oxford University Press, 1996.

Lucey, Michael "A Literary Object's Contextual Life." In *A Companion to Comparative Literature*, edited by Ali Behdad and Dominic Thomas, 120–35. Malden, MA: Wiley-Blackwell, 2011.

Lucey, Michael. *The Misfit of the Family: Balzac and the Social Forms of Sexuality.* Durham, NC: Duke University Press, 2003.

Lucey, Michael. *Never Say I: Sexuality and the First Person in Colette, Gide, and Proust.* Durham, NC: Duke University Press, 2006.

Lucey, Michael. "On Proust and Talking to Yourself." *Qui Parle* 26, no. 2 (2017): 281–93.

Lucey, Michael. "Proust and Language-in-Use." *Novel: A Forum on Fiction* 48, no. 2 (2015): 261–79.

Lucey, Michael. "'La recherche que l'on peut dire formelle': Proust with Bourdieu." In *What Forms Can Do: Attending to the Real in 20th and 21st Century French Culture*, edited by Patrick Crowley and Shirley Jordan. Liverpool: Liverpool University Press, forthcoming.

Lucey, Michael. "Sexuality, Politicization, May 1968: Situating Christiane Rochefort's *Printemps au parking*." *differences* 12, no. 3 (2001): 33–68.

Lucey, Michael. "When? Where? What?" In *After Sex? On Writing since Queer Theory*, edited by Janet Halley and Andrew Parker, 221–44. Durham, NC: Duke University Press. 2011.

Maget, Frédéric. "De Missy à 'La Chevalière.'" In *Colette*, edited by Gérard Bonal and Fréderic Maget. *Cahiers de l'Herne*, no. 97 (2011): 248–53.

Maingueneau, D., and G. Philippe. "Les conditions d'exercice du discours littéraire." In *Les modèles du discours au défi d'un "dialogue romanesque": L'incipit du roman de R. Pinget "Le Libera*," edited by Eddy Roulet and Marcel Burger, 351–77. Nancy: Presses Universitaires de Nancy, 2002.

Maniglier, Patrice. *La vie énigmatique des signes: Saussure et la naissance du structuralisme.* Paris: Scheer, 2006.

Marks, Elaine. "Lesbian Intertextuality." In *Homosexualities and French Literature*, edited by George Stambolian and Elaine Marks, 353–77. Ithaca, NY: Cornell University Press, 1979.

Marx-Scouras, Danielle. *The Cultural Politics of "Tel Quel": Literature and the Left in the Wake of Engagement*. University Park: Pennsylvania State University Press, 1996.

Mavor, Elizabeth. *The Ladies of Llangollen*. Harmondsworth: Penguin, 1973.

McHale, Brian. "Free Indirect Discourse: A Survey of Recent Accounts." *PTL: A Journal for Descriptive Poetics and Theory of Literature* 3 (1978): 249–87.

Merleau-Ponty, Maurice. *Phenomenology of Perception*. Translated by Colin Smith. London: Routledge & Kegan Paul, 1962.

Meunier, Jean-Peirre, and Brigitte Léardée. *La biguine de l'Oncle Ben's: Ernest Léardée raconte*. Paris: Editions Caribéennes, 1989.

Michel Journiac. Exhibition catalog. Strasbourg: Éditions des musées de Strasbourg, 2004.

Miller, Christopher L. *Blank Darkness: Africanist Discourse in French*. Chicago: University of Chicago Press, 1985.

Moi, Toril. *Simone de Beauvoir: The Making of an Intellectual Woman*. Oxford: Blackwell, 1994.

Montfort, Eugène. *Apollinaire travesti*. Paris: Pierre Seghers, 1948.

Moran, Richard. *Authority and Estrangement: An Essay in Self-Knowledge*. Princeton, NJ: Princeton University Press, 2001.

Muñoz, José Esteban. *Cruising Utopia: The Then and There of Queer Futurity*. New York: New York University Press, 2009.

Muñoz, José Esteban. *Disidentifications: Queers of Color and the Performance of Politics*. Minneapolis: University of Minnesota Press, 1999.

Nancy, Jean-Luc. "Concealed Thinking." In *A Finite Thinking*, edited by Simon Sparks, 31–50. Stanford, CA: Stanford University Press, 2003.

Nealon, Christopher. *Foundlings: Lesbian and Gay Historical Emotion before Stonewall*. Durham, NC: Duke University Press, 2001.

Noguez, Dominique. *Duras, Marguerite*. Paris: Flammarion, 2001.

Parker, Andrew. "Foucault's Tongues." *Mediations* 18, no. 2 (1994): 80–88.

Patton, Cindy. *Inventing AIDS*. New York: Routledge, 1990.

Peirce, Charles Sanders. "Pragmatism (1907)." In *The Essential Peirce: Selected Philosophical Writings, Volume 2 (1893–1913)*, edited by the Peirce Edition Project, 398–433. Bloomington: Indiana University Press, 1998.

Philippe, Gilles. *Le discours en soi: La représentation du discours intérieur dans les romans de Sartre*. Paris: Champion, 1997.

Pichois, Claude, and Alain Brunet. *Colette*. Paris: Fallois, 1998.

Piégay-Gros, Nathalie. "Domesticité et subalternes." In *Robert Pinget: Matériau, Marges, Écriture*, edited by Martin Mégevand and Nathalie Piégay-Gros, 129–43. Saint-Denis: Presses Universitaires de Vincennes, 2011.

Piégay-Gros, Nathalie. "La folie, la faute et le secret." *Europe* 82, no. 897–98 (2004): 88–100.

Pinget, Robert. *L'affaire Ducreux et autres pièces*. Paris: Minuit, 1995.

Pinget, Robert. *15 Rue des Lilas*. Translated by Barbara Wright. In *Barbara Wright: Translation as Art*, edited by Madeleine Renouard and Debra Kelly, 133–298. Champaign, IL: Dalkey Archive, 2013.

Pinget, Robert. *L'inquisitoire*. 1962. Paris: Minuit (Double), 1986.

Pinget, Robert. *The Inquisitory*. Translated by Donald Watson. Champaign, IL: Dalkey Archive, 2003.

Pinget, Robert. *Le Libera*. Paris: Minuit, 1984.

Pinget, Robert. *The Libera Me Domine*. Translated by Barbara Wright. New York: Red Dust, 1978.

Pinget, Robert. "Pseudo-principes d'esthétique." In *Nouveau roman: Hier, aujourd'hui*, volume 2, edited by Jean Ricardo and Françoise van Rossum-Guyon, 311–50. Paris: UGE (10/18), 1972.

Pinget, Robert. *Quelqu'un*. Paris: Minuit, 1965.

Pinget, Robert. *Robert Pinget à la lettre: Entretiens avec Madeleine Renouard*. Paris: Belfond, 1993.

Pinget, Robert. *Someone*. Translated by Barbara Wright. New York: Red Dust, 1984.

Pollak, Michael. *Les homosexuels et le sida: Sociologie d'une épidémie*. Paris: Métailié, 1988.

Poskin, Anne. "Colette et 'l'Argus de la presse.'" *Études françaises* 36, no. 3 (2000): 113–26.

Povinelli, Elizabeth A., and George Chauncey. "Thinking Sexuality Transnationally: An Introduction." *GLQ: A Journal of Lesbian and Gay Studies* 5, no. 4 (1999): 439–50.

Prince, Gerald. *Métaphysique et technique dans l'oeuvre romanesque de Sartre*. Geneva: Droz, 1968.

Proust, Marcel. *À la recherche du temps perdu*. Edited by Jean-Yves Tadié. 4 vols. Paris: Gallimard (Pléiade), 1987.

Proust, Marcel. *Swann's Way*. Translated by Lydia Davis. New York: Penguin, 2004.

Provencher, Denis M. *Queer French: Globalization, Language, and Sexual Citizenship in France*. Aldershot: Ashgate, 2007.

Querlin, Marise. *Femmes sans hommes (choses vues)*. Paris: Éditions de France, 1931.

Rawls, Anne Warfield. "Interaction as a Resource for Epistemological Critique." *Sociological Theory* 2 (1984): 222–52.

Renouard, Madeleine, and Jean-Claude Liéber. "*L'Inquisitoire, Le Libera*: (pré)histoire(s) du texte." *Roman 20–50* 30 (2000): 31–44.

Ringer, Loren. "*Saint Genet" Decanonized: The Ludic Body in "Querelle*." Amsterdam: Rodopi, 2001.

Rowley, Hazel. *Tête-à-Tête: Simone de Beauvoir and Jean-Paul Sartre*. New York: HarperCollins, 2005.

Ruffel, David. "Pinget Queer." Translated by Maria O'Sullivan. *Romanic Review* 104, nos. 1–2 (2013): 127–45.

Rumsey, Alan. "Agency, Personhood and the 'I' of Discourse in the Pacific and Beyond." *Journal of the Royal Anthropological Institute* 6 (2000): 101–15.

San Francisco Human Rights Commission LGBT Advisory Committee. *Bisexual Invisibility: Impacts and Recommendations*. March 2011. http://sf-hrc.org/modules/showdocument.aspx?documentID=989.

Sanzio, Alain. "*L'homme blessé*: Un nouveau désordre amoureux." *Masques*, no. 19 (Automne 1983): 119–22.

Sapiro, Gisèle. "Pour une approche sociologique des relations entre littérature et idéologie." *COnTEXTES* [electronic journal], no. 2 (2007). URL: http://contextes.revues.org/165. DOI: 10.4000/contextes.165.

Sarkonak, Ralph. *Angelic Echoes: Hervé Guibert and Company*. Toronto: University of Toronto Press, 2000.

Sartre, Jean-Paul. "À propos de John Dos Passos et de '1919.'" In *Critiques littéraires (Situations, I)*, 14–24. Paris: Gallimard (Folio), 1993.

Sartre, Jean-Paul. *Carnets de la drôle de guerre, Septembre 1939–Mars 1940*. Nouvelle édition. Edited by Arlette Elkaïm-Sartre. Paris: Gallimard, 1995.

Sartre, Jean-Paul. "Une idée fondamentale de la phénoménologie de Husserl: L'intentionnalité." In *Critiques littéraires (Situations, I)*, 29–32. Paris: Gallimard (Folio), 1993.

Sartre, Jean-Paul. *The Imaginary: A Phenomenological Psychology of the Imagination*. Translated by Jonathan Webber. London: Routledge, 2004.

Sartre, Jean-Paul. "Introducing *Les Temps Modernes.*" In *"What Is Literature?" and Other Essays*, translated by Jeffrey Mehlman, 247–67. Cambridge, MA: Harvard University Press, 1988.

Sartre, Jean-Paul. "John Dos Passos and *1919.*" In *Literary and Philosophical Essays*, translated by Annette Michelson, 88–96. New York: Criterion, 1955.

Sartre, Jean-Paul. *Lettres au Castor et à quelques autres*. Edited by Simone de Beauvoir. 2 vols. Paris: Gallimard, 1983.

Sartre, Jean-Paul. "Présentation." *Les Temps Modernes*, no. 1 (1945): 1–21.

Sartre, Jean-Paul. *Saint Genet: Actor and Martyr*. Translated by Bernard Frechtman. Minneapolis: University of Minnesota Press, 2012.

Sartre, Jean-Paul. *The War Diaries of Jean-Paul Sartre, November 1939–March 1940*. Translated by Quintin Hoare. New York: Pantheon, 1984.

Schultz, Gretchen. "Baudelaire's Lesbian Connections." In *Approaches to Teaching Baudelaire's "Flowers of Evil,"* edited by Laurence M. Porter, 130–38. New York: Modern Language Association, 2000.

Schütz, Alfred. *On Phenomenology and Social Relations: Selected Writings*. Edited by Helmut R. Wagner. Chicago: University of Chicago Press, 1970.

Schütz, Alfred. "The Stranger: An Essay in Social Psychology." *American Journal of Sociology* 49, no. 6 (1944): 499–507.

Scott, Joan Wallach. *Parité! Sexual Equality and the Crisis of French Universalism*. Chicago: University of Chicago Press, 2005.

Scott, Joan Wallach. *Politics of the Veil*. Princeton, NJ: Princeton University Press, 2007.

Sebhan, Gilles. *Tony Duvert: L'enfant silencieux*. Paris: Denoël, 2010.

Sedgwick, Eve Kosofsky. "Affect Theory and Theory of Mind." In *The Weather in Proust*, edited by Jonathan Goldberg, 144–63. Durham, NC: Duke University Press, 2011.

Sedgwick, Eve Kosofsky. "Anality: News from the Front." In *The Weather in Proust*, edited by Jonathan Goldberg, 166–82. Durham, NC: Duke University Press, 2011.

Sedgwick, Eve Kosofsky. *Epistemology of the Closet*. Berkeley: University of California Press, 1990.

Sedgwick, Eve Kosofsky. "Queer and Now." In *Tendencies*, 1–20. Durham, NC: Duke University Press, 1993.

Sedgwick, Eve Kosofsky, Stephen M. Barber, and David L. Clark. "This Piercing Bouquet: An Interview with Eve Kosofsky Sedgwick." In *Regarding Sedgwick: Essays on Queer Culture and Critical Theory*, edited by Stephen M. Barber and David L. Clark, 243–62. New York: Routledge, 2002.

Sentein, François. *Nouvelles minutes d'un libertin (1942–1943)*. Paris: Gallimard (Le Promeneur), 2000.

Silverstein, Michael. "Contemporary Transformations of Local Linguistic Communities." *Annual Review of Anthropology* 27 (1998): 401–26.

Silverstein, Michael. "'Cultural' Concepts and the Language-Culture Nexus." *Current Anthropology* 45, no. 5 (2004): 621–52.

Silverstein, Michael. "'Direct' and 'Indirect' Communicative Acts in Semiotic Perspective." *Journal of Pragmatics* 42 (2010): 337–53.

Silverstein, Michael. "The Improvisational Performance of Culture in Realtime Discursive Practice." In *Creativity in Performance*, edited by R. Keith Sawyer, 265–312. Greenwich, CT: Ablex, 1997.

Silverstein, Michael. "Language and the Culture of Gender: At the Intersection of Structure,

Usage, and Ideology." In *Semiotic Mediation: Sociocultural and Psychological Perspectives*, edited by Elizabeth Mertz and Richard J. Parmentier, 219–59. Orlando, FL: Academic Press, 1985.

Silverstein, Michael. "Languages/Cultures Are Dead! Long Live the Linguistic-Cultural!" In *Unwrapping the Sacred Bundle: Reflections on the Disciplining of Anthropology*, edited by Daniel A. Segal and Sylvia J. Yanagisako, 99–125. Durham, NC: Duke University Press, 2005.

Silverstein, Michael. "The Limits of Awareness." In *Linguistic Anthropology: A Reader*, edited by Alessandro Duranti, 382–401. Oxford: Blackwell, 1990.

Silverstein, Michael. "Metapragmatic Discourse and Metapragmatic Function." In *Reflexive Language: Reported Speech and Metapragmatics*, edited by John A. Lucy, 33–58. Cambridge: Cambridge University Press, 1993.

Silverstein, Michael. "Postscript: Thinking about the 'Teleologies of Structuralism.'" *Hau: Journal of Ethnographic Theory* 6, no. 3 (2016): 79–84.

Silverstein, Michael. "Shifters, Linguistic Categories, and Cultural Description." In *Meaning in Anthropology*, edited by Keith H. Basso and Henry A. Selby, 11–55. Albuquerque: University of New Mexico Press, 1976.

Silverstein, Michael. "The Voice of Jacob: Entextualization, Contextualization, and Identity." *ELH* 81, no. 2 (2014): 483–520.

Silverstein, Michael. "What Goes Around . . . : Some Shtick from 'Tricky Dick' and the Circulation of U.S. Presidential Image." *Journal of Linguistic Anthropology* 21, no. 1 (2011): 54–77.

Silverstein, Michael. "The Whens and Wheres—as Well as Hows—of Ethnolinguistic Recognition." *Public Culture* 15, no. 3 (2003): 531–57.

Silverstein, Michael, and Greg Urban. "The Natural History of Discourse." In *Natural Histories of Discourse*, edited by Michael Silverstein and Greg Urban, 1–17. Chicago: University of Chicago Press, 1996.

Simons, Margaret A. "Lesbian Connections: Simone de Beauvoir and Feminism." *Signs* 18, no. 1 (1992): 136–61.

Sinfield, Alan. "Lesbian and Gay Taxonomies." *Critical Inquiry* 29 (Autumn 2002): 120–38.

Soupault, Philippe. *Terpsichore*. Hazan: Paris, 1928.

Southworth, Helen. *The Intersecting Realities and Fictions of Virginia Woolf and Colette*. Columbus: Ohio State University Press, 2004.

Stephens, Elizabeth. "The Bad Homosexual: Genet's Perverse Homo-Politics." *Sexualities* 15, no. 1 (2012): 28–41.

Thurman, Judith. *Secrets of the Flesh: A Life of Colette*. New York: Knopf, 1999.

Tilburg, Patricia A. *Colette's Republic: Work, Gender, and Popular Culture in France, 1870–1914*. New York: Berghahn, 2009.

Tinsley, Omise'eke Natasha. *Thiefing Sugar: Eroticism between Women in Caribbean Literature*. Durham, NC: Duke University Press, 2010.

Valentine, David. *Imagining Transgender: An Ethnography of a Category*. Durham, NC: Duke University Press, 2007.

Vicinus, Martha. *Intimate Friends: Women Who Loved Women, 1778–1928*. Chicago: University of Chicago Press, 2004.

Vološinov, V. N. *Marxism and the Philosophy of Language*. Translated by Ladislav Matejka and I. R. Titunik. Cambridge, MA: Harvard University Press, 1986.

Walker, David H. "Literature, History and Factidiversiality." *Journal of European Studies* 25 (1995): 35–50.

Warner, Michael. *Publics and Counterpublics*. New York: Zone Books, 2002.

Weiner, Susan. *Enfants Terribles: Youth and Femininity in the Mass Media in France, 1945–1968.* Baltimore: Johns Hopkins University Press, 2001.

Wekker, Gloria. *The Politics of Passion: Women's Sexual Culture in the Afro-Surinamese Diaspora.* New York: Columbia University Press, 2006.

White, Edmund. *Genet: A Biography.* New York: Knopf, 1993.

Wickberg, Daniel. "Homophobia: On the Cultural History of an Idea," *Critical Inquiry* 27, no. 1 (2000): 42–57.

Williams, James S. "A Beast of a Closet: The Sexual Difference of Literary Collaboration in the Work of Marguerite Duras and Yann Andréa." *Modern Language Review* 87, no. 3 (1992): 576–84.

Williams, Raymond. *Marxism and Literature.* Oxford: Oxford University Press, 1977.

Wortham, Stanton. "Accomplishing Identity in Participant-Denoting Discourse." *Journal of Linguistic Anthropology* 13, no. 2 (2003): 189–210.

Zobel, Joseph. "Rue Blomet ou Paris by Night." In *Le soleil partagé: nouvelles,* 45–83. Paris: Présence africaine, 1964.

Index